Composition Theory for the Postmodern Classroom

Edited by
Gary A. Olson
Sidney I. Dobrin

Foreword by
Jacqueline Jones Royster

Afterword by
Linda Brodkey

State University of New York Press

For Milton and Ruth Dobrin, in memory of Geneva Harbin
And for Evelyn Ashton-Jones and the dedicated members
of JAC's editorial staff from 1986 to 1995

Published by
State University of New York Press, Albany

Printed in the United States of America
Edited and designed by Gary A. Olson and Sidney I. Dobrin

For information, address State University of New York
Press, State University Plaza, Albany, N.Y., 12246

Production by Christine Lynch; marketing by Nancy Farrell

Library of Congress Cataloging in Publication Data

Composition theory for the postmodern classroom /
  edited by Gary A. Olson and Sidney I. Dobrin; foreword
  by Jacqueline Jones Royster; afterword by Linda Brodkey.

        p. cm.—
Includes bibliographical references and index.
        ISBN 0-7914-2305-0 (ch: acid-free) —
        ISBN 0-7914-2306-9 (pb: acid-free)
1. English language—Rhetoric—Study and Teaching—Theory, etc.
2. Postmodernism.   I. Olson, Gary A., date.   II. Dobrin, Sidney
I., date.

PE1404.C627 1994
808'.042'07—dc20   94-8605
                                                                CIP

10   9   8   7   6   5   4   3

Contents

The Essay and Composition Theory

Gender, Culture, and Radical Pedagogy

Rhetoric, Philosophy, and Discourse

Acknowledgments

We would like to acknowledge the support and efforts of the numerous individuals who helped make the journal and thus this project a success: the many scholars who contributed their finest work to the *Journal of Advanced Composition* over the last decade, especially those represented in this collection; the members of the Editorial Board; the tireless members of the editorial staff during this period, including Evelyn Ashton-Jones, Nina Marilyn Minor, Joseph Moxley, Fred Reynolds, Phillip Sipiora, Karen Spear, Todd Taylor, Irene Ward, and Kristin Woolever; the administrations of the Universities of Idaho, Kansas State, Southern Mississippi, and South Florida for financial and clerical support of the journal; the hundreds of devoted *JAC* manuscript reviewers; and the many editorial assistants who served the journal over the last ten years. Special recognition is due to William T. Ross, chair of the Department of English, and Rollin Richmond, dean of the College of Arts and Sciences at the University of South Florida, both of whom took a personal interest in the success of the journal. Finally, we would like to thank Priscilla Ross at SUNY Press for her editorial acumen and unflagging encouragement, Todd Taylor for his work on the index, and the anonymous manuscript reviewers of this book for their constructive suggestions. All of these individuals, and no doubt some whom we have failed to include, have made this project possible.

Foreword

JACQUELINE JONES ROYSTER

To say that research and scholarship in rhetoric and composition have blossomed over the last thirty years is by all stretches of the imagination an understatement. In point of fact, what we have experienced might easily be labeled both revolution and evolution. A survey of session titles from the last three decades of the Conference on College Composition and Communication, a listing of scholarly journals that have emerged in the last twenty years, including the *Journal of Advanced Composition*, a general description of the network of professional organizations that have been organized to meet special needs and interests within this disciplinary community, and a cataloging of workshops, conferences, and conventions that have taken place across the nation all offer evidence of an exponential increase in scholarly activity in this arena at a level that would suggest profound shifts in thinking and operational patterns.

An even closer look at this domain reveals that there has been a remarkable transformation in our notions of what constitutes the scholarly enterprise as we have brought definition, clarity, and substance to a discipline that is still variously articulated. Colleagues have reinvented and refined traditional modes of inquiry and created new paradigms, efforts that have given rise to a matrix of innovative mechanisms for quantitative and qualitative analyses, for theoretical and pedagogical designs. We have rethought the terms of engagement, the ways and means of theory and practice, and a complex of relationships and interrelationships in a commingling of people, places, practices, and ideas. Across this disciplinary landscape, our insights and concerns shape and reshape themselves as a never-ending story that encourages us, if we will allow it, to imagine ourselves in polytonal fashion to be this, that, and the other, usually all at once.

In essence, we have reached out abstractly and concretely across boundaries of knowledge and experience to enhance our understanding of the written word as a human phenomenon. From the evidence before us in theory and practice we have accepted with renewed vigor the challenge of refashioning conceptual frames to make better sense of ourselves as language users and to identify reasonable, workable strategies for passing along a broader and deeper understanding to newer generations. It seems more possible than ever before to acknowledge multiple ways of envisioning the world and representing reality. We are becoming more accustomed to recognizing varieties of lived experiences and learning experiences, and thereby more accustomed to looking for variety as we endeavor to support academic growth and achievement. This flurry of activity suggests that our concerns are wide-ranging and fluid and that our most consistent imperative as educators is to bring to bear on contemporary academic challenges a collectivity of observations, discoveries, insights, and expertise in the interest of learning, achievement, and scholarly excellence.

The basic point is that we have, in fact, succeeded rather well in recreating ourselves as teachers and scholars in rhetoric and composition and in generating a noteworthy mixture of research, scholarship, and innovative practice. We have engaged in thirty years or so of an intense gathering and processing of information and experience and an equally intense application of insights and assumptions within disparate institutional environments. It seems appropriate, therefore, that at this juncture we would seize the opportunity to reflect on our handiwork, to reconsider it analytically and dialectically, and, given the distance over which we have come, even to historicize what we include in our most generous definition of rhetoric and composition.

Composition Theory for the Postmodern Classroom offers such an opportunity. This collection of essays from ten years of the *Journal of Advanced Composition* (*JAC*) reminds us that *JAC* has been a central resource for the presentation and consideration of "theory" in composition studies. These essays act as springboards for reflecting on the ways in which we interrogate and problematize in this discourse community. They capture the spirit of our conversations as these conversations were manifested in a particular moment in time and continue still in the making. Also, given the ways in which the discipline seems to be in a continual state of flux, they lend insight as we labor periodically to reseat ourselves within this contemporary context in terms of philosophy, ethics, knowledge bases, and classroom practice.

Further, this collection underscores something else that is quite essential to codes of conduct in rhetoric and composition. We have discovered in this field the distinct advantage of rereading and doing so systematically as good training for strength, flexibility, durability, and long-range vision. Experience has taught us that revisiting texts helps to keep us in focus with a clearer sense of the intertextuality of discourse over time and space. Rereading helps to clarify, not just roots, but root systems as they serve to nourish our thinking and push us to levels of reflection, abstraction, and hypothesizing that actually have the capacity to refocus what we see, how we see it, why we see it as we do, and, perhaps most of all, what we can do with ourselves as teachers, scholars, and students once we do acquire vision.

Composition Theory for the Postmodern Classroom comes into place, then, at a critical moment. We have worked assiduously to flesh out the ways and means of composition for a new era. This text helps to document our way.

In addition, we catch ourselves now in the midst of a fast-flowing, hazard-ridden stream, compelled to be held accountable for the truths and consequences of our choices and actions. This collection demonstrates that our vessels for negotiating these troubled waters may be oddly built but still reasonably sound. Above all, the fast-flowing nature of the current in composition studies is a constant reminder of two things. One is the desirability of a Janus view, a view that learns from the past and looks toward the future with informed eyes. The second is the advantage of making good use of lulls in a storm, moments to question progress, to reflect on thought and action, to renew body and spirit, and to reread the map. *Composition Theory in the Postmodern Classroom* encourages us to reread the map and to come away with a clearer notion, not just of how far we have come, but also where we are going and why our going there makes such very good sense.

Introduction

Composition Theory for the Postmodern Classroom is a collection of the most outstanding scholarly articles published in the *Journal of Advanced Composition* over the last decade. As the journal in the discipline of rhetoric and composition most associated with "theory," *JAC* has promoted scholarly inquiry that crosses disciplinary borders in ways that are productive and useful to composition. Over the last decade, the journal has attempted to push at the borders of rhetoric and composition by encouraging scholars to engage the discourses of theorists in other fields in substantive and significant ways. The result of such encouragement both by *JAC* and by other forums and individuals has been to revolutionize how compositionists view the field, its scholarship, and the teaching of writing. Rather than being restricted to the narrow confines of a field circumscribed by empirical method, composition scholars now engage regularly in important intellectual dialogues across a wide range of disciplinary borders. The essays in this collection chronicle the kinds of attempts made over the last decade to conduct such productive dialogues.

Part One, **The Process of Writing**, contains four essays investigating various kinds of writing and the ways in which such writing is produced. Calling for a "much more comprehensive notion of process," James Kinneavy draws on Martin Heidegger's concept of interpretation to expand our notion of the writing process. In an essay that went on to win the 1992 James L. Kinneavy Award for the most outstanding article published in *JAC*, Jasper Neel uses two different conceptions of writing imported from ancient Greece as a framework for comparing and contrasting the kind of writing done by a technical writer with that done by a literary critic. In another article that won the James L. Kinneavy Award (1991), Patricia Sullivan maintains that the graduate curriculum in English departments must be reconceptualized as "a scene of writing as well as a scene of reading" in order to help prevent literature and composition from being perceived as separate intellectual activities, as they most certainly are in most graduate curricula today. In an essay contained in the first issue of a composition journal devoted exclusively to gender issues (volume 10.2), Mary Kupiec Cayton explores how long-term writer's block contains gender-specific components and how women's attempts to enter male-centered discourse communities can often lead to writing paralysis for many women.

Part Two, **Theory and the Teaching of Writing**, is a collection of four essays that suggest ways in which theory and pedagogy converge. In his often-cited "Some Difficulties with Collaborative Learning," David Smit questions whether the body of scholarly literature used to justify collaborative pedagogies does indeed supply a convincing rationale for using collaborative practices in composition classes. In the first article ever to win the James L. Kinneavy Award (1988), Reed Way Dasenbrock draws on the scholarship of Jacques Derrida to claim that compositionists have overemphasized the similarities between writing and speaking and in so doing have negatively influenced their own writing pedagogies; he contends that Derrida's critique of "presence" will enable compositionists to develop a better understanding of various aspects of the teaching of writing. In a shocking discussion of the consequences of composition teachers' writing assignments, Sandy Moore and Michael Kleine relate a narrative of how a writing student, Sandy, was victimized because of an assignment she prepared for her writing teacher, Michael. Concerned that the educational system is not able to meet the needs of African American students, Thomas Fox calls for a reconceptualization of literacy and composition pedagogy, suggesting that we begin such a reconceptualization by becoming familiar with Afro-American literary theory.

The last decade has seen increased attention in the scholarly literature to the nature and function of "the essay." Some have asserted that compositionists should "teach" belletristic essays in their composition courses as an effective way to sensitize students to sophisticated issues of style and form; others have claimed that this is simply a back-door attempt to return to a pedagogy in which the teaching of "literature" and canonical works displaces true composition pedagogy. The chapters in Part Three, **The Essay and Composition Theory**, address some of these issues. W. Ross Winterowd argues that the essay should be "the central genre in composition instruction," so long as we expand our notion of "essay" in the light of poststructuralism to include exploratory, nonconclusive discourse. Douglas Hesse, however, is highly suspicious of recent attempts to make literary nonfiction central to composition pedagogy, maintaining that it is in our students' and our own best interest to question critically many of the underlying assumptions of this position. In a playful, entertaining, belletristic essay of her own, Lynn Bloom declares that teachers of writing should regularly compose and publish their own literary nonfiction so as to justify their "authority" as writing teachers and to "enliven and enhance" the genre, their teaching, and the profession itself.

Part Four, **Gender, Culture, and Radical Pedagogy**, presents seven articles on the kinds of social and cultural issues that have been central to *JAC* and to recent theoretical scholarship in the field. David Bleich contends that the traditional academic styles of learning are thoroughly informed by sexist values, so much so that even well-meaning people find such sexism difficult to detect and change. Robert Wood goes one step further in insisting that even "radical pedagogy" is informed by androcentric values, often resulting in the suppression of female students' intellectual development. Perhaps one reason why radical pedagogy can have such an effect is that, according to Henry Giroux, many Western scholars and educators have misappropriated the work of Paulo Freire, denuding it of its profoundly radical and postcolonial nature. Writers such as Michael Murphy, however, believe that composition theory and pedagogy will remain ineffective as a radical discourse so long as it continues to adhere to modernist strategies of resistance; instead, argues Murphy, we must transform composition into a thoroughly *post*modern discipline focused especially on cultural studies. While Joseph Harris supports this turn in composition toward cultural studies, he cautions those who engage in cultural critique in the composition classroom not to assume that students necessarily are gullible, unsophisticated readers of culture. John Trimbur suggests that composition studies has not paid enough attention to its own "narrativity," and he presents an analysis of the narrativity of Mike Rose's *Lives on the Boundary* as an example of how to gain critical insight into the conjunctures of discourses and practices. Finally, Carrie Leverenz examines the multicultural classroom.

The final section, **Rhetoric, Philosophy, and Discourse,** focuses on another important strain in recent composition scholarship: investigations of the relationships among epistemology, philosophy, and discourse. J. Hillis Miller employs Friedrich Nietzsche's early writings on rhetoric as an example of the kind of close connection between reading and writing that he defends in his essay. Thomas Kent is also interested in the close connection between reading and writing and, drawing on the work of philosopher Donald Davidson, proposes an alternative view of how we produce discourse. Joseph Petraglia provides a critique of the basic premises underlying composition's understanding of social construction, and Richard Coe analyzes Kenneth Burke's never-before published revision of his famous definition of *humanity.* This reading of Burke, posits Coe, provides critical insights that have implications for the teaching of composition.

Together these twenty-two essays represent the breadth and strength of composition scholarship that has engaged fruitfully with critical theory in its many manifestations. In drawing on the critical discourses of philosophers, feminists, literary theorists, African Americanists, cultural theorists, and others, these compositionists and others like them have enriched the scholarly discourse of the field, broadened our intellectual conceptions of the multiple roles and functions of discourse, and opened up an infinite number of questions and new possibilities for composition theory and pedagogy. As composition continues through the 1990s toward the new millennium, the discipline will continue to grow and be redefined, but it will owe an important debt to the scholars in this collection and those like them who during the 1980s and early 1990s had the vision and courage to take the bold and unpopular step of engaging with important theoretical discourses.

Gary A. Olson
Sidney I. Dobrin

The Process of Writing

The Process of Writing:
A Philosophical Base in Hermeneutics

JAMES L. KINNEAVY

There is no doubt that among those concerned with composition and the teaching of writing, one of the dominant concerns is the process of writing. Anyone who has attended the annual Conference on College Composition and Communication in the past five years can attest to this fact. Indeed, writing across the curriculum and the process method of teaching composition are probably the two most important innovations in the field of composition in the past ten years. Whole programs have been restructured to enable teachers to teach by the process method. At my own institution, John Ruszkiewicz added this dimension to an already fairly elaborate composition program. Many of us who have been teaching composition for a good number of years have substantially altered our own techniques of teaching to incorporate more process emphasis.

The Process of Writing: The Current Scene
This large-scale movement in the teaching of writing has some obvious advantages. It focuses attention on the student as writer and enables the teacher and the student's peers to assist in the ordeal of writing. Student-teacher conferences, collaborative writing, peer consulting, the importance of several drafts—all receive much attention. In my opinion and that of many others, the final product that results is immeasurably superior to the cold one-shot products of the traditional paradigm. The process approach allows those with a background in classical rhetoric to reassert the importance of invention over organization and style—and, of course, this was the overwhelming priority in the comprehensive rhetorics of the classical period, especially in Aristotle. Reasserting the significance of process tends to place the student at the center of pedagogical concern—and students like this and usually say so in strong affirmations in teacher and class evaluations.

Yet the process revolution, if it may be called a revolution, has not been implemented without some problems. One of these has been the neglect and disregard, on the part of some, of almost any concern with product at all. About three years ago, a major publishing company asked me to review a manuscript avowedly, almost heroically, dedicated to the process approach. The author, I might add, is an important figure in the field of rhetoric and is also a good friend of mine. I became concerned, as I progressed through the text, that the students were continually engaged in exercises that did not relate to a whole paper. By page 153, after about four complete chapters, the students still had not been asked to compose a whole paper; this was about one third of the way through the book. Process so enthroned and separated from any relation to product can be as meaningless as grammar or vocabulary taught in isolation from the actual act of writing. The book, I might add, was subsequently published.

Another major concern of mine has been that process is often very narrowly conceived. Many scholars who have written on process have taken it as axiomatic that the act of writing begins when a student puts pencil to paper and starts to produce a sequential manuscript. The early and significant monograph of Emig, the work of Macrorie, the several books by Elbow, the experiments of Flower and Hayes, the studies by Matsuhashi, and many other "process-oriented" publications almost take this position as self evident. It gives itself to experimentation, lends a neat beginning and closure to the act of writing, and can be easily incorporated into attempts to evaluate writing—but I think it is entirely too narrow a view of the process of writing.

In fact, this view is almost totally at variance with the practice of almost any professional writer I know. James Michener spent years learning about the history of Texas before writing his recent novel on that state (judging by the results, he should have taken a few more years). Journalists and reporters have to pound their beats, interview people, look up records, take notes, and so on before they start sequential writing. The research for a talk I gave on the Greek rhetorical origins of the Christian concept of faith took five years—and was only possible then because I had twenty years of training in rhetoric and a good number of years in theology. Professional writers don't just sit down and begin an exercise in free writing.

What is needed is a much more comprehensive notion of process. I began to think of this three or four years ago, and, in fact, I considered and rejected several possible alternatives among the process philosophers. Eventually, I turned to a notion of process which I had found in hermeneutics and which I had seen applied in three rather different areas by eminent thinkers. Martin Heidegger's general concept of the process of interpretation has been applied brilliantly to Biblical interpretation by Rudolf Bultmann, whom many consider the most outstanding theologian of this century to date. It has been applied to the humanities by Georg Gadamer, an eminent name in modern philosophy. And it has been applied to literary criticism and philosophy by such deconstructionists as Derrida, Spanos, Bove, and others. Heidegger's concept of process seems particularly relevant to composition.

It is, of course, a theory of interpretation, but more general than Biblical or legal hermeneutics, and even more general than the so called general hermeneutics of Schleiermacher or Dilthey, which really are limited to the humanities. For Heidegger, all understanding involves interpretation, from perception to speech, from poetry to science, from ordinary conversation to philosophy. Consequently, in applying Heidegger's concept of interpretation to writing, I am not enlarging the area of interpretation or applying a reading theory to writing; rather, I am applying a general theory of interpretation to one kind of interpretation.

Heidegger's Theory of Forestructure

Heidegger's theory of interpretation begins with what he calls the "forestructure." He contends that all interpretation must begin with the mental structure which the interpreter brings to the object being interpreted. Indeed, the interpreter has no other alternative but to interpret everything with the knowledge that he or she has. This is so obvious that it hardly seems revolutionary. Yet it does have revolutionary consequences. It means, for instance, that every interpretation must be unique, since every interpretation, even by the same person, is made from a somewhat different perspective. My interpretation of, for instance, a former student of mine is different now that he is a professor than it was when he was a student not long ago; my forestructure has changed since then. The changing of the context is possibly the most important of the notions of poststructuralism—and this notion is Heideggerian. Let us see what Heidegger sees as constituting this mental context, this forestructure. The application to composition is, I believe, extremely fertile.

Heidegger uses the concept of forestructure throughout *Being and Time*. It is a recurring tool which he applies to different issues throughout the book. First, he treats it in his analysis of interpretation in general (150-153, 157; pagination is to the glossed German pagination in the English translation by John Macquarrie and Edward Robinson, London: SCM Press, 1962). Then he applies forestructure to the interpretation of the nature of assertion (157). He uses it in his analysis of mankind's (*Dasein's*) hermeneutical situation (232-234) and employs it three times in his analysis of the notion of care (311-312, 317, 327). In addition, there are briefer uses of the forestructure in other parts of the book.

The word "forestructure" is a literal translation of the German term *Vorstruktur*, a typical Heideggerian coinage. The three components of the forestructure—forehaving, foresight, and foreconception—are also literal translations of *Vorhabe, Vorsicht*, and *Vorgriff*; and *Vorgriff* is also a coinage. In fact, all of the words have somewhat idiosyncratic meanings, as we will see. Let me consider each.

Forehaving

In interpreting anything, a person approaches the object to be interpreted already with some sense of having the thing in mind, even if ever so tentatively and provisionally. The passages about "forehaving" in *Being and Time* all insist on this pre-possession of intention. The interpreter has the thing in advance, like an appropriation (150); it has a definite character; there is a unitary view of the full phenomenon (157). The whole of the entity is perceived (232). Twice conscience is said to be a fore having (268, 290). Speaking of the analysis of the notion of care (*Sorge*), Heidegger says, in a passage which brings together the three terms of the forestructure:

> The hermeneutical Situation which was previously inadequate for interpreting the meaning of the Being of care, now has the required primordiality. Dasein has been put into that which we have in advance, and this has been done primordially—that is to say, this has been done with regard to its authentic potentiality-for-Being-a-whole; the idea of existence, which guides us as that we see in advance, has been made definite by the clarification of our ownmost potentiality-for-Being; and now that we have concretely worked out the structure of Dasein's Being, its peculiar ontological character has become so plain as compared with everything present-at-hand, that Dasein's existentiality has been grasped in advance. (311)

A concise summary of the three dimensions of the forestructure is seen at the end of the treatment of care:

> If resoluteness makes up the mode of authentic care, and if this itself is possible only through temporality, then the phenomenon at which we have arrived by taking a look at resoluteness, must present us with only a modality of temporality, by which, after all, care as such is made possible. Dasein's totality of Being as care means: ahead-of-itself-already-being-in (a world) as Being-alongside (entities encountered within-the-world). When we first fixed upon this articulated structure, we suggested that with regard to this articulation the ontological question must be pursued still further back until the unity of the totality of this structural manifoldness has been laid bare. *The primordial unity of the structure of care lies in temporality.* (327)

The summative phrase of the three dimensions is this statement: "The unity of the totality of this structural manifoldness has been laid bare." Unity, as we shall see, characterizes foresight. Totality is the usual term connected with forehaving. And structural manifoldness is usually related to foreconception.

The main meaning of *Vorhabe* in German does not come through in the literal translation of "forehaving." In German, it means intention, design, object, purpose. Consequently, the intention is seen as having a totality to it in the forestructure. There is a definite character to it, the full phenomenon, the whole entity; the totality of the being is appropriated.

The exact nature of this totality will be more apparent when the other two dimensions are analyzed.

Foresight

"Foresight" is the literal translation of *Vorsicht*, but does not convey the insistence on the notes of caution and circumspection that the German word highlights. We have already seen some of the uses of the term. An early rather full treatment of the three dimensions can be seen in the following passage, given in the general notion of interpretation. While reading this passage, think of the interpretation given the use of a tool by a gardener, not of a scientific and derivative interpretation, as of a difficult text or poem:

> The ready-to-hand is always understood in terms of a totality of involvements. This totality need not be grasped explicitly by a thematic interpretation. Even if it has undergone such an interpretation, it recedes into an understanding which does not stand out from the background. And this is the very mode in which it is the essential foundation for everyday circumspective interpretation. In every case this interpretation is grounded in *something we have in advance—in a fore-having*. As the appropriation of understanding, the interpretation operates in Being towards a totality of involvements which is already understood—a Being which understands. When something is understood but is still veiled, it becomes unveiled by an act of appropriation, and this is always done under the guidance of a point of view, which fixes that with regard to which what is understood is to be interpreted. In every case interpretation is grounded in *something we see in advance—in a fore-sight*. This fore-sight "takes the first cut" out of what has been taken into our fore-having, and it does so with a view to a definite way in which this can be interpreted. Anything understood which is held in our fore-having and towards which we set our sights "foresightedly," becomes conceptualizable through the interpretation. In such an interpretation, the way in which the entity we are interpreting is to be conceived can be drawn from the entity itself, or the interpretation can force the entity into concepts to which it is opposed in its manner of Being; In either case, the interpretation has already decided for a definite way of conceiving it, either with finality or with reservations; it is grounded in *something we grasp in advance—in a fore-conception*. (150)

This is probably Heidegger's most extended treatment of foresight. On several occasions, the idea of foresight is linked with that of unity—foresight seems to provide the unity of the object which is being envisaged as a whole (157), providing the "unity of those structural items which belong to it and are possible" (232); and of course the notion of unity appears in the summation formula about care: "The unity of the totality of this structural manifoldness has been laid bare" (327).

Secondly, foresight is several times explicitly said to be made possible by the idea of existence. Again, speaking of care, Heidegger says, "the idea of existence, which guides us as that which we see in advance, has been made possible by the classification of our inmost potentiality-for-Being" (311). The same idea is repeated a few pages later.

Foresight, therefore, always has the idea of a unity which is projected onto the object which is intended. It seems to be that which makes the parts cohere as a whole, and it is existentially grounded.

Foreconception

I have already cited several important passages explaining foreconception. *Vorgriff* is usually connected with the notion of being able to conceptualize the object (150, 312). This conceptualizing is sometimes explicitly seen to be a recognition of the structure of the object being interpreted. Thus, speaking of *Dasein*, Heidegger says, "Ontological Interpretation projects the entity presented to it upon the Being which is that entity's own, so as to conceptualize it with regard to its structure" (312). And, in the passage discussed above, foresight provides the "unity of those structural items which belong to it and are possible" (232).

The summary formula for care, cited above, also in dudes the notion of a structure: "The unity of the totality of this structural manifoldness has been laid bare." The perception of this structure is sometimes referred to as an "articulation": "To any assertion as a communication which gives something definite character there belongs, moreover, an Articulation of what is pointed out, and this Articulation is in accordance with significations" (157). The word "articulation" preserves both in German and in English its original Latin meaning of distinct segments separated by joints. For our purposes, "articulus" also means the parts of a discourse, both a German and a Latin meaning. And Heidegger, of all people, would have been very aware of both meanings.

Now, let me draw together all of these segments of forestructure. Forehaving means primarily an intention, which is conceived as a whole, a totality, a full phenomenon. Foresight means a look at something which understands the unifying character which holds the totality together. And foreconception means the grasping of the structural manifoldness of the object. If foresight emphasizes the unity of the whole, foreconception emphasizes the perception of the distinct parts which make up the whole.

Application to the Process of Composing
With this notion of forestructure in mind, let me now apply the concept to the process of composition.

When an author wishes to write about something, to interpret this something to future readers, he or she brings to the act of writing a forestructure. This forestructure is constituted by the entire history of the author, including complex cultural conventions which have been assimilated. Against this background, the something which is to be written about is interpreted. Consequently, any writing project I undertake immediately takes a long look into my past. I sort out related objects, meanings, and structures which I have encountered in the past which are similar to or markedly different from the object being interpreted in an attempt to understand the object I have focused on.

My past enables me to see the object as a whole separate from other wholes, as a unity, and as a complex structure with interrelated parts. With this unified and structured whole, I intend to do something. This is the first glimpse I get of the object. As I begin to examine and use the object, I may immediately have to revise my perception of the whole, of the unity, of the structure, and of the intent I had.

Heidegger uses the metaphor of the hermeneutic circle to show the continuing dynamic character of this forestructure (314-16). A simple example may help to explain this circularity. When I begin a sentence, you assume that I have a full sentence meaning in mind, and you relate each word separately to the provisional whole you have projected by context. Each word refines and changes the original whole, so that the meaning of each word is determined by the meaning of the developing wholes, and these words themselves determine the developing wholes. So the meaning of the parts depends on the wholes, and the meaning of the wholes depends on the meanings of the parts. There is a circularity. But it is a necessary circularity. This is the hermeneutical circle.

And it applies to composition. The original forestructure, made up of an intended whole, a unity, and a structural complexity, is continually modified as the richness of the object causes the writer to change his or her original views of his or her intention, unity, and structure. Continually, these modifications are made up against the changing background. There is continually a look at the object and a return to the background to interpret it. Recursion is not an accident; it is a necessity.

The metaphor of the circle, however, should not suggest anything like a closed system between the forestructure and the object being interpreted. Both object and forestructure may require radical alterations, even transformations. And the process of interpretation may cause the interpreter to go far afield from his or her own early forestructure and from the first simple perception of the object of interpretation. The metaphor should not at all suggest the closed system or internal heuristic methodologies which are sometimes read into the work of Emig, Elbow, Flower and Hayes, and others.

The rich dialectical movement in the hermeneutic back and forth between the object and the interpreter is true of many applications of Heidegger's hermeneutic. Heidegger used his hermeneutic to make revolutionary interpretations of many philosophic figures, and he called such re-interpretations "destructions," following Nietzsche. Derrida initially used the same term, but eventually came to call his radical re-interpretations "de-constructions." In his case, they often involve a thorough and meticulous examination of whole sets of cultural assumptions, often unconscious, underlying the position of the piece being deconstructed. This kind of dialectic also involves a serious re-consideration of the object and of the forestructure on the part of Derrida's readers.

Thus the dialectic of the hermeneutic circle can involve recursions, external excursions, transformations of both object and forestructure, and continual new unions of the two.

Even as the author moves through the usual stages of invention, organization, and stylistic choices, these recursions, excursions, and mutual transformations continue. The object continually feeds back into the forestructure to force new accommodations—conceptual, structural, stylistic, and so on. A stylistic accommodation can be made at any stage; so can an organizational change; so can an invention adjustment of any type, ethical, pathetic, or logical (to use the traditional Aristotelian terms); so can a change of genre or medium; so even can a change of audience.

I have tried to suggest this flexibility by mapping the Heideggerian hermeneutic onto the traditional rhetorical sequence of invention, disposition, and style in the accompanying figure. Even this figure, however, does not include the situational and cultural contexts which are implied by changes of audience, genre, and medium. The figure implies that there is a general progressive movement from invention to organization to style, although even within this progression there are continual recursions and jumps ahead. Secondly, it attempts to illustrate graphically that the three dimensions of the Heideggerian forestructure operate throughout the entire hermeneutic process. There is a sustained revision of intent and notion of the whole, of unity and unifying factors, and of relations of part to part. These constant revisions are necessitated by the progressions, regressions, egressions, and ingressions of the dialectical movement.

The Forestructure in the Writing Process

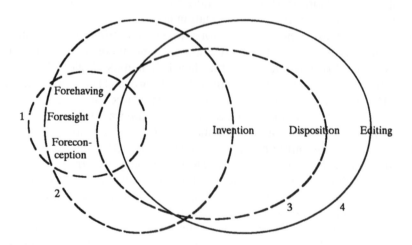

Circle 1 represents the original forestructure. Circle 2 represents one of the forestructures as it has been adapted at one point in the process of invention—the project has been considerably expanded at this point. Circle 3 represents a somewhat scaled-down version of the project during one stage in the process of organization; but organization, while reacting on the forestructure, also involves invention, whence the overlap with it. Circle 4 represents the final project after some changes have been brought about in the editing stage, which has also involved both organization and invention.

Such a view of process should give us a more flexible, more recursive, more exploratory, and especially more pluralistic view of the writing process than we now seem to have almost unconsciously adopted. In particular, it would militate against an almost monolithic notion floating in the journals that there is a single process underlying all invention, prewriting, writing, and editing stages. Certainly, a different kind of totality, unifying principle, and relationship between parts and whole are to be found in the invention, organization, and style of a narrative than in a careful expository taxonomy, or in a political speech. Each of these types demands a different kind of totality, unifying principle, and notion of structural organization—in effect, also a different style. The forestructure brought to each will necessarily differ radically, as will the absorption of the interpreted subject by the forestructure and the resulting dialectic between the two.

There may be generic kinds of forestructures—for example, narrative versus taxonomic—but each individual case will still be far from formulate. The individual writer, the individuating circumstances, and the particular subject or content will all change even generic kinds of forestructures. Our current linguistic and rhetorical inventions and organizations and styles have especially failed to take into account different subject matters; they are, as it is said, content-free. Now, different writing-across-the-curriculum movements are beginning to teach us that disciplinary communities think, organize, and discourse differently—in effect, have different invention, organization, and style behaviors, at least in their internal communications. Hopefully, there are also common thinking, organizational, and style behaviors which will still enable us to communicate at some level with other groups and with the public. All of this suggests a variety of forestructures for different authors, audiences, and subject matters.

This notion of a structure also strongly opposes a linear view of process that takes into account only the time a person sits down and turns out sequential prose, even if in different drafts. Egressions from the hermeneutic circle—or apparent egressions—may sometimes take hours or weeks or months, even years. They may entail reading entire books, lengthy laboratory experiments, interviews, and so on. The extemporaneous freshman theme, written to no one in particular, about nothing in particular, with no publishing medium considered, and in an information vacuum, cannot continue to be the assumed model for process or product.

Heidegger's forestructure has been a useful model in other areas of discourse production and analysis. Hopefully, it can give some depth to our own problems in rhetoric and composition.

Dichotomy, Consubstantiality, Technical Writing, Literary Theory: The Double Orthodox Curse

Jasper Neel

Imagine this scene. A technical writer employed by a large computer manufacturer must update the documentation for a redesigned fluid-mechanics process control system. No new hardware has been developed, but the software, which each end user must reinstall and reconfigure, has changed considerably. The writer has one month in which to delete all the outdated material, write approximately seventy-five screens of new material, and ensure that the new documentation seems both uniform and univocal. The revised documentation, which will exist only on-line and will offer hypertext navigational features, will require about two-hundred screens. The statistical process control (SPC) oversight program will require an additional twenty screens.

Imagine a second scene. An associate professor of literature who specializes in reader-response criticism must publish a book in order to be promoted. The professor must take into account all that has already been written about reader response and must be careful to demonstrate how the new book corrects and expands prior books. Since this professor has tenure, there is no particular deadline, but writing the book is a daunting task: first because the professor must find a university press interested in publishing yet another theory book in the area of reader response, and second because the professor must write a book that will please at least two unknown and anonymous referees. Though the literature professor must use MLA documentation style and generate a text that other professors will recognize as "a book," no particular rules about length, style, or delivery system constrain the writing process.

For now, let these scenes form a split-screen backdrop as I try to articulate two different conceptions of writing that come to us from ancient Greece. My purpose in articulating these conceptions is to use them as a field in which to compare the above writing scenes. I want to know whether the two scenes are the same, merely similar, or absolutely different. More importantly, I want to know whether the two scenes imply similar, different, or mutually exclusive pedagogies. I recognize that the reader-response school does not encompass all literary theory just as software documentation does not encompass all technical writing. I use reader response and software documentation merely as extreme examples. I want to work at the extremes to see what, if anything, they show about the middle, if any such place exists.

An Ancient Dichotomy
Writing, as Plato would have it, is at best an innocuous pastime; at worst, it is a dangerous distraction capable of generating the illusion of false wisdom and incapable of communicating true knowledge. "It shows great folly," Plato's Socrates says near the end of Phaedrus, "to suppose that one can transmit or acquire clear and certain knowledge of an art through the medium of writing, or that written words can do more than remind the reader of what he already knows on any given subject" (275c). According to Plato, when it comes to writing, one must believe "that nothing worth serious attention has ever been written in prose or verse" (279e). "Any serious student of serious realities," Plato says in the "Seventh Letter,"

> will shrink from making truth the helpless object of men's ill-will by committing it to writing.... When one sees a written composition, whether it be on law by a legislator or on any other subject, one can be sure, if the writer is a serious man, that his book does not represent his most serious thoughts; they remain stored up in the noblest region of his personality. (344b-c; see also 343b)

Aristotle does not deal quite so harshly with writing as does Plato, but he carefully places it two removes from its "content." "Spoken words," he says in the second paragraph of *De Interpretatione*, "are the symbols of mental experience and written words are the symbols of spoken words." While Aristotle admits that all people do not have the same writing or the same speech, "the mental experiences, which these directly symbolize," he argues, "are the same for all, as also are those things of which our experiences are the images" (16a5-10). I take this last clause to imply that some reality exists outside mental experience and is the universal of which mental experience is the image. I take the whole passage to imply that mental experience, the "content" that language must carry, is the same for everyone and that it exists both prior to and outside of any sort of language, whether spoken or written. In *De Anima* Aristotle repeats this quadripartite division into reality-experience-expression-inscription (431a1-10).

One can with some certainty describe the epistemological and ontological assumptions that Plato and Aristotle make about writing. Both exclude it entirely from the process of knowing, thereby separating it from invention. After this first move, however, an apparent disagreement occurs. Aristotle seems willing to allow writing to serve authorial intent. Although he does not allow writing a role in the *episteme*, neither does he condemn it utterly. Plato, of course, goes much further by separating writing absolutely from the best of a person's thought and self.

These notions of writing have widespread support. Nearly everyone who bothers to consider the matter at all agrees that writing represents speech, which in turn represents thought. Provoked to go beyond this initial notion, a few would agree with Plato, but most would agree with Aristotle. Even such trendy theorists as Richard Rorty and Jacques Derrida, when pressed to discuss the matter at all, seem to regard the teaching of writing as a classical, traditional undertaking (Olson, "Social" 6-9 and "Derrida" 4-7).

Outside university humanities departments, the Platonic and Aristotelian notions of writing predominate. Carolyn Miller has shown how the Aristotelian "windowpane" notion, expounded most forcefully in this century by A.J. Ayer, has dominated technical writing since it first appeared in the 1940s in the aerospace and electronics industries. Building on her essay, David Dobrin has explored the tradition of Cartesian rationalism that comes to us through Bacon, Locke, Burke, Spencer, and the early Wittgenstein.

There is, of course, an alternative notion of writing. But one must work a little harder to find its ancient roots. One can begin with Heraclitus, who seems to have considered all existence as a dance of opposites, with no entity able to exclude its opposite. "In writing," according to one of his few extant fragments, "the course taken, straight and crooked, is one and the same." Were one to set up a Heraclitean thought-writing duality, one would have a forever self-recreating, transmogrifying dance of opposition, resulting in a Janus-faced notion (Stokes 478). While one can argue, as many classical scholars do, that Heraclitus built his philosophy on a unified logos, the Heraclitean "unity" is a unity of opposition resembling Saussurean "difference" if not Derridean "différance." In the *Refutatio Heresiorum*, Hippolytus quotes Heraclitus as saying, "They do not understand how that which differs with itself is in agreement: harmony consists of opposing tension, like that of the bow and the lyre." Plutarch renders the most famous Heraclitean dictum: "It is not possible to step twice into the same river. (It is impossible to touch the same mortal substance twice, but through the rapidity of change.... The combination and separation are simultaneous)..." (McLean and Aspell 35).

When one claims to see Heraclitean notions of writing in the works of Protagoras and Gorgias, one must argue inferentially because history has left us so few texts. Even so, the few scraps that remain imply notions rather different from those of Plato and Aristotle. Protagoras taught that all arguments carry within themselves their opposites; Gorgias, using a rhetorical strategy sometimes labeled "apogogic," assumed a plurality of voices for any possible argument (Barrett 9-18; see also Guthrie, Kerferd, and Sprague). Protagoras has been roundly condemned for millennia for his radical humanism ("man is the measure of all things") and his agnosticism. Gorgias has been condemned with equal vigor for his relativism: "Nothing exists," he wrote, "and if anything did exist humans could not know it, and if they could know it, they would have no means to communicate what they knew" (Freeman 125-39; Romeyer-Dherbey 7-52).

Just as one can summarize Plato and Aristotle, one can also summarize Heraclitus, Protagoras, and Gorgias. From their perspective, there is no prior place where thinking and meaning can prepare themselves for transportation in writing. If, as Heraclitus would have it, one cannot step twice into the same stream, then one cannot describe that stream as anything other than a brief, now lost, historical moment that was in the process of change even during the moment described. If, as Gorgias would have it, nothing exists, then the quadripartite Aristotelian notion of reality-experience-expression-inscription is nothing more than anthropocentric ego glorification. If, as Protagoras would have it, humankind is the measure of all things and if humans have no way to know about the existence of the gods, then Plato's divine Forms fade into triviality, if not willful self-delusion. As a result of all this, writing no longer plays a tertiary role. Rather, the unfinished and unfinishable process of writing permeates every aspect of whatever would like to present itself as outside of and prior to writing.

For the sake of convenience, I will call the Platonic-Aristotelian notion of writing classical; the Heraclitean-Protagorean-Gorgian notion sophistic.

A Modern Dichotomy

In spite of powerful theoretical work by Bazerman (6-17, 318-32), who tries to show the "situated, purposeful, strategic, symbolic activity" that makes all technical writing "rhetorical"; in spite of studies by Michael Halloran, Greg Myers, and Jone Rymer that show the rhetorical processes of scientific writing; in spite of important pedagogical efforts by Paul Anderson to bring a kind of reader response to technical writing; in spite of the work by Dobrin and Miller mentioned above; in spite of Merrill Whitburn's entire career; the classical notion dominates both theory and praxis in the field of technical writing. One can attend an STC convention or local chapter meeting or read through the dozens of technical writing texts published each year without ever suspecting all this theory exists. For example, in explaining how to write what they call "functional documents" (a phrase that would make a theorist's imagination race), Flower, Hayes, and Swarts articulate the "'scenario principle,' which states that functional prose should be structured around a human agent performing actions in a particularized situation" (42). Readability in technical writing, according to Jack Selzer, "is simply the efficiency with which a text can be comprehended by a reader, as measured by reading time, amount recalled, questions answered, or some other quantifiable measure of a reader's ability to process a text" (73). In her Herculean effort to make "document design" into a legitimate professional specialization, Karen Schriver makes clear that technical "writers need to find ways to design text that anticipates a quick, probably passive reading." Her method is to begin with "empirical findings about users' needs" and then specify "ways to design text that meets those needs" (319-20).

The textbooks are even more forthright. "Technical writing," argue Kelley and Masse, "is writing about a subject in the pure sciences or the applied sciences in which the writer informs the reader through an objective presentation of facts" (6). "The primary . . . characteristic of technical and scientific writing," Britton contends, "lies in the effort of the author to convey one meaning and only one meaning in what he says" (11). "Because readers use a technical document," Lannon explains, "it must be based on facts, and it must have one single meaning. Poetry and fiction, then, would not be forms of technical writing because they are largely based on intuition, feelings, and imagination" (4). "Technical writing is meant to get a job done," says Markel. "Everything else is secondary" (5). "Our readers are busy people who are interested only in facts," Blicq urges. "Information they do not need irks them. For these people we must keep strictly to the point" (41). "Technical writing is ideally characterized by the maintenance of an attitude or impartiality and objectivity, by extreme care to convey information accurately and concisely, and by the absence of any attempt to arouse emotion" (Mills and Walter, 5). And so on.

Look what a difference one finds when one moves to the sophistical notion of writing. Louise Phelps describes writing in that world as "marked by themes of loss, illusion, instability, marginality, decentering, and finitude" (5). Foucault and Derrida (however bitter their own disputes may have been and however much each would resent being called a sophist) articulate and exemplify the notion of writing I am describing. At the end of the Introduction to *The Archaeology of Knowledge*, after having foregrounded a notion of history as discontinuous and put the notion of "self" radically in question, Foucault turns to a sort of apologia for his *oeuvre* where he describes the sort of writing he does and approves. He concludes the description by shifting abruptly to the form of a hostile question followed by a canny answer. "Aren't you sure of what you're saying?" his made-up questioner demands,

> Are you going to change yet again, shift your position according to the questions that are put to you, and say that the objections are not really directed at the place from which you are speaking? Are you going to declare yet again that you have never been what you have been reproached with being? Are you already preparing the way out that will enable you in your next book to spring up somewhere else and declare as you're now doing: no, no I'm not where you are lying in wait for me, but over here, laughing at you?

"What," comes the canny reply,

> do you imagine that I would take so much trouble and so much pleasure in writing, do you think that I would keep so persistently to my task, if I were not preparing—with a rather shaky hand—a labyrinth into which I can venture, in which I can move my discourse, opening up underground passages, forcing it to go far from itself, finding overhangs that reduce and deform its itinerary, in which I can lose myself and appear at last to eyes that I will never have to meet again. I am no doubt not the only one who writes in order to have no face. Do not ask who I am and do not ask me to remain the same: leave it to our bureaucrats and our police to see that our papers are in order. At least spare us their morality when we write. (17)

Technical writers need no particular ingenuity to discover themselves as the "bureaucrats" and "police" who keep society's papers (machines, social services, marketing structures) "in order" so that the Foucauldian project can play itself out secure in the certainty that electricity will flow to the word processor, food will be in the market, criminals will not attack in the night.

At the end of "Plato's Pharmacy," having reduced the writer of *Phaedrus* to a state of ear-stopping confusion and uncertainty, Derrida writes and describes the play of writing: "The walled-in voice" that is written into *Phaedrus*,

> strikes against the rafters, the words come apart, bits and pieces of sentences are separated, disarticulated parts begin to circulate through the corridors, become fixed for a round or two, translate each other, become rejoined, bounce off each other, contradict each other, make trouble, tell on each other, come back like answers, organize their exchanges, protect each other, institute an internal commerce, take themselves for a dialogue. Full of meaning. A whole story. An entire history. (169-71)

The kinds of dichotomies I am making are obvious: between ancient Greek and modern Euro-American theory, between sophistical and Platonic notions of epistemology, between theory and praxis, between technical writing and literary theory, and so on. I want to keep those dichotomies as clear as possible for a while longer, working constantly to stay at the extremes.

A Practical Dichotomy

The technical writer in the scene I have described writes in a densely structured, highly determined environment. The process control and its computerization have already been invented. The system already works. While the writer must make frequent decisions about order and emphasis as well as about what the reader already knows, "topic" and "focus" are rigidly controlled. Company guidelines, which are embedded in a host publishing system that includes a required seven-level markup language, largely determine what the final document will look like. The task analysis and usability testing stages in the company's standard documentation procedure give the writer both a rigidly determined mandate and a clear evaluation of the text's successes and failures. Because much of the former documentation survives and the writer has insufficient time to rewrite it, the syntactic style has already been set, leaving little room for significant modification. A company editor will read the final text to ensure that it looks and sounds like other company publications.

These straightening factors are, however, mitigated by the comfort zone in which the writer writes. The writer remains comfortable because there is no question about the documents's value. Without documentation, the computerization remains largely useless. Although no end user is likely to read the entire text, nearly every end user will read parts of it, and no customer would even consider buying the equipment without documentation. Both the value of the writer's work and the certainty of the reader's motive remain beyond question.

Which of the two conceptions of writing informs this technical writer's situation? Almost certainly the classical. The most comfortable fit in that model occurs with Aristotle. The technical writer knows that the computer-controlled process constitutes the "reality" to be described. It exists without the documentation. Thus, the writer must learn how the computerized equipment controls the process and how to install both hardware and software. Then the writer must explain this knowledge in a CD-ROM text, conduct usability testing to ensure the effectiveness of the documentation, and revise the text in light of what the usability testing shows. Company guidelines dictate a three-part structure: first an overview explaining what the system does and protecting the manufacturer from liability suits; then an installation procedure; and finally a reference guide. Depending on what the task analysis shows, the writer may or may not include a tutorial. Someone in manufacturing will write an SPC monitoring program to ensure that the flow rate, temperature, pressure, and a host of other variables remain within defined parameters. Installing and assuring the reliability of the SPC program will be treated as a separate and particularly important part of the documentation package. Because the hypertextual function will operate across the boundaries separating the different parts of the text, at the level of hypertext the document becomes one large Aristotelian "field."

Elements of Plato do occur in this scene, even though they may remain hidden. Most, if not all, technical writers would accept Plato's dicta against the writing they do on the job. They would readily agree that their most serious thoughts do not appear in their texts. While they would hope that these texts tell the "truth" about technical processes and in fact communicate information about such processes, they would also agree that this sort of "truth" is not the most interesting sort. Process control documentation, in Plato's words, does not deal with "serious realities," merely with a technical process. Pirsig remains the paradigmatic figure here: the technical writer supporting himself as a servant of industry while seeking "Quality" on his own time.

The sophistical model plays no significant role here. Heraclitus may be right about the ontology of streams, but he is wrong about process controls. Considerable difference exists between a straight and a crooked description of the process. When, for example, some aspect of the process begins to operate outside the SPC parameters, the program will tell the operator to shut down the system. This command has no meaningful opposite. All operators will be drilled *ad nauseam* on how and why to stop the process when the program tells them to do so. Perhaps more to the point, a genuine reality test exists: either the process control update works or it does not work. Gorgias is plain wrong. The process to be controlled and the system for control both exist. The writer can learn about both and communicate the appropriate knowledge to the reader. Indeed, the technical writer's company stands legally liable if the documentation is incorrect or if the product does not do what the documentation claims.

In sum, the technical writer writes in a quite orthodox, classical world. In this world, writing (which may include all types of graphics) functions best when it functions as a conduit for verifiable, technical information. At the same time, the writing has nothing to do with, or at least operates many removes from, the writer's soul, where the best parts of the writer remain stored up to be employed and deployed for more important matters. Yes, the writer must decide on the 250 linkages for the hypertext function, linkages whose labels and chaining sequences depend on the writer's experience and intuition. Yes, many technical writers now control the product interface by participating in product design from the beginning. Nevertheless, writing in the technical writer's world fits almost perfectly into the classical conception.

Making one's way in the world as a reader-response critic, on the other hand, is rather different. To begin with, one must make obeisance to the Bleich-Fish-Holland triumvirate. And if one chooses to focus at length on describing readers, one must also take into account a trinity of hallowed theorists (Booth, Gibson, and Ong) who have already described the "implied reader," the "mock reader," and the "fictionalized audience." Since the triumvirate has already made the outrageous normal, one cannot succeed by being outrageous, which merely seems normal, and one runs the risk of vanishing entirely if one presents oneself as merely normal. Worse yet, the trinity has already staked out the simple and elegant modes of describing the reader. As a result, one must find some way of appearing normally outrageous while at the same time showing how to complicate the simple, elegant trinitarian notions.

Whereas reality for the technical writer exists in the form of hardware and software that, correctly installed and configured, moves vast quantities of viscid liquid through a pipe; reality for the reader-response critic exists in the form of a reader's responses to (canonized?) literature. Whatever mode of validation one chooses (by appealing to a discourse community as Fish does, to subjective experience as Bleich does, to some sort of psychological modeling process as Holland does, or, as Peter Rabinowitz has recently done, by describing a multilayered reader whose roles range from actual reader and narrative reader to authorial reader and critical reader), the reality available for the reader-response critic differs markedly from that for the technical writer. No tangible, physical substance moves from the literary text to the reader's intellect. No absolutely reliable verification procedure to evaluate the reading process exists. In other words, one cannot easily imagine writing an SPC monitoring program to record violations of the reading specifications and stop the process if the reader makes too many parameter violations.

Which of the two conceptions of writing informs the literary critic's situation? Almost certainly not the classical. The critic utterly reverses

Plato's notion of writing by assuming that writing is the most significant act a person can undertake. One can also infer that Aristotle's quadripartite notion gets reversed. Writing, or the ability to write, generates experience and teaches both writer and reader how to "criticize" anything that attempts to present itself as "reality." The "close reading" of literary texts coupled with the writing that grows from that reading is, to the critic, the single most important undertaking available for human beings. Whether one reads the triumvirate, the trinity, or such recent players as Rabinowitz, one cannot help noticing the absolute value placed on the writing that grows out of the reading of literature.

If Pirsig is the technical writer's model, Kafka and Hartman are the literary theorist's models. For Kafka, in an utter reversal of Plato's denunciations, writing replaced all forms of oral communication and became the only way he could think: "I hate everything that does not relate to literature," he wrote in his diary. "Conversations bore me (even if they relate to literature), to visit people bores me, the sorrows and joys of my relatives bore me to my soul. Conversation takes the importance, the seriousness, the truth, out of everything I think" (292). Hartman (as does his colleague Harold Bloom) gives this same seriousness to the writing of literary criticism, arguing that "we have entered an era that can challenge even the priority of literary to literary-critical texts." Hartman sees Longinus' criticism as being equal to the texts it treats, Derrida's as equal to the texts he (dis)interprets (17).

The sophistical seems to be the conception of writing that informs the critic's text. Almost every aspect of reader-response criticism exists as a Heraclitean opposition. To begin with, such criticism knows itself through its opposition to any of the criticisms that imply a closed, complete, accurate reading. Any particular modification of reader response (Rabinowitz's recent book being a good example) knows itself by differing from the triumvirate on one hand and from the trinity on the other. Notions about canon reformation that usually grow out of reader response exist by opposing the traditional, Anglo-male canon of the past. Just as one cannot step into the same stream twice, one cannot open the same book twice. Humanity, with all its inconsistencies, truly is the measure of everything. And nothing exists if by "existence" one means the articulation of a definitive reading of a given text. In short, writing—the never-finished processes of restatement, replacement, revaluation, and repetition—serves no greater end. The unending process of (re)writing is itself the end.

Note the differences between the undertakings of the theorist and the technical writer. Theorists neither expect nor desire that their books be the last on critical theory. They recognize at all points that their books can be unwritten. Indeed, they hope that their books will be unwritten because attempts to unwrite their books imply that those books have become so important that future theorists must account for them or get rid of them before offering their own interpretations. In other words nothing about a reader-response critic's book claims to be "correct." The joy of the book is that the new theorist can enter an old field, one presumably tilled to exhaustion, and raise a new, bountiful crop. The metaphor is apt because Plato uses it to distinguish the long, slow dialectical process toward truth from the short, easy process of using writing for trivial pastimes (*Phaedrus* 276c).

In contrast to the critic, the technical writer must fix anything in the documentation that is wrong. If, after the equipment is shipped, errors or ambiguities turn up, the writer must correct the documentation, bringing it in line with the reality of the process control. As long as the equipment remains the same, the documentation remains the same.

A Political Dichotomy

Now I can return to the questions with which I began. Are the technical writer and the theorist the same, merely similar, or utterly different? Are the pedagogical situations in literary criticism and technical writing the same, similar, or different?

Aristotle contends that arguing both sides of a question has the salutary effect of teaching the correct position because proofs are always easier to generate for the "right" side of any issue (*Rhetoric* 1355a). Although one can certainly imagine how to argue that reader-response criticism and process control software documentation are alike, one can (perhaps with more ease) imagine how to argue that they differ profoundly. The differences are obvious. Whereas the technical writer documents a computer-controlled mechanical process, a process that must be activated and maintained following the instructions, the theorist offers nothing of the sort. People had read literature for millennia before the appearance in 1938 of Louise Rosenblatt's *Literature as Exploration*, the text usually considered to be the first attempt at reader-response theory. No one having trouble reading will ever refer back to Rosenblatt or Fish or even Booth to discover what has been configured or installed improperly or where the error in the system of reading lies. An act of reader-response criticism includes no product liability disclaimer because no critic has ever worried that someone might sue if the reading procedure described fails to work (whatever "work" might mean in such a scenario). The "knowledge" that emerges from hallowed texts such as *The Rhetoric of Fiction* or *Is There a Text in This Class?* is not technical; one cannot know it in the way one can know how to operate a process control system.

What of pedagogy? Does training in one form of writing support teaching in the other? All technical writing teachers know what literature faculty would say. The notion of an experienced technical writer offering a long list of successful technical manuals as justification for teaching literature courses would be regarded as perversely evil by every literature faculty. Of course, literature faculty do not object to literature professors teaching technical writing. As we all know, most professors of technical writing were trained in literature, and a shockingly high percentage (certainly more than 75 percent) of them have never written a technical manual of any sort. Worse yet, most of them, in Schriver's words, work as "untenured instructors or part-time adjunct faculty" because their literature colleagues regard their world as "atheoretical, anti-humanistic, smacking too much of the material world, and uninteresting" (323).

Do the pedagogies differ as profoundly as the acts of writing? Obviously I think they do, and I will end by trying to contrast the two pedagogies. One pedagogy values ambiguation and the increase of complexity. Tracing the increasing complexity of trinitarian notions of reader response shows this. Walker Gibson's 1950 essay describing the "mock reader" consists of five pages. Wayne Booth's 1961 book includes about thirty pages on the "implied reader." Walter Ong's 1977 book includes about sixty-five pages describing the "fictionalized audience." Peter Rabinowitz's 1987 book contains more than 150 pages on the roles of and rules for being a reader.

Looking from the perspective of the triumvirate, anyone can see how much more complex notions of the reader are now than they were in 1968 when Norman Holland published *The Dynamics of Literary Response*. This book, which had been preceded in 1938 by Rosenblatt's, was followed in 1972 by Wolfgang Iser's *The Implied Reader*, in 1975 by Holland's *5 Readers Reading*, in 1978 by Iser's *The Act of Reading* and David Bleich's *Subjective Criticism*, and then in 1980 by Stanley Fish's *Is There a Text in This Class?* and Jane Tompkins' collection of essays *Reader-Response Criticism*. After 1980, reader response expanded across North America developing into a full-fledged methodology as widespread and dominant as the New Criticism ever was. Each successive reader-response text makes the notion of reading more complicated, more fraught with layers, uncertainties, and difficulties. With the appearance in 1989 of Fish's *Doing What Comes Naturally*, the notion of "naturalness" in the reading process had taken on a kind of complexity comparable to that in quantum theory.

In contrast, the technical writer works constantly to make the documentation less complicated, briefer, less necessary. The currently impossible (but not unthinkable!) ideal would be a computerized process control system that installs, configures, and operates itself. In short, one pedagogy calls for an increasingly plurisignificant, increasingly expansive notion of writing, while the other calls for an increasingly univocal, increasingly reductive notion. More literary interpretation is better than less; there cannot possibly be enough. Less computer documentation is better than more; any at all is too much.

Professors of literary interpretation will go to almost any length to avoid telling students what to do in their papers. The single most annoying question posed to such professors goes like this: "If you'll just tell me what you want, I'll try to do it." Professors have to bite their tongues to avoid replying, "You reveal your naivete about intellectual matters by asking me to turn you into a trained technician." After all, specific directions about what to do defeat the purpose and limit the student's creativity. The notion of a rigidly standard essay format with codified rules for organization, structure, authorial voice, evidence, syntax, and interpretation violates the point of literary interpretation. Students must work their own way through their assignments just as Rabinowitz, as a relative latecomer in 1987, had to create his own way to participate in the exceedingly crowded field of reader response. Every honest professor of literary interpretation would admit that a paper that gets "A" from one professor might very well get "D" from another and vice versa. New insight, surprise, idiosyncracy—these are the qualities that please the theorist.

In a technical writing class, however, it would be quite ordinary for students to write in a hierarchical markup language rigidly controlled both by the host publishing system and by the standard format for the particular task at hand. It would be quite ordinary for technical writing professors to articulate the rules of format, appearance, content, organization, structure, authorial voice, syntax, and evidence (if such a notion as "evidence" obtains). In extreme cases, students might be asked to document software. The "grading" procedure for their documents would consist of having a representative member of the target audience try to run the program. If the documentation works with no glitches or bugs, "A"; with just a few, "B"; with several but not enough to halt the program, "C"; with enough to threaten the program's execution, "D"; if the program fails, "F." Professors merely watch their linked terminals as users try to implement documentation. Everyone starts at "A." As bugs, glitches, and failures multiply, the grade drops. While different professors might draw slightly different lines between "A" and "B," no student whose documentation runs smoothly would get a grade below "B," and no student whose documentation fails to run the program would get a grade above "F." Most important of all, however, the technical writing professor will (or certainly should) build usability testing into the documentation process. Thus, only students who do not follow the assignment through its proper steps could ever reach the point of having their documentation fail. In other words, a properly run software documentation class leaves no room for failure. The whole point is the elimination of chance, guesswork, surprise and idiosyncracy. Each writing task has a specific technical function to enable. Close collaboration among students as well as between students and professor ensures that, by the end of the term, everyone has an operational text, a text that has already been tried and found successful in the usability testing stage. Perhaps this is why the mere existence of a course entitled "Technical Documentation" both mystifies and horrifies most literature faculty.

And so we have these extremes. When they are drawn this way, technical writing suffers a sort of double orthodox curse. Literary theorists cannot help holding technical writers in contempt; the theoretical assumptions of literary theory demand it. Sophistical theory would not even allow technical documentation to present itself to the world as writing. It would be like trying to run a DOS program on an Apple with no interface software. To the theorist working from a sophistical base (and obviously I do not believe a theorist can operate from any other base), technical documentation simply is not interesting. Bruffee, for example, may claim social constructionism for writing in general, and Edward Barrett may apply that notion to the virtual environment of a hypertextual situation, but mentioning "social construction" to the theorist whose work supposedly enabled it produces nothing but a snort of condescension, as both the Rorty interview (Bruffee's response notwithstanding) and the repeated sneers of Stanley Fish clearly show. Barrett can claim that through the ideology of social construction, hypertext "escapes from the collapsed inner world of the machine and enters history" (xiv), but you can bet no theorists are reading his arguments, or even know where to look for them.

At the other extreme the technical writer does have a classical base, but this classical base reduces technical writing either to trivial pastime or to slavery. Worse yet, the literary theorist can (and usually does!) leap into the classical world and claim to be on a Platonic, dialectical journey toward Truth, a journey that never ends, a journey in which writing does in fact function as a pastime record of lovers' dialectical discussions in the office and the classroom.

How do we begin some sort of Rogerian argument? Technical writing teachers can initiate such a discussion in two ways. First, they can show that the extreme case of software documentation for an SPC-monitored process control system does not encompass all of technical writing. They can explain the complexities of proposals, of reports, and of technical writing assignments that involve the writer in a ground-up way so that the writer has input from the beginning. Second, technical writing teachers can study critical theory so as to understand what it shows not only about canonized literature but also about technical writing. They can bring poststructural analysis to bear on almost any technical writing situation, showing its full complexity and trying to avoid the tendency toward oversimplification. Certainly they can use poststructural analysis to debunk plain language notions or simplified English programs.

But Rogerian argument does require an interlocutor. If technical writing teachers attempt some sort of rapprochement (Rogerian or otherwise), will there be anyone to talk with? In submitting this essay to *JAC* I rest quite confident that no subscriber will have difficulty with it. Even though it relies on Foucault, Derrida, reader-response theory, classical rhetoric, contemporary theories of argument, and the jargon of both composition studies and software documentation, all readers of *JAC* will understand my jargon with no trouble whatsoever. To what degree is that true of literature professors? How many of them would know what Rogerian argument is? How many would imagine that they could learn about teaching literature by reading *Technical Communication* or listening to a talk by Karen Schriver?

As long as we inhabit a political structure where one can qualify to teach technical writing by studying literature but not the reverse, is a conversation possible? Or are we forced to operate at the extremes I have described? In other words, can the middle become a hospitable neighborhood only through the good will and effort of the people who operate at what the other people regard not as an opposite extreme but as an intellectual vacuum?

Where are the departments that are truly strong at both extremes, yet have a Rogerian discussion of the differences going on? The sort of department I mean would offer work in technical and professional writing comparable to that at Rensselaer or Carnegie Mellon and literary theory comparable to that at Duke or Berkeley. Am I wrong in assuming that technical writers can and do move all the way from one extreme to the other, while literature professors do not see themselves either at an extreme or as part of any sort of continuum that would, if followed far enough, reach to the writing of software documentation for a process control?

Works Cited

Anderson, Paul V. *Technical Writing: A Reader-Centered Approach*. New York: Harcourt, 1987.

Aristotle. *De Anima (On the Soul)*. *Aristotle: On the Soul, Parva Naturalia, On Breath*. Trans. W.S. Hett. Cambridge: Harvard UP, 1936. 2-203.

——. *De Interpretatione*. Trans. E.M. Edghill. *The Works of Aristotle*. Ed. W.D. Ross. London: Oxford, 1928. 16a-23b.

——. *Rhetoric and Poetics*. Trans. W. Rhys Roberts and Ingram Bywater. New York: Modern Library, 1954.

Barrett, Edward. "Introduction." *Society of Text: Hypertext, Hypermedia, and the Social Construction of Information*. Ed. Edward Barrett. Cambridge: MIT P, 1989. xi-xviii.

Barrett, Harold. *The Sophists: Rhetoric, Democracy, and Plato's Idea of Sophistry*. Navato, CA: Chandler, 1987.

Bazerman, Charles. *Shaping Written Knowledge: The Genre and Activity of the Experimental Article in Science*. Madison: U of Wisconsin P, 1988.

Bleich, David. *Subjective Criticism*. Baltimore: Johns Hopkins UP, 1978.

Blicq, Ron S. *Technically—Write! Communications in a Technological Era*. 3rd ed. Englewood Cliffs, NJ: Prentice, 1986.

Bloom, Harold. *The Anxiety of Influence: A Theory of Poetry*. New York: Oxford UP, 1973.

Booth, Wayne C. *The Rhetoric of Fiction*. Chicago: U of Chicago P, 1961.

Britton, Earl. "What is Technical Writing? A Redefinition." *The Teaching of Technical Writing*. Ed. D.H. Cunningham and H.A. Estrin. Urbana: NCTE, 1975. 23-33.

Bruffee, Kenneth A. "Response to the *JAC* Interview with Richard Rorty." *Journal of Advanced Composition* 10 (1990): 145-46.

——. "Social Construction, Language, and the Authority of Knowledge: A Bibliographical Essay." *College English* 48 (1986): 773-90.

Derrida, Jacques. "Différance." *Margins of Philosophy*. Trans. Alan Bass. Chicago: U of Chicago P, 1982. 1-27.

——. *Dissemination*. Trans. Barbara Johnson. Chicago: U of Chicago P, 1981.

Dobrin, David. "What's Technical About Technical Writing?" *New Essays in Technical and Scientific Communication: Research, Theory, Practice*. Ed. Paul V. Anderson, R. John Brockman, and Carolyn Miller. Farmingdale, NY: Baywood, 1983. 227-50.

Fish, Stanley. *Doing What Comes Naturally*. Durham: Duke UP, 1989.

——. *Is There a Text in This Class?* Cambridge: Harvard UP, 1980.

Flower, Linda, John R. Hayes, and Heidi Swarts. "Revising Functional Documents: The Scenario Principle." *New Essays in Technical and Scientific Communication*. Ed. Paul V. Anderson, R. John Brockman, and Carolyn Miller. Farmingdale, NY: Baywood, 1983. 41-58.

Foucault, Michel. *The Archaeology of Knowledge and The Discourse on Language*. Trans. A.M. Sheridan Smith. New York: Pantheon, 1972.

Freeman, Kathleen. *Ancilla to the Pre-Socratic Philosophers*. Cambridge: Harvard UP, 1966.

Gibson, Walker. "Authors, Speakers, Readers, and Mock Readers." *College English* 11 (1950): 265-69.

Guthrie, W.K.C. *A History of Greek Philosophy*, Vol 1. Cambridge: Cambridge UP, 1967.

Halloran, S. Michael. "The Birth of Molecular Biology: An Essay in the Rhetorical Criticism of Scientific Discourse." *Rhetoric Review* 3 (1984): 70-83.

Hartman, Geoffrey. *Saving the Text: Literature, Derrida, Philosophy*. Baltimore: Johns Hopkins UP, 1981.

Holland, Norman. *The Dynamics of Literary Response*. New York: Oxford UP, 1968.

——. *5 Readers Reading*. New Haven: Yale UP, 1975.

Iser, Wolfgang. *The Act of Reading*. Baltimore: Johns Hopkins UP, 1976.

——. *The Implied Reader*. Baltimore: Johns Hopkins UP, 1972.

Kafka, Franz. *The Diaries of Franz Kafka*. Ed. Max Brod. Trans. Joseph Kresh. 2 vols. New York: Schocken, 1948.

Kelley, Patrick, and Roger Masse. "A Definition of Technical Writing." *The Technical Writing Teacher* 4 (1977): 94-97.

Kerferd, G.B. *The Sophistic Movement*. Cambridge: Cambridge UP, 1981.

Lannon, John M. *Technical Writing*. 3rd ed. Boston: Little, 1985.

Markel, Michael H. *Technical Writing: Situations and Strategies*. 2nd ed. New York: St. Martin's, 1987.

McLean, George F., and Patrick J. Aspell, eds. *Readings in Ancient Western Philosophy*. New York: Appleton, 1970.

Miller, Carolyn R. "A Humanistic Rationale for Technical Writing." *College Writing* 40 (1979): 610-17.

Mills, Gordon H., and John A. Walter. *Technical Writing*. 5th ed. New York: Holt, 1986.

Myers, Greg. "The Social Construction of Two Biologists' Proposals." *Written Communication* 2 (1985): 219-45.

Olson, Gary A. "Jacques Derrida on Rhetoric and Composition: A Conversation." *Journal of Advanced Composition* 10 (1990): 1-21.

——. "Social Construction and Composition Theory: A Conversation with Richard Rorty." *Journal of Advanced Composition* 9 (1989): 1-9.

Ong, Walter. *Interfaces of the Word: Studies in the Evolution of Consciousness and Culture.* Ithaca, NY: Cornell UP, 1977.

Phelps, Louise Wetherbee. *Composition as a Human Science: Contributions to the Self-Understanding of a Discipline.* New York: Oxford UP, 1988.

Pirsig, Robert. *Zen and the Art of Motorcycle Maintenance.* New York: Bantam, 1974.

Plato. *Phaedrus and the Seventh and Eighth Letters.* Trans. Walter Hamilton. New York: Penguin, 1973.

Rabinowitz, Peter J. *Beyond Reading: Narrative Conventions and the Politics of Interpretation.* Ithaca, NY: Cornell UP, 1987.

Romeyer-Dherbey, Gilbert. *Les Sophists.* Paris: Presses Universitaires de France, 1985.

Rosenblatt, Louise. *Literature as Exploration.* 1938. New York: Barnes, 1976.

Rymer, Jone. "Scientific Composing Processes: How Eminent Scientists Write Journal Articles." *Writing in Academic Disciplines.* Ed. David Joliffe. Norwood: Ablex, 1988.

Saussure, Ferdinand de. *Course in General Linguistics.* Trans. Wade Baskin. 1959. New York: McGraw, 1966.

Schriver, Karen A. "Document Design from 1980-1989: Challenges That Remain." *Technical Communication* 36 (1989): 316-31.

Selzer, Jack. "What Constitutes a 'Readable' Technical Style." *Essays in Technical and Scientific Communication: Research, Theory, Practice.* Ed. Paul V. Anderson, R. John Brockman, and Carolyn Miller. Farmingdale, NY: Baywood, 1983. 71-89.

Sprague, Rosamond K., ed. *The Older Sophists.* Columbia: South Carolina UP, 1972.

Stokes, Michael C. "Heraclitus of Ephesus." *The Encyclopedia of Philosophy.* Ed. Paul Edwards, et al. Vol. 3. New York: Macmillan, 1967. 477-81. 4 vols.

Tompkins, Jane. *Reader-Response Criticism: From Formalism to Post-Structuralism.* Baltimore: Johns Hopkins UP, 1980.

Writing in the Graduate Curriculum: Literary Criticism as Composition

PATRICIA A. SULLIVAN

In 1900, the Pedagogical Section of the Modern Language Association sent a questionnaire to its members asking their opinion as to whether rhetoric was a proper subject for graduate work in English, and, if they felt that it was not, what they regarded as "their strongest reasons for excluding it from the list of graduate studies" (Mead xx). In reporting the results of the survey, W.E. Mead acknowledged that "owing to the prevalent vagueness of conception as to what Rhetoric really is and should cover, the various reports read a little like debates on a question in which the meaning of leading terms has not been agreed upon" (xx). Nonetheless, he was able to conclude that those professors who viewed rhetoric as a "science" generally felt that it had a legitimate place in the graduate curriculum, while those who construed rhetoric to mean "the arts of discourse" or "composition" felt that it was not a proper subject for graduate work. Those in the latter group shared what we would now call a "current-traditional" view of composition, as the following excerpts from Mead's report attest:

> Regarding Rhetoric as the art of speaking and writing correctly, I am of the opinion that it is an unsuitable subject for graduate study.

> Rhetoric should be mastered in its practical aspects before the student completes his undergraduate study; but as a science I believe it is eminently suited for graduate work.

> A graduate student should, of course, be able to present in appropriate literary form the results of labor in his chosen field; but he should have done preparatory work to that end before he became a graduate student.

> Mere theme-writing, however sublimated or raised even to the nth power, ought never to be a part of the credits for a higher degree.

> The object of teaching Rhetoric is not theoretical but practical, as propadeutic to composition and literature, and the undergraduate course should suffice for this. The graduate course should be literature itself, which has no limit. (xxii-xxx)

Equated with "speaking and writing correctly," "theme-writing," and presenting "results" in "appropriate literary form," writing was perceived as a set of skills that a student "mastered" before undertaking the graduate study of "literature itself." Such skills were presumably manifest in the papers the student composed, so that flaws in form could be taken as signs of intellectual deficiency, perhaps even an inherent unsuitability to the demands of literary study, as one of the more surly responses to Scott's questionnaire suggests: "When a man has obtained his A.B. degree, he ought to be able to write his language with sufficient correctness to be responsible in the future for his own style. If he has not thus learned to write reasonably well he probably never will learn" (xxii).

In the decades that have passed since the MLA conducted its survey, developments in literary theory and composition have radically altered the nature of English studies. Literary theory has come to concentrate on the activity of reading, the processes by which readers reconstruct texts. Contemporary theories of reading revise the relationship between texts and readers, displacing the authority and autonomy of texts by recognizing the constitutive powers of language and readers' creative capacities as language users. Accordingly, to read and interpret a literary work is to shape or modify or reconstitute the work "itself" (or what was formerly viewed as a static, autonomous object) so that the text that was formerly accorded an independent status is now viewed as a function of our scholarly and critical discourse. In a similar vein, composition theory has shifted its emphasis from the formal product to the activity of composing—the complex interplay of linguistic, cognitive, rhetorical, social, and cultural processes by which texts come into being. From the generative rhetorics and expressivist pedagogies of the 1960s to more recently articulated social and cultural theories of writing, composition has steadily moved in the direction of a constitutive theory of discourse, one which emphasizes both the agency of the writer and the importance of context in the production of meaning. Literary studies and composition, then, would now seem to share a common theoretical basis and not merely a common home in English departments. Indeed, as Jay Robinson has pointed out, "Theories linking reading and writing are becoming the dominant ones among those who study either reading or composition—theories that reconceive reading as the active construction of texts and their meanings; theories that reconceive writing as an act of perpetual making, perpetual revision, with publication or submission for a grade an arbitrary stopping point" (492).

In his introduction to *The Social Mission of English Criticism*, Chris Baldick addresses the pedagogical implications of contemporary theories of criticism and observes that "the real content of the school and college subject which goes under the name 'English literature' is not literature in the primary sense but criticism"; the student "is required to compose, not tragic dramas, but essays in criticism" (4-5). Significantly, Baldick not only identifies the "real content" of literary studies as criticism but also reminds us that criticism must be composed, that a student's work in literary studies—whether it goes by the name of interpretation, criticism, or analysis—entails acts of writing as well as reading. In limiting this insight to a school and college subject, however, Baldick, like many other scholars and educators today, implicitly reinforces the notion that composition properly belongs in the undergraduate curriculum, a notion which still allows us to represent literature and composition as separate intellectual activities in graduate courses. While graduate programs now admit rhetoric as an area of concentration or specialization for the Ph.D., it is rhetoric conceived as a "science," a method of analyzing the art of discourse rather than the practice of this "art" in its own right. Most graduate faculty assume that graduate students, by definition, "already know how to write," and thus writing assumes a secondary and often marginal role in graduate education. The written product, but not the writing process, compels the attention of graduate faculty. In this respect, graduate courses today still bear a remarkable resemblance to the tacit curriculum which Mead uncovered in the MLA survey ninety years ago. Despite development of theories which emphasize the processes and contexts of interpretation, we are still tied to current-traditional modes of writing instruction, for while we have allowed contemporary critical theories to inform our teaching of literature, we have not investigated the ways such theories problematize our assumptions about writing. In the remainder of this essay, I will explore the disjuncture between theory and practice to argue for a reconceptualization of the nature and role of writing in the graduate curriculum.

Writing in Graduate Literature Courses

To discern whether developments in critical theory and composition research were having a discernible impact on the pedagogical practices of graduate faculty and on the writing practices of graduate students in literary studies, I conducted a two-part study of graduate-student writing. First, I surveyed graduate students in English at six universities to learn what kinds of writing they had been assigned in their courses that term and the rhetorical frameworks in which these assignments had been cast.[1] I followed the survey with case studies of two master's and two doctoral students enrolled in four different literature seminars (Twentieth-Century American Literature, Studies in Hawthorne, Studies in Shakespeare, and Restoration Drama) at one of the universities I surveyed.[2] For each case study, I observed courses, interviewed the student before, during, and after the course, collected drafts and revisions of the writing he or she did in response to course assignments, and interviewed the professor of the course at the end of the term. My intent in presenting this study is not so much to offer the results of data-driven research as to highlight and illustrate, through the actual experiences of graduate-student writers, the broader theoretical issues underlying this essay.

From the survey, I learned that a great deal of writing is assigned in graduate courses in English, but writing is seldom taught as a process integral to the study of literature. The most common writing assignment reported by the one hundred graduate students who completed the survey was a term paper of fifteen pages or more. Seventy percent of the graduate students reported that they were assigned term papers of at least fifteen pages in their courses (with creative writing workshops and teaching practica excepted) during the term that the survey was conducted. Somewhat less frequently assigned were short (three to five page) and medium length (six to fifteen page) papers; forty-five and fifty-one students, respectively, reported they were assigned at least one paper of those lengths. Journals, essay exams, one-to-two-page "response" or "position" papers, and bibliographies comprised the other types of writing assigned. Of ninety-five students who responded that they had written or were writing at least one paper of medium length or longer, less than twenty percent reported that their professors had assigned or suggested paper topics or had discussed in class how to formulate arguments, conduct research, or develop ideas. Less than ten percent reported that their professors had asked to see or respond to drafts before the final version was evaluated, had asked the students to share their written work with other students in the class, or had specified an audience or suggested a forum other than the professors themselves.

In many respects, the four case studies confirmed the findings of the survey. In three of the four courses I observed, lengthy term papers were assigned and were due at the end of the term; little discussion occurred with regard to the papers in terms of their purpose, method of development, audience, or forum. In one of these courses (American Literature), the term paper was preceded by a short, analytical essay which was due at midterm; in another course (Shakespeare), a series of two-page "position" papers preceded the term paper; and in the third (Hawthorne), the term paper was the sole writing assignment. In the fourth course I observed (Restoration Drama), students were asked to keep a journal, which was collected and graded both at midterm and at the term's end but which was read only by the professor. Each of the four students who participated in the study reported that a term paper was the most commonly assigned writing task in their graduate experience, and none could recall receiving explicit instructions about content, purpose, or audience. Finally, with the exception of the student enrolled in the Shakespeare seminar, none of the students read or responded to another graduate student's paper in the courses I observed, and only one student said that he had done so in a previous graduate course.

The results of my survey and case studies suggest that under the current pedagogical model, the completed assignment is privileged over its production, the written product over the writing process. A pedagogical distinction is drawn, in other words, between course content and course assignments, between subject matter and what the student writes. Writing is separated from the study of a subject (an author or period) and relegated to the bottom tier of a tacit hierarchy of discursive practices—of reading, speaking, and writing. The most important "object" of three of the seminars I observed, both in terms of their subject matter and their *raison d'etre*, was the set of literary texts studied. (In none of these courses was secondary sources—scholarly or critical articles—made part of the required reading that the class discussed as a group.) The most important activity of these courses was reading. That is, students read the assigned set of literary texts to cover or to "know" the material and to critique, interpret, or otherwise analyze the texts themselves. Such "readings" were shared either through class discussion or through an oral report that was the responsibility of an individual student. Since students were expected to give formal evidence of their reading of literary texts and their awareness of critical issues, they were asked to write. But unlike the literary texts themselves and class discussion of those texts, the student's writing was not valued for what it contributed to the course and to other students' understanding of the issues. Rather, it was valued primarily for its evaluative properties as an academic exercise, as the basis for a grade.

I should point out that contemporary theories of criticism were mentioned and in some instances discussed at length in all but one course (Studies in Hawthorne, which was tacitly informed by the tenets and close-reading methodology of New Criticism.) In Restoration Drama, for example, the professor took pains to show how Dryden presaged poststructuralist, reader-response, and dialogic theories in his "Essay on Dramatic Poesy." Class discussion in Studies in Shakespeare frequently turned to feminist critiques of character, scene, and plot; and the professor incorporated such critiques in the list of topics he periodically distributed to the class for written analysis in their position papers and for in-class discussion. And in Twentieth-Century American Literature, the professor transformed his frequently acknowledged ambivalence toward contemporary critical theory into an ongoing, reflexive commentary upon the current state of literary studies, invoking its central pragmatic problem—"what you're to do as a critic"—to defend his own belief that "one should look closely at the text." In none of these courses, however, did awareness of theory translate into a comparable theory or pedagogy of writing. That is, each course reflected a text-based, product-centered approach to composition. Students were expected to produce critical essays, term papers, and a journal; but in each case, it was up to the student to discover a significant topic or issue, determine lines of reasoning that would resolve the issue, construct the audience to whom the discourse would be addressed, and devise a purpose for communicating. In some courses, professors acknowledged that a particular critical approach would make a difference in the way students read a particular text or set of texts, but no suggestion was made that such an approach might similarly influence the students' writing—the shape, voice, argument, or style of their discourse.

Although many of us wish to claim in theory that a distinction between literature and its interpretations is no longer tenable, our practices continue to emphasize the substance, not the act, of interpretation, for we continue to attend only to the ends, and not the means, of written production. The contexts for writing in many graduate literature courses are, in this sense, arhetorical, for writing does not take place within, or as a fundamental part of, the courses themselves. Writing is nearly always a matter of individual performance, a solitary act rather than a social or collaborative experience. This act most often occurs at the conclusion of course work, in the form of a term paper, so that a student's critical or scholarly discourse is removed from the course itself as a context for inquiry and learning. And the student's work is most often read by a single reader, the professor; students do not write for one another. Thus, acts of writing are both marginalized and privatized in the graduate classroom; literary texts are given precedence over the texts that the students themselves compose, and even in courses where theory is made part of the interpretive context, such theories are not translated into a comparable theory or pedagogy of writing.

Implicit in this pedagogical model, as I noted earlier, is the assumption that graduate students "already know how to write" by virtue of their higher educational status. This assumption is, I believe, the cognitive corollary of a current-traditional theory of writing and a product-oriented pedagogy: writing itself is conceived as a set of skills that a student "masters" at some point in his or her educational life. The point at which an individual makes the transformation from "novice" to "expert" may vary from student to student, but it is presumed to occur before the student attains a bachelor's degree so that the teaching of writing to graduate students is held to be redundant or superfluous.[3] If writing problems manifest themselves in a text a graduate student composes, such problems can be attributed to personal deficiency, not institutional *praxis*.

Recent composition scholarship, particularly that which takes a social view of the writing process, has shown "mastery" to be an exceedingly arbitrary concept; writing well is as much a function of context—the particular task at hand and the situation or situatedness of the writer—as of personal experience. The writer, regardless of ability, is subject to the conventions and constraints that inform his or her particular rhetorical situation. But for graduate students in literary studies, the arts of rhetoric are still equated with "speaking and writing correctly" and "presenting results in appropriate literary form"—in short, with the set of skills the student presumably mastered before undertaking graduate study. And so graduate students are simply asked to set these basic skills in motion and bring their professors the finished product, which is then evaluated according to how well it approximates an ideal, but apparently unteachable, text.

The assumption that writing is an automatic process is so deeply embedded in the collective unconscious (indeed, I would argue, in the political unconscious) of English departments that the term "composition" has come to serve, as James Slevin points out, as a synecdoche for "all the activities that are in fact undertaken within composition" (547). Most often the term designates a specific course—usually first-year English—so that composition is construed as an activity that only undergraduates engage in. The labels "First-Year English" or even "Advanced Composition" serve the institutional function of putting composition in its proper place, but they also allow us to suppress and evade the rhetoricity of our own discipline: the ways complex interrelations of topic, audience, voice, genre, gender, culture, convention, disciplinary context, and self become folded into our own and our students' construction or reconstruction of texts. The institutionalized suppression and evasion of writing, moreover, leads us to reenact modes of instruction at the graduate level—such as assigning papers that will be read only when the course is over—that mirror an earlier world, a world or *Weltanschauung* that has been superseded by constitutive theories of reading and writing. The problem with such traditional modes, as David Punter argues, is that they "do almost nothing to help students to understand what literary *work* might be; . . . an enormous weight [is] placed on written production, and at the same time this production is required to fit into pre-established molds" (220). As a result, Punter says, "an alienated self, formed according to the imagined desires of the institution, attempts to speak to another alienated self, caught between subjectivity and convention..." (221). Punter's representation of the student writer as a self caught between subjectivity and convention is particularly apt of the graduate-student writer, whose discourse emanates from the dual (and oftentimes conflicting) ethos of both "graduate" and "student." Elsewhere I have discussed the conflicts this dual ethos or double perspective engenders for graduate students' perceptions of audience as they write essays on literature (Reader). Here I wish to focus on two additional problems that graduate students encounter in the act of writing as a result of the current disjuncture between theory and pedagogical practice: problems of invention (the processes by which they formulate issues to write about) and argumentation (the manner of discourse in which these issues are explored and resolved.)

Invention, Tradition, and Individual Talent

In "The University and the Prevention of Culture," Gerald Graff writes, "A literary education that operationally boils down to a series of blunt confrontations with texts 'in themselves' will leave students at a loss as to what they are to say about literature. For the problem is that literary texts in themselves go only so far in telling us what we are supposed to say about them" (78). As a critical theorist, Graff identifies the problem of "what to say" about literary texts as a problem of reading, a problem whose solution depends on students' training in critical approaches that counter New Criticism's emphasis on the text itself. Graff nominates "speech act theory, pragmatism, and various forms of reader-response criticism" as possible contenders to the New Critical throne because each takes into account the linguistic codes and cultural values that exist, not in the text, but in the interaction between text and reader. While I share Graff's misgivings about text-oriented theories of reading which ignore the agency of the reader and contingencies of context, I wish to reconstrue the problem of what to say about literature as a problem of writing«more specifically, as part of a problematic of writing that both presumes and subsumes what Graff has posed as a problem of reading. The student who is assigned a piece of writing must have something to say, and if that writer is a graduate student, he or she must often say it for fifteen pages or more. While other disciplines routinely assign topics for research projects and papers at the graduate level, English studies nearly always leaves finding a topic part of the writing task, a task, moreover, that is completed as an addendum to rather than integral part of the course which forms the occasion for inquiry. While graduate students talk about literary texts in class, thereby having the benefit of a communal exchange of ideas, they most often write papers as individual, autonomous "subjects," isolated from the "interpretive community" which provided a forum for their ideas as members of a class.

The experiences of the two doctoral students who participated in my study, Karen and John, cast into relief what Graff has posed as a problem of reading and what I have posed as a problem of writing: both students found themselves at a loss of "what to say" at some moment of their writing processes as they endeavored to compose critical discourse to meet their respective writing assignments. At the outset of her seminar on Hawthorne, Karen confided that she wished professors would propose topics more often because, she noted, "there's always more to be said, but it isn't always obvious." Karen's course focused exclusively on the Hawthorne canon—the author's novels, tales, and sketches—which the class read closely and analyzed, in Karen's words, "mainly to cover the material." As Karen read the assigned texts in the course, she became intrigued by Hawthorne's use of a particular narrative technique in his fiction. As she put it, "There's a storyteller telling a story about a story, and I see it over and over again, and that's intriguing to me, and I want to sit down and analyze when and where he does it and why he does it." She hoped to explore Hawthorne's use of storytellers in her term paper. By the end of the course, however, Karen felt she could not begin to answer the question of why Hawthorne used that particular technique without knowing more about the narrative tradition in which Hawthorne was writing, and the seminar's emphasis on coverage and close reading of Hawthorne's works themselves left her with no time to conduct inquiry into outside sources. She felt she lacked the "right context" to explore her topic further, so she went to see her professor with that specific problem in mind: "I told him what I was interested in but that the more I thought about it the more I felt, 'There's just no topic here.' I asked, 'What am I going to write about once I get past the first paragraph?'"

In essence, Karen posed a question about writing; she could say, in her first paragraph, what she had observed about Hawthorne's use of a story-teller, and she could point out when and where he used this device; but she could not say why. Karen's professor, however, deferred to her judgment that she had no topic and suggested she think of something else to write about. If she could not see what directions her topic might lead her given her close readings of the Hawthorne canon and whatever criticism she might read in the allotted time, he told her, she should probably choose a different topic.

John identified himself in our initial interview as "a historical scholar," interested in "historical accuracy rather than aesthetic evaluation," but he noted (in a remark similar to Karen's wish that professors would suggest topics more often) that he was becoming "somewhat disillusioned with scholarship" because he has "this finite sense that all that can be written has." Nonetheless, John, like Karen, discovered a topic to write about during his seminar on Restoration Drama. Midway through the seminar, John became taken with Dryden's *All for Love* and wanted to explore his "intuitive feeling" that Dryden's version of the Antony and Cleopatra story was the "superior work." He began reading and meticulously summarizing other versions of the play and some works of secondary criticism on *All for Love* in his journal to gauge critical responses to the plays, and this activity consumed much of his time for the remainder of the course. He then went to speak to a former professor and mentor about issues that remained to be resolved with respect to the Antony and Cleopatra plot beyond the critical responses he had catalogued; however, he was told, in effect, that there was virtually nothing left to be done. In essence, the professor confirmed the fear John had expressed many weeks earlier, his "finite sense that all that can be written has."

Karen's experience speaks to the immediate problem a student encounters when a literature course is primarily devoted, in Graff's words, to a blunt confrontation with texts themselves: the close reading model in the Hawthorne seminar left Karen without a coherent theoretical context for framing, developing, and evaluating her ideas, and so she was left wondering what to say in her term paper "beyond the first paragraph." Karen's difficulty in developing her topic, in other words, can be traced to constraints inherent in the course itself. John's experience, on the other hand, reveals a potential dilemma for graduate students that transcends the immediate course as the context for writing—what work there is left to do, what the student can contribute to an ongoing conversation or to what Adena Rosmarin calls the "interpretive history of a work" that hasn't already been said. Unlike the constraints that Karen encountered, John had ample time to read outside sources and to read intertextually, and his professor's assignment of a journal afforded him multiple opportunities to probe and refine his topic. Nonetheless, he too reached a point at which he wondered what to say, what work was left to be done.

Although specific features of each student's discourse situation were different, the problems Karen and John experienced in writing and the strategies by which they set out to resolve these problems were similar in some significant and revealing ways. First, both students found themselves trying to invent an *issue* for writing; that is, while each had a specific topic in mind, even a general theoretical approach (narrative and reception theory, respectively), these topics and theoretical approaches were not enough in and of themselves to propel the students into writing sustained, formal discourse. It was not in the act of reading or interpretation or analysis of works themselves that Karen and John found themselves at a loss as to what to say, but in what each as a writer had to bring to those texts, to the topics they had discovered through their transactions with the texts. Second, both students sought out their professors to help them formulate an issue and conceive a way of exploring or resolving it. That is, preparatory to actually writing or drafting their texts, Karen and John sought to construct themselves as writers by constructing a rhetorical situation for their work; they engaged in dialogue with an actual interlocutor (a professor) who represented the authorial audience of their prospective texts, that is, "Hawthorne critics" or "Dryden scholars." And third, both were told that they had chosen unfruitful topics of inquiry, that writing along the lines of the topic they had already conceived was pointless. By engaging their actual reader in the invention stage of their work, both students cast their professor (or in John's case, a previous mentor) in the role of co-writer or collaborator—a role both professors resisted, deferring the problem of what to say back to the student.

Karen and John both recognized what we too often forget in our assumption that writing is an "automatic process": graduate students in literary studies encounter a vast tradition of literary texts and scholarship in their courses, but they must read against this tradition in order to have something to say in their own texts. To write, in other words, they must have the sense that the subject or topic of their discourse is an issue that requires intellectual work. This issue is neither self-evident in the texts that students read nor immanent in students' transactions with texts; rather, it is a function of the critical resources that they bring as *writers* to their readings or reconstructions of texts. Graff's contention that certain contemporary critical approaches have a heuristic value that New Critical practice no longer enjoys offers a partial solution to the problem of invention, then, for having something to say about literature is clearly dependent on the literary-critical frameworks in which texts are read. Had the Hawthorne seminar incorporated theoretical discussions of narrative and allowed more time for secondary reading, for example, Karen might have felt better prepared to answer the question she had formulated. But I would caution against our seeing specific theories and approaches as a panacea to the problem of invention, for like literary texts themselves, critical theories "go only so far" in telling students what they're supposed to say about them, or more to the point, what they're to do with them and why. The exigencies which give rise to writing are no more inherent within critical approaches themselves than they are within the texts that students read. The issues which compel critical discourse must still be invented by a writer who has both a personal and professional stake in the criticism he or she produces. Karen and John, through their interactions with professors, sought not only to create a rhetorical context which would give purpose and meaning to their inquiries about Hawthorne and Dryden but to insert themselves within this context as authors or rhetors. However, so long as the questions of what to say and why it's important to say it remain confined to a pragmatics of reading—construed as a problematic of reader, text, and (theoretical) context but not writer, text, and (rhetorical) context—graduate students cannot locate themselves within the interpretive history of a literary work as coauthors or co-makers of this history. In other words, if students' writing is not perceived as an integral part of the study of a subject but only as a discursive exercise through which they demonstrate individual ability, they cannot fully participate in the critical and scholarly discourse that a graduate course is intended to engender. Chances are they will discover, like Karen and John, that they are not active agents in the construction of a scholarly tradition, a tradition that seems to go on independently of anything they might do.

Academic Genres

As my survey and case studies revealed, a term paper of at least fifteen pages is the most common writing assignment in graduate courses in English studies, the predominant mode of writing by which graduate students do their academic work. The fifteen-to-twenty-five-page term paper would seem, moreover, to be a distinctly (though not exclusively) graduate-level genre; the term papers which the four graduate students in my study reported that they wrote as undergraduate English majors generally fell into the eight-to-ten-page range, and all but one of the students said that they had never written a longer paper as undergraduates. Most likely, the term paper is the most frequently assigned writing task because it is perceived as preparatory to the scholarly essay or journal article, which requires research and a more complex and extensive treatment of a topic than a shorter paper allows. The term paper, in this sense, may be viewed as a kind of discursive "training ground," one in which graduate students gain practice conducting sustained inquiry into a topic. It is one of the ways that they learn the argumentative processes and bibliographic procedures that are the "tools of the trade" in literary studies. Also, such learning presumably has a cumulative effect: by writing a succession of term papers and reading different professors' responses to their work, students acquire knowledge of the formal features and conventions of literary criticism and enhance their skills in argumentative discourse.

But whether the term paper, as currently conceived and taught, truly has the effects which graduate faculty imagine and desire is a questionable assumption at best. For in truth, the term paper is not "taught" at all; it is assigned. This assignment is usually cast only in generic terms—a twenty-page research paper or a critical analysis—so that the work that students will do is already represented as a text, not as a process of inquiry. Whatever discursive practices are required to write the paper take place in what Patricia Bizzell has called a "black box," out of view of the professor (49). The professors who participated in my study, in fact, explicitly stated that such processes cannot or ought not be taught because discussion of the writing task would mean intervening in the writing process either in superfluous or counter-productive ways. One professor said he did not feel it was necessary to teach the term paper as a process of inquiry because "graduate students already know about such things"; another said that students learn the conventions of critical discourse "from their reading rather than having them spelled out"; and another said that to teach the term paper as a discursive practice would "inhibit students' creativity" and induce them to write "formulaic stuff." Perhaps because graduate faculty are accustomed to viewing their own scholarly and critical practices as acts of reading (or interpretation or criticism) rather than acts of writing, they naturally assume the role of readers (or critics or evaluators) of their students' texts rather than as teachers of the discursive processes by which texts are composed.[4] In any case, they commonly expect graduate students to have mastered the arts of discourse well enough to produce term papers "as easily and inevitably," in Bizzell's words, "as a hen lays eggs" (49).

From the students' perspective, writing term papers can be a gratifying and rewarding experience, a place to test out their own theories, to engage other critics' voices, to make discoveries and bring new challenges to the literary tradition. But the process of producing argumentative discourse (the predominant mode of discourse in literary studies) proves neither easy nor inevitable, as the reports of the graduate students who participated in my study reveal. To be sure, all of the graduate students I interviewed were able to say, in general, what constitutes a literary argument; in fact, all sounded remarkably similar: "You have to have a thesis, prove it with textual evidence, counter possible criticisms" and so forth. But the actual process of constructing a formal argument proved difficult when the students were engaged in writing sustained discourse on their chosen topics. Hank, one of the master's students in my study, had studied structuralism in a previous course and decided to write a term paper in his American Literature seminar on a certain "binary opposition" he had discerned in Sylvia Plath's short stories. But he said he needed to go to the library and get his professor's book to see how his professor "constructed an argument." The other master's student, Lisa, did considerable research in preparation of her term paper in the Shakespeare seminar, but she asked me and later her professor whether simply reporting on the various theories that have been advanced to account for *Othello*'s popularity in the Old South "constituted an argument." Karen said that her greatest difficulty in writing on the topic she had finally chosen for her term paper (the relation between Hawthorne's use of storytellers and his often ambiguous endings) was "interweaving disparate ideas into a coherent argument." In the professors' evaluations of the students' writing, the most frequently discerned problem was some flaw in the students' reasoning: Hank "tried to make his thesis do too many disparate things"; Lisa "didn't seem to understand what constitutes literary evidence"; the text "didn't warrant some of the claims that [Karen] made." Significantly, these comments came at the "end" of the students' writing, as evaluations of the students' finished texts, and at the end of the course, when the students had no opportunity to revise or rethink the arguments they were trying to make for the actual reader of their work.

If we are searching for reasons why graduate students have difficulty with argumentation, we would do well to focus on the writing situation or context in which these arguments are composed. In the cases of the three students I have described here, this "context" was narrowed to the term paper itself. Each student had to produce a text-based form of argument, one which demonstrated its own logic rather than engaged an actual reader in a dialogical process. The students were not exchanging ideas with an interlocutor, in other words, but submitting a linear, fully formed argument to a textual critic, who then evaluated the argument's premises, evidence, and so forth. The product-oriented or formalist conception of argumentation evident in the professors' comments was also reflected in the students' own accounts of what constitutes an argument: the "thesis-proof" model to which each of the students pointed as the defining structural feature of the critical essays they were to compose. While this model may have "fit" neatly with the activities of close reading and explication that the students likely practiced at the undergraduate level, the longer paper that graduate students in literature are routinely asked to write calls for more elaborate and complex forms of argumentation, for a dialectical interplay of critical voices and perspectives—in short, for a discursive practice that goes well beyond the thesis-proof model with which they are most familiar. The problems the students encountered in drafting their arguments and the flaws the professors perceived in their students' texts might have been addressed more effectively had the students been given opportunities to engage in argument—to test their ideas, lines of reasoning, and evidence—with actual readers in the process of writing their term papers. But once again, such interventions were perceived by the professors in my study as either superfluous because students already know how to produce critical discourse or as impediments to students' individual creativity.

Those aspects and features of critical discourse that are not thought to be the function of already learned skills or a matter of inspiration are often assumed to be a function of the student's reading: students will learn to compose critical discourse by reading critical discourse and internalizing its structures, strategies, vocabulary, and style. While this assumption is no doubt true, Baldick's assertion that students compose "not tragic dramas, but essays in criticism" bears repeating here, for students in literature courses are reading and writing in two distinct genres. In most literature courses, graduate students read a set of literary works—for example, the complete works of Hawthorne, Twentieth-Century novels and poems, or Shakespeare's plays. They may or may not read "secondary" or non-literary works such as scholarly essays or critical reviews as part of the required reading of the course. (In one of the courses I observed, Twentieth-Century American Literature, students were instructed *not* to do outside reading for their term papers because other critics' notions might interfere with their own perceptions of the literary texts under study.) In their papers, however, graduate students are asked to produce a kind of discourse that bears almost no resemblance to the plays, novels, short stories, and poems they are writing about. Literary texts, the primary reading in most courses, assume an evidentiary role in the papers the students must compose. The texts that might serve as examples of the kind of critical work students are expected to emulate in their writing—critical reviews or scholarly essays on particular literary works—are not always read in class in conjunction with the literary texts themselves. And when secondary works are included in a course, they are not "read" as examples of the kind of work that professionals in English do. They are not analyzed for the way a critic frames an issue, establishes its significance, builds a case, and resolves the issue, but as further pieces of evidence the student might incorporate in his or her own argument. Thus, the literary essay, one of the predominant genres by which professionals do their work in literary studies, is not taught as such. We teach literary genres by asking students to read and analyze examples and variations of the kind, but we assume that the term paper, as both a mode of writing and a method of inquiry, teaches itself.

Reconceiving the Graduate Course
My study indicates that in the graduate curriculum, literature and composition are still represented as separate intellectual activities, the study of literary texts occupying center stage, the production of student texts a peripheral role at best. Graduate faculty tend to teach literature in the primary sense but assume that graduate students will master (or have mastered) the writing of scholarly and critical texts on their own. Literary criticism is still imagined as the "reading" an individual student produces rather than as a discourse he or she participates in. This individualized, privatized notion of reading and displacement of writing leaves students without a social context in which to develop and explore disciplinary issues, practice academic genres, or engage in argument with real (as opposed to idealized) others.

The persistence of product or text-oriented pedagogies of reading and writing in the graduate curriculum has implications, I think, both for students undertaking graduate study and for the profession itself. Such pedagogies tend to deny to the graduate student an active and defining role in shaping the critical and scholarly discourse of the discipline. And they contradict the very process approaches, including collaborative writing and peer response, that graduate teaching assistants are adapting in undergraduate writing courses.[5] If the purpose of graduate education is to train students in the roles they will assume as future practitioners of our profession, then our current modes of instruction are serving, in effect, to perpetuate the very models of inquiry and teaching that contemporary theories of reading and writing seek to displace at all levels of the English curriculum.

If we are to translate theory into practice, it will be necessary to revise text-oriented approaches to literature and practice ways of reading that call upon all of the resources available to the reader, including his or her experiences or "transactions" with the text in the act of reading. But though such a revision may represent a dramatic change in the way literature has traditionally been taught in the university, it still allows us to forget that criticism—the real content of literary studies—must be composed, that it is writing that ultimately defines graduate students' work and role in the academy. Along with text-oriented approaches to reading, then, we must also revise our view of composition as an art that graduate students have already mastered, for such a view gives rise to the currently dominant product-oriented model of composition that fails to recognize the social and constitutive nature of writing and commits us, at best, to a paradox: at the same moment we proclaim that literary texts are not self-interpreting, our practices reinscribe the belief that our students' interpretations are somehow self-generating.

The move from text-oriented to reader-oriented theories of literary criticism, in short, must be accompanied by a similar move from text-oriented to writer-oriented theories and pedagogies. It is not only the reader's relation to the text but the writer's relation to the texts and contexts of literary studies that must be the real "content" of English studies. If, indeed, interpretation is the only game in town, as Stanley Fish says, then the text the student writes must be the most important text in the class, the processes by which this text comes into being the real subject of any seminar. As Graff has observed, reader-response and pragmatic theories, which regard reading as the active construction of meaning, grant students an authority which was formerly held to be a property of the text "itself." And cultural criticism, feminism, and the new historicism, which concentrate on the social conditions and political circumstances under which texts are produced, offer graduate students more to say and exigencies for saying it. But it is not enough to grant authority to the reader nor to bring history and culture back into the classroom unless graduate students see themselves as makers of this history and culture through their acts of authorship.

Composition scholarship has shown that to become a practitioner of a discipline, one must not only learn the discursive terms of that discipline but must participate in its discourse as a rhetor, as an author whose texts have the power to alter knowledge in that field (see, for example, Bazerman). Graduate students must be able to reflect on their own work as developing scholars and critics, as members of a community who have an active role and stake in the knowledge generated by the course which formed the original occasion for inquiry. To become authorities on Shakespeare, Austen, Dickinson, or Derrida, students must first become authors, and their acts of authorship must occur in settings that are self-consciously rhetorical. The graduate course in English studies must be conceived as a scene of writing as well as a scene of reading, a discursive site in which literary history is truly conceived as history in the making.

Notes

[1] I surveyed English departments at Florida State University, Ohio State University, Pennsylvania State University, the University of California at San Diego, the University of Oregon, and the University of Utah. I wish to thank both my colleagues and the graduate students at these institutions who assisted with the survey.

[2] I have changed the names of the four graduate students who participated in this study to preserve their anonymity.

[3] Early cognitive research in composition may have unwittingly contributed to this assumption via studies in which graduate students were placed in "expert-writer" control groups against which the writing of "novices" was measured.

[4] The tacit hierarchy of discursive practices I discerned in the graduate seminars I observed—where the reading and in-class discussion of literary texts took precedence over the writing that students did about those texts—accords in many respects with the English apparatus Roberts Scholes has discerned and delineated in *Textual Power*. According to Scholes, consumption is privileged over production, reading over writing, and literature over non-literature; hence the greatest gap is between literature and composition—the reading (or interpretation or criticism) of literary texts and the writing of pseudo non-literature (or student essays). Scholes' schema serves to explain, in part, why literature faculty more easily assume roles as readers and critics of the finished texts of their students than as readers or collaborators of work in progress: they are accustomed to seeing themselves as "consumers" of texts, as critics and scholars of the "already written" rather than as teachers of writing. The texts of their students, moreover, inhabit the area of pseudo-non-literature. But Scholes overlooks in his apparatus what graduate faculty overlook in their roles as teachers and readers of literature: criticism, including a book like *Textual Power*, must be composed. We do not merely "consume" literature; our readings, interpretations, and criticisms of literature and of the academy entail acts of production—of composition.

[5] Irene Gale similarly observes that "many graduate courses, even in rhetoric and composition, are based on the presentational model, in that the professor lectures and requires one or two research papers due at the end of the term but offers no avenue for peer response to emerging papers." Arguing that it is "inconsistent to teach teaching assistants to teach writing as a process on the one hand while on the other to force them as students to magically produce finished products," she calls for graduate courses designed to let teaching assistants "deal with writing problems they face as students and professionals" (46-47).

Works Cited

Baldick, Chris. *The Social Mission of English Criticism: 1848-1932*. Oxford: Clarendon P, 1987.

Bazerman, Charles. "What Written Knowledge Does: Three Examples of Academic Discourse." *Philosophy of the Social Sciences* 11 (1981): 361-87.

Bizzell, Patricia. "Composing Processes: An Overview." *The Teaching of Writing*. Ed. Anthony R. Petrosky and David Bartholomae. Chicago: U of Chicago P, 1986. 49-70.

Gale, Irene. "Conflicting Paradigms: Theoretical and Administrative Tensions in Writing Program Administration." *Writing Program Administrator* 14 (1990): 41-50.

Graff, Gerald. "The University and the Prevention of Culture." *Criticism in the University*. Ed. Gerald Graff and Reginald Gibbons. Chicago: Northwestern UP, 1985. 62-82.

W.E. Mead. "Report of the Pedagogical Section," Proceedings for 1900, *PMLA* 16 (1901): xix-xxxii.

Punter, David. "University English Teaching: Observations on Symbolism and Reflexivity." *Demarcating the Disciplines*. Minneapolis: U of Minnesota P, 1986. 215-36.

Robinson, Jay. "Literacy in the Department of English." *College English* 46 (1985): 492-98.

Rosmarin, Adena. "The Narrativity of Interpretive History." *Reading Narrative*. Ed. James Phelan. Columbus: Ohio State UP, 1989. 12-26.

Scholes, Robert. *Textual Power: Literary Theory and the Teaching of English*. New Haven: Yale UP, 1985.

Slevin, James. "Connecting English Studies." *College English* 48 (1986): 543-50.

Sullivan, Patricia. "Writers' Conceptions of Audience in Graduate Literature Courses." *Reader: Essays in Reader-Oriented Response and Criticism* 21 (1989): 22-34.

What Happens When Things Go Wrong: Women and Writing Blocks

Mary Kupiec Cayton

When I began writing this paper, I expected to have some difficulty. Like many people, I have a history of painful writing blocks. The odd thing about my blocks is that they haven't interfered with my journal writing, personal communication, administrative memos, lecturing, or other forms of teaching. They have only come into play in my formal academic prose.

Over the years, I have observed that I am not alone. Many of my undergraduate women students, in particular, tend to have far more difficulties with and vocal misgivings about academic prose than my male students do. They are talented, motivated young women who write frequently in journals, who have exciting ideas, who explain themselves articulately when they talk and when they write informally in the first person. However, they freeze, balk, or resist when it comes to negotiating the challenges of academic prose.

During a six-year period when I taught at the School of Interdisciplinary Studies at Miami University, I had the opportunity to watch a variety of male and female undergraduates as they blocked—and unblocked—on yearlong senior projects. In the Western Program (as it is called), students design their own majors after completing two years in a core curriculum; during their senior year, they complete an academic project in their area of focus. As coordinator (for two years) of the workshop that brought together all those working on senior projects, I was able to observe the seniors' progress and hear what they said about their work, both in formal workshops and individual conferences held over the course of the year. I collected drafts of work in progress, asked for self-reports at regular intervals, and administered a self-report inventory at the end of the process.

What I noted were visible differences between women and men students in the ways that they described their writing blocks. My impression from written reports of their experiences was that women and men writers tended to block with about an equal degree of frequency. Most described at least one major occasion of blocking during the course of their projects. Many women, however, seemed to block for longer periods of time than did their male counterparts, and they also seemed to experience more prolonged and overt psychological distress over their failure to make progress. Their experience—as well as my own—led me to investigate the possibility that some kinds of writer's block, particularly those involving academic prose, might have gender-specific components. I was especially interested in the question of how men and women might approach and negotiate long-term writing projects differently.[1]

Current Scholarship on Writing Blocks

Most of the existing literature treats the paralysis that many writers suffer from time to time as an equal opportunity problem. A cognitive model, perhaps best exemplified by Mike Rose's work, points to "rule rigidity" among blocked writers. That is, inflexible or conflicting composing rules and planning strategies channel writers into "narrowed interpretive planning or composing styles" (72). Writers get "stuck" because they don't know what to do next, or because they don't have a sufficient repertoire of choices to help them move beyond counterproductive and limiting sets of heuristics.

A second model, focusing on the affective components of writing blocks, sees anxiety of various sorts as the root of the problem. For example, John Daly and Michael Miller posit within the writer a dispositional characteristic that they call "writing apprehension." Someone suffering from writing apprehension characteristically avoids writing tasks and feels anxious about them. In his own review of the literature on this construct, Daly addresses the issue of gender, but he finds the data mixed and, thus, concludes that it is likely that gender differences do not strongly influence writing apprehension. Another proponent of the affective model, Robert Boice, provides a therapeutic behavior modification regimen designed to help blocked writers. As an addendum to his work, Boice tantalizingly notes that although he has not particularly discussed its political implications, for a variety of reasons he knows that women may experience more bars to writing than men do, and he believes that the issue of gender bias in the world of academic writing needs to be investigated (213-14).

Reed Larson's research also locates writing dysfunction in the affective realm, but he presents situational characteristics that contribute to it rather than locating the source of the problem in some inherent characteristic of the writer. Overarousal—a state characteristic of students "unable to establish expectations for themselves that were consistent with what they could realistically do" (23)—led to high anxiety among the subjects he studied; underarousal, or boredom, characterized those students unable to conceive of the task as a problem-finding situation. Presumably, both men and women are subject to states of over- or underarousal. Whether individuals are particularly vulnerable to either state by virtue of their gender is a question that Larson does not raise.

Both cognitive and affective models of blocking behavior have tended to focus on the individual subject, without considering an individual's social positioning as a possible factor in blocking behavior. In contrast, contextualists—including Lynn Bloom, David Bartholomae, Patricia Bizzell, and Rose in his later work—have begun to suggest that difficulty in mastering writing tasks may be (in Bloom's words) a "function of the interaction between the individual and his or her environment rather than a function of one or the other acting alone" (119). According to the contextualist view, communication problems, including problems in written communication, result in part from a problematic fit between the cultural expectations and understandings that an individual brings to a given task and those that the environment demands for effective functioning.

Because women and men stand in different kinds of relationships to established knowledge and the knowledge conventions that transmit power and authority, we might expect the blocking they experience in their writing tasks to differ. For both women and men, engaging in academic discourse means envisioning oneself as having sufficient cultural authority to utilize a privileged language associated with authority. Moreover, it also entails experiencing oneself as accepted by others as possessing appropriate cultural authority. In some cases, it may also involve a third component: grappling with the power relations inscribed in the discourse itself. All three of these factors can (and sometimes do) become problems for male writers. However, by virtue of their social positioning and long-standing exclusion from cultural authority, it is difficult for women to escape them.

Men's Reports of Writing Blocks

These models differed substantially in their ability to predict the senior-thesis writers' reports of what happened when things went wrong in their writing. The thirty-five men in the workshop tended to talk about their periods of being blocked in strategic terms, as the cognitive model might predict. Druid, for example, reported getting stuck when he "didn't know a good general direction or rule to go by." As he recounted, "I was . . . at the mercy of my inspiration." Jonathan wrote that he had problems when he "could not find a way to analyze the data." Like Druid and Jonathan, many of the men in the workshop seemed to think of their project as a problem to be solved, with greater or less economy of effort. To the extent that they described their blocking in any detail (and they were less apt to do so than the women), their problems fell into three different categories, all of which the "gender-neutral" literature on writing blocks might have predicted.

The first centered on finding an acceptable strategy for conceptualizing, researching, and presenting the project. Many of the men reported an initial period of intimidation at the beginning of the project, when they began to discover the enormity of the topic they had chosen. For example, Greg, by his own admission a frequent blocker, reported "trouble getting a handle on or deciding on an approach" to his project on U.S. intervention in Grenada. Ron, who hardly ever had trouble writing, remembered that his only block occurred when he was "narrowing down the topic to exactly what I was going to do." Until these writers were able to narrow the topic successfully, they remained anxious, unable to identify the most useful strategies for investigation. Cognitive and affective components both entered into their writing blocks.

Andy's and Gary's experiences with blocking suggest a second type of situation that stymied some of the male writers. For them, competing tasks took time away from project development, and the result was a loss of momentum (or what another affective theorist, Mihaly Csikszentmihalyi, has called "flow") that made writing difficult. At the outset, Andy was scared to begin his project, a fantasy novel, but after writing about a hundred pages, he seemed to hit his stride. An individual with multiple involvements in the community, however, he then became "busy with other things for several weeks and couldn't keep at it." As a result, he "lost contact and didn't want to start again." (Ironically, the situation of multiple competing responsibilities is one that Tillie Olsen associates with women's writing barriers.) Fortunately, Andy's block lasted only about three weeks. Gary, a student government vice-president, often found his extracurricular involvements demanding more time than his classwork. "The only time I got stuck," he wrote, "was when I was very busy with non-class activities."

The third kind of blocking that male students reported occurred toward the end of their projects, and it classically fit Larson's underarousal model. Several described themselves as bored with their topics, and they had to exert a mighty, if unenthusiastic, effort to finish. Eric, who almost did not finish his project designing a public relations strategy for a particular client, wrote simply that "the project got tedious." Jeff's project, a well-conceived experimental design investigating burn-out among special education teachers, left him burned out in the final weeks of project preparation. If he had it to do over again, he wrote at the end of the process, "I might do something that had more of 'me' in it. You see, doing a project like mine was 'safe' in that it followed a very set pattern—in writing style, as well as research style. So something that was a bit more *me*, more heartfelt if you will, may have given me a greater sense of self-growth, although I did feel satisfaction from completing this."

Women's Reports of Writing Blocks

In contrast to their male peers, the thirty-eight women exhibited patterns that the existing cognitive literature on writing blocks would have been far less likely to predict. While the men most frequently wrote about their cognitive progress in analyzing issues, the women more often wrote about themselves and the affective processes involved.[2] Many exhibited affective blocks, and even more exhibited a concern about mediating between themselves and the demands of an (academic) audience. When the women spoke about being stuck or having difficulty making progress on their projects, the problems they spoke about tended to fall into four general categories:

Difficulties with Audience
They reported problems imagining an audience and meeting the sometimes conflicting needs of different audiences. Many doubted their ability to interest any real audience and expressed skepticism that the audiences they had in mind would respond favorably or appropriately to what they had to offer.

Difficulties with Ethical Responsibility to the Subjects of the Projects
In cases where individuals or groups (either living or deceased) were the focus of their work, they feared overstepping boundaries by reducing persons to oversimplified versions of themselves. They expressed concern that their work might be merely exploitative—using the experiences of their subjects for personal gain, or characterizing them in a way that they would not characterize themselves.

Difficulties Utilizing Research from Secondary Sources
Many felt lost in their research material or overwhelmed by it, in peril of losing what it was they wanted to say as they tried to accommodate themselves to their sources. Alternatively, many claimed to have become stymied by a lack of materials—an inability to encounter anything at all that seemed to pertain to the problem they had in mind or that sparked a reaction of any sort.

Difficulties with Voice
Trying to write academic prose seemed to give many of them a sense that they were obliterating themselves from the project; nevertheless, when they wrote of their own experiences in a voice that they felt comfortable with, they expressed doubts that the problems they addressed were anything other than idiosyncratic, and they feared that no one would attend to their message.

In short, for these women—in a way that was not true for most of the men—their writing became a vehicle for finding an appropriate definition of self and the relationship of the self to the world outside.[3]

Connecting with Others: Support, Nonsupport, Conflict
The real, live people on the receiving end of their writing concerned many of these women writers enormously. When unable to imagine who might want to hear about an issue, when dealing with conflicting claims of audiences, when forced to imagine the audience as a "generalized other," a majority of the women blocked. Nikki, a writing-center peer tutor who frequently served as a concrete audience for the work of others, in general had little trouble writing. She sometimes used the class itself as her audience, addressing it

directly and adding at the end of a long, technical paper, "Oh, yea! Thanks for listening!"

But not all of the women were as confident of the interest of intended or concrete audiences. For example, Genelle, writing a project on women's communication patterns with other women, consistently had difficulty getting the two (male) members of her small workgroup to listen. About midway through the first semester, she noted in a journal entry that they seemed to ignore her project whenever the three of them got together to share writing: "It was really odd on Tuesday. We met and when Ted or Jeff each talked about their project, they completely ignored me." Trying to explain to herself why this seemed so, she wrote: "They have a lot in common because they take the same classes, and have a lot of the same problems, and they really understand a lot about each other's project. Maybe they don't think I can give them any worthwhile advice, or maybe I don't comment on what they want commented on, or I don't comment enough. I don't know." While Genelle continued to try to find a way to communicate with them, she encountered a major period of blockage in her writing.

When she was required to submit a well-structured proposal on her project for another class, she produced a seventeen-page proposal on which both her sociology professor and her (male) senior project advisor gave her an "A-." She was pleased with herself—until she encountered her small group again:

> They talked about [my proposal] and said they were glad that I finally did produce something but that they couldn't really tell anything by it. That was fine. It didn't make me feel great because I thought I had done something really substantial and they just blew it off. Then Ted said that some of the writing was really bad and Jeff agreed with him. They didn't offer any suggestions, didn't show me where it was bad. They just said some of it was really bad and that I needed to have spent more time on it.

Recalling her advisor's praise, Genelle was able to brush off the criticism—temporarily. But then she began to doubt herself: "I thought they must be right. My research prof probably doesn't know anything about writing and Geoff [her advisor] was probably busy."

What we can learn from Genelle's experience (aside from some of the limitations of collaborative peer groups) goes beyond Genelle's own experience. The refusal of important concrete audiences to acknowledge the legitimacy of Genelle's project, communicated through a refusal to discuss anything but technical details, left her feeling without an audience. In an extreme way, her experience may mirror the experience of other women determined to pursue issues significant to them in academic prose. The response from well-intentioned others is sometimes stylistic criticism and often none at all, perhaps because they may not be familiar with a problem, or they may lack a sense of its significance, and, thus, they may be at a loss for any response to make other than technical or procedural. Nor is Genelle's experience unique to undergraduate women, as Angela Simeone notes in

Academic Women: "Because research on women is perceived as being outside of the mainstream, biased, political, unimportant, and/or inaccurate, women whose interests and work lie in this area are at an obvious disadvantage in being published" (71). For an undergraduate, this dismissal or marginalization may simply take the form of silence—a non-response that communicates that the message has not been taken seriously as a stimulus to dialogue.

In Janet's case, failure to find interested others led to problems in sustaining motivation on her project, an examination of the nature and impact of adventure-oriented environmental education programs. In her first semester self-evaluation, Janet evinced a good deal more self-confidence than Genelle ever did; yet she, too, had made only sporadic and mediocre progress on her project all semester long. "I like my idea," she wrote. "It's relevant to myself and (if I may be so bold) the world. I think it's developed pretty well. I kind of feel alone in thinking about it." At the end of her evaluation, almost as an afterthought, she wrote that she had received feedback from her advisor only once all semester.

The point, in part, is that women (particularly women who take their own experiences seriously) may be more likely than their male counterparts to receive questionable responses or no response at all from individuals operating out of male-centered disciplinary communities. Yet many males also received precious little encouragement from advisors. Perhaps a better reading of the situation is that audience reaction (or nonreaction) may have played a heavier role in these women's motivation to write than in men's. Women were far more likely than men to mention lack of response or a sense of isolation as an important factor in their attitude toward their projects. If, as Dale Spender notes, women have culturally been expected to "restrict their own opportunities for expression by concentrating on the development of male [conversational] topics" (49), then the lack of a response to work that represents risk-taking self-expression may be particularly devastating. Most men, Spender indicates, have had more experience being taken seriously in conversation simply by virtue of their sex. Women often have had more experience acting the part of the good listener or the facilitator of mixed-sex conversations, rather than the part of the initiator of important topics that others are likely to take seriously.

With surprising frequency, women also expressed a sense of having failed audiences, handing in notes of apology with rough drafts or chapter drafts of their projects. Amy, whose project on the negative effects of tracking in public schools was characterized by a mechanical and forced prose that belied her intensity of feeling about the project, even apologized for the self-evaluation she wrote: "Mary, I'm sorry this isn't much of an evaluation. I thought about this for two days and it still turned out awful."

Just as paralyzing as these situations was the situation of the writer who kept in mind audiences with conflicting claims. As Anne Aronson suggests, these women suffered from Virginia Woolf's "Angel in the House" syndrome—the necessity for keeping everyone happy that leaves a writer unsettled, unable to write, and manifestly unhappy. "I'm having trouble not getting sidetracked while trying to please three very different advisors," Jenny wrote in a project on more effective ways to teach ancient history in high schools. "The advice of my advisors is very good, but if I were able to do all that they suggest, I would be working on forty projects in addition to my own." Genelle found herself "being pressured to take approaches that [she] didn't want to take," but added, "This was my own fault because I was not aware of the exact approach I wanted; so I took suggestions and became dissatisfied, but failed to voice that concern because I felt intimidated. I also felt guilty because I thought I was creating problems for everyone, and so for a while I tried to pursue others' suggestions for my project." In the absence of a clear agenda or method for the project, these writers looked to please the "experts"—and they ended up feeling co-opted, confused, and angry.

Christina explicitly identified her own particular writing block as being *"paralyzed in face of audience*—I can't write this; there are too many views to take care of. What *words* will I use? How do I ever start off?" She considered dropping out of college for a while in order to avoid the project required for graduation. After several agonizing months of work with her advisor trying to break the logjam, she stumbled onto a strategy that worked for her. She rejected an academic approach to her project, an examination of women's power to subordinate themselves by unquestioningly accepting patriarchal linguistic constructions. Instead, she drafted letters to particular individuals—her mother, her best friend, younger women she knew—thinking of herself as entering into dialogue with these concrete others whose needs and points of view she could anticipate. She then took "excerpts from those letters and put them together to make [her] essay."

Those writers able to identify themselves as part of a group who would need or be interested in what they produced were most successful in completing the project without serious hindrance, overcoming occasional stoppages and blocks without excessive agony. Nikki, for example, directed her prose on battering within lesbian relationships to three audiences with overlapping concerns, audiences in which she counted herself a member: persons interested in stopping battering within intimate relationships, feminists committed to the welfare of all women, and women committed primarily to other women. Sherry, a premed student, found a focus and a purpose through critical theory, which enabled her for the first time to see herself as an intellectual. Through reading Michel Foucault and Terry Eagleton for another of her classes, she decided that "the role of an intellectual is to expose those practices which contribute to or undermine the existing power structure." She also discovered a focus for her project on electronic fetal monitoring: to "create women's dialogue that will help people reclaim some of the power that the medical professional seems to monopolize." In both cases, these women saw themselves as engaging in a dialogue with others like themselves in some way, others who would need what they wrote.

The problems of these senior women with audience might provide support for Peter Elbow's exhortation that at certain stages of the writing process we might be well advised to "close our eyes as we speak"—that is, to ignore the audience.[4] This is useful advice, perhaps, in some instances, except that for many of these women, the impetus for writing often seemed to come from a sense of connection to audience. Carol Gilligan's research on women's moral development suggests that many women in our culture may be particularly attuned to values and issues connected with relationship. For each of the women above, the question of audience became an issue of how to establish, maintain, and responsibly contribute to a connection with the other or a group of others. In the absence of the ability to envision the other, or envisioning the other as hostile or indifferent to the message, these women often ceased to be able to make progress.

Gilligan's theory of women's moral development also helps place in context another aspect of these women's blocking. In several cases, they backed off from the material they were analyzing, hesitating to make generalizations that would oversimplify, misrepresent, or speak for another. Rita, trying to find an appropriate form and voice for a project on Vincent van Gogh, wrote, "I had to figure out how to say something that is not some kind of slander against the subject of my project because *it was his life after all*! (I still haven't totally resolved my feelings on this one)." Tammy, a white middle-class woman acutely aware of her difference from the black and white South African women that she wrote about, said, "By using stories of women's lives offered in books that compile many interviews, I am removing the actual story of the woman to the third degree. This bothers me. I do not want to speak for these women!" The awareness of difference, increasingly apparent to some of these women as they wrote their projects, led them to be overly cautious about doing anything that would obscure, flatten, or distort the difference between themselves and their subjects. Their responsibility (as they saw it) to respect the integrity of the experience of others often left them floundering for a focus in their project, since nothing short of complete fidelity to the experience of their subjects would do. This heightened awareness of difference and hesitation about overgeneralization marked several of the women but few of the men.

Personal Involvement, Acceptability, and Self-Representation
The two other prominent difficulties women mentioned—problems utilizing research from secondary sources and problems finding a voice that felt both appropriate and comfortable—both involved several concerns: assessing the degree of personal involvement in the project that was practicable for the writer, assessing its acceptability to potential audiences, and fighting to assert and maintain presence of the self in the material being discussed. As

the subtitle of the book by Mary Field Belenky and her colleagues, *Women's Ways of Knowing*, suggests, the development of self, voice, and mind are inextricably linked for most women. Differing strategies for developing an appropriate representation of self in prose seemed to lead to either boredom or anxiety, depending on the particular strategy chosen.

Some of the men (such as Jeff and Eric) seemed far more frequently to become bored with their projects before the end. Motivation to write often became a problem, and deadlines became the motivation to write. As Greg noted of his project, it was "a matter of just going ahead and doing what I was supposed to do or had to do to get the job done according to my standards." There were women who exhibited the same pattern of boredom in their projects—and they were usually those whose projects evidenced the least struggle with academic discourse conventions. For them, mastering discourse conventions became the problem to be solved. They were unable to see those conventions and methods as means of investigating problems of their own devising, and the project took on a life of its own from which they eventually found themselves distanced and alienated. For example, asked what she had gained from her project on the role of international law in developing nations, Jennifer answered, "This project made me realize that I don't want to pursue a masters and Ph.D. in political science, as I find the reading material dreadfully boring." Joy, an honors student whose technically superb investigation of the effectiveness of area labor-relations committees indicated a more thorough understanding of the discourse conventions in her particular field (social psychology) than did the project of any other student, reflected in retrospect that her work on the project was "rather erratic . . . I don't think I did enough fundamental rethinking of the project after the first semester." After meeting the expectations of a certain type of academic prose in her writing, she doubted that she would ever attempt an examination of such an issue again. Betsy lost interest in her project on the vernacular architecture of barns halfway through it. Only when she departed from conventional academic prose and focused on oral histories of the farmers and farms did her enthusiasm for the subject return: "I am really excited about continuing studying people and including interviews in my field work," she wrote at the end of the project. Any intrinsic interest in vernacular architecture or academic research on vernacular architecture had been lost by the wayside. (The same was true, however, of the projects of at least two of the men: interviews bolstered an interest in projects that they feared were in danger of becoming "over-academicized.")

Far more common than the bored writers, however, were those who became overstimulated and anxious during the course of their projects. Anxiety seemed to stem from two sources: the fear that the writer's own perspective might become lost in the welter of materials encountered, or the anxiety accompanying failure to find materials that adequately addressed the problem as the writer had formulated it in her own mind. Julia, at the end of a semester of difficulty in locating sources that addressed the problems of the woman journalist, asserted, "I still fight to retain my vision." Often women went to the library expecting to find materials that did not exist—that they themselves would need to write if they were to exist at all. Liz, for example, talked about how proud she was that she had persisted in digging through boring books to find the materials she needed for a study of women's development organizations in Senegal and Kenya; yet, she added, "I feel the need to find one book that totally substantiates what I've written." As with many women writers, the likelihood that she would find such a book was substantially less than that of a writer who had chosen a topic more central to male academic discourse. Tammy, after hours in the library, returned to lament her "difficulty finding the necessary resources": "While the books I have read address certain questions of oppression, and discuss the lives of the women involved in South Africa, they fail to mention the need for sisterhood, the drive a woman feels to 'bond' with other women against oppression." Not finding resources that explicitly addressed the values problem as she had constructed it left her floundering for structure and direction.

The bored women strongly resembled the "procedural knowers" that Belenky and her colleagues studied: women "absorbed in the business of acquiring and communicating knowledge" (95). Having mastered the procedures, they had not yet found a mode of connecting to the problem they studied, and they rapidly lost interest. The overanxious women described above stood on the verge of procedural knowing. However, their insistence on pursuing questions neglected in traditional male-centered discourse communities left them in danger both of losing connection with the project and of losing any sense of effective procedures and strategies for exploring a problem through research.

Another group of overstimulated or anxious women fell into the category that Belenky and her colleagues call "subjective knowers." Passionately involved in the subjects of their projects—in many cases they themselves were indirectly the subject of their projects—they responded to the threat of having their points of view procedurally invalidated by discrediting the validity of academic discourse altogether. Melissa, Christina, and Cat, for example, flatly resisted the notion of writing in academic prose or making any accommodation to it. "At the beginning I knew that my voice would not be heard in a 'research' paper or even an analytic essay, but I knew no familiar form with which to write true to my voice," Christina wrote at the end of her project. She finally wrote a persuasive essay based on minimal research, an essay that she believed adequately represented herself to her audience. Still, at the end of the process, she added, "I wonder sometimes...if I am somewhat unapproachable, operating in my own world—my own particular notion of how things are."

Melissa struggled all year on a project on the experiences of Southeast Asian refugee women in the United States. Her advisor was a sociologist who insisted on a methodologically rigorous, empirically based project, believing that anything else was not scholarship but mere "journalism." She expressed doubt throughout the year that his notion of "scholarship" was any more valuable than the detailed and personal oral histories she wanted to collect. She compromised between his conception of the project and her own by writing a schizophrenic project: half for her advisor, in which she had no interest, and half for herself, in which he had no interest. "There is an inner struggle I have been experiencing," she wrote at midyear. "First, how much of myself *should* be in the final project? Secondly, what kind of an audience *should* I address? (Now replace 'should' with 'do I want to' and you have my inner struggle.)"

Cat absolutely balked when pushed to connect her own work in photography with that of other photographers:

> This paper is not going to be scholarly. This paper is supposed to be what I want to write, self-pity or whatever. I want to say: I feel like I am getting fucking *nowhere*. I feel like I am fucking being patronized. Somewhere I got the feeling that this project was an *independent* endeavor, a culmination showing maturity and experience. . . . One of the biggest frustrations of my undergraduate years has been that I don't feel I have been "taught to think" for myself. I've been taught to think for someone else, to be a sort of brown-nosing grade-grubber trying to figure out what the prof wants.

For Cat, the pressure to connect with any academic, disciplinary, or artistic community was pressure to deny her own needs and impulses.

Some women resolved the tension between self and a learning that seemed to obliterate the self by self-consciously searching for a "voice" that would maintain the right of the self to be present in the work. In her project, Rita combined standard academic prose with short stories written from van Gogh's point of view (as she imagined it) and with a form she called "creative essays," a form that she "wrote in a fit of egotism, thinking [she] could be another John Berger." Sarah, whose project on feminist therapies for eating disorders largely relied on academic prose, interpolated fictionalized versions of her own journal entries—implicit indications to the reader that the person who wrote the academic essay, as a victim of eating disorders, remained passionately involved in the subject even if the prose style seemed to discount that involvement. Robin struggled endlessly with her advisor, a psychologist, over the question of "voice" and ultimately refused to write as he requested. Instead, as a recovering drug addict herself, she chose to write a manual directed to "the suffering addict." In a blistering year-end evaluation of her advisor and of academic writing in general, she wrote proudly that her project finally had "very little to do with the 'academic' world." She added, "What happened to the kid in all of this? Well, I will not forget that person because I was once there."

A Question of Identity in Academic Discourse Communities

Two decades of feminist work suggest that negotiating a discourse that has historically and systematically labeled women's perspectives as "other" carries with it certain emotional risks. Elizabeth Flynn succinctly summarizes the problem when she poses the question, "What does it mean to compose as a woman?":

> [Feminist research and theory] argue that men have chronicled our historical narratives and defined our fields of inquiry. Women's perspectives have been suppressed, silenced, marginalized, written out of what counts as authoritative knowledge. Difference is erased in a desire to universalize. Men become the standard against which women are judged. (425)

To enter into a discourse shaped principally by men's experience and values may leave some women uncomfortable with, even anxious about, some of the ways of thinking it demands. Thus, women's location vis-à-vis male-centered discourse communities may lead as a matter of course to nonfunctional or contradictory strategies or paralyzing "rule rigidity." Mary Daly's work demonstrates dramatically the sense in which the very words we use depict a patriarchal reality. Spender and Robin Lakoff both observe the necessity of being "bilingual" to operate effectively as a member of a muted group: that is to say, as women, we must constantly translate our own concerns (for which we may be struggling to find a language) to those of the dominant (male) language. For many women, the process of writing academic prose may nearly always involve an extra step: the clarification of an issue in the language of one's own experience, and its translation into a mode of discourse that may have no readily available structure to accommodate it. As Julia Penelope and Susan Wolfe put it:

> Patriarchal expressive modes reflect an epistemology that perceives the world in terms of categories, dichotomies, roles, stasis, and causation, while female expressive modes reflect an epistemology that perceives the world in terms of ambiguities, pluralities, processes, continuities, and complex relationships. (126)

Although I am somewhat uncomfortable with the dualism implicit in Penelope and Wolfe's assertion, I am still persuaded that the social positioning of women in our culture usually leads us toward adopting the "female expressive modes" they describe.

While men entering academic discourse communities may be more likely to see themselves as apprentices mastering a process that will allow them to contribute to a generalized body of knowledge, women are—for good reason—more likely to see themselves as outsiders with misgivings about entering the circle of the elect. For many of the women I worked with, the process of undertaking an independent academic research project involved a serious examination of what their relation would be to received bodies of knowledge, procedures, and methods. Those who could be self-consciously critical of those procedures and conventions—or those who could remain detached from them—seemed to fare best in terms of being able to conceive, carry out, and complete a senior project. Those willing to trust their own experiences and to formulate problems for study accordingly, but who lacked a language of critique, frequently found themselves unable to proceed for long periods of time.

If writing is necessarily a social activity in which, as Marilyn Cooper puts it, "a person is continually engaged with a variety of socially constituted systems" (367), it is also necessarily a political one. The experience of women writing suggests that we should be wary of calls for students to learn to write uncritically within discourse communities.[5] If we teach women students only to reproduce existing discourse conventions as ways of reaching particular audiences, we run the risk of placing them in situations in which conflicting strategies, anxiety, boredom, or writing apprehension may appear as a matter of course. To ask them to enter into discourse uncritically is to ask them to enter into a relationship with others and with language itself, and many may feel uncomfortable doing this. For the women I studied, the issue of "voice" was not merely a pragmatic one of reaching the audience they desired; more often, it involved a question of identity itself, and how much control they had over language in the face of discourse communities that they often experienced as hostile to their self-definitions.

At the same time, however, we need be cautious about approaches to process that are solely expressive or cognitive in orientation.[6] Although these tend to provide suggestions that unblock some writers temporarily, they do nothing to address the values conflicts at the heart of the dilemmas experienced by the women writers I studied. Any assessment of factors involved in the writing process that purports to be gender-neutral runs the risk of obscuring the ways in which certain writing contexts may be more fraught with peril and internal contradictions for women than for men.

Moreover, though the differences in negotiating academic discourse conventions that I have found have mainly to do with gender, it is important to note that the population of students I studied—both women and men—were nearly all white and upper-middle class. Of the four black students who registered for the senior project workshop, two dropped out (in different years) midway through the first semester. A third ended up needing four semesters to complete the process. I wonder now about the extent to which they may have experienced powerful values dilemmas that differed in kind from those of individuals marginalized solely by gender. Patricia Hill Collins, for example, describes an Afrocentric feminist epistemological orientation that includes some of the concerns voiced by the women whose project development I observed, but which differs in yet other ways from the orientation toward knowledge of Eurandrocentric culture. Research by neither the cognitive nor affective schools has captured the roles that race, class, or other marginalizing factors may play in making writers uneasy with the identity construction required by academic discourse and in blocking their writing altogether.

Despite their many instances of blockage, the news from the women I studied on the whole was encouraging. As Jenny put it at mid-year, *"I'll get there but it gonna hurt."* For me, Chris, whose project concerned the loneliness lesbian women in small towns face, summed up both the pain and the triumph of the women who persisted in asking hard questions about the conventions (and identities) that discourse communities made available to them:

> I still have many questions. I wonder if my project makes sense to the audience. I wanted it to make sense for I wonder what I can do with my information and knowledge. I feel the need to *do* something more... and I'm sure I will somehow. I wonder what my mother and the women who filled out my survey will think. Did I write what they believe? Will my mother understand it? Can I really make a difference by saying what I know or believe? Is there a way to have everyone understand what happens in my head? Will I find many people to help me make changes—or many people I can help? Did [my project discussant] think I didn't have enough theory? Was my language too passive? Should I make minor changes for the library copy? Will my project help other students? Should I have done something else?—
>
> I couldn't have.

Notes

[1] I do not want to claim what I found among Western Program students to be universally the case. In many ways, the Western Program is unique. A self-conscious alternative to the standard undergraduate curricula in many large state institutions, it is a living-learning community that was set up a decade and a half ago as an embodiment of progressive Deweyan educational ideals. In its emphasis on active learning through seminar participation and its writing-intensive, issue-oriented curriculum, the School of Interdisciplinary Studies provides a different kind of initiation into academic discourse than do most discipline-based programs that require a student to choose from a list of predefined majors. For instance, in their required core curriculum, Western Program students typically do not focus in any self-conscious way on the particular types of discourse conventions appropriate to different disciplinary communities. The audience for which they write in the most immediate sense includes their peers and the faculty of the Western Program community, with whom they share both curricular and co-curricular experiences. Moreover, because of the critical bias of the program's curriculum, more women students undertake senior projects with feminist themes than one might ordinarily expect to be the case.

[2] Had I used strict protocols on the actual composing behavior of these women students, I may indeed have found at the heart of women's blocking the "rule rigidity" that the men mentioned in their self-reports. It may also be that some men suffered from the same sorts of affective blocking I found in the women's self-reports, and that more probing would have encouraged them to articulate more about these difficulties. Nevertheless, the self-report procedure was the same for both men and women, and the questions and assignments that they responded to were the same. When asked to describe the factors that led to their blocking, the men nearly always responded in task-oriented terms; women, in contrast, nearly always drew on language that suggested issues of identity and relationship to audience.

[3] In their study of the careers of academic women, particularly those on the margins of the academy, Aisenberg and Harrington discovered in the scholarly work of many a similar focus on personally meaningful issues and a similar identity investment in their scholarly work. The women that they studied tended to be preoccupied in their work with social transformation and the contexts of power, and they frequently crossed disciplinary boundaries or undertook projects

unconventional for their disciplines. Often, their failure to adhere to standard disciplinary agenda brought with it high professional costs (83-106).

[4]Roth makes this suggestion as well.

[5]See Reither; Bizzell.

[6]Lester Faigley makes this case in advocating a social view of composing that entails awareness of the contexts in which writing takes place. James Berlin has also issued powerful calls for an approach to rhetoric that "attempts to place the question of ideology at the center of the teaching of writing" (492).

Works Cited

Aisenberg, Nadya, and Mona Harrington. *Women of Academe: Outsiders in the Sacred Grove*. Amherst: U of Massachusetts P, 1988.

Aronson, Anne. "Remodelling Audiences, Building Voices." Conference on College Composition and Communication. Atlanta, GA, March 1987.

Belenky, Mary Field, Blythe McVicker Clinchy, Nancy Rule Goldberger, and Jill Mattuck Tarule. *Women's Ways of Knowing: The Development of Self, Voice, and Mind*. New York: Basic, 1986.

Berlin, James. "Rhetoric and Ideology in the Writing Class." *College English* 50 (1988): 477-94.

Bizzell, Patricia. "Cognition, Convention, and Certainty: What We Need to Know about Writing." *Pre/Text* 3 (1982): 213-43.

Bloom, Lynn Z. "Anxious Writers in Context: Graduate School and Beyond." Rose, *When a Writer* 119-33.

Boice, Robert. "Psychotherapies for Writing Blocks." Rose, *When a Writer* 182-218.

Collins, Patricia Hill. "The Social Construction of Black Feminist Thought." *Signs: Journal of Women in Culture and Society* 14 (1989): 745-73.

Cooper, Marilyn. "The Ecology of Writing." *College English* 48 (1986): 364-75.

Csikszentmihalyi, Mihaly. *Beyond Boredom and Anxiety*. San Francisco: Jossey-Bass, 1975.

Daly, John A. "Writing Apprehension." Rose, *When a Writer* 43-82.

Daly, John A., and Michael D. Miller. "The Empirical Development of an Instrument of Writing Apprehension." *Research in the Teaching of English* 9 (1975): 242-49.

Elbow, Peter. "Closing My Eyes as I Speak: An Argument for Ignoring Audience." *College English* 49 (1987): 50-69.

Faigley, Lester. "Competing Theories of Process: A Critique and a Proposal." *College English* 48 (1986): 527-42.

Flynn, Elizabeth A. "Composing as a Woman." *College Composition and Communication* 39 (1988): 423-35.

Gilligan, Carol. *In a Different Voice: Psychological Theory and Women's Development*. Cambridge: Harvard UP, 1982.

Lakoff, Robin. *Language and Woman's Place*. New York: Harper, 1975.

Larson, Reed. "Emotional Scenarios in the Writing Process: An Examination of Young Writers' Affective Experiences." Rose, *When a Writer* 19-42.

Olsen, Tillie. *Silences*. New York: Delacorte, 1978.

Penelope (Stanley), Julia, and Susan J. Wolfe. "Consciousness as Style; Style as Aesthetic." *Language, Gender and Society*. Ed. Barrie Thorne, Cheris Kramarae, and Nancy Henley. Cambridge, MA: Newbury, 1983. 125-39.

Reither, James A. "Writing and Knowing: Toward Redefining the Writing Process." *College English* 47(1985): 620-28.

Rose, Mike, ed. *When a Writer Can't Write: Studies in Writer's Block and Other Composing Process Problems*. New York: Guilford, 1985.

——. *Writer's Block: The Cognitive Dimension*. Carbondale: Southern Illinois UP, 1984.

Roth, Robert G. "The Evolving Audience: Alternatives to Audience Accommodation." *College Composition and Communication* 38 (1987): 47-55.

Simeone, Angela. *Academic Women: Working Towards Equality*. South Hadley, MA: Bergin, 1987.

Spender, Dale. *Man Made Language*. 2nd ed. Boston: Routledge, 1985.

Theory and the Teaching of Writing

Some Difficulties with Collaborative Learning

David W. Smit

Theories of collaborative learning and collaborative writing are finally gaining recognition. Sessions at the Conference on College Composition and Communication convention devoted to the research and practice of collaborative methods jumped from six in 1987 to eleven in 1988 to twenty-two in 1989. Articles on the subject are appearing in all the major journals with an interest in composition, including *College English*, the *Journal of Advanced Composition*, *Research in the Teaching of English*, and *Rhetoric Review*. The field even recognizes a list of semi canonical texts: Edwin Mason's *Collaborative Learning*, M.L.J. Abercrombie's *The Anatomy of Judgment*, John Dewey's *Experience and Education*, and Thomas Kuhn's *The Structure of Scientific Revolutions*. Also, proponents of collaborative learning often cite Kenneth Bruffee's ground breaking articles, "Collaborative Learning and the 'Conversation of Mankind'" and "Social Construction, Language, and the Authority of Knowledge: A Bibliographical Essay." Perhaps, then, we should stop and critically survey this phenomenon, if for no other reason than that the term "collaborative learning" applies to such a wide range of pedagogical theories and methods. The support for such theories and methods depends on a truly eclectic body of theory, presupposition, and evidence, much of it not directly related to composition at all. In this essay, I will examine some of the major theories that support collaborative learning in composition, especially the assumptions, evidence, and relationships between theory and practice. I am less interested in the theories themselves, which have received comment elsewhere, than I am in the pedagogical application of the theories.[1]

The problem begins with what we mean by "collaborative learning." The term applies to any pedagogical theory or method that advocates or involves using groups, everything from free group discussions to teach close observation to adults to highly structured systems for organizing lower elementary classrooms into teams of students who have their progress regularly charted in order to earn rewards for their achievements. In composition, the most common forms of collaborative learning are peer response groups and peer tutoring, although various kinds of group projects using teams of researchers, drafters, and editors are also used. I often find it difficult to sort out the claims of collaborative theorists so as to discover just what kind of pedagogy they are recommending when they champion the benefits of collaborative learning. No matter what particular methods they promote, collaborative theorists can cite an impressive body of theory and evidence in support of their claims. However, I question whether this body of theory provides an adequate basis for a collaborative pedagogy and whether it clearly demonstrates that collaborative methods improve writing.

Usually, collaborative theorists offer three arguments in favor of collaborative learning: (1) traditional classroom methods have failed to teach students what they most require—a critical stance toward authority and the ability to cooperate to solve problems of social concern—and therefore we need to restructure both education and society to promote these values, (2) collaborative learning mirrors the social nature of language and writing, and (3) empirical studies demonstrate the positive effects of collaborative methods.

Collaborative Learning and Social Change

Edwin Mason hotly argues that our present educational system needs to be restructured. He writes, for example, that in our society,

> Systems in which the simple right of human beings to relationship, to membership (*full membership*) of the species and of some protecting group within it, are not recognized; systems in which relationship is not given, but has to be earned—these must be cleared away. We are directly teaching mistrust of humanity wherever we make the young compete for esteem. There is a natural drive towards this which needs no reinforcement; indeed it needs countering and can only be countered by experience of successful collaboration with others in which everybody's self-esteem is enhanced and in which questions of esteem eventually simply fall out of mind. (42)

Mason further argues that our very survival as a species depends on our educational system's ability to foster a new kind of nonhostile, noncompetitive personality in students and an attitude which questions traditional certainties and promotes a new relationship between authority and the larger group. According to Bruffee, traditional pedagogical methods—lecturing, recitation, and their various combinations subtly teach the opposite values, such as the following:

> Knowledge is what a teacher says.
> Answers are more important than questions.
> Ignorance is the same thing as stupidity.
> I am what someone else says I am.
> Fear thy neighbor.
> Think because it pays off.
> Stay in line.
> Learning is preparing to do.
> Teaching is telling.
> The goal of education is to complete it.　("The Way Out" 469)

To Bruffee (and to Mason), the best way to counter these false values is to change "the way students are organized for learning," to create a "polycentralized collaborative learning community which places faculty at the edge of the action, once they have set the scene, a position from which they may respond to needs which the students discover for themselves" ("The Way Out" 465-66).

Bruffee acknowledges the explicitly political nature of collaborative pedagogy; and like Mason, Paulo Freire, Henry Giroux, Kyle Fiore, Nan Elsassar, and other collaborative theorists, he argues that all education is political: "The purpose of education—hence the job teachers are hired to do—is to induct people into the mores and values of 'the state,' that is, the prevailing culture" ("Kenneth A. Bruffee Responds" 77). Thus, the most significant issues of educational theory and practice involve the mores and values we choose to promote in education and the best way to "induct people" into them.

Of course, it is a matter of personal opinion and judgment whether cooperation is superior to competition, whether a critical stance toward authority is more appropriate than acceptance, and whether knowledge is dependent upon the constraints of time, place, and point of view. All of these propositions are highly debatable, and whether we accept the argument for social change will depend in large part on the degree to which we accept these assertions. But even if we do accept them, I am still not convinced that the best way to accomplish a more cooperative society, a more critical stance toward authority, and a more open and relative view of knowledge is through a particular pedagogical method.

Are collaborative methods *necessarily* better at teaching the values and abilities that collaborative theorists wish to transmit to their students? At least two arguments seriously question the inherent superiority of collaborative methods for achieving the very goals its adherents cherish. First, I am sympathetic to the values Mason and Bruffee advocate, and yet I learned my values from traditional lecture and recitation methods. I presume others did also. The best of my teachers did not indoctrinate me into one limited view of knowledge or restrict the scope of my questioning. They were open about why they accepted what they held to be true; they respectfully granted other points of view their own arguments and reasons. True, these teachers did control their own classrooms: they did a great deal of talking, and when they promoted discussion, they did so in order to get students to understand a particular point. However, I did not feel manipulated; I did not learn to fear my neighbor or stay in line; I did not come to believe that ignorance is the same as stupidity. Despite the fact that these teachers did not use collaborative methods, they did promote the values of collaborative theory by illustrating a mind at work and by transmitting a set of values by example.

Although there is some empirical evidence that certain collaborative methods are superior to traditional methods in promoting cooperation and even altruism (see Slavin, *Cooperative Learning* 117-18), most of this research has been conducted on highly structured forms of classroom management in the elementary grades. No one, so far as I know, has conducted such studies for methods of collaborative learning. Since traditional methods can be effective, we should not overlook them when we consider some of the problems of collaborative pedagogies.

Indeed, the problems inherent in collaborative methods constitute a second reason for questioning their superiority. Thomas Johnson feels that collaborative methods promote "authoritarian leveling toward the norm through peer pressure," which he associates with the techniques for social engineering used by "Naziism, Fascism, and Communism" (76). Although Johnson's reaction may be extreme, Greg Myers voices similar concern. Myers points out that collaborative methods in most cases do not reflect conditions outside the school or university and that accomplishing the social goals of collaborative theory would require a radical change not just in academic structures but in the entire society: "Our problems will not be solved just by new methods, or new theories, or new knowledge" (170). Social change can only be accomplished by a massive change in attitude and a revolutionary movement to change society based on these new attitudes. Such a revolutionary agenda seems to be beyond the scope of a single pedagogical method.

Even if we grant that a particular pedagogical method can be part of revolutionary change, it is not at all clear that collaborative methods are the best means for accomplishing these social goals. Bruffee, for example, grants that "conformity, anti-intellectualism, intimidation, and leveling down of quality" are potential dangers for collaborative learning, but he argues that they can be overcome with "a demanding academic environment" ("Conversation" 652). The impulse of groups to foster conformity, or at best to arrive at consensus, must be in constant tension with the right of group members to voice their individual differences and the creation of an atmosphere in which they feel free to do so. Many of the published reports on collaborative learning indicate that rather than consensus collaboration may promote a wide variety of points of view; students often do not agree in their responses to the work of their peers, and their responses are often quite different from those of their teachers.[2] Thus, collaborative methods seem to have created a dilemma. On the one hand, they may unleash irreconcilable differences in assumptions, values, and points of view; on the other hand, the emphasis on achieving consensus may result in unnecessary peer pressure to conform to what the group decides. Of course, the goal is a proper balance between individual differences and group consensus, but given the tension inherent in the method, it seems excessive to claim that it is intrinsically better than other pedagogical techniques in achieving a change in values.

The Social Nature of Language

The philosophy that language, indeed all knowledge, is a social product is called social construction. Bruffee writes,

> A social constructionist position in any discipline assumes that entities we normally call reality, knowledge, thought, facts, texts, selves, and so on are constructs generated by communities of like-minded peers. Social construction understands reality, knowledge, thought, facts, texts, selves, and so on as community-generated and community-maintained linguistic entities—or, more broadly speaking, symbolic entities—that define or "constitute" the communities that generate them. . . . ("Social Construction" 774)

Even if we grant the tenets of social construction, however, it is not at all clear that collaborative methods best implement that philosophy. As an example of the reasoning involved in this claim, I turn to "Let Them Write—Together" by Lisa Ede and Andrea Lunsford, although Bruffee has made many of the same claims with the same reasoning in his article on social construction. In a schematic form, Ede and Lunsford argue as follows:

- "Learning always occurs as part of an interaction either between the learner and the environment or, more frequently, between the learner and peers."

- "One effect of what we may, without too much exaggeration, call an epistemological revolution is a new view of the role of language, a view which no longer defines language as incidental to the creation of knowledge or belief . . . but as itself constitutive of knowledge."

- "In this view, an individual writing alone is still participating in social experience, since the language he or she grows into as a child comes with its own rich history. Even when writing alone in a garret, in other words, the writer is not alone."

- Therefore, teachers ought to promote collaborative writing. (120-21)

Obviously, this reasoning assumes a great deal. I understand the warrants of the argument to be these: (1) Classroom practice ought to reflect "real world" experience, and (2) collaborative writing as a pedagogy more effectively models language as a socially constituted medium and knowledge as a social product than individual writing does.

Of course, if all language is social, then all pedagogies that use language are social, too. In some sense, then, all experience with language is "real world" experience, and the question becomes what "real world" experience the classroom should reflect. The language of a lecture or recitation class could be just as formative in developing a student's concept of writing as a collaborative pedagogy. The rationale for a lecture class might be that students need to *hear* language, to listen to concepts being elaborated on and worked through, in order to have models for their own usage and patterns of thinking. The rationale for a recitation class might be that it is modeled after the way children learn language through interaction with others, testing their concepts and usage by trying them out and seeing how well other people understand them. Thus, the claim that language always occurs as part of an interaction between the learner and the environment seems an inadequate premise on which to base a collaborative pedagogy. By the definitions of social construction, all pedagogies use language socially, and the collaborative theorist must demonstrate how collaborative methods more closely model the "real world" than other pedagogies.

Thus, Ede and Lunsford argue that writers interact frequently in the "real world" and that therefore the writing class ought to reflect this reality. Ede and Lunsford base their conclusions on a survey of "200 randomly selected members of six professional organizations" (a total of 1,200), 87% of whom "reported that they sometimes wrote as part of a team or group." In addition, "59% of those who participated in co- or group writing projects indicated that they found such collaboration to be 'productive' (45%) or 'very productive' (14%)" ("Why Write" 72, 76).

A number of questions arise here. The most significant, of course, is why writing done by professionals on the job is more "real worldly" than writing done, say, by free-lance writers who specialize in articles for sports magazines or by corporation executives dashing off memos to their subordinates. If writing should reflect "real world" experience, what aspects of the "real world" should it reflect and on what grounds? I would have serious reservations about creating a writing course, even an advanced one, entirely on the model of writing done in professional associations, unless the course were specifically labeled as such.

But another question can be raised about the basis of Ede and Lunsford's confident assertion that 87% of their professional respondents wrote as part of a team or group. Apparently the figure of 87% is from the unpublished results of a follow-up questionnaire to their published survey. The data published in *Rhetoric Review* suggests a variety of interpretations. Consider the figures for the amount of time professionals spend writing collaboratively:

Percentage of Time Spent in Writing Activities

Writing alone	81%
Writing with one person	10%
Writing with small group (2-5)	7%
Writing with large group (6 or more)	2%
Total	100%
	("Why Write" 78)

Note that the professionals claimed they wrote alone an overwhelming 81% of the time. However, that figure may be contradicted by the survey of how frequently the professionals surveyed used the various forms of collaboration:

Frequency of Organizational Patterns

Organizational Patterns	Very Often	Often	Occasion-ally	Never
A. Group plans and outlines. Each member drafts a part. Group compiles the parts and revises the whole.	6%	18%	48%	28%
B. Group plans and outlines. One member writes draft. Group revises.	5%	22%	4%	29%
C. One member plans and writes draft. Group revises.	8%	26%	44%	22%
D. One person plans and writes draft. One or more persons revise draft without consulting the author.	4%	8%	21%	67%
E. Group plans and writes draft. One or more persons revise draft without consulting the authors.	1%	2%	18%	79%
F. One member assigns writing tasks. Each member carries out individual tasks. One member compiles parts and revises.	7%	18%	41%	34%
G. One person dictates. Another person transcribes and revises.	2%	8%	19%	71%

("Why Write" 80)

No more than 34% of the professional respondents use any method of collaboration more than occasionally, and the most frequently used form of collaboration is "One member plans and writes draft. Group revises." The other methods are used about 25% more than occasionally. Once again, the question arises: do these kinds of writing occur frequently enough even in this particular and limited segment of the "real world" to justify an entire pedagogy based upon them? Which of the seven kinds of interaction should we teach—any or all?

Ede and Lunsford suggest that peer response is the best way to introduce students to the realities of collaboration, but the values they find in peer groups have little direct connection with preparing students for the realities of collaboration in the professions:

> We believe that using such peer response groups is the best and most effective way to introduce students to collaborative or group writing. Teachers who use such groups in their classes report a number of benefits: group members provide an immediate, concrete audience, often the first one a student has encountered; interest level is generally high, since students are inherently interested in what their peers think; the teacher becomes a helper rather than a judge; and emphasis is put on revision, with its obvious rewards. ("Let Them Write" 123)

Peer response groups may indeed provide these benefits, but unless Ede and Lunsford want to recommend more particular strategies for guiding peer groups, peer response as it is commonly reported in the literature will not adequately prepare students for the rigors of even one kind of professional collaboration—one member planning and drafting and the team revising—which professionals use more than occasionally only 34% of the time.[3]

Language may indeed be a social construct, and knowledge may indeed be socially negotiated; however, it does not follow that collaborative methods are thereby the best way to teach writing. Such an assertion depends on what aspects of social reality collaborative methods are designed to reflect and how well the collaborative method reflects that reality.

The Effectiveness of Collaborative Learning
Ede and Lunsford are confident that collaborative methods accomplish a good deal:

> Evidence in support of this hypothesis [that learning always occurs as part of an interaction between learner and environment or between learner and peers] has been provided by Abercrombie, Bruffee, and Garth, who have studied the collaborative learning process in detail. Their studies confirm that students often learn both skills (such as writing) and content material more effectively and efficiently when they do so as part of a group. ("Let Them Write" 120)

Certainly, several researchers have shown that collaborative pedagogies have positive effects. Students in classrooms which use collaborative methods do seem to develop certain skills and learn certain content "more effectively and efficiently" than by other methods. However, whether these improved skills result in better writing is open to question. The studies most often cited by collaborative theorists demonstrate not improved writing but the enhancement of certain skills which we might call "precursors" to good writing. Take the study by M.L.J. Abercrombie, for example. Abercrombie does not address the teaching of writing at all. Her first study involves teaching medical students how to observe more closely and how to make appropriate inferences based upon these observations. The method which Abercrombie taught her medical students—"free group discussion"—forced students to compare their observations and inferences with those of other members of the group, and in the process the students saw how limited and governed by presupposition their judgments really were.

Similarly, consider Bruffee's essays. He asserts that "students' work tended to improve when they got help from peers" ("Conversation" 638), and he cites a collection of essays on college peer groups edited by Theodore Newcomb and Everett Wilson. But none of the essays in that volume deals specifically with writing instruction. In "The Brooklyn Plan" Bruffee does mention that students working with peer tutors demonstrated an increased .ability to think through problems and to relate the concrete and the specific in their writing, but he offers only the most general of illustrations in support of his assertion. He also found that students in the Brooklyn peer tutoring program developed an increased amount of self-esteem.

So it is with the volume edited by Bouton and Garth and cited by Ede and Lunsford, as well as many other studies: few of them analyze the effects of collaborative pedagogy on writing per se. Instead, they demonstrate that students improve such things as feeling good about the class, having better attitudes toward writing, having an increased ability to interact in small groups and participate in discussion, and being able to critically analyze the writing of others.[4] These improvements are valuable in and of themselves and provide, I think, an adequate rationale for instituting collaborative pedagogies. But feeling good about writing and a writing class, being able to interact well in small groups, and being able to critically analyze the writing of others are at best preconditions to writing well.[5]

The studies which analyze the effects of collaboration on writing have much more ambiguous results. Angela O'Donnell and her colleagues (1985) found that pairs of writers working together with few guidelines could produce instructions that were more "communicative"—that is, the instructions included a statement of purpose, used illustrations, referred to illustrations, used and enumerated the steps of the process, and correctly ordered the steps—than writers working alone. However, in a later study (1987) O'Donnell and company found that neither paired writers nor individual writers who rewrote a set of instructions used this experience to improve their performance on a later assignment. When revising, the pairs of writers did produce more complete instructions than the individual writers, but they also focused on different levels of information: the pairs of writers used more "descriptive information," while the individual writers used more "procedural information" in their revisions. The advantages of group writing in this series of tasks are not clear cut.

Many studies do show that collaboration improves writing, but the pedagogies in these studies are so complex that collaboration alone may not be the reason for the improvement. Most of the activities in these collaborative pedagogies are highly structured, focus on practice (not on talking about writing in general) and provide students with substantial response to their writing; the pedagogies they are compared with are not as highly structured, involve much less practice, and provide students with much less response to their writing. John Clifford's study is a good example. In Clifford's experiment, collaborative classes systematically engaged in the following activities: brainstorming, free writing, small group analysis of the free writing, student summaries of progress, drafting, small group responses to these drafts, another student evaluation of the draft, and further revision. Almost all of the class time was devoted to workshops of one kind or another. The control classes, however, reviewed grammar and mechanics, analyzed readings from a text, received instruction in "the patterns, strategies, and conventions of traditional rhetoric," and studied samples of student work as examples of rhetorical principles (44). Any additional class time was spent on discussion of the problems in the last assignment and explaining how to do the next one. Clifford's collaborative classes showed significantly greater gains in a pre/post test evaluation of writing than the control classes. However, it may be that the tight focus of the experimental classes, or the amount of response given at the various stages of the writing process, or even the time devoted to practice contributes as much to the improved writing of Clifford's students as collaboration.

The studies cited by George Hillocks in *Research on Written Composition* provoke the same reservations. Hillocks found that an environmental mode and a focus on inquiry were the most beneficial pedagogies for improving writing. All of these pedagogies are collaborative in one way or another. Inquiry techniques ask students to analyze a set of data collaboratively in order to help them "develop skills or strategies for dealing with the data in order to say or write something about it" (211). Environmental modes of instruction also rely heavily on "small-group problem-centered discussions" in order to give students practice in working on "concrete materials and problems, the working through of which not only illustrates the principle but engages students in its use" (122). Like Clifford's study, which Hillocks cites as an example of the environmental mode, environmental and inquiry pedagogies are more highly structured and more focused on practice than the control groups. It remains to be seen, then, whether collaboration, or structure, or time spent in practice, or some combination of factors is the dominant reason for improved writing in these studies.

Adopting a Critical Attitude

When we devise teaching strategies, we need to adopt a critical attitude: we need to analyze claims about the advantages of particular strategies over others, and above all, we need to be aware of the assumptions, reasoning, and kinds of evidence various theorists use to support their claims.

Properly executed, collaborative practices may constitute an effective pedagogy; but to be certain, we need a great deal more evidence—evidence clearly rooted in consistent theory, and tightly reasoned and documented by the methods best suited to test the hypotheses of that particular theory, whether the theory be historical, philosophical, critical, experimental, clinical, formal, or ethnographic, to use Stephen North's terms. We need to know more about the dynamics of groups and the tensions they create between individual creativity and social conformity. We need to know more about exactly what produces effective writing in collaborative pedagogies—the structure, the amount and range of response, or the sheer time spent in practice.

Whether collaborative learning will lead to a new order of social relations, whether it more adequately mirrors language as a social activity, whether it improves writing more than other techniques—all of this is still open to question.

Notes

[1]For a Sympathetic bibliographical essay, see Trimbur. The only major critical essay I know of is by Myers, but critical response has appeared in letters to the editor by Beade, Foster, and Johnson.

[2]For example, see Danis, Flynn, Gere and Abbot, Newkirk, and Ziv.

[3]For an argument that "contingencies specific to an organization" are quite different from those in the classroom, see Harrison.

[4]For summaries of this research see Bishop, Gere and Abbott, Hill, and Slavin.

[5]Bruffee asserts that students need to be an "astute and demanding" audience before they can be "clear effective writers" ("Some Practical Models" 641).

Works Cited

Abercrombie, M.L.J. *The Anatomy of Judgment*. London: Hutchinson, 1960.

Beade, Pedro. "More Comments on 'Social Construction, Language, and the Authority of Knowledge: A Bibliographical Essay.'" *College English* 49 (1987): 707-08.

Bishop, Wendy. "Research, Theory, and Pedagogy of Peer Writing Groups: An Annotated Bibliography." 1986. ERIC ED 276 035.

Bouton, Clark, and Russell Y. Garth, eds. *Learning in Groups*. San Francisco: Jossey, 1983.

Bruffee, Kenneth A. "The Brooklyn Plan: Attaining Intellectual Growth through Peer-Group Tutoring." *Liberal Education*. 64 (1978): 447-68.

——. "Collaborative Learning and the 'Conversation of Mankind.'" *College English* 46 (1984): 635-52.

——. "Collaborative Learning: Some Practical Models." *College English* 34 (1973): 634-43.

——. "Kenneth A. Bruffee Responds [to Thomas Johnson]." *College English* 48 (1986): 77-78.

——. "Social Construction, Language, and the Authority of Knowledge: A Bibliographical Essay." *College English* 48 (1986): 773-90.

——. "The Way Out." *College English* 33 (1972): 457-70.

Clifford, John. "Composing in Stages: The Effects of a Collaborative Pedagogy." *Research in the Teaching of English* 15 (1981): 37-53.

Danis, Francine. "Weaving the Web of Meaning: Interaction Patterns in Peer Response Groups." 1982. ERIC ED 214 202.

Dewey, John. *Experience and Education*. New York: Collier, 1963.

Ede, Lisa, and Andrea Lunsford. "Let Them Write—Together." *English Quarterly* 18 (1985): 119-27.

——. "Why Write...Together: A Research Update." *Rhetoric Review* 5 (1986): 71-81.

Elsasser, Nan, and Vera P. John-Steiner. "An Interactionist Approach to Advancing Literacy." *Harvard Educational Review* 47 (1977): 355-69.

Fiore, Kyle, and Nan Elsasser. "'Strangers No More': A Liberatory Literacy Curriculum." *College English* 44 (1982): 115-28.

Flynn, Elizabeth. "Freedom, Restraint, and Peer Group Interaction." CCCC Convention. San Francisco. Mar. 1982.

Foster, David. "More Comments on 'Social Construction, Language, and the Authority of Knowledge: A Bibliographical Essay.'" *College English* 49 (1987): 709-11.

Freire, Paulo. *Pedagogy in Process*. New York: Seabury, 1978.

——. *Pedagogy of the Oppressed*. New York: Continuum, 1970.

Gere, Anne Ruggles, and Robert D. Abbott. "Talking about Writing: The Language of Writing Groups." *Research in the Teaching of English* 19 (1985): 362-81.

Jerks, Henry A. *Theory and Resistance in Education*. South Hadley, MA: Bergin and Garvey, 1983.

Harrison, Teresa M. "Frameworks for the Study of Writing in Organizational Contexts." *Written Communication* 4 (1987): 3-23.

Hill, Gayle W. "Group versus Individual Performance: Are N+1 Heads Better Than One?" *Psychological Bulletin* 91. (1982): 517-39.

Hillocks, George. *Research on Written Composition*. Urbana: NCRE-ERIC, 1986.

Johnson, Thomas S. "A Comment on 'Collaborative Learning and the Conversation of Mankind.'" *College English* 48 (1986): 76.

Kuhn, Thomas. *The Structure of Scientific Revolutions*. 2nd Ed. Chicago: U of Chicago P, 1970.

Mason, Edwin. *Collaborative Learning*. New York: Agathon, 1972.

Myers, Greg. "Reality, Consensus, and Reform in the Rhetoric of Composition Teaching." *College English* 48 (1986): 154-74.

Newcomb, Theodore M., and Everett K. Wilson, eds. *College Peer Groups*. Chicago: Aldine, 1966.

Newkirk, Thomas. "Direction and Misdirection in Peer Response." *College Composition and Communication* 35 (1984): 301-11.

North, Stephen M. *The Making of Knowledge in Composition: Portrait of an Emerging Field*. Upper Montclair, NJ: Boynton, 1987.

O'Donnell, Angela M., et al. "Cooperative Writing: Direct Effects and Transfer." *Written Communication* 2 (1985): 307-15.

———. "Effects of Cooperative and Individual Rewriting on an Instruction Writing Task." *Written Communication* 4 (1987): 90-99.

Slavin, Robert E. "Cooperative Learning." *Review of Educational Research* 50 (1980): 315-42.

———. *Cooperative Learning.* New York: Longman, 1983.

———. *Cooperative Learning: Student Teams.* 2nd ed. Washington, DC: NEA, 1987.

Trimbur, John. "Collaborative Learning and Teaching Writing." *Perspectives on Recent Research and Scholarship in Composition.* Ed. Ben W. McClelland and Timothy R. Donovan. New York: MLA, 1985. 87-109.

Ziv, Nina D. "Peer Groups in the Composition Class: A Case Study." 1983. ERIC ED: 229 799.

Becoming Aware
of the Myth of Presence

REED WAY DASENBROCK

It has been a fundamental axiom of writing instruction for generations that good writing is like speech inasmuch as it has "voice" and is aware of its audience. And this comparison seems to make sense, because both activities draw on a common reservoir of language skills. But why, then, do so many students have trouble writing when they seem to have so little trouble speaking?

The argument of this essay is that teachers of writing have in several crucial respects over-emphasized the similarities between speaking and writing and, in so doing, have reinforced what Jacques Derrida has called the "metaphysics of presence." Like most of Western culture, we have treated writing as if it were speech or essentially a substitute for it, even though the problems students have with writing are precisely with those aspects of writing that don't work like speech. Moreover, the relation between writing and speaking, as well as the methods by which we write and speak, are changing rapidly in response to technological innovations—computers, tele-communications, dictation systems, and the like. These innovations have changed the "scene of writing" in ways that teachers of writing need to be aware of. I want to argue that Derrida's critique of presence enables us to come to a sharper understanding of how these new developments affect the teaching of writing. I am not one of those who believe that Derrida can be "found everywhere," that the entire world can and should be read through lenses polished in Paris; in fact, the pedagogical model I want to develop finally is not one that Derrida would endorse. But I find Derrida's discussion of the relation between speech and writing (particularly in Part I of *Of Grammatology*, "Writing before the Letter") entirely relevant to current issues in the teaching and study of writing.[1]

Logocentrism: Privileging the Spoken Word

One of the key themes of Derrida's thought is the concept of *presence/absence*. Derrida sees the metaphysics of presence, which he also calls "logocentrism," as the dominant tradition in Western thought from Plato and Aristotle to the present. Logocentrism is the privileging of the *logos*, or spoken word, over the written word, and Derrida rather sweepingly asserts that the Western tradition has always privileged the spoken word or oral language over the written. In oral communication, the speaker is present to an audience, and, according to this tradition, this presence ensures full, unmediated communication; writing, in contrast, is seen as secondary to speech. As Rousseau has said, writing is "nothing but the representation of speech" (qtd. in Derrida, *Of Grammatology* 27). We resort to writing only when the more secure method of face-to-face communication is impossible—when the person we wish to communicate with is absent. Thus, writing is seen as a system for transcribing speech, a system that functions as a supplement to speech in the absence of the speaker, and the specific differences that exist between the written and the spoken codes are a function of the perceived difference between their natures.

Although Derrida has been faulted by his critics for ignoring examples which tend not to support his point, he has gathered an impressive array of passages in which key Western thinkers privilege speech over writing, presence over absence.[2] Plato's attack on writing as a falling away from the purity of speech is perhaps the *locus classicus*.[3] Aristotle also viewed writing as secondary to speech: "Spoken words are the symbols of mental experience and written words are the symbols of spoken words" (qtd. in Derrida, *Of Grammatology* 36). And Derrida has criticized such contemporary thinkers as Saussure, Levi-Strauss, and J.L. Austin for their analogous privileging of the oral over the written (*Of Grammatology* 27-73, 101-40; "Signature"). Moreover, a sense of the spoken word as vital is, of course, crucial to the Judeo-Christian tradition: "In the beginning was the Word." And "God *said*, 'let there be light.'"

It is difficult, perhaps, for many of us to share Derrida's agitation about this dominance of logocentrism. Derrida speaks of "the historical-metaphysical reduction of writing to the rank of an instrument enslaved to a full and originally spoken language" (*Of Grammatology* 29) as if writing were the victim of a nefarious authoritarian conspiracy. But, certainly, Derrida is correct in arguing that the way we customarily regard writing ignores the differences between writing and speaking, between reading and listening. I found it, for example, far more natural two sentences ago to write "Derrida speaks of" though I have never heard him say these words. We speak of what Shakespeare "says" in Sonnet 129 or of what an author is "telling us," and these metaphors are the marks of a metaphysics of presence that treats writing as if it were speech or, more precisely, that assimilates writing under a model of communication based on speech. Though the writer is absent when we read, we ignore that fact and treat the writer as if he or she were present, speaking to us in an unmediated way. This response ignores everything that is different (and much that is problematic) about writing, the essence of which is that the writer's writing functions in the absence of the writer. We see the differences between speaking and writing as contingent, not essential, as mere "devices" writing must use in order to approach the full, unmediated presence speech has unproblematically. The value of speech thus comes from its presence, and, in Derrida's view, the metaphysics of presence conflates speech and presence, thus automatically denigrating writing as absence.

Derrida argues that this metaphysics of presence, this logocentrism, utterly pervades the Western intellectual tradition; good evidence for this view is provided by the fact that even the discipline of the study of writing has continued in many important respects to be logocentric. For instance, the aim of one influential pedagogy—Zoellner's "talk-write"—is to increase students' written fluency by leading them from talking to writing.[4] Further, the tradition of rhetoric originated in the study of oral, not written, discourse, and the continuing influence of classical rhetoric on composition studies helps reinforce logocentric language and concepts. We find it more natural to refer to a writer's "awareness of an audience," as if the writer were on stage declaiming, than to refer to a readership; we also refer to the importance of a writer "finding his or her own voice," again as if the writer were speaking. Moreover, we teach writing orally and seem unaware of the resulting tension. Many of us conduct conferences, believing that comments given in person will be more effective than written comments even though our oral comments are about writing. Others work extensively with peer groups, in which a writer tries to say what he or she means and peers provide oral responses to the writing. In any of these situations, if the writer's meaning is unclear, we ask, "What are you trying to *say* here?"

Despite some important exceptions, much research in composition is also still enmeshed in logocentric assumptions. The relationship between speaking and writing is an important topic in composition studies, but the trend in these studies has been largely to emphasize the similarities—not the differences—between speaking and writing (for example, see Kroll and Vann). Moreover, armed with Derrida's critique, we can find traces of logocentrism in many other aspects of composition theory and practice today: in the methods of protocol analysis, in references to "inner speech," and in references to disciplinary or interpretive communities of discourse. However, it would be wrong to present all the approaches and theories in composition today as unequivocally logocentric. For example, in a spirit largely (if not totally) compatible with Derrida, those theorists who stress writing as a mode of learning—rather than as a mode of putting down on paper what one has learned—reverse the logocentric vision of writing as mere transcription.[5] But Derrida suggests that logocentrism is so pervasive that we must keep reminding ourselves that it is writing—not rhetoric, not invention, not inner speech—that we study and teach. All too readily, anyone working from Western cultural assumptions comes to see speech and writing as hierarchically related and, therefore, subsumes writing under a model of communication which privileges speech over writing, presence over absence.

Student Writers and the Metaphysics of Presence

Derrida's description of the metaphysics of presence also explains much about the state of mind of the average college writer. The "basic" writer, so Mina Shaughnessy and others have argued, is often overly aware off—and therefore intimidated by—the differences between speaking and writing. But the "average" college writer, sufficiently at ease with writing to have avoided the intimidation the basic writer experiences, far more often ignores these differences, treating writing as if it were speech or simply a device for transcribing it. A number of serious problems in student writing stem from this unarticulated premise about writing.

Most students, of course, have had much more experience with the spoken than with the written code, so it should come as no surprise that many of the most common errors found in student writing stem from excessive reliance upon the spoken code as a guide to writing. No one seems to know how to use an apostrophe anymore, largely because no one has ever spoken an apostrophe. Many spelling mistakes, and most of the frequent ones, arise from the same source: when in doubt about the spelling of a word, the student sounds it out and then writes it down as he or she hears it. This simple speech-based rule of thumb is often unreliable, so the student writes *piticular* instead of *particular*, *temperament* instead of *temperament*. Other examples of common errors that arise from transcribing speech as writing are *most all* instead of *almost all*, *should of* instead of *should have*, and *suppose* and *use* as past-tense forms.

Punctuation, of course, is a feature of writing, not of speech, but four punctuation marks—the period, comma, exclamation point, and question mark—correspond fairly straightforwardly to the intonations and pauses of speech. And these are the forms of punctuation to be found in student writing. The dash, parenthesis, semicolon, colon—those forms of punctuation that cannot be indicated in speech—do not appear spontaneously in much student writing. But extensive reliance on the comma and the period does not mean that even these punctuation marks are used correctly. The punctuation errors that students make, unlike those concerning plurals and the apostrophe, do not typically arise from students' having forgotten the rules they were taught about comma use; these errors often come, on the contrary, from having learned one "rule" extremely well. For example, I hear semester after semester about a basic rule of comma usage taught across the nation: use a comma to indicate a pause. This rule is a wonderful example of the privileging of speech over writing: punctuation exists to indicate something in speech—pauses—that writing lacks. But, clearly, writing is richer, not poorer, than speech in this regard. Moreover (and this is the source of the problem), most of us pause for other reasons as well, and we do so quite haphazardly.[6] This means that following the punctuate-when-you-pause rule leads to some very oddly punctuated sentences.

These are some of the common mechanical and sentence-level errors that appear in students' writing, and we should be able to see the pattern in these errors. The pattern should tell us that our students make errors precisely where the connection or overlap between speaking and writing breaks down. Acting on the unarticulated premise that writing is simply transcribed speech, students make errors in those aspects of writing that require discriminations not found in speech. Where mastery of the spoken code suffices, the average college writer today does an acceptable job; it is where the written code works rather differently from speech that most student writing begins to manifest problems.

This phenomenon can be seen on a level beyond the surface and grammatical features I have described so far: in the problems students have creating a coherent text. The issue of how we produce formally coherent texts is, of course, enormously complicated, and I wish to point out only a few aspects of this problem here. One important means of creating coherence is the use of cohesive ties. Halliday and Hasan demonstrate that cohesion is realized by five means: reference, substitution, ellipsis, lexical cohesion, and conjunction. Though studies have shown that better writers use all of these cohesive devices more frequently than poorer writers do, the difference is largest, according to Witte and Faigley, in their use of conjunction (196; also see Gebhard). Conjunction is established primarily by what Halliday and Hasan call the "discourse adjunct," the conjunctive adverb or prepositional phrase (such as *consequently* or *on the other hand*) that signals the connection between sentences, and it is surely used less frequently in conversation. The "discourse adjunct" is under-utilized in student writing, I would argue, precisely because it is less frequently used in speech. The only conjunctive adverb students seem to use extensively in their writing is *however*, but even this word is usually used incorrectly as a conjunction. Even the simple word *nonetheless* strikes the student ear as unnecessary and foreign—unnecessary because it adds no new information about the referential subject and foreign because such an indication of the logical relation between two parts of a discourse is more a part of the mechanism of formal written discourse than part of the repertoire of conversational speech. But by refusing to employ devices that don't *sound natural*, students cut themselves off from fully learning the mechanisms of writing, some of which admittedly do not sound natural. Does anyone speak in footnotes?

The footnote is just one example of the devices employed in written texts but not characteristic of conversation and that, therefore, students tend to resist. Introductions, conclusions, transitional phrases, the apparatus of scholarship contained in notes and in bibliographies—all are part of the formal repertoire of writing and deliberately call attention to their written formality as a way of signaling the coherence, the *integritas*, of a written text.[7] Students, by and large, have difficulty with these devices, preferring a more purely referential, subject-oriented prose that calls much less attention to itself as writing.

Though our students run into many different kinds of problems creating coherent texts, a remarkable number of these problems are traceable to a common root: they are not characteristic of the conversational speech our students have mastered. And as long as our students have not mastered the facets of writing not found in speech, they are going to continue to have problems in all these areas, from "surface" conventions like the apostrophe to larger whole-discourse units. Another way of putting this is that our students' problems are a function of their logocentrism, their privileging of oral over written discourse. And it is difficult to make students aware of their logocentrism because it is part of the much larger culture of logocentrism Derrida has described. Our students regard writing as a transcription of speech, a supplement to speech that we resort to only when face-to-face communication is impossible, because they have been taught—consciously or unconsciously—to regard writing this way. They see writing this way, in short, because their culture does. Understanding this phenomenon is helpful in itself because it can lead us, instead of uselessly blaming our students' mysterious recalcitrance about apostrophes, to see how and why these errors are reinforced by the culture as a whole.

Articulating the Myth

In the writing classroom, therefore, we must discuss the myth of presence, make our students conscious that we all subscribe to such a myth. We need to articulate for our students a more complex and sophisticated view of writing, showing them that writing is not a supplement to speech but a different form of language in its own right, with advantages over speech as well as disadvantages. But such theoretical teaching must complement—not displace—the more concrete teaching of the specific problems that result from the myth of presence. Only a combination of the two will really do the job.

How can this be done? How can we make students aware of the myth of presence? (Here, beyond giving us a useful theoretical framework, Derrida is not going to help us very much.)[8] First, we can lead students to see from their own experience how writing can be of use in its own right and not just as a form of communication to resort to when face-to-face communication is impossible. The difference between letters and conversations on the telephone is one useful example. Even, or especially, if they do not receive many letters, most students feel that a letter "means" more because of its permanence and because, as reluctant writers themselves, they think that more work went into it. Love letters, for instance, have a value that conversations on the telephone do not exactly replace. Complaint letters provide another useful example; everyone has had to complain to someone about something, and it is easy to see that to get results one has to complain by letter, because organizations seldom keep accurate records of the phone calls they receive. And almost every student has had a similar experience with job applications.

By means of such examples within their experience, most students can be brought to see the distinctiveness and usefulness of writing as a system of communication in its own right and not just a device for recording speech.

Ironically, perhaps, the use of oral presentations and formal public-speaking practice can also help make students conscious of the myth of presence. A good presentation is almost always scripted and written in advance; a terrible presentation is one that partakes of the spontaneous, disorganized nature of every day conversation. So the introduction of such elements in a writing course suggests that writing may, on occasion, be prior to speech, not the other way around.

I also think it important to insist on students' typing (or now, word processing) formal essays precisely because typed text looks more foreign to the student than the student's own handwriting. That foreignness brings home the lesson of absence. It enables the student to see his or her own work more as others would see it, which means that the student sees its errors and weaknesses more readily and, more importantly, that he or she realizes *that* others might see it: "Someone could read this who doesn't know me at all, who doesn't even know that a 'me' wrote it." Writing, students will see, is indeed a different activity from having a conversation with a friend. It can also be valuable to discuss these matters in class as well as have students experience them; I always speak in my writing classes about what it feels like to see my own work in print and how I often see errors at that point that I never saw before. Mature writers as well as immature ones have to grapple with the problems of absence; such problems are, indeed, part of the nature of writing.

A Pedagogy of *Absence/Presence*

But, of course, introducing examples from public speaking and discussing differences between writing for ourselves and writing for publication reveal that the presence/absence distinction is not exactly the same as the speaking/ writing one; they are at least partially—and also usefully—distinguishable. There are, however, *intermediate cases*, kinds of writing close to the presence of speaking—a note to a friend or a note to oneself, for example. In these kinds of writing, we can use the code we often use in speech because we are not concerned with the intelligibility of our message to a large audience and may, in fact, be trying to prevent such intelligibility. Our almost-present audience may indeed welcome and certainly won't mind the more personal and intimate writing which behaves like speech. And in these situations in which we can write more the way we talk, more colloquially and informally, correctness is no longer an issue. Thus, the problems of absence are not part of the nature of writing as much as they are part of the broader category of communicating in the absence of the recipient. There are also intermediate forms of *speech* which have some of the characteristics I have been ascribing to writing. In public speeches, for example, the audience—though physically present is relatively absent in much the same way readers are. This absence means that the language used in public speech falls between that appropriate for face-to-face communication and that appropriate for writing. Indeed, as I have already said, such speeches are generally written in advance, though written from the idea of being spoken, and this perfectly establishes public speech as an intermediate case.[9]

Moreover, the presence/absence concept just sketched is being radically transformed by new technologies of communication. Something as simple as Post-It notes, in making writing detachable and readily disposable, creates a new kind of writing more like speech in its impermanence. Electronic mail makes writing radically present even across great distances; other electronic media, particularly television and video storage, make public speech possible in contexts of absence—despite a powerful illusion of presence. In contrast, audio mail and dictation/transcribing technologies (recently studied in Halpern and Liggett) present speech situations in which speech functions much like writing or is designed to be transformed into writing.

It is impossible to predict the effect these new technologies will have on writing, since we are experiencing transformations we cannot see the end of. But I want to relate Derrida's thoughts on presence/absence and speech/writing to these new technologies. On the one hand, the new technologies demonstrate incontrovertibly that we need a partial distinction between speaking/writing and presence/absence. On the other hand, Derrida's distinctions—modified in this way—give us a powerful theoretical perspective on the new technologies. The new technologies help shatter or deconstruct any simplistic speech/writing model and help blur the overly neat speaking/writing distinction that this essay began with and that most research in this field assumes (and that is represented by the disciplinary distinction between departments of English and departments of speech and communication). This blurring means that if we stick to the old speaking/writing problematic, we won't be giving our students the distinctions that will help them cope with and adapt to the changing scene of writing. We need to shift our thinking from speaking/writing to presence/absence because our students are writing in a world desaibed more adequately by the presence/absence problematic. And Derrida has given us the terms with which to describe this new world of writing.

What our students need to learn, in short, is to move from presence to absence, not just from speaking to writing. And showing that the writing/speaking difference is less fundamental than the presence/absence difference is a crucial part of leading our students to negotiate both differences. Playing a random set of messages left on a telephone answering machine, for example, quickly shows students how this form of communication shares some characteristics with writing. Communicating successfully here requires a very different sense of language than does conversation; normal context-dependent or presence-oriented speech doesn't work well in this context. In contrast, Post-It notes circulating among departmental colleagues are largely unintelligible removed from their original context, in just the way comparable snippets of conversation among the same people ("What did you decide about that thing I gave you?") would be. Such presence-oriented, contextually-dependent notes are far easier to compose than are messages left on the answering machine of a stranger. This observation helps show students that their writing problems are only partially a function of their inability to master the specific conventions of writing as opposed to those of speech; and, probably more importantly, it shows that these problems are partially a function of their inability to master the general conventions of communicating in the absence of a recipient.

It is not writing that is so difficult for our students but communicating in the absence of a reader. The aspects of writing that give them trouble are not there to give English teachers things to find wrong with their writing but to ensure communication in a situation of absence. When communicating to someone who is absent, one must master two skills not necessary for those who communicate in the presence of their audience. First, one's communication must partake of certain formal characteristics which mark it as a coherent piece of discourse; second, it must be error-free because an absent audience has none of the tolerance for error allowed a present speaker. Students need to see this, not only to learn to write but also to learn other modes of communication characterized by absence. And they will learn these modes of communication more quickly if they encounter them aware of what these modes have in common with writing as well as of how they differ.

Notes

[1] The essays collected by Atkins and Johnson avoid this issue altogether, focusing instead on the relationship between reading and writing. Crowley's early essay is the pioneering work to explicitly relate Derrida's critique of the metaphysics of presence to issues in the teaching of writing, although she emphasizes less the speaking/writing issue than the related one that language is not primarily a representation of ideas and therefore should not be valued only for its clarity or transparency. Derrida is never mentioned in Kroll and Vann or in either of Tannen's collections of essays.

[2] Schafer provides considerable support for Derrida's claim. In an excellent summary of the work that has been done on the similarities and contrasts between speech and writing, Schafer shows how until quite recently linguistics neglected this topic because it took the spoken word as primary and, thus, as its principal object of investigation.

[3] Connors has recently argued that Plato's attack on writing (in the *Phaedrus*) lines up with his attack on rhetoric (primarily in the *Gorgias*) and on poetry (primarily in *The Republic*) because all three are one-way modes of communication "that cannot be questioned" (55), as opposed to the dialectical reasoning Plato wants opened up through the insistent questioning of Socrates. This argument redraws Derrida's distinction but doesn't obliterate it. What Socrates represents is the presence of dialogue; and, to anticipate a point made later, the public speech of rhetoric and poetry would, in this view, approach the condition of writing in relative absence.

[4] Liggett's useful bibliography lists a number of studies influenced by Zoellner's work.

[5] See Emig and Elbow, for example. I say "not totally" both because of Elbow's insistence on the importance of voice in writing and also because both writers would agree with the reservations about Derrida's position explained in note 8 below.

[6]Shaughnessy subscribes to the speech-based notion that writing is primarily a way to transcribe speech when she suggests that "the writer perceives periods as signals for major pauses and commas as signals for minor pauses." But she goes on to provide an excellent summary of the different reasons for pausing when we speak: "Pauses mark rates of respiration, set off certain words for rhetorical emphasis, facilitate phonological maneuvers, regulate the rhythms of thought and articulation, and suggest grammatical structure" (24).

[7]Schafer suggests that the problems inexperienced writers have with transitions and with opening and closing their texts comes from the fact that in conversation we get help from the other party in these acts (23-37). Writing, a monologue not a dialogue, requires the writer to do these things alone.

[8]I say this because Derrida's position is that, because of its acontextuality or "iterability" (the fact that writing can be significant fully stripped of its originating context), writing can never unequivocally transmit authorial intention; it can never work in quite the way its author would want. This is, of course, a hotly disputed position; my sense, which I assume most teachers of writing share, is that this is not a view likely to be enabling in the writing classroom, however useful and enabling Derrida's discussion of the absence/presence distinction can be. A number of people disagree with me, however; see the Atkins and Johnson collection.

[9]Hirsch cites radio broadcasting and writing to oneself as examples that blunt the absoluteness of the distinction between speaking and writing:

> From the structure of these speech situations, it is evident that the distinctive features of written speech do not depend on its merely being written down. A radio talk is, functionally speaking, written discourse. A private note is, functionally, oral speech. Moreover, we encounter utterances which belong equally in the two functional categories, for instance, a rather formal conversation, or a very informal and elliptical letter to a close friend. As with most generic distinctions in speech, one discovers a continuum where one had hoped to discover definitive classifications. *But a good reason for keeping the functional distinction between speech and writing is that the typical, privative character of written speech creates the main difficulties in teaching and learning composition.* (22; emphasis added)

Works Cited

Atkins, G. Douglas, and Michael L. Johnson. *Writing and Reading Differently: Deconstruction and the Teaching of Composition and Literature.* Lawrence: UP of Kansas, 1985.

Connors, Robert J. "Greek Rhetoric and the Transition from Orality." *Philosophy and Rhetoric* 19 (1986): 38-61.

Crowley, Sharon. "Of Gorgias and Grammatology." *College Composition and Communication* 30 (1979): 279-84.

Derrida, Jacques. *Of Grammatology.* Trans. Gayatri Chakravorty Spivak. Baltimore: Johns Hopkins UP, 1976.

———. "Signature Event Context." *Glyph I* (1977): 172-97.

Elbow, Peter. "The Shifting Relationships between Speech and Writing." *College Composition and Communication* 36 (1985): 283-303.

Emig, Janet. "Writing as a Mode of Learning." *College Composition and Communication* 28 (1977): 122-28.

Gebhard, Ann O. "Writing Quality and Syntax: A Transformational Analysis of Three Prose Samples." *Research in the Teaching of English* 12 (1979): 211-31.

Halliday, M.A.K., and Ruqaiya Hasan. *Cohesion in English.* London: Longman, 1976.

Halpern, Jeanne W., and Sarah Liggett. *Computers and Composing: How the New Technologies Are Changing Writing.* Carbondale: Southern Illinois UP, 1984.

Hirsch, E.D. *The Philosophy of Composition*. Chicago: U of Chicago P, 1977.

Kroll, Barry M., and Roberta J. Vann, eds. *Exploring Speaking-Writing Relationships: Connections and Contrasts*. Urbana: NCTE. 1981.

Liggett, Sarah. "The Relationship between Speaking and Writing: An Annotated Bibliography." *College Composition and Communication* 35 (1984): 334-40.

Schafer, John. "The Linguistic Analysis of Spoken and Written Texts." Kroll and Vann 1-31.

Shaughnessy, Mina P. *Errors and Expectations: A Guide for the Teacher of Basic Writing*. New York: Oxford UP, 1977.

Tannen, Deborah, ed. *Coherence in Spoken and Written Discourse*. Norwood: Ablex, 1984.

——., ed. *Spoken and Written Language: Exploring Orality and Literacy*. Norwood: Ablex, 1982.

Zoellner, Robert. "Talk-Write: A Behavioral Pedagogy for Composition." *College English* 30 (1969): 267-320.

Toward an Ethics of Teaching Writing in a Hazardous Context–The University

SANDY MOORE AND MICHAEL KLEINE

Prelude

The following essay is a collaborative effort by a writing teacher and a writing student to make sense out of a situation we experienced together when Sandy Moore, the writer, responded to an assignment given by Michael Kleine, the teacher. In an advanced persuasive writing course, Michael asked students to experiment with the major Aristotelian categories of persuasion: ceremonial, forensic, and deliberative discourse. For the ceremonial assignment, Sandy chose to write an essay of blame about patrons of her workplace, a restaurant/bar. Though ceremonial discourse aims to praise or blame its subject before a public audience, Sandy did not intend to publish the essay outside the context of the classroom. Aware of the charged nature of her essay, Sandy wanted to use the university classroom not as a place from which to launch a public attack on a private workplace; instead, she hoped that the classroom would provide a safe place in which to practice persuasive discourse and to develop her rhetorical skills.

A rumor that the essay had been written (true)—and that Sandy and another employee planned to publish it or something like it outside the classroom (false)—reached some of the patrons of the establishment where Sandy worked as a waiter and shift leader. Near the State Capitol of Arkansas, the restaurant and lounge was frequented by lobbyists and legislators. Although neither the legislators and lobbyists nor Sandy's boss ever read the written text, Sandy was fired.

Both of us were disturbed deeply by what happened to Sandy—for different reasons. Thus, we offer the following "Fugue" for two voices, a counterpoint that has helped us come to an understanding of the ethical problems Sandy's experience poses for writing students and teachers. We conclude with a "Coda" that considers how the experience affected the composition of our own essay.

Fugue

I Wrote a Paper for a Class and Lost My Job—Sandy Moore

For two and a half years I waited tables at a restaurant and bar across the street from the Arkansas State Capitol. The restaurant was frequented by members of the General Assembly, State officers and employees, lawyers, lobbyists, and the political "in crowd." I regularly waited on a particular group of legislators and lobbyists. I knew their drinks, their districts, their special interests. We spoke on a first-name basis.

The tabs were large and my tips were good, but I was physically tired of making forty trips to the bar for this group over a two-hour period each night I worked. I was emotionally exhausted from holding my tongue after the nightly barrage of "Honeys," "Sugars," "Sweethearts," and drunken statements such as "Woman, fetch me another drink." I didn't like strange men's hands rubbing my leg, and I was offended by the cruel racist and sexist jokes I overheard at each table. One night a lobbyist was verbally abusive to me in front of the group because I would not date him. After three double scotches, he whined that I "didn't have time" for him. My employer would not have supported me if I had suggested that sexual harassment was taking place; he would have asked what I was doing to provoke the customer. I knew a public statement would put my job at risk, so I wrote a paper for a class as an outlet for my frustration; and I wrote it in a university writing situation, one I believed to be safe and benign.

When my paper was returned, I filed it with other writings I probably wouldn't read again. One month later the assistant manager at work called to inform me I had been suspended from my job; I was accused of planning to write a free-lance article for the *Arkansas Gazette* or *Arkansas Democrat* about the "goings on" of the legislators and lobbyists at the restaurant.

I admitted a paper existed, and my employer asked to see it. I refused. No one had seen it outside the classroom, and publication for a general audience was not my intent. I naively thought that my job was secure because I was a shift leader and the trainer at work, had been employed over two years, was always on time and rarely sick, and had told the truth. It never entered my mind that I could lose my job over a false rumor. Apparently, a co-worker had mentioned my paper and her own writing aspirations—possibly in the same sentence—at a private party for one of the senators. Within two days rumors were circulating that we planned to write a free-lance article for a local paper and that we were leaking conversations we overheard to the press.

I remember the owner's words two days later: "I cannot let you come back to work. After talking with numerous legislators and lobbyists it [the paper] has done some damage and has been a detriment to the business. You are fired because this paper that you have written . . . and some of the conversations that you had with [a female lobbyist], the lobbyists, and others about the goings on of their business has [sic] become a detriment to their business." The owner explained that my co-worker was fired because of what "could have or may have been written."

The co-worker and I had never discussed collaborating on anything beyond lunch. My accusers didn't even know what my paper said, and none of them had confronted me directly. I thought that people with power, money, and influence only preyed on other people with power, money, and influence. What did they have to fear from a writing student?

The ACLU couldn't help. Because I did not have an employment contract, I was employed "at will," and I could be fired for any reason. Two civil rights attorneys told me I had no legal recourse; my civil rights had not been violated. (In order for me to have any recourse in a civil suit, I needed proof that one of the legislators had made threats involving the publication of my paper.) I talked with an attorney friend who was willing to file a cause of action based on the tort of Outrage, but the restaurant filed for Chapter Eleven Bankruptcy the week after I was fired, listing the IRS as a creditor. My friend felt the chances of getting a judgment against my employer in a bankruptcy court were unlikely, and a bankruptcy judge would never give my claim priority over a claim by the federal government.

I talked to newspaper reporters. I collected articles related to my situation and did volunteer work for the ACLU. I learned how to use the law-school library as I investigated the legality of the action taken against me. I wrote summaries of law journal articles for a technical writing class I was taking. I warned my fellow creative-writing students to guard their papers. I wrote thirty letters to government officials, twenty-six of which remain unanswered. I tried to understand what had happened and blamed myself. I wrote again and again, wanting someone, anyone, to tell me they were sorry. I had been humiliated and abused. I didn't have a job. I had no money. I was in pain and no one seemed to care.

I conferenced with students in the writing center at my university, where I worked as an intern, about the content of their papers. I wondered if I needed to tell them not to name names, to be careful. Did I need to invite them to censor themselves because of my own fear? Never before had I worried about the content of school papers; I had believed that my academic writing was somehow protected. I thought I was safe so long as I chose not to take my writing outside the university. I was naive to think I could mention a paper about my workplace to a fellow employee. So, in a sense, it was my choice to take my paper out of the context of the persuasive writing class.

The week immediately after I was fired, I went out, rented movies, watched the television I rarely turn on, and did everything except write. The first time I did pick up my pen, I censored myself. I backtracked and read over my writing to make sure I didn't say anything that could be used against me. I added disclaimers to charged or questionable statements. I was miserable.

In retrospect, to say I lost my job because I wrote a paper for a class now seems too simplistic. There are several questions I must ask now:

- Is freedom of speech a right *given* by the Constitution, or is it a basic human right that *should be protected* by the Constitution? Currently, the First Amendment only protects us against governmental interference. Should private citizens, specifically employers, be allowed to encroach on the freedoms of private-sector employees as they desire? Should government employees be able to rob me of my civil rights when they are backed by a powerful lobby who will lie on their behalf?

- The Employment at Will Doctrine, which has been upheld by the courts since late in the nineteenth century, states that absent a fixed-term contract of employment, employers "may dismiss their employees at will . . . for good cause, for no cause or even for cause morally wrong" (*Payne v. Western A.R.R.*, 81 Tenn. 507, 519-20, 1884). As long as states lack Wrongful Discharge Legislation, will at-will employees continue to risk the loss of their civil rights?

- The courts have carved out a few protections by ruling that employers cannot discriminate for reasons based on race, religion, gender, disability, or for a reason that goes against public policy. (The public policy exception is vague, differs by state, and is decided on a case-by-case basis.) If the physical differences and belief systems of employees are protected, why isn't the freedom to express an opinion protected?

- Does a waiter break an implied confidence if he or she discusses a customer's purchases or actions? Would public consumers lose their right to privacy if an employee's free speech were protected from the employer?

- Is my situation a sign of a politically corrupt system, one in which a coercive lobby enjoys the right to squelch individual liberty in order to preserve its own special interest? Should lobbyists be made more accountable? According to Arkansas Law, a lobbyist is not required to name a recipient of a favor unless more than $24.99 is spent. If the host's group is large, the average spent on each individual might be less than the maximum allowed by law, but the total might be far more than $24.99. This loophole allows many legislators to go unnamed in the lobbyist's reports to the Secretary of State.

- Was the action the legislators, the lobbyists, and my employer took against me consistent with the action they would have taken against a man? My situation might be one that rarely occurs, but it seems to represent an abuse of power that my own political representatives are at least capable of.

- Is freedom of speech in jeopardy in the university as well as in the workplace? Should universities be allowed or forced to control a student's oral or written expression? Or should the university protect students from "outside" interference? Freedom of speech is fundamental in a free society. Without it, students and millions of at-will employees are not free to speak. We have a Constitutional amendment that guarantees our right to express ourselves, but we are not necessarily protected against the consequences of exercising that right if someone is offended by our actions, even if we tell the truth and, sometimes, especially if we do.

Throughout my life I have been told not to break rules, that I am somehow responsible if others are bad or mean or if things go wrong. I felt I had broken a rule—one I was not aware existed—and my hand was slapped. Now I realize that when I went to work I did not take any kind of loyalty oath or vow of secrecy. I am not responsible for the public actions of the men and women about whom I wrote. I wrote about adults who are responsible for their own actions, and it cost me dearly. I did not write with spite or malice. I expressed an opinion, an expression that is my Constitutional right. I have the right to write. I do not have the right to slander or abuse, but I have the right to express my opinion in writing. I also have the right to feel secure in my job and the right to due process.

It was not just that I wrote critically about patrons of my workplace; it was that I wrote about the wrong people—people lacking in principle. I was honest, and now I believe my subjects feared that the average person, their constituents, would be appalled at the behavior I observed. I got too close to the truth, and I was expendable. The legislators' and lobbyists' right to privacy in a public place was more important than my right to earn a living.

When I lost my job, I lost my seniority, and, for awhile, my self-esteem and my belief in my ability to make sound decisions. Now when I look in the mirror each morning I see an intelligent, strong, and independent thirty-six-year-old woman who has the right to demand that she not be referred to as "girl" or "honey." I am not afraid to be called a "bitch" because I show my outrage and ask that I be treated with courtesy and respect. My belief in the fairness and intelligence of Arkansas' legislators is lost forever. Much of the lobbying effort is corrupt. Although I have no recourse through the courts, and no way to recover my financial losses, I am determined to be heard. I will continue to seek recourse through my writing. Employers should not be allowed to fire someone indiscriminately, nor should legislators be allowed to infringe on the rights of their constituents. Legislators should not be allowed to abuse the system they themselves created. I have a responsibility to my fellow students and at-will employees to speak out against such abuses.

Four pieces of unseen typewritten paper, filled with the words of a student, created havoc among powerful lobbyists and legislators in Arkansas. Clearly, writing is powerful, and a voice keeps screaming in my ear, "Don't stop. Keep writing. Become their greatest nightmare!"

Arrested Without Charge—Michael Kleine
When Sandy called to tell me that she had been fired over the essay she had written for class, I felt like Joseph K. in Kafka's *The Trial*—arrested without charge, guilty of something, but uncertain of what. I had been teaching writing since 1971, and to my knowledge a student had never before been fired for writing an essay for class. After the phone call, I tried to convince myself that I had done nothing wrong, merely given an open-ended writing assignment. I wanted to believe that my sense of having been arrested was caused more by moral outrage over an abuse of political and economic power than by anything for which I personally could be held responsible. Now, nearly a year after Sandy's phone call, I still feel a sense of outrage; but I also recognize that I was culpable, that in my teaching I had perhaps not committed a crime of commission, but that certainly I deserved to be charged with a crime of omission: in my naivety, I had failed to tell students the whole truth about writing.

Like many contemporary writing teachers, the belief system underlying my pedagogical theory and practice was influenced from early on by the work of people like James Britton and Peter Elbow, compositionists who advise us to tap the expressive energy of our students and to encourage students to write without fear, to play the "believing game." Although my later reading of ethnographers and social activists—people like Shirley Brice Heath and

Paulo Freire—may have caused me to shift my perspective and language (from a focus on *developing* the "voice" and "confidence" of the individual writer to a focus on *empowering* the writer in various "discourses," "communities," and "ideologies"), my teaching goals have remained relatively constant. I want written discourse to be available and meaningful to my students. I want them to make a personal commitment to their written expression, to write freely about their experiences, their visions of reality, their reading. Most of all, I want them to be empowered to participate in the construction of knowledge and the shaping of the world.

For the past twenty years or so, I have done my best to celebrate empowered writing with my students and with other writing teachers across the country. Because I encourage students to import their own discourses into my writing class and to shape those discourses there, I count myself participant in a pedagogy of "liberation" and permission, an advocate of free speech in writing. In technical writing courses, I have asked students to address problems from their workplaces and institutional worlds, to use the class as a place to practice acts of proposing and reporting that might in fact make a difference in those places and worlds. In persuasive writing courses, I have always directed students to write to "real audiences" about "real-world problems," and I have always encouraged them to find their own personal space in persuasive discourse.

But now I reread the two paragraphs above and discover that linguistically they embarrass themselves—and me. I notice the repetition of "I want" and the avoidance of "they want." I notice that words like "liberation," "permission," and "free" are mixed with words like "asked" and "directed"—that the notion of empowerment is problematized by the fact that it is more or less required by an agent of power, by the teacher, by me. My written celebration of empowered writing deconstructs. In the context of what happened to Sandy, it rings false—or at least oxymoronic: I celebrate "mandated empowerment"; I contradict myself.

When Sandy was fired, I was forced to confront the rationalizations that had enabled me to celebrate the freedom I had imposed on my students. Because I never forced students to disclose expressively when they were uncomfortable, never forced them to submit proposals and reports they wrote in class to supervisors at their workplaces, never forced them to publish the persuasive pieces they wrote outside the classroom, I felt rather smug. In that smugness, I believed that I had helped create a kind of sanctuary, a safe writing context where one could more or less import external contexts and write freely, not having to worry about the repercussions of external publication. I believed that my students were protected from the outside, that they could take risks with their writing, that they could experience the power of writing without having to deal with the possibility that power flows two ways: that it is capable of flowing outward and changing the world, but that it is also capable of flowing back toward the writer and doing harm.

What happened to Sandy changed everything for me, destroyed my pedagogical illusions and forced me to come to terms with my own power, my own responsibility. There is no sanctuary, no protected context. Writing is potentially harmful, both to the world and to the writer. Teaching writing is more problematical than I ever knew: when we give a writing assignment, we do more than ask students to take linguistic risks; we may in fact be asking them to take personal risks and job risks. Indeed, the more we ask students to invest in writing about non-academic contexts, the greater the risk we ask them to take.

Shortly after Sandy's phone call, I asked her whether she would like to discuss what had happened with the rest of the class. I assumed that the class, which was comprised of many older and non-traditional students, would be sympathetic and supportive. Sandy thought the same thing and agreed to lead a discussion of what happened to her because of the paper she had written. Although some of the students shared our outrage, others, especially several older male students, sympathized with the employer who fired Sandy. Some believed that a kind of implicit contract between employer and employee had been violated when Sandy decided to write about her place of work. Even though her writing was not read in final form by anyone besides me, and not at all by her accusers, they argued that Sandy had entered into a fiduciary relationship with the employer when she accepted money for her work, and that outside disclosure of insider conversation and activity constituted a breach of such a relationship. Others questioned the protected status of discourse within the university and even between teacher and student. They argued that a text, once written, can easily be dislocated from its context, and that once it is dislocated it can become a kind of unguided missile, capable of exploding and doing damage wherever it lands.

I will never forget a story that one of the students told me after class. She had written a report for a technical writing course concerning a problem at her workplace. She said that she wrote the report with full knowledge that if it had been read accidentally by the "wrong people" (meaning the ostensible audience for the report) she herself would have been fired. She went on to explain that at one point she had been writing part of the report at her word processor at work when she was called away from her desk. When she returned to her desk and reread on her screen what she had just written, she came to a dark realization: even though she was writing the report for class, the text itself, if read in the workplace, might lead to her dismissal. I asked her how a report written with the intention of improving the workplace might lead to her dismissal. She said, "Oh, it wouldn't be because I was writing a report about work, but because I was writing a report about work for somebody who didn't work there: my teacher."

The classroom discussion surprised me. Apparently some of my students had known all along that what writing teachers want for them and request of them may not be safe. Especially those students who had experienced the politics of workplace writing understood that certain contexts and subjects are best avoided—even in the "freedom" of the classroom. Before Sandy's experience and the classroom discussion of it, I probably would have rationalized most of my writing assignments in this way: "I ask students to bring their own worlds of experience and feeling, their own discourses, into the classroom, and there we work on translating those discourses into writing that would be effective if it were read by audiences outside of the classroom." Now, in my darker moments, I want to say, "I pay students with grades to import and disclose discourses that are none of my business and in so doing force them to betray the private discourse communities of friends, families, workplaces, and various institutions."

I asked myself why Sandy's experience surprised me so much. In order to come to terms with this question, I was forced to meditate on my own status as a tenured academic writer—a privileged status, I understand now, that had led me to believe in the university as a sanctuary, as a protector of free speech. Before I was tenured, I probably was just as wary of speaking freely about my own workplace, the university, as any other untenured assistant professor. Aware of the political realities of a multi-leveled tenuring process, I believed I was free to talk and write about ideas without fear of job retaliation, but only insofar as those ideas were safely dislocated from the interests and ideologies of those who had the power to judge my case after six years of speaking softly.

However, as I approached tenure time several years before Sandy was fired, I coauthored a risky article with a colleague about problems with corporate writing. The article was published and later read by executives at a local corporation. Although my colleague and I had not identified the specific corporation we had studied in order to write the article (we had called it "Corporation X"), some of the corporate executives suspected that their corporation was the subject of the article. They telephoned us several times, first to express their anger and then to persuade us to disclose the true identity of the corporation we had studied. Not knowing why the corporation wanted us to make such a disclosure, we refused. The executives then complained to the university and requested that our administrators pressure us to disclose the corporation's true identity. I was up for tenure at exactly this time and, needless to say, worried that the university might apply such pressure and deny me tenure. But administrators at my university politely refused to comply with the corporation's request and explained that such compliance would undermine academic freedom. I was later given tenure. In other words, I was not fired and to this day I receive a paycheck from the university.

In part because of my experience, I came to trust the university as a force of protection, as a kind of sanctuary. After all, it had risked alienating a powerful local corporation to protect the academic freedom of two of its professors. And because the university had protected me and my job, I overgeneralized that it functioned as a protector of the academic freedom of all within, of each member of the "academic community." Although I still believe that the university should strive to protect the speech and writing of those within, at least from its own institutional power, Sandy's experience now forces me to question my belief that the university is capable of protecting the discourse of faculty and students equally. It is true that the university is *capable* of protecting the discourse that transpires therein from itself, from its own power to monitor, control, and retaliate. And it is also true that the university is *capable* of protecting the jobs of its employees, its professors, when they speak or write freely. However, Sandy's experience demonstrates clearly that despite such capability, students are inevitably vulnerable—that their jobs and personal lives are at risk every time they write for us: even if a professor doesn't retaliate powerfully and harmfully for a student's expression of value, belief, or knowledge, some outside force might retaliate. Thus, student discourse is in no way protected. For students, the university is not a sanctuary.

I see, now, that I am situated in an institution that both empowers me and expects me, because I am a writing specialist, to require that students express themselves in writing. Ironically, it is my effort to erase my own institutional position and power that puts students most at risk in external institutions and constructions of power. When they cease speaking and writing the discourse of the classroom and begin importing the discourses of "outside," they are no longer securely situated in either discourse. What they write within the university context, if discovered outside of that context, might be perceived as a kind of disclosure, or even betrayal, of a private discourse. In fact, my power is never really erased. Indeed, it now seems a kind of originating power, a force of exigence, that requires students to speak and write and that potentially complicates their relationships with other forces of power.

Perhaps my inability to connect with the experience of writing as a student in the 1990s can be explained further by reflecting on what it was like to write as a student in the 1960s. The rhetorical situation within the university was different back then—for me and, I suspect, for many others who now teach courses that focus on writing. Back then I did not take "writing courses." Most of the papers I wrote concerned dead literary figures and anthologized literary texts. The audience was clearly the professor. In fact, few of my papers were read by my peers. As long as I gave the professor what he wanted, writing was safe.

Since the Vietnam era, the writing revolution has resulted in a scrutiny of the school-writing rhetorical situation and a critique of a pedagogy that establishes the teacher as only audience and rewards the replication and perpetuation of a static academic discourse. Specialized writing courses require students to experiment with non-academic discourses. As they complete an English major at my university, upper-division students write literary nonfiction, technical and professional proposals and reports, expository pieces about themselves and their non-academic areas of knowledge, and persuasive pieces that aim to change the world outside the university. They are constantly encouraged to write for non-academic audiences, either to find or construct audiences other than the teacher. Thus, my own students experience a complicated rhetorical situation that I never had to face myself, a situation in which they must negotiate a text in and for two totally different worlds. Neither world, the classroom world or the one outside the classroom, is safe. Both worlds are capable of a response that may seem retaliatory to students. In my class, I tend to promote writing that evokes an external audience. If students do what I ask them to do, especially in a persuasive writing class, then they run the risk of offending the external audiences they evoke. What, then, am I to do?

Telling the Story

My familiarity with the schemas of academic discourse leads me to a superficial and easy answer to my own question: I must write a final "implications" section that will somehow make up for the unusual form of this essay. But this answer, by itself, does not suffice. Somehow what Sandy wrote, and what I am trying to write here, problematizes the ordinary discourse of composition theory. An implications section, by itself, is impossible to write. The implication is, at last, that I must write this essay with Sandy, that I must tell this story—to as many audiences as I can. And because my own understanding of the nature of the harm done by *not* telling such a story in the past is limited, because I cannot understand completely the feelings of my students, I must tell it collaboratively.

In my own classroom I must reiterate the tale told above. I must make space for honest discussion of the complex rhetorical situation that students face when they write to and for external audiences while at the same time they contend with the demands of the classroom context. Such discussion should not only help the students understand what they face, but it should also help me understand what it is I ask them to do when I request suasive writing, when I ask them to take rhetorical risks, when I encourage them to import discourses external to the classroom.

I will no doubt continue to encourage students to experiment with a variety of rhetorical contexts, but never again without warning and never again without vigilant protection of work in progress and of completed texts. Such protection would involve considering, with the student, the consequences of an actual reading by the intended audience. If such a reading would result in harm to the student, then I would need to suggest that any collaborative activity within the classroom be safeguarded. A student facing potential rhetorical risk should be allowed to decide whether to share his or her writing with a peer group. Upon request, I would need to pledge to the student that I would not show any given piece of writing to anyone else, including trusted colleagues.

Finally, I must problematize in this essay and in my classroom the notion of free speech and free writing. Writing students and teachers alike need to come to terms with the myth that free speech is protected as a right that can be exercised without fear of retaliation. Indeed, our speech is only protected by our government from the government itself. The government does not protect us from each other when we speak freely. Thus, free speech is not a given for the speaker or writer: it is more a process that begins in the knowledge that its use, its exercise, might bring harm to the user; at the same time, the exercise of free speech in the face of possible harm asserts the value of such exercise and works to promote that value universally.

It saddens me that my own future teaching of writing may involve not only the rhetorical action of encouraging free speech in writing, but also of warning about the possible consequences of such speech. Nevertheless, what happened to Sandy has persuaded me that such a warning is ethically requisite. At the same time, it seems ethically requisite that writing teachers encourage free speech among students and freely speak, ourselves, a discourse that celebrates its value.

Perhaps it is time for all of us who assign and supervise writing from positions of power to move away from the kind of "objective research" that tends to erase our presence and our ethical responsibility. If we told stories about ourselves and the consequences of what we do, and if we encouraged students to tell us stories about what happens to them because of what we do, then we could engage in a dialogue on the ethics of teaching writing, a dialogue that perhaps has been deferred for too long.

Coda

Michael—On Writing the Above Essay

Through our collaboration, Sandy and I learned more than what the text above tells: our process of exchanging and consolidating drafts helped us construct not only a shared understanding of the relationship between power and writing, but also a kind of reciprocal understanding of the position of the "other"—writer understanding teacher, teacher understanding writer. Moreover, the process of revising and editing this essay clearly revealed to us how much our mutual awareness of the possibility of retaliation affected, and infected, our composing process ("sanitizing process" might be a better phrase). For us, revising was mainly a process of deletion—deletion of any specific discussion that could possibly injure either or both of us, or even injure *JAC*, if it were read by the "wrong people"—powerful people external to the academic audience we *think* we address here. Editing was a process of erasure, erasure of the names of specific lobbyists and legislators, erasure of the name of the workplace, erasure, even, of the names of students in the classroom.

We wanted to write this "Coda" to make sense of our own writing, of our collaboration. But as I reread my part of the "Coda," I fear that it makes us seem paranoid. And this fear makes me want to gloss the gloss. The writing above is not only erasure. It is also iteration in writing of a story we both want to tell. In publishing the story, we want to change things, to make things better. At the same time, both of us have come to understand the necessity of self-protection. And so we engage in a rhetoric of cautious blame, of simultaneous iteration and erasure. Every future act of writing will seem to be an act of free expression and, at the same time, an act of discretion.

Sandy—On Writing the Above Essay

During one of our editing sessions, I wrote a note to Michael telling him I was not afraid of telling the truth and naming names if doing so would strengthen our paper. He said our audience wouldn't be familiar with local names and places, so specifics were not necessary. Something about this interaction made me uncomfortable.

After countless re-writes and hours of meditating on this piece, I realize that, again, my intentions do not match the reality of the writing situation. All writing is discretionary and potentially harmful, from papers I write for class to the journals that lay haphazardly around my house. I must protect what I put on paper, and, by doing so, perhaps I can protect myself. Outcomes, however, are unpredictable, and I do not have control over the reactions of unexpected audiences. Unless I intend to publish what I have written, I will guard my work with great care. Never again will I write a paper for a class without first changing names and places. Nor will I discuss my ideas about work in progress.

I can honestly say that by naming my accusers in this paper I would intend to inflict harm. By censoring myself, I do not absolve them of responsibility for their actions. I believe that the individuals involved should be exposed to their constituents, but I will attempt to do that by writing to a different audience through another vehicle.

For now I must be satisfied with sharing my story in the hope that others will be aware of the risk involved in writing about real-life situations, even if that writing is done in the classroom. I also hope that this piece might stir up just a little trouble for the Employment-At-Will Doctrine and promote an awareness of the need for Wrongful Discharge Legislation to protect all citizens.

My sense of being a victim is slowly being replaced by the return of my sense of humor. Sometimes I sit back and think, "Hmmm. Isn't writing fun?"

Repositioning the Profession: Teaching Writing to African American Students

Thomas Fox

I begin this essay by urging writing teachers of all backgrounds to face higher education's continuing inability to meet the needs of African American students (see both Brooks and Ogbu for a sense of some of these problems as they relate to literacy). Because literacy—in the form of placement and proficiency tests and required writing courses—frequently works to exclude African American students, our greatest obligation is to transform literacy education for these students. Incumbent in this transformation is the reconception of African American literacy and writing pedagogy in more deeply understood cultural and historical contexts. Afro-American literary theory provides fertile ground for this reconception to begin.

Literacy and African American Students
Literacy issues for African Americans have been obscured, unfortunately, by a focus on a narrowly understood black English, despite the efforts of Labov, Smitherman, and others to place the language of African Americans in a more fully understood social and historical context. And despite Labov's early and thorough argument against the deficit theories of the 1960s, such theories are resilient and return in new forms (see Smitherman-Donaldson, Fox). The emphasis on discrete grammatical features of black English has diverted attention from more serious issues, among them the separation of literacy instruction in school from the literary history of African Americans.

African American students do not usually leave school because they fail to master an academic discourse. Instead, as the research of John Ogbu suggests, schools have failed to make good on the promise that literacy instruction in the schools will reward African American students socially and economically. Equally serious is the fact that schools have failed to change the perception (and reality in most cases) that for African American students literacy instruction entails "deculturation without true assimilation" (151). That is, schools have failed to integrate literacy instruction with the experience and history of African Americans, and we have failed as a society and a profession to prove that literacy will result in a more rewarding life. African Americans have known all along that a casual and easy relationship between literacy and economic success does not exist. J. Elspeth Stuckey, in *The Violence of Literacy*, states bluntly what Ogbu's research suggests, "Perhaps one of the consequences of literacy is its failure to end the violence of an unfair society" (124).

Writing teachers who recognize the urgent need to reconceive writing pedagogy can look to Afro-American literary theory for strategies of reading and interpreting African American student writing that are free from a narrow understanding of dialect "interference," strategies free from the residue of deficit theories of language that still govern the reading of African American student writing, strategies that instead see African American literacy in social, economic, and historical contexts. Recent literary and composition theories have conceived of writing as dialogic, as invoking stances towards institutions, history, and culture. Particularly useful for this essay is the concept of "position." As characterized by Houston A. Baker, Mae G. Henderson, Cheryl A. Wall, and others, position refers to political relationships between the literary critic and culture, history, and institutions. This geographic metaphor has the advantage of ridding concepts of race, class, and gender from determinist and essentialist associations. So while African American student writing is informed by its position in the history of what Du Bois calls "race rituals," a unitary concept of "race" does not determine or characterize that writing. Instead, a series of intersections between race and history, race and institutions, race and gender, and so on, informs it. This sense of position as "intersection" avoids reductive and simplistic accounts of African American writing and more generously accounts for its multiplicity and diversity.

"Position" as a central concept in the exploration of African American student writers requires a pedagogy that would investigate the ways in which history, culture, institutions, social relations, and race intersect and influence writing. Min-zhan Lu argues in "Writing as Repositioning" that such a pedagogy "would require that both we and our students see writing as a process in which the writer positions, or rather, repositions herself in relation not to a single, monolithic discourse but to a range of competing discourses" (18). Importantly, Lu includes the teacher in this process. Such a disclosure of position on the part of the teacher would help particularize and "locate" the teacher's authority. To paraphrase Cheryl A. Wall's discussion of critical practice, particularizing the teacher's position would "not claim a 'privileged' status," and would help guard against the "false universalism" that has "rendered black women and their writing mute" (2).[1]

Authentication: Demonstrating Literacy

Afro-American literary theory can help writing teachers and their students map cultural and historical positions toward literacy. Representing the diversity of opinion among Afro-American literary theorists is beyond the scope of this article. (See the exchange between Joyce, Gates, and Baker in

New Literary History for an indication of the truly complex issues facing these writers.) The theorists I have chosen to discuss seem most relevant to teachers of writing. Robert Stepto's 1979 study, *From Behind the Veil*, is a good place to begin because it most directly addresses ideas about literacy. Ostensibly, Stepto's study attempts to expose the intertextual relationships among literary texts, to deal with literary relations rather than relations between history and literature or society and literature. Fortunately, as Houston Baker points out, history and society creep into and enrich his study (*Blues* 94-97).

One of the most useful parts for writing instructors is Stepto's exploration of "authentication," the means by which African American writers guarantee the "credibility" of their text. Guaranteeing credibility was of obvious and primary concern with narratives written by former slaves, whose act of literacy itself cast doubt on the authenticity of the text. Early slave narratives were framed with "authenticating" documents, letters and prefaces written by white guarantors. William Lloyd Garrison's preface to Frederick Douglass' autobiography is a handy example. Garrison assures readers of the authenticity of the text, stating that Douglass wrote "his own Narrative, in his own style, and according to the best of his ability" (qtd. in *Veil* 17). Stepto is most useful when he presents authentication as a rhetorical problem, involving audience and purpose. Although authenticating documents appear to bolster the author's credibility, "the issue is really the audiences'—white America's—credulity: their acceptance not so much of the former slave's escape and newfound freedom, but of his literacy" (8). This is the heart of the authentication problem; white audiences were quite willing to believe that slaves escape but unwilling to believe that slaves write.

Stepto moves from the authenticating documents of slave narratives to show how authenticating strategies have become part of the tradition of African American literature in the twentieth century. For instance, Stepto argues that Richard Wright's *Black Boy* is an after-the-fact authentication of *Native Son*, validating the latter work as fiction and artifice. *Black Boy*, he says, differentiates Wright from his main character Bigger Thomas, primarily through demonstrating "profound differences in degrees of literacy" (130). The great moments of learning to read in *Black Boy* are noticeably absent in *Native Son*, for instance.

A central strategy of African American writers is to seek authorial control and legitimacy in the face of an audience that seeks to deny the very literacy that African American authors demonstrate. Demonstrating literacy, in this context, is an act of liberation, an extension of the famous example of Frederick Douglass' writing his own pass to freedom. Our nation's race rituals have shaped the way African American writers—and white readers reading African American writers—understand literacy, and these attitudes have defined what Stepto sees as the predominant quest in African American writing: the quest for literacy and freedom.

In what way do African American students feel obliged to authenticate their writing in the classroom? An African American student at my university described her university experience as

> a good training ground for blacks. On campus the racism is covert, but in the community it's blatant—the people out there feel no need to hide it. If a black wants to learn how to get along in hostile America, this is a good place to start. This is our "Green Beret" training place.

Part of "hostile America's" attitude towards African American students is the association of illiteracy with African American language. One of the means by which African American student writers authenticate their texts is by "proving" their literacy. Sometimes, in the first three weeks of first-year composition, I see a literacy story. Consider the following excerpt from Joe's response to Richard Rodriguez's *Hunger of Memory*:

> One day my family was sitting in the living room watching T.V. and my mom said, "Joe, how are you doing in school?" I replied, "Just fine," then she said, "Read to me."
> I didn't know of anything that I hated more than reading. I had to get my little book and stumble through the words, paragraphs, and pages. I would get so irritated that I would lie, cry, or just say, "No, I'm not doing it anymore!" I knew my friends' moms didn't make them read out loud, so why was my mom doing this to me? She finally told me that she was doing this to help me. "I don't need your help," I told her, and like a woman she explodes. Then she gives me a choice. She put the book on one end of the table and a belt right next to it. We're standing on opposite ends of the table and she says, "You better get to the book before I get to the belt. The one off the table first will be the one used tonight." That night I read for the first time without complaining.

Joe uses this story to open his discussion of Rodriguez, attesting to his English teacher and his classmates his family's longstanding commitment to literacy. He goes on to state how his changed attitude toward his parents differentiates his educational experience from Rodriguez's. He concludes,

> I learned to put my hate and aggravation away. Once when I picked up a newspaper and watched the news, the subject was illiteracy. People who can't read. I thought, how did they grow up not knowing how to read, getting past the teachers and most of all their parents? Some of them didn't go to school but some of them did. That was the first time I was thankful that my parents made sure I could read.

All student writers authenticate their texts in one way or another. But as Stepto shows us, African American writers have an intensified need to authenticate their texts by stressing or "marking" their own literacy. Joe differentiates himself quite effectively from "people who can't read," even those who went to school. And he locates the source of his literacy squarely and securely in his family.

Here's another example, this one written in the second week of class in response to a childhood memory question. Marsha opened with the following paragraph:

> When I first said, "Da Da," I believe that was when my mom decided I was a genius. She began molding me to be an academic achiever. I was well prepared when I started school at the age of three. My mother had already taught me kindergarten basics such as numbers, the alphabet, etc.

She goes on to describe first grade:

> I started first grade at Martin Luther King Elementary School. Despite the fact that I had a really good teacher, all the work seemed really simple. I already had all the little yellow and red series books and the fun with Dick and Jane books at home, and I had read them all.

By citing and describing their experiences in literate households, both Marsha and Joe authenticate more than the narratives they write for English class. They authenticate their place in the classroom in the eyes of the white teacher and the mostly white classmates. Ultimately, in part because these students were enrolled in a non-credit basic writing workshop, they seek to authenticate their place in the university.

Literacy and Economy

Houston A. Baker, in *The Journey Back*, has this to say about the university and literacy for African American students:

> The type of literacy guaranteed by the academy today is still not calculated to provide anything approaching an adequate definition of black life in America. Instead, the university remains a bastion of racism, complacency, and incompetence, striving desperately to maintain the status quo. (130-31)

What are the effects of authentication on African American student writers? For the authors that Stepto discusses, authentication is but a necessary fact and is sometimes even a beneficial one, leading an author like Douglass, for instance, to discover and chart the relationship between literacy and freedom. Baker sees the relationship of the author to this kind of literacy more problematically. Considering Douglass, for instance, Baker states,

> The angelic Mrs. Auld, however, in accord with the evangelical codes of the era, has given Douglass the rudiments of a system that leads to intriguing restrictions. True, the slave can arrive at a sense of being only through language. But it is also true that, in Douglass's case, a conception of the preeminent form of being is conditioned by white, Christian standards. (*Journey* 36)

In *The Journey Back*, but especially in *Blues, Ideology, and Afro-American Literature*, Baker seeks an understanding of literature grounded in culture, defined anthropologically in *The Journey Back* and economically and socially in *Blues, Ideology, and Afro-American Literature*. He sees literacy and language more as Paulo Freire sees education: as either liberating or domesticating. More accurately, Baker shows that acts of literacy can be both liberating and domesticating. Literacy has the potential to constrain African

American writers even as it liberates them. Both of Baker's books offer much to the teacher of African American writers by positioning African American authors not only in a literary tradition (as *From Behind the Veil* does), but in a cultural, collective one. Most original, and to my mind most applicable to writing teachers, is Baker's economic analyses of African American narratives in the first chapter of *Blues, Ideology, and Afro-American Literature*.

Drawing on the work of Frederic Jameson and Hayden White, Baker seeks to "reinvent" the relationship between the literary work and its "social ground." By understanding writing as a "commodity," something of economic worth, Baker seeks to disclose both the "deprivations of material resources that have characterized African life in the New World" and "the profoundly brilliant expressive strategies designed by Africans in the New World" (*Blues* 31).

To take Douglass, again, as an example, Baker states that there is a "bifurcation of voices" in Douglass. One voice, the result of "the deprivations," speaks a "developmental history that leads from Christian enlightenment to the establishment of Sabbath schools" (*Blues* 43). The other voice, a "sotto voce," is Douglass' brilliant ability to read the culture, especially economically. Baker reads Douglass' path to freedom as the path to becoming a "*salaried* spokesman, combining literacy, Christianity, and revolutionary zeal in an individual and economically profitable job of work" (*Blues* 49).

Recent explorations of education, like Aronowitz and Giroux's *Education Under Siege*, or slightly earlier ones like Richard Ohmann's *English in America* or Paulo Freire's idea of the "banking concept" of education in *Pedagogy of the Oppressed*, have made it possible for us to understand the classroom in economic terms. The classroom is a "free market" where enterprising students compete to earn the grade that we reward them with. Especially for African American students from economically disadvantaged backgrounds, the economic metaphor carries extra force. Demonstrating literacy is crucial to their financial situations; continued financial aid is but the most obvious manifestation of the fact that university education represents hope for economic freedom for many African American students. One of my favorite students, Kathy, wrote the following essay; she was asked, in a final paper, to analyze the essays that she had written during that semester. Here is an excerpt:

> The form that my essays take is very simple if you haven't already notice. I was taught all my life in writing any kind of paper always have an introduction, body, and conclusion. I tried to stay with this pattern and sometimes I do if I'm trying to impress somebody.... While growing up I use to love to write. I wrote down all my feelings and thoughts. This was the best way I could express myself. I use to take my time and make sure that all my commas were in the right place and all my sentences were complete ones and not run ons. ... Since I've been in college my whole outlook has changed. Its gotten to the point where instead of me actually sitting down, thinking the situation or problem out that I have to write about, I just write what I feel the teacher might want to hear. Yes I even done this in my class for you. ... Writing has become like an enemy to me lately.

Kathy's paper is interesting because she articulates her own sense of oppression at the hands of literacy through the currency of literacy. On one hand, this writing is liberating; she has come closer to naming her oppressor than most first-year students. Elsewhere in this essay, Kathy shows that racial issues underlie her "enemy." That "somebody" that she has to impress is her white teacher—if not actually me, then her white sociology teacher or her white history teacher. Frankly, this writing was also rewarding. Kathy knew me well enough to know that I could take the bad news and appreciate the candor. She "earned" a good grade, received "credit" for the required course, and continued on her presumed path to getting a good job by getting a good education. In a sense, she did what she said she does: she just wrote what she thought the teacher wanted to hear, and it was a commercial success.[2] But there is a trace of what Baker calls the vernacular, the *sotto voce*, and the missing past tense markers are but a speck of the trace. The commercial success of this essay is what also allows her to speak those haunting words, the ones I didn't want to hear, "Writing is like an enemy to me lately," and to include me in her critique of writing in the university.

Finally, and most importantly, she can articulate the consequences of the dilemma that contemporary race rituals put African American students into, the sense of anger and sadness at having to submit to the economic demands of the university classroom. Kathy was an exceptionally courageous student, one willing to use literacy, in the classroom, if not as a means of liberation at least as a means of exploring the relationship between self, race, language, and education.

Defining Self; Reclaiming History

Defining "self" is a central concern of literary theorist Barbara Christian, whose collection of articles, *Black Feminist Criticism*, appeared in 1985. Christian opens her book with a description of a conversation between her ten-year-old daughter and herself. She is sitting at a table surrounded by books, a pencil and a pad of paper in front of her. Her daughter begins to ask, as my children do, simple, direct questions about her mother's vocation. She eventually asks what Christian calls "one of her whoppers":

> "What good does it do?" Knowing that the reading will turn into writing, she looks at the low table, books, pen and pencil: "What are you doing?" (xiv)

The anecdote works beautifully, for Christian suggests that the task of the African American feminist critic is to explore and create definitions, definitions of the self made necessary by the damaging and dangerous definitions of African American women imposed by a white, patriarchal society. Christian argues for the specificity of the task of defining for African American women writers:

> Of course, many literate persons might say that the commitment to self-understanding ... is at the core of good fiction and that this statement is hardly a dramatic one. Yet, for Afro-American women writers, such an overtly self-centered point of view has been difficult to maintain because of the way they have been conceptualized by black as well as white society. The extent to which Afro-American women writers in the seventies and eighties have been able to make a commitment to an exploration of self, as central rather than marginal, is a tribute to the insights they have culled in a century or so of literary activity. (172)

This perspective is echoed by Gloria T. Hull and Barbara Smith in one of the more well-known collections of African American feminist research, *But Some of Us Are Brave:*

> The opportunities for Black women to carry out autonomously defined definitions of the self in a society which through racial, sexual, and class oppression systematically denies our existence have been by definition limited. (xviii)

The point is not so much that African American women write from a vacuum so much as from an erasure, for a vigorous history of African American women's literacy does of course exist (see Gates). So Smith's groundbreaking article, "Towards a Black Feminist Criticism," begins, "I do not know where to begin." And she goes on to explain that the invisibility of African American women, "which goes beyond anything that either Black men or white women experience," makes it difficult for her to begin. First, there is the "numbing" "massive silence"; second, there remains such a great deal of truly groundbreaking work to do: reconstructing a history of an erased literature. While not excluding the common oppression that both African American men and women endure, composition instructors will benefit from paying specific attention to the "double oppression" that African American women face.

This perspective on African American women's writing may help composition teachers understand the contexts from which African American student writers, especially women, write. Alice wrote the following paper in class. We had just finished discussing the scene in Malcolm X's autobiography in which he learns to read in prison and concludes that he had "never been so truly free." The class created a writing topic about the "prisons" we face:

> The prison I have is my own fault. It deals with me pressuring myself to succeed in life, because I don't want the problems of being unable to do what I want and when I want. If I didn't think negative of myself not being able to succeed in life my new life would not be such a headache. I'm coming to the problem where I really don't know my captivity, it could be me, trying to get myself ahead in life without having the patience I need to really get ahead in life. If I didn't go through the problem of bewildering myself then maybe it wouldn't be so rough for me to be patient and wait for the future ahead. But no not me I see such a bright future ahead for myself that I don't know how to pace myself in waiting for it. I picture in my mind everyday on how I see my future. It's good, but I'm tired of dreaming, that's all, I'm just tired and I want reality in my hands right now.

Baker's ideological analysis works well with this essay, too, especially since Alice goes on later in the paper to explain that one of the reasons she feels so pressured is that her parents are paying for her education. The economic freedom of "being able to do what I want when I want" contrasts with the headache of reality. But the story of the self coming to terms with dreams that are difficult to achieve and a reality that induces headaches seems to me to be the real story. The gulf between the self existing in the "bright future" and the one in the bewildering present motivates her to work toward a self-definition that may lead to a greater sense of self-determination. More than anything else, I sense a person who is defining herself. She seems engaged in what Smith, Christian, and other African American feminists argue is necessary and important: the process of defining herself centrally, not marginally.

Toward A More Inclusive Literacy
These explorations of texts by African American student writers suggest changes for the writing classroom. For African American students, the presence of African American literature by women and men is a special necessity. African American students will benefit from exploring the way African American writers have wrestled with the problem of authentication, struggled toward freedom through writing, overcame or were overcome by economic demands, and worked toward writing themselves into the center of American culture. For many African American students, writing themselves into the history of African American literature is no easy task, for that history has been kept from them. The following essay was read at a public reading by Ray Fed, a first-year student at California State University, Chico:

> Disappointed
> I'm mad! Do you know why I'm so mad? Good! I'll tell you why I'm so mad! Well, for one thing I didn't know about Frederick Douglass, W.E.B. Du Bois, Malcolm X, Nat Turner, or Sojourner Truth. Doesn't that piss you off? It pissed me off for the simple fact that it wasn't until now, at the age of eighteen, that I hear of some famous African-Americans who didn't take any bullshit from slavemasters or any other racist organization. What? You don't understand? Dammit, I'm mad because all my life I've been denied the truth of my heritage because of the education system in America.

Writing instructors need to present literacy as something that includes the contributions of African Americans, and, I argue, there's a special urgency to include pre-twentieth century writing by African Americans. Jacqueline Jones Royster argues that for women students, African American literary history confirms that "there has been more going on in what black women write than just novice beginnings, practice or five finger exercises in thought and expression.... They have established themselves not just as readers and writers but as master artisans and visionaries" (104). Yet, the history of literacy for most African American students means solely a history of oppression (as Ray's essay makes plain); the central symbol is of the slave who was prevented from reading and writing by the master. Rarely are students shown the history of remarkable resistance and the use of writing not only to gain one's own freedom (as in Frederick Douglass' case) but for the collective fight against injustice. And although imaginative literature has played a special role in African American intellectual history (as Barbara Christian points out in "But What Do We Think We Are Doing?"), powerful examples of nonfiction help fill out the variety of writing: Ida B. Wells-Barnett's fiery and eloquent essays against lynching, autobiographical slave narratives such as Harriet Jacobs' *Incidents in the Life of a Slave Girl* or Frederick Douglass' autobiography, or (just past the twentieth century) W.E.B. Du Bois' *The Souls of the Black Folk*. These texts function more than as prose models for students to copy; they work to provide historical and political contexts within which African American student writers can position themselves. African American literature, presented in the context of these cultural issues, argues forcefully against the separation of school literacy from the traditions of African American writing, against the notion that learning to write is learning to be white.

Recently, I was told a story about Tim, a bright articulate student who failed a timed essay test on our campus. I know his writing and know it to be powerful, humorous, and intelligent. I know he's done well in our composition courses; I've heard admiring comments from his teachers. His response to the failure was this: "I better learn to write like a white man and fast!" It is a telling response. One thing it does *not* tell me is that we need to teach this student the conventions of academic discourse *and fast*! I'd argue, first, that he already knows them (at least well enough to pass the test), and, second, the failure of the test was not a failure of academic conventions; it was a failure on the part of my institution to demonstrate (before and during the test) that Tim's language and experience are *already* a part of the university. It was a failure of the test to assure Tim a position *within the university* from which to write.[3]

Teaching texts by African American authors teaches "positions" of literacy (social and cultural positions) that go beyond learning to write like a white man, from Ishmael Reed's "writin' is fightin'" to writing for freedom as explored by Frederick Douglass and echoed by many others (including Malcolm X's sense of liberation after learning to read and write in prison) to the brave and complex and varied explorations of gender and race by contemporary African American women writers. These "positions" are far more likely to encourage equality in universities than pedagogies that stress learning the master's voice.

Simply adding texts by African American writers is not enough. Composition teachers need to see these texts as forming the "social ground" from which African American students write. More than ever, writing teachers need to abandon a simplistic skills approach to writing, which for African

American students has meant an unnecessary concentration on the verb forms of standard English. Instead, we need to elaborate a model of classroom behavior informed by the central questions of race and gender relations suggested in this essay. The purpose of this classroom is to build articulate and powerful writers in the university, writers who can participate in and shape an academic culture that desperately needs their presence. The ongoing annoying questions of whether or not to teach standard English withers in its insignificance.

If recent literacy theory has taught us anything, it is that literacy—as an idea and as a practice—is defined by the social relations in which it occurs. It is therefore obvious that adding new texts alone will not change literacy instruction for African Americans (although it is one of the necessary changes). Additionally, and this seems especially crucial for the white teacher or the teacher of color who is unfamiliar with the cultural contexts of African American students, teachers and students both have to learn to enter into a dialogic relationship. Here again, the concept of "position" plays a central role. Baker describes the successful Afro-American literary critic as I would like to describe the successful teacher of African American students: someone who knows "where and how to listen" and "where and how to see" ("Beautiful" 147). Such a teacher needs to be informed about the social ground from which students write, a knowledge that needs to come from study of African American texts, but also through listening and "seeing" their own students. Explorations for such classrooms abound, most of them influenced by Paulo Freire's dialogic theories of learning, which demand of teachers that they constantly interpret and "unveil" their students' realities. Such productive relationships between white faculty members and African American students are rare and difficult; yet there is no other way than to disclose "position," show a willingness to listen and to change, and demonstrate, in overt ways (texts, assignments, and daily classroom demeanor), a desire to include and legitimate the experiences and language of African Americans.

Finally, to really change the power relations between faculty and African American students, we need to redouble our efforts to attract African American writing teachers, teachers who learned through their own experience the connections between literacy and African American culture. Along with supporting strong and effective affirmative action in hiring, we also need to increase the number of qualified applicants by vigorously recruiting and financially supporting African American students for our undergraduate and graduate programs in writing. Most of all, we need to become a profession that ceases excluding African Americans and begin welcoming the strengths and experiences of African American students and future teachers.

Notes

[1] The original passage refers to the position of black women critics and reads, "Making our positionality explicit is not to claim a 'privileged' status for our positions. . . . Making our positionality explicit is, rather, a response to the false universalism that long defined critical practice and rendered black women and their writing mute."

[2] For a detailed discussion of this student's work, see Fox, chapter 5.

[3] Clearly, Tim's response shows how crucial writing-across-the-curriculum programs are to innovative composition programs. Without the support of other teachers in other disciplines, progressive writing courses are isolated and insignificant.

Works Cited

Aronowitz, Stanley, and Henry A. Giroux. *Education Under Siege: The Conservative, Liberal and Radical Debate Over Schooling*. South Hadley, MA: Bergin, 1985.

Baker, Houston A. *Blues, Ideology, and Afro-American Literature: A Vernacular Theory*. Chicago: U of Chicago P, 1984.

——. *The Journey Back: Issues in Black Literature and Criticism*. Chicago: U of Chicago P, 1980.

——. "There is No More Beautiful Way: Theory and Poetics of Afro-American Women's Writing." *Afro-American Literary Study in the 1990s*. Ed. Houston A. Baker, Jr. and Patricia Redmond. Chicago: U of Chicago P, 1989. 135-54.

——. "In Dubious Battle." *New Literary History* 18 (1987): 363-69.

Brooks, Charlotte K., ed. *Tapping Potential: English and Language Arts for The Black Learner*. Urbana: NCTE, 1985.

Christian, Barbara. *Black Feminist Criticism: Perspectives on Black Women Writers*. New York: Pergamon, 1985.

——. "But What Do We Think We're Doing Anyway: The State of Black Feminist Criticism(s) or My Version of a Little Bit of History." *Changing Our Own Words: Essays on Criticism, Theory, and Writing by Black Women*. Ed. Cheryl A. Wall. New Brunswick: Rutgers UP, 1989. 58-74.

Douglass, Frederick. *Narrative of the Life of Frederick Douglass, An American Slave, Written by Himself*. 1845. New York: New American, 1968.

Du Bois, W.E.B. *The Souls of Black Folk*. 1903. New York: Signet, 1969.

Fox, Thomas. *The Social Uses of Writing: Politics and Pedagogy*. Norwood, NJ: Ablex, 1990.

Freire, Paulo. *Pedagogy of the Oppressed*. Trans. Myra Bergman Ramos. 1970. New York: Continuum, 1980.

Gates, Henry Louis, Jr. "'What's Love Got to Do with It?': Critical Theory, Integrity, and the Black Scholar." *New Literary History* 18 (1987): 345-62.

Gates, Henry Louis, Jr., ed. *The Schomberg Library of Nineteenth-Century Black Women Writers*. New York: Oxford UP, 1988.

Henderson, Mae G. "Response." *Afro-American Literary Study in the 1990s*. Ed. Houston A. Baker, Jr. and Patricia Redmond. Chicago: U of Chicago P, 1989. 155-63.

——. "Speaking in Tongues: Dialogics, Dialectics, and the Black Woman Writer's Literary Tradition." *Changing Our Own Words: Essays on Criticism, Theory and Writing by Black Women*. Ed. Cheryl A. Wall. New Brunswick: Rutgers UP, 1989. 16-37.

Hull, Gloria T., and Barbara Smith. "Introduction: The Politics of Black Women's Studies." *But Some of Us Are Brave*. Ed. Gloria T. Hull, Patricia Bell Scott, and Barbara Smith. Old Westbury, NY: Feminist P, 1982.

Jacobs, Harriet. *Incidents in the Life of a Slave Girl.* 1861. Cambridge: Harvard UP, 1987.

Joyce, Joyce A. "The Black Canon: Reconstructing Black American Literary Criticism." *New Literary History* 18 (1987): 335-44.

——. "'Who the Cap Fit': Unconsciousness and Unconscionableness in the Criticism of Houston A. Baker Jr. and Henry Louis Gates, Jr." *New Literary History* 18 (1987): 371-84.

Labov, William. *Language in the Inner City*. Philadelphia: U of Pennsylvania P, 1972.

Lu, Min-zhan. "Writing as Repositioning." *Journal of Education* 172.1 (1990): 18-21.

Malcolm X, and Alex Haley. *The Autobiography of Malcolm X*. 1964. New York: Ballantine, 1973.

Ogbu, John U. "Opportunity Structure, Cultural Boundaries, and Literacy." *Language, Literacy, and Culture: Issues of Society and Schooling*. Ed. Judith Langer. Norwood, NJ: Ablex, 1987.

Ohmann, Richard. *English in America: A Radical View of the Profession*. New York: Oxford UP, 1975.

Reed, Ishmael. *Writin' is Fightin'*. New York: Athenuem, 1988.

Royster, Jacqueline Jones. "Perspectives on the Intellectual Traditions of Black Women Writers." *The Right to Literacy*. Ed. Andrea Lunsford, Helen Moglen, James Slevin. New York: MLA, 1990.

Smith, Barbara. "Toward a Black Feminist Criticism." *But Some of Us Are Brave*. Ed. Gloria T. Hull, Patricia Bell Scott, Barbara Smith. Old Westbury, NY: Feminist P, 1982. 157-75.

Smitherman, Geneva. *Talkin' and Testifyin': The Language of Black America*. Boston: Houghton, 1977.

Smitherman-Donaldson, Geneva. "Discriminatory Discourse on Afro-American Speech." *Discourse and Discrimination*. Ed. Geneva Smitherman-Donaldson and Teun A. van Dijk. Detroit: Wayne State UP, 1988.

Stepto, Robert. *From Behind the Veil: A Study of Afro-American Narrative*. Urbana: U of Illinois P, 1979.

Stuckey, J. Elspeth. *The Violence of Literacy*. Portsmouth, NH: Boynton, 1991.

Wall, Cheryl A. "Introduction: Taking Positions and Changing Words." *Changing Our Own Words: Essays on Criticism, Theory and Writing by Black Women*. New Brunswick: Rutgers UP, 1989. 1-15.

Wells-Barnett, Ida B. *On Lynchings*. New York: Arno, 1969.

The Essay and Composition Theory

Rediscovering the Essay

W. Ross Winterowd

The essay is—and, for reasons that the following discussion will advance, should be—the central genre in composition instruction. However, if the essay is to serve as the kind of writing through which students realize their full potential as liberally educated beings, they, and we, need an expanded conception of what the essay is and what it can do.

Traditionally, of course, essays are classed as *informal* and *formal*. A set of truisms adequately characterizes the *informal* essay (by such practitioners as Swift, Lamb, Hazlitt, De Quincey, Twain, Thurber, and White). It is personal and not as highly structured as the formal; it is likely to be anecdotal; and the author has no obligation to assume a disinterested stance toward issues. On the other hand, the *formal* essay (of, for instance, Addison, Johnson, Arnold, Mill, Newman, Pater, and Emerson) is nonpersonal, highly structured, and goes beyond "conveying information," attempting to convince readers of the validity of a particular vision of experience or reality. However, as Dillon says,

> It does not seek to engage the reader in a course of action . . . but rather in a process of reflection, and its means of convincing are accordingly limited to the use of evidence and logical proof and the posture of openmindedness. These methods are also associated with the liberally educated person, who is meditative, reflective, clear-headed, unbiased, always seeking to understand experience freshly and to find things of interest in the world. (23)

My argument (not really startling or original in this post-structuralist age) is that students should have the right *not* to be conclusive—as they must be in formal essays—but rather to *explore* themselves and their worlds in informal essays. *Exploratory* discourse, as James L. Kinneavy points out, is the result and manifestation of cognitive dissonance, a condition of "wonder, instability, or discomfort" that comes about when observed facts clash with accepted premises or dogmas, precipitating the search for a new model of experience (102-03). For Montaigne, the essay was exploratory; as Zeiger points out, Montaigne "essayed" his ideas, examining them from various points of view, ready to abandon them if the *assay* (from the same French root as essay) proved they were fool's gold (455).

Students should, like Montaigne, have the right to use their essays to assay.

A New Understanding of Coherence in the Essay

From lyric poetry—not very popular nowadays, I think—we can learn much about attitudes, little about opinions; much about sense impressions, little about ideas. Such also is the case with many particularly satisfying informal "expository" essays that do not provide significant information or advance arguments, but, rather, as Kenneth Burke would say, dance attitudes. The lyric in prose gains its coherence from what Burke calls *qualitative progression*, in which "the presence of one quality prepares us for the introduction of another" (*Counter-Statement* 124), not from the syllogistic progression that structures formal essays.

In "Form, Authority, and the Critical Essay," Keith Fort serendipitously and convincingly explains what should have been, but was not, the obvious: available forms determine attitudes. If, for instance, the only form available to students for their responses to literature is the conventional expository essay, with its clear-cut topic and its tree-able structure, then the attitude expressed must affirm the discursiveness of literature. The prose lyric breaks out of the syllogistic, linear Western form and, in so doing, frees itself of the strictures of discursiveness.

The essential difference between the coherence of the formal essay and that of the informal essay can be expressed metaphorically. In its superstructure, the well-formed formal essay is a branching tree diagram or organizational chart with the topic, enthymeme, or macro proposition (Van Dijk 42) at the top. In an image adapted from Kintsch (7-8), the form of an informal essay is that of a galaxy, with dense clusters of bright stars related as subsystems within the whole as it spirals through the universe.

The prevailing dogma is that a clear-cut topic (in the scientistic language of Van Dijk, a "macro proposition") is essential to coherence, but Witte and Faigley give a more useful view of coherence as "those underlying semantic relations that allow a text to be understood and used . . . conditions governed by the writer's purpose, the audience's knowledge and expectations, and the information to be conveyed" (202). In effect, *any text will be coherent if the reader takes it to be so*, and a case in point is *The Waste Land*, which Cleanth Brooks interprets as a perfectly coherent whole (138-59), and which Graham Hough likens to a painting with "pointillist technique in one part . . . and the glazes of the high renaissance in another" (38).

One of Wolfgang Iser's points is that readers must fill "gaps" in the text and, thus, are actively involved in constructing, not merely recovering, meaning. A passage quoted in Clark and Clark demonstrates that readers also construct global representations (that is, coherent wholes) from the individual sentences of a text:

> The two of them glanced nervously at each other as they approached the man standing there expectantly. He talked to them for about ten minutes, but spoke loudly enough that everyone else in the room could hear too. Eventually he handed over two objects he had been given, one to each of them. After he had said a few more words, the ordeal was over. With her veil lifted, the two of them kissed, turned around, and rushed from the room arm in arm, with everyone else falling in behind. (161)

Readers eventually realize that the scene is a wedding, even though no individual sentence in the passage says as much, and the text becomes a coherent whole.

Clark and Clark also quote a story from a study by Bransford and Johnson. One group of readers was given the title "Watching a Peace March from the Fortieth Floor" and another group the title "A Space Trip to an Inhabited Planet." Because of one sentence in the passage "The landing was gentle and luckily the atmosphere was such that no special suits had to be worn"—the readers of "A Space Trip to an Inhabited Planet" found the passage much more coherent than did the readers with the other title:

> The view was breathtaking. From the window one could see the crowd below. Everything looked extremely small from such a distance, but the colorful costumes could still be seen. Everyone seemed to be moving in one direction in an orderly fashion and there seemed to be little children as well as adults. The landing was gentle and luckily the atmosphere was such that no special suits had to be worn. At first there was a great deal of activity. Later, when the speeches started, the crowd quieted down. The man with the television camera took many shots of the setting and the crowd. Everyone was very friendly and seemed glad when the music started. (163)

The point is, of course, that the problematic sentence fits readers' (sci-fi) world knowledge about space travel and conflicts with views from the fortieth floor.

But the best way to demonstrate the expressive and cohesive range of the essay is to examine specimens by contemporary writers. I will begin with a discussion of a formal essay by Stephen Jay Gould; next I will turn to informal essays by Joan Didion, Lewis Thomas, and Loren Eiseley.

A Formal Essay by Stephen Jay Gould

The title is "Natural Selection and the Human Brain: Darwin *vs.* Wallace," and the first sentence is "In the south transept of Chartres cathedral, the most stunning of all medieval windows depicts the four evangelists as dwarfs sitting upon the shoulders of four Old Testament prophets—Isaiah, Jeremiah, Ezekiel, and Daniel." Gould then refers to Newton's aphorism: "If I have seen further, it is by standing on the shoulders of giants." This point leads him to mention a book on pre-Newtonian uses of the metaphor and Gould's explanation that the author, Columbia sociologist of science Robert K. Merton, "devoted much of his work to the study of multiple discoveries in science" (47), which is exactly what happened in the case of Darwin and Wallace.

A reader might ask why Gould would devote nearly a whole page of his essay to a lead-in when he might have begun directly by stating that Darwin and Wallace almost simultaneously developed theories of natural selection. The answer is obvious: Gould needed to establish his *ethical* argument by setting a tone and taking a stance.

Despite its dramatistic structure, "Natural Selection" is an example of Burke's *syllogistic progression*, "the form of a perfectly conducted argument, advancing step by step" (*Counter-Statement* 124). The body of the essay is an explanation of the dialectic whereby Darwin and Wallace developed nearly identical theories of natural selection and of the way in which the theories diverged. In other words, the essay is essentially an analysis of scientific logic—but in terms of a human drama.

The disagreement between Wallace and Darwin hinges on the doctrine of strict selectionism, to which Wallace clung: all evolutionary developments must have been the result of adaptation for survival of the fittest. Darwin argued, however, that adaptive change in one organ of a creature can lead to nonadaptive change in another organ, and that an organ developed for one function can perform another non selected function as well. Gould writes, "In 1870, as he prepared *The Descent of Man*, Darwin wrote to Wallace: 'I grieve to differ from you, and it actually terrifies me and makes me constantly distrust myself. I fear we shall never quite understand each other'" (52).

The crisis came when Wallace attempted to understand the evolution of the human brain. He knew that the brains of savages were as large as those of civilized humans and that "since cultural conditioning can integrate the rudest savage into our most courtly life, the rudeness itself must arise from a failure to use existing capacities, not from, their absence" (54). As Wallace said, "Natural selection could only have endowed savage man with a brain a few degrees superior to that of an ape, whereas he actually possesses one very little inferior to that of a philosopher" (55). The human brain must have been created by a Higher Power. Ironically, then, as Gould says, Wallace's hyper-selectionism led directly back to the creationism that it was intended to replace.

Thus, in his essay Gould has cast a technical discussion in the form of a drama, fashioning characters—Alfred Russell Wallace and Charles Darwin—that "humanize" the information. These are quite different from the "composite characters" that Hallowell says are one of the devices of the new journalism. Nonetheless, the informativeness of the essay is its primary interest; the *technical* brilliance of the author in conveying that information engages only the specialized reader, not the common reader. "Natural Selection" contrasts starkly with the essays discussed below.

An Appositional Essay by Joan Didion

Joan Didion's "Los Angeles Notebook," an attitudinal characterization of Los Angeles, is a series of five sketches in eight pages, adding up to an ideal example of *qualitative progression* in a prose lyric. Here are the subjects of the sketches:

> 1) **The Santa Ana wind:** "The Pacific turned ominously glossy during a Santa Ana period, and one woke in the night troubled not only by the peacocks screaming in the olive trees but by the eerie absence of surf" (217-18).
> 2) **A late-night radio talk show:** "So it went, from midnight until 5 a.m., interrupted by records and by occasional calls debating whether or not a rattlesnake can swim. Misinformation about rattlesnakes is a leitmotif of the insomniac imagination in Los Angeles" (221).
> 3) **Wearing a bikini to a supermarket on a hot afternoon:** "That is not a very good thing to wear to the market but neither is it, at Ralph's on the corner of Sunset and Fuller, an unusual costume. Nonetheless a large woman in a cotton muumuu jams her cart into mine at the butcher counter. *'What a thing to wear to the market,'* she says in a loud but strangled voice" (222).
> 4) **The bored sophistication of movie people:** "A party at someone's house in Beverly Hills: a pink tent, two orchestras, a couple of French Communist directors in Cardin evening jackets, chili and hamburgers from Chasen's" (223).
> 5) **Piano bars:** "A drunk requests 'the Sweetheart of Sigma Chi.' The piano player doesn't know it. 'Where'd you learn to play the piano?' the drunk asks. 'I got two degrees,' the piano player says. 'One in musical education.'" (224).

Through what Chris Anderson calls her "radical particularity" (4), Didion creates an attitudinally coherent essay. "Her habitual gesture as a stylist is to isolate the ironic or symbolic or evocative image and then reflect on its possible significance" (Anderson 134). "Los Angeles Notebook" is a series of these irnages in *apposition*.

In "Brain, Rhetoric, and Style," I characterize the "appositional" essay (135-36) as follows:

> 1) The topic is implied, not stated directly. (I would now say that the reader may derive or create a topic or macro proposition.)
> 2) As opposed to the rigid organization of what I called the "propositional" (that is, "discursive") essay, appositional organization is flexible.
> 3) Examples are specific (as in the "radical particularity" of Didion).
> 4) As opposed to the backgrounded style of the propositional essay, the appositional style is foregrounded. To use the foregrounded style is "to present phenomena in a fully externalized form, visible and palpable in all their parts, and completely fixed in their spatial and temporal relations" (Auerbach 6).
> 5) Finally, the appositional essay has great presence.

In fact, these characteristics are a pretty good description of an essay such as "Los Angeles Notebook."

Lewis Thomas and the Sham Enthymeme

If asked to state the thesis of the title essay in Lewis Thomas's collection, *Late Night Thoughts on Listening to Mahler's Ninth Symphony*, the typical reader, attempting to explain the nearly unsayable lyric experience in discursive terms, would probably say something like this: "The realization that human-kind can annihilate itself is depressing." But this is much like boiling "To His

Coy Mistress" down to the aphorism *carpe diem*, and it demeans the experience that the essay provides—as a colleague of mine once said, you sell your soul for a pot of message.

In this essay, only the unsayable, the lyric, makes sense; the discursive, the expository, is madness.

The very title evokes the swelling lament of the symphony's first movement, but Thomas is preoccupied with the final movement, the *adagio*—an indeterminate text which once had been "a metaphor for reassurance, confirming my own strong hunch that the dying of every living creature, the most natural of all experiences, has to be a peaceful experience." But now the meaning has changed. From the call of the horns and the inconstancy of the strings fading almost into silence and then surging back, Thomas derives a meaning that he conveys through a panoramic image of worldwide thermonuclear devastation, concluding specifically with the area that he loves more than any other part of earth, the Engadine.

Now, Thomas makes a prosaic statement about his reconciliation to the idea of death, but then modulates from this statement to another image: that luminous blue and white ball, the earth as seen from outer space, "the great round being, "seen as an organism with a mind which Thomas would be a small part of after his death.

What has transformed the meaning of the Ninth into "a hideous noise" is the thought of the young, who could, like Thomas, have discovered Wallace Stevens, Brahms, and Beethoven; who, from the records of their forebears, could have derived assurance of the future, but who must now live with the *facts* of the thermonuclear age. The melody near the end of the Ninth no longer says "We'll be back, we're still here, keep going, keep going" because a freakish intertextuality—the discursive facts of a pamphlet on *MX Basing* and a television talk on civil defense by a government official—has changed the symphony's conclusion into the unintelligible cacophony of silo hatches opening. Thomas has gone as far as language will carry him, but that isn't far enough. To "say" what needs to be said, young people would need to invent a new kind of music, for the old kind is inadequate, and human language, with its rational statement of the facts, is merely a curse to be exorcised, an unbearable torment.

Unlike Didion's "Los Angeles Notebook," Thomas's "Late Night Thoughts" does have an easily derivable enthymeme or macro proposition, stated earlier (somewhat invidiously, to be sure): "The realization that humankind can annihilate itself is depressing." But, paradoxically, the "real" message is that the real "message" is unsayable, even unthinkable—beyond comprehension and, hence, beyond expression. One might say, then, that Thomas's enthymeme is a sham.

A tree diagram of "Los Angeles Notebook" is one-dimensional:

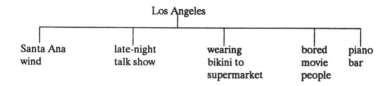

A tree of "Late Night Thoughts" is a superstructure that could well be that of a discursive essay:

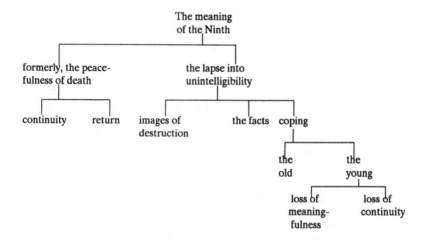

But neither "Los Angeles Notebook" nor "Late Night Thoughts" advances an argument, as does Gould's "Natural Selection"; nor is either informative in the sense of reducing the reader's uncertainty about a topic or of supplying fresh data; nonetheless, both are, in my opinion at least, particularly satisfying and convincing.

Organic Form in Loren Eiseley's Essays

Leafing through the works of Loren Eiseley, one finds, page after page, brilliant metaphors, such as this one from the first page of *The Unexpected Universe*: "Every man contains within himself a ghost continent—a place circled as warily as Antarctica was circled two hundred years ago by Captain James Cook." Or this one from the first page of *The Immense Journey*: "Some lands are flat and grass-covered, and smile so evenly up at the sun that they seem forever youthful, untouched by man or time. Some are torn, ravaged and convulsed like the features of profane old age."

Throughout the essays, one also finds anecdotes from which the teller draws lessons. One of the most dramatic, though too long to quote in its entirety, begins "The Angry Winter":

> I had been huddled beside the fire one winter night, with the wind prowling outside and shaking the windows. The big shepherd dog on the hearth before me occasionally glanced up affectionately, sighed, and slept. I was working, actually, amidst the debris of a far greater winter. On my desk lay the lance points of ice age hunters and the heavy leg bone of a fossil bison. No remnants of flesh attached to these relics. The deed lay more than ten thousand years remote. It was represented here by naked flint and by bone so mineralized it rang when struck. As I worked on in my little circle of light, I absently laid the bone beside me on the floor. The hour had crept toward midnight. A grating noise, a heavy rasping of big teeth diverted me. I looked down.
>
> The dog had risen. That rock-hard fragment of vanished beast was in his jaws and he was mouthing it with a fierce intensity I had never seen exhibited by him before.
>
> "Wolf," I exclaimed, and stretched out my hand. The dog backed up but did not yield. A low and steady rumbling began to rise in his chest, something out of a long-gone midnight. There was nothing in that bone to taste, but ancient shapes were moving in his mind and deter mining his utterance. Only fools gave up bones. He was warning me.
>
> (93-94)

There follows an essay, concerning evolution and ecology, among other topics, which ends with another anecdote. When he was a young man, Eiseley set out for a long walk on a "sullen November day," finally, at twilight, reaching the town cemetery. There among the dead, he found life: a jackrabbit.

> We both had a fatal power to multiply, the thought flashed on me, and the planet was not large. Why was it so, and what was the message that somehow seemed spoken from a long way off beyond an ice field, out of all possible human hearing?
>
> The snow lifted and swirled about us once more. He was going to need that broken bit of shelter [provided by a slab]. The temperature was falling. For his frightened, trembling body in all the million years between us, there had been no sorcerer's aid. He had survived alone in the blue nights and the howling dark. He was thin and crumpled and small.
>
> Step by step I drew back among the dead and their fallen stones. Somewhere, if I could follow the fence lines, there would be a fire for me. For a moment I could see his ears nervously recording my movements, but I was a wraith now, fading in the storm.
>
> "There are so few tracks in all this snow," someone had once protested. It was true. I stood in the falling flakes and pondered it. Even my own tracks were filling. But out of such desolation had arisen man, the desolate. In essence, he is a belated phantom of the angry winter. He carried, and perhaps will always carry, its cruelty and its springtime in his heart. (119)

It would appear that Eiseley the essayist is a practicing Romantic, following the leads of his anecdotes and metaphors, not aiming them—as does Gould, for instance—toward a clear-cut semantic intention.

As a long-time admirer of Eiseley's work, one who has with great pleasure been reading and rereading the essays for twenty years, I can say without intending criticism that the essays are structurally alogical, but not quite, either, examples of qualitative progression. They gain their structure through the "perspective by incongruity" that results when Eiseley follows the implications of his "representative anecdotes" (Burke, *Grammar* 59-61).

We need to ponder Burke's "perspective by incongruity." It is, he says, "a method for gauging situations by verbal 'atom cracking.' That is, a word belongs by custom to a certain category—and by rational planning you wrench it loose and metaphorically apply it to a different category" (*Attitudes* 308). Then, of course, you follow the particles set free in the "cracking." The result is a "*dramatic* vocabulary, with weighting and counter-weighting, in contrast with the liberal ideal of *neutral* naming in the characterization of processes" (*Attitudes* 311).

Structurally, another of Eiseley's essays, "The Hidden Teacher," is a series of anecdotes:

> 1) **A retelling of the Job story:** "A youth standing by, one Elihu, also played a role in this drama, for he ventured diffidently to his protesting elder that it was not true that God failed to manifest Himself. He may speak in one way or another, though men do not perceive it" (48-49).
>
> 2) **An anecdote of a spider** (discussed below).
>
> 3) **An anecdote of a seed:** "Its flexible limbs were stiffer than milkweed down, and, propelled by the wind, it ran rapidly and evasively over the pavement. It was like a gnome scampermg somewhere with a hidden packet—for all I could tell, a totally new one: one of the jumbled alphabets of life" (56-57).
>
> 4) **An anecdote of a mathematical genius:** "Like some heavy-browed child at the wood's edge, clutching the last stone hand ax, I was witnessing the birth of a new type of humanity—one so beyond its teachers that it was being used for mean purposes while the intangible web of the universe in all its shimmering mathematical perfection glistened untaught in the mind of a chance little boy" (58).
>
> 5) **An anecdote of an archaeologist at Palenque:** "After shining his torch over hieroglyphs and sculptured figures, the explorer remarked wonderingly: 'We were the first people for more than a thousand years to look at it'" (60).
>
> 6) **An anecdote of a young linguistics student who ultimately became Eiseley's revered professor:** "The young student published a paper upon Mohegan linguistics, the first of a long series of studies upon the forgotten languages and ethnology of the Indians of the Northeastem forest. He had changed his vocation and turned to anthropology because of the attraction of a hidden teacher. But just who was the teacher? The young man himself, his instructor, or that solitary speaker of a dying tongue who had so yearned to hear her people's voice that she had softly babbled it to a child?" (62-63).
>
> 7) **An anecdote of a dream, in which a writer sees his dead father and mother through a window and then realizes that he is looking only at his own reflection:** "My line was dying, but I understood. I hope they understood, too" (66).

The anecdote of the spider is a synecdoche for the structure of Eiseley's essay:

> I once received an unexpected lesson from a spider.
>
> It happened far away on a rainy morning in the West. I had come up a long gulch looking for fossils, and there, just at eye level, lurked a huge yellow-and-black orb spider, whose web was moored to the tall spears of buffalo grass at the edge of the arroyo. It was her universe, and her senses did not extend beyond the lines and spokes of the great wheel she inhabited. Her extended claws could feel every vibration throughout that delicate structure. She knew the tug of wind, the fall of a raindrop, the flutter of a trapped moth's

> wing. Down one spoke of the web ran a strout ribbon of gossamer on which she could
> hurry out to investigate her prey.
> Curious, I took a pencil from my pocket and touched a strand of the web. Immedi-
> ately there was a response. The web, plucked by its menacing occupant, began to vibrate
> until it was a blur. Anything that had brushed claw or wing against that amazing snare
> would be thoroughly entrapped. As the vibrations slowed, I could see the owner
> fingering her guidelines for signs of struggle. A pencil point was an intrusion into this
> universe for which no precedent existed. Spider was circumscribed by spider ideas; its
> universe was spider universe. All outside was irrational, extraneous, at best, raw material
> for spider. As I proceeded my way along the gully, like a vast impossible shadow, I
> realized that in the world of spider I did not exist. (49-50)

Stripped of its context, the lesson that Eiseley learned from the spider is nugatory: the realization that "among the many universes in which the world of living creatures existed, some were large, some small, but all, including man's, were in some way limited or finite" (51); however, the anecdote validates the lesson, just as a fable validates the moral or a lyric poem validates whatever enthymeme can be derived from it.

In any case, Eiseley tells us that many times he has pondered his encounter with the orb spider and that "a message has arisen only now from the misty shreds of that webbed universe"(51). The message, though, turns out to be a question that leads to a *non sequitur*:

> Was it that spidery indifference to the human triumph?
> If so, that triumph was very real and could not be denied. (51)

Paraphrased, these sentences say, "If the message was that spidery indifference to the human triumph, that triumph was very real and could not be denied," and this simply does not compute. However, the lapse in *syllogistic progression* hardly matters, for the reader is following the implications of the anecdotes, which are heuristic.

What is the triumph? One cannot, as a matter of fact, be certain. It is either the emergence of the human species or the scientific achievement of tracing that emergence:

> I saw, had seen many times, both mentally and in the seams of exposed strata, the long
> backward stretch of time whose recovery is one of the great feats of modern science. I
> saw the drifting cells of the early seas from which all life, including our own, has arisen.
> The salt of those ancient seas is in our blood, its lime is in our bones. Every time we walk
> along a beach some ancient urge disturbs us so that we find ourselves shedding shoes and
> garments, or scavenging among seaweed and whitened timbers like the homesick
> refugees of a long war. (51)

The "refugees of war" metaphor opens a new pathway for Eiseley to follow: "And war it has been indeed—the long war of life against its inhospitable environment, a war that has lasted for perhaps three billion years" (51)—from the first seething of chemicals in a world without oxygen through the age of the ferns to the human brain, "so frail, so perishable, so full of inexhaustible dreams and hungers" (52).

To fault Didion, Thomas, and Eiseley because they follow leads other than the logical is to miss the whole point of these prose lyrics, which advance by what might be called *anecdotal progression*. To disregard these kinds of essays in the classroom is to delimit the range of discourse available to students and, thus, to delimit their capacity for thought and expression.

Works Cited

Anderson, Chris. *Style as Argument: Contemporary American Nonfiction*. Carbondale: Southern Illinois UP, 1987.

Auerbach, Erich. *Mimesis: The Representation of Reality in Western Literature*. Trans. Willard R. Trask. Princeton: Princeton UP. 1953.

Brooks, Cleanth. *Modern Poetry and the Tradition*. Chapel Hill: U of North Carolina P, 1960.

Burke, Kenneth. *Attitudes Toward History*. 3rd ed. Berkeley: U of California P, 1984.

———. *Counter-Statement*. Los Altos, CA: Hermes, 1953.

———. *A Grammar of Motives*. Berkeley: U of California P, 1969.

Clark, Herbert H., and Eve V. Clark. *Psychology and Language*. New York: Harcourt, 1977.

Didion, Joan. "Los Angeles Notebook." *Slouching Towards Bethlehem*. New York: Dell, 1968. 217-24.

Dillon, George L. *Constructing Texts*. Bloomington: Indiana UP, 1981.

Eiseley, Loren. "The Angry Winter." *The Unexpected Universe*. New York: Harcourt, 1969. 93-119.

———. *The Immense Journey*. New York: Vintage, 1959.

Fort, Keith. "Form, Authority, and the Critical Essay." *College English*. 32 (1971): 629-39.

Gould, Stephen Jay. "Natural Selection and the Human Brain: Darwin *vs.* Wallace." *The Panda's Thumb*. New York: Norton, 1980. 47-58.

Hough, Graham. *Reflections on a Literary Revolution*. Washington, DC: Catholic U of America P, 1960.

Iser, Wolfgang. *The Act of Reading*. Baltimore: Johns Hopkins UP, 1978.

Kinneavy, James L. *A Theory of Discourse*. Englewood Cliffs, NJ: Prentice, 1971.

Kintsch, Walter. *Psychological Processes in Discourse Production*. Technical Rept. 99. Institute of Cognitive Science. Boulder: U of Colorado, 1980.

Thomas, Lewis. *Late Night Thoughts on Listening to Mahler's Ninth Symphony*. New York: Bantam, 1984.

Van Dijk, Teun A. *Macrostructures: An Interdisciplinary Study of Global Structure in Discourse, Interaction, and Cognition*. Hillsdale, NJ: Erlbaum, 1980.

Wintered, W. Ross. "Brain, Rhetoric, and Style." *Linguistics, Stylistics, and the Teaching of Composition*. Ed. Donald McQuade. Akron: U of Akron P, 1979. 151-81.

Witte, Stephen P., and Lester Faigley. "Coherence, Cohesion, and Writing Quality." *College Composition and Communication* 32 (1981): 189-204.

Zeiger, William. "The Exploratory Essay: Enfranchising the Spirit of Inquiry in College Composition." *College English* 47 (1985): 454-66.

The Recent Rise of Literary Nonfiction: A Cautionary Assay

Douglas Hesse

> An additional special feature of the 1990 Convention will be a series of sessions dedicated to reclaiming the *literary status of the essay*.
> *Program* of the 1990 CCCC Convention

> The first to come as a group, of a desire sprung within themselves, they were the first American democracy—and it was they, in the end, who would succeed in making everything like themselves.
> William Carlos Williams, "Voyage of the Mayflower"

Composition teachers and scholars should be wary of recent efforts to settle the writing world for "literary nonfiction," especially when this project has, as yet, been so uncritically conceived. Convention, I know, dictates a more essayistically measured opening, and I promise reassuring qualifications and uncertainties. But the land rush toward "the personal essay" has come so furiously that there is a need for cautionary urgency.

When this movement began depends on where you choose to stake the first claim. Perhaps in Dennis Rygiel's 1984 *College English* article, or Ronald Weber's 1980 *The Literature of Fact*. Or Tom Wolfe's 1973 *The New Journalism*, or Robert Scholes and Carl Klaus' 1969 *Elements of The Essay*. Perhaps in a textbook that devoted separate sections to "Logical Composition" and "Literary Composition," and located the essay in the borderland between them. That was Charles Sears Baldwin's 1902 *College Manual of Rhetoric*. Perhaps earlier: Samuel Newman's 1827 *Practical System of Rhetoric*, which included histories, letters, and essays among the five genres of literature. Beyond, of course, is Hugh Blair.

It is apt, then, to speak of the current interest in literary nonfiction in terms of *reclamation*. That interest includes such works as Chris Anderson's *Literary Nonfiction*, Graham Good's *The Observing Self*, Alexander Butrym's *Essays on the Essay*, W. Ross Winterowd's *The Rhetoric of the "Other" Literature*, several books in preparation, and articles in virtually all of the profession's journals. There are undergraduate and graduate courses in the area and textbooks for them. The past several CCCC meetings have featured living and breathing authors. In 1990 there were some eighteen sessions directly related to literary nonfiction, most concerning the essay.

Perhaps the best sign of any concept's having "arrived" is the possibility and necessity that the assumptions pushing it should be examined. In the case of literary nonfiction, writing teachers should examine contentions that its various genres offer the kind of natural and "student empowering" discourse that more "academic" genres do not. To explain why, I'll discuss reasons for the current interest in the essay as literature and examine positions voiced in several relatively recent articles.

I should note that the critique that follows comes from an insider. I have published essays in both Anderson's and Butrym's volumes, and I regularly lead a writing workshop in nonfiction prose. My own professional self-interest, then, is in the continued ascendancy of the essay. However, I fear that if we do not challenge some current assumptions, we stand strangely disengaged from several important issues in rhetorical, genre, and cultural theory. The result may be to insulate students from vital questions about relationships among language, individualism, and discursive formation. While I quite favor students' reading and writing the sorts of texts generally collected as "personal essays," the justification for doing so should be something more than the naive celebration of "the literary."

Motivations Nostalgic and Territorial

Three motives may account for the rise of interest in the essay as literature. First, briefly, is the lure of nostalgia. I suspect that many of us were seduced by a certain way of studying literature before we were more powerfully seduced by rhetoric and composition. Our pasts were infused with the pleasures of close reading, interpretation, and the analysis of "finished texts." One effect of declaring the essay as literature, then, is to invite compositionists occasionally to return to our aestheticized roots. Such a return can be for good or ill, depending on whether we ponder what we're up to and what it holds for our students.

A second motivation is less nostalgic than territorial. To put it crassly, in a landscape crowded with scholars, one way to gain *Schreibensraum* is to declare new territories open for colonization. Suddenly there are not only virgin texts to explore but a virgin genre, not only countries but continents. And like early priests or prospectors, scholars who first stake claims will not only publish more richly but also largely determine future citizenship in the territory. To the ranks of The Leading Milton Scholar can be added The Leading Dillard.

Naming this territory by asserting the *literariness* of the essay is a gesture with corporate as well as individual payoffs. In a by-now well-worn argument, Terry Eagleton points out that one function of labeling texts as literary is to justify our attending to them. By announcing that what "literary scholars" can do with "their" texts (novels, plays, short stories, poems) "we" can do with "ours" (essays, autobiographies, articles), compositionists seek, consciously or not, to enhance their status in the profession. James Berlin argues that positivistic rhetoric endures because literary interests have needed it: "To demonstrate the unique and privileged nature of poetic texts, it has been necessary to insist on a contrasting set of devalorized texts" (28). It might be the case that composition studies similarly needs the category of "literary nonfiction" to assert its place in the hierarchy of discourse comprising the modern English department. As English departments became increasingly centered on the interpretation of texts, it became increasingly important for compositionists to identify texts of their own.

But what does it mean in canon-shattered 1991 to claim a domain of texts under the flag of literariness? In his introduction to *Literary Nonfiction*, Chris Anderson observes that "the word *literary* masks all kinds of ideological concerns, all kinds of values, and is finally more a way of looking at a text, a way of reading ... than an inherent property of texts" (ix). Anderson is right, of course, but there are important consequences that he doesn't pursue. (I make the point not to fault Anderson's achievement in this introduction and the book it precedes but to outline the intricate questions he has staged.) If "literary" is finally a way of reading, why is that way of reading "invited by" or, more properly, "deemed appropriate for" a certain class of texts? Anderson characterizes the various approaches in *Literary Nonfiction* as "aesthetic, linguistic, rhetorical, formalist, psychoanalytical, poststructuralist, feminist, and deconstructionist" (x). Yet, these ways of reading can be performed on any text, the ability to do so depending not on the text itself but on the resourcefulness and inclination of the reader.

Apologists for literary nonfiction must confront the fact that, despite the plurality of reading strategies available, the name "literary nonfiction" signifies those texts apparently most susceptible to certain interpretive practices. In other words, before any of those ways of reading—which can all be used with any text—can be performed with a piece of literary nonfiction *as* literary nonfiction, that piece must first be labeled as an appropriate object of study. We should acknowledge that the way into this hermeneutic cyclotron is narrowly circumscribed. The assay of a nonfictional work's literariness is against an aesthetic Mohs scale, with lyric poetry at diamond and weather reports at talc. In terms of the personal essay, older works in the canon consist, of course, of received texts that have demonstrated their mettle in withstanding analysis: the works of Hazlitt, Lamb, Stevenson, Woolf, Orwell, and so on. Newly canonized essays (by Dillard, Didion, Hoaglund, Selzer, Thomas, Ehrlich, and so on) have, above all, "organic form," then surprising combinations of language, new juxtapositions of experience and readings and ideas, a vision and voice that are "personal"—but personal in just the appropriate ways. To belabor the point: a work does not become "literary nonfiction" because it supports, say, a psychoanalytical or any other kind of reading. Essays become literature as readers attribute to and recognize in them a certain aesthetic and way of constructing individual subjectivity—that is, a particular voice and stance toward the world. The terms "literary" and "aesthetic," as they have been used in relation to "literary nonfiction," are synonymous.

The politics of canon formation is old news these days, but we in composition studies must understand that its issues pertain to us, too. It is particularly important that when we adopt stances no longer valorized for other genres we at least do so self-consciously. For example, it is no longer professionally sufficient to publish purely New Critical readings of short stories, novels, and poems. But the declaration of literary nonfiction subtly implies that, since we're at an early stage in criticism of these genres, it is possible, even necessary, to trace imagery and symbolism and argue for the aesthetic integrity and autonomy of the work. To establish the literariness of literary nonfiction, the implication continues, we must be able to demonstrate that these works can sustain aesthetic readings. Such reasoning is reflected in comparisons of the essay's celebrated "organic form" to that of the lyric poem. George Dillon aptly observes, "We will discover a great deal of good writing when we can find ways of esteeming it without estheticizing it" (209). The motivation for embracing these new ways extends beyond political or theoretical correctness to pedagogy. For writing teachers, the reading of essays as an act of cracking aesthetic codes may hearken uncomfortably to pre-process, pre-reader-response, pre-social construction, prose model days, a concern John Clifford has underscored. One way to address it is to discard the "literary" measure of the worth of nonfiction to focus instead on more broadly rhetorical, cognitive, and political aspects. And, in fact, these dimensions have partially accounted for the rise of interest in the essay.

Motivations Ideological and Power-Full

The third motivation for interest in the personal essay, an ideological one, is most clearly seen in the historical context in which it takes place, for the phenomenon recapitulates issues contested in nineteenth and early twentieth-century English departments. The fall of rhetoric and the rise of literature, first at Harvard, then throughout American universities in the 1880s and 1890s, is a story familiarly told by Berlin and many others. What has not been fully explored is the role that literary nonfiction played in literature's rise. At the same time that proponents of Hugh Blair's belletristic rhetoric were advocating the study of fine writing, English departments were being formed around the study of texts. The two strands, both emphasizing the analysis of completed works over the production of new ones, combined with Romantic views of the author, were synergistic in the rise of literature. Of course, it cannot be argued that belletrism caused the downfall of rhetoric and composition in nineteenth-century American colleges any more than it can be argued that personal essays may undermine rhetoric in composition studies today. And, of course, it's beyond the space of this essay to argue whether such a demise is good or bad. However, others have hinted at this prospect. James Slevin, for example, warns strongly against the "literary appropriation of rhetoric" when he complains, somewhat unfairly, that Eagleton focuses on rhetoric in interpretation of texts rather than in the development of student writers (6-10). To the extent that emphasis on the interpretation of nonfiction elides emphasis on its production, such fears may be justifiable.

The rise of the personal essay, then, might be seen as but the fuller arrival of efforts begun a century ago. But why now? The question is best answered, I think, as a backlash against postmodern theory, for the "personal essay" seems to offer a defensive position against threats to the autonomy of individual writers. For example, Donald Stewart has expressed many concerns about social constructionism. He scorns its failure to account for individual genius and its reinforcement of academic discourse conventions that are obscurantist "rubbish" (67, 70). He argues for self-assertive individual prose that resists the potential for "totalitarian societies in which the individual is completely subjected to the will of the group" (71, 74). The *personal* essay, with its insistent declaration that "I am writing from my personal experience a piece that none other could write in just this way," becomes a privileged genre in the resistance.

In slightly different terms, this is the position that Kurt Spellmeyer takes when he warns that by reifying discourse communities we disempower students. Spellmeyer embraces the essay as a "common ground" on which students can meet and come to terms with the academy and its ideas. His argument is a strong one, and I will consider it closely. But first I should like to point out some apparently paradoxical claims made for the essay. We should detect a rich discordance in, for example, Pat Hoy's being able to celebrate the personal essay as holding values espoused by Matthew Arnold and Cardinal Newman (288, 291) at the very same time that Jean-François Lyotard declares "the essay is postmodern" (81).

The weak argument for the personal essay as defense against social constructivism—embraced most directly in articles by Ross Winterowd, Lynn Bloom, and William Zeiger—begins by accepting the genre as personal thought shaped organically. It celebrates the view articulated by Samuel Johnson and perpetuated throughout the history of the genre that personal essays are relatively "formless" and thereby "pure," uncompromised and, most significantly, unconventionalized. As literature, the personal essay triumphantly stands beyond the tyranny of form.

In an analytic gesture common at least since Hugh Walker published *The English Essay and Essayists* in 1915, Ross Winterowd distinguishes in *JAC* between "formal" and "informal essays." Students have been allowed too long only to write the former, Winterowd argues, to the detriment of new ideas and original thinking. Working with the same opposition, Zeiger claims that the conventional academic essay artificially limits the thoughts and feelings that students may express (210). In contrast, according to Zeiger, the personal essay is unfettered and, most symptomatically, "natural." His argument is worth summarizing in some detail. The essay, he claims, is shaped both by "organic form" (that is, the coherence of its imagery) and by "abstract form." "Abstract form," he explains, has its source "outside the essay. It represents a pattern not of art but of life" (210). What is more, the form of the personal essay "generally derives from 'natural' schemata dwelling within the mind and projected outward," and these schemata arise from "physical sensation" (211). Finally, according to Zeiger, persuasion depends on the reader's ability to recognize already-familiar patterns that are "invested with a natural authority" (213). Here is a foundationalist argument straight from eighteenth-century faculty psychology and pre-Saussurian linguistics.

In imagining the essayist as free and the essay as natural, these writers imagine a type of writing that does not—in fact, cannot—exist. To say of the essay that "there are no rules, no constraints except one: the work simply has to be true" is to imagine these texts as purely independent of other texts (Bloom 89). It is paradoxical simultaneously to hold this position and yet to advocate collecting those unconstrained writings under a generic term, "literary nonfiction" or "personal essay." Annie Dillard's pronouncement that for the essay "No subject matter is forbidden, no structure is proscribed" is an odd assertion when Dillard herself relies so heavily on the work of previous essayists (qtd. in Bloom 92). For example, compare her "Death of a Moth" with Virginia Woolf's "The Death of the Moth," or her "Total Eclipse" with Woolf's "The Sun and the Fish." My point is this: *Even "informal" essays are historically situated and generically contextualized.* Any single "informal essay" exists in the genre "informal essay." Susan Miller makes this point concisely in a response to Spellmeyer: "Written language... is read only after it becomes embedded in local or wider discourse communities that give it significance beyond its physical status as graphic marks" (332). To invite students to "explore the world" or "create themselves" through personal essays is to have them focus a certain type of lens on certain types of experience to create a certain type of self. This is not to claim that the range of possibilities for the genre—or even for personal agency—are narrowly bounded and fixed. But the genre does cast a trajectory for those who would write in it.

While we should encourage students to explore their own experience, we should not mistake the individual as the *focus* of exploration for individualism in the *form* of exploration. To their credit, Winterowd and Zeiger have discussed tropes and formal patterns characteristic of essays. While I certainly don't dream the narratological dream of a grammar of the genre, continued attention to essay conventions will temper beliefs in the essay as free discourse. What we need further (and it sounds unbearably trendy) is a cultural critique of the genre. What draws us to the personal essay? Which voices do we prize or reject? What does the history of the genre mean for those writing and reading it?

Essays and Empowerment

Understanding that the personal essay is "open" only in particular ways substantially qualifies the claim that writing essays empowers students. Students *are* empowered by essaying. But we should be clear about how and to what extent.

To begin this analysis, consider the contention that "students should have the right *not* to be conclusive" (as they must be in formal essays) "but rather to *explore* themselves and their world in informal essays" (Winterowd, "Essay" 146). There are two sources of power implied here, one inherent in the genre but one dependent on the teacher's stance. There is, first, the epistemic power of exploration and new combination, which like metaphor, creates by gathering and juxtaposing experiences, ideas, and texts, however imperfectly, that the student has not combined before. For the products of this exploration to be authorized, however, they must be accepted by another as sufficient. This acceptance is more than a matter of the author's desiring it. It is governed by the reader's perception of "fit" between the essay and the essay tradition, unless that reader is willing to suspend all judgment and accept the text, whatever it is.

Here I am at a crucial point, for we need to recognize two levels of acceptance, and between them turns the trickiest problem of the power of literary nonfiction.

At one level, teachers may simply grant the student's right to explore, viewing the products of that exploration with full tolerance, as they normally might journals or first drafts. At this level, "personal essay" becomes less form than mode, collapsing into something like Britton's expressive discourse, writing whose aim is the author's homesteading for her or himself a plot of language. Acceptance at this level consists of teachers evaluating not the quality of the performance but its existence. Anything goes so long as it goes (who, after all, can judge even "effort" without comparing the performance to existing texts?), and the student is empowered with the right to speak. But speaking and having one's words accepted as well-formed or significant are two very different things—the difference, in fact, between Britton's expressive and poetic discourse. There are quite different kinds of power held, then, by two students who *publicly* receive equally positive responses for having essayed, but one of whose texts the teacher *privately* regards as "clichéd, unoriginal, and boring," the other's as "insightful, well-written, and stimulating."

This brings me to the second level of acceptance and power, the level at which questions of genre and "literariness" impinge. As soon as teachers raise the issue of quality, of what even constitutes a personal essay, they create the need for a comparative standard. The measure of "quality" entails a holding of "this against that." To rally around essays as literary objects is to assert that standards of measure in composition courses should include works whose aims are aesthetic and experiential, not only those whose aims are rational and transactional. I wholly embrace this effort.

But consider carefully wherein power lies. An essay is successfully literary only if the larger category, literature, exists. Hermeneutics notwithstanding, works cannot assert their own literariness except in relation to other works. Power lies not in the author's freedom but in her or his producing a text recognizable as an appropriate move in the language game of essaying.

Lest I be criticized for too-narrowly using "the literary status of the essay" to argue that power at the second level is gained only through favorable comparisons of student texts to "literature," I assert that my claim is a more general one. For example, the quality of a student's "exploratory text" is determined by comparisons of it to previously-written "exploratory texts." The text in question must bear at least some family resemblance, to use Wittgenstein's concept, to other texts to which it is compared. When Spellmeyer argues that we should have students "bring to bear" extra-textual knowledge on texts (something I quite agree with), this bearing does not take place in a vacuum. Spellmeyer himself notes that we must provide students with strategies for using this knowledge. Mastering the genre of personal essay, its topoi and rhythms and stances, involves no more or less the practice of conventions than learning to write lab reports.

Let me elaborate and then qualify my citing of "conventions," for I, too, fear the new foundational ways in which discursive formations have been invoked to preserve the status quo. Spellmeyer discusses a student who writes successfully about an essay by Sartre. He cites the student's beginning her text with a story of a diseased pet rat as a sign of her ability to hold Sartre "in abeyance . . . in order to consider the text of her experience in a new light. . . . Retrospectively she realizes that her own behavior could be explained in existential terms" ("Common" 274). Such an analysis misstates what this student writer has achieved. She has crafted a text whose arrangement suggests that she analyzed her experience retrospectively and "naturally" out of her reading of Sartre. But the assignment, after all, was to read and respond to Sartre's essay, *not* to write about experience and see where this leads. I say this neither to diminish the student's achievement nor to question Spellmeyer's preference for this piece over the other he quotes. Instead, I want to correct his interpretation of what the "Dying Rat" author has done. She has employed a strategy of personal essays—namely, she has delayed contextualizing the significance of a personal experience. As teachers we prize the move she has made because it matches our expectations of the essay tradition in which such moves are made.

Now for the qualification. Drawing on Gadamer's theory of method, Spellmeyer rejects a view of conventions as "static schemata," a view which "obscures both the historical character of knowledge and its openness to the present" ("Kurt" 335). In doing so, he is right to assert the futility of pinning down discourse with unchanging rules. He is even right to locate in historicity the possibility for students to produce "new" texts. But the theoretical shift from "conventions" to "historicity," however correct, does not neatly transform the situation in which readers read texts, especially when they are required to make judgments. Spellmeyer is right to speculate that

> if we permitted our students, not only freshman writers but undergraduates at all levels, to join in our ongoing conversations—to talk with our texts in their own language, without forcing themselves to speak as we speak, or to think as we think—the voices that have given us our words would gradually infuse their speech as well. ("Kurt" 336)

There are pragmatic limitations to this pedagogy of immersion; we teach in sixteen-week terms or, at most, four-year spans of writing across the curriculum. But these concern me less than the implications of the essay *as* essay for achieving the writing ends of "open" student participation in our discourse. By invoking any genre, any corpus of prototypical texts—regardless of the merits of that genre over any other, including the formal academic essay—one necessarily and, in this case, paradoxically draws the writing borders in which students might most easily dwell. *Is* the essay the genre most like the language students bring to the course? No, at least not the "essay as literature," not the essay of Lewis Thomas or Annie Dillard or E.B. White. The essay does not become "natural discourse" simply by asserting it as such.

Toward Reflective Stewardship
To the writing of literary nonfiction is attributed a third power, that of motivation. Before our students we dangle like a fat dew worm the prospect of becoming E.B. White, trying to hook them into the larger boat of discourse. Lynn Bloom makes this argument most directly. The extent to which she is right«and my own experience suggests that she is«is largely a reflection of how the ideologies of literary nonfiction mirror the culture in which it is taught and read. Literary nonfiction is motivating because it sounds chords of the romance of writing, of the value of aesthetic sensibility, of the rugged individual, of a Frederick Jackson Turner style open frontier of discourse. There is a quandary for teachers here. By presenting these ideologies as the case for all writing (which I can imagine no one seriously advocating), they would risk reinforcing in students a questionably romantic view of writing. But the alternative, relegating these texts to a special class of leisured writing, marginalizes the genre.

What, then, to do with "the literary status of the essay," a concept so ripe for deconstruction? I'm tempted to advocate a double stance, one as scholars and one as teachers. It is not asking much to realize how messy our theoretical house is. As scholars we cannot claim the literariness of some nonfiction and simultaneously ignore literary theory at large, dismissing questions of agency, subjectivity, intertextuality, and ideology. We cannot deride current theory and act as if literary nonfiction behaves differently. But to what extent should we bring this theory into the classroom? Is there some value in critiquing, in our offices and journals, the concept of literary nonfiction at the same time we preserve, in our classrooms and assignments, the enabling fictions of "personal experience" and "individual voice" and "natural form" and "freedom from conventions"? As a way of mediating these, Schilb turns to Gerald Graff's solution of "teaching the controversy." But such a solution, while perhaps in the best rhetorical tradition, is unsatisfying in the way that meta-pedagogies tend finally to be.

In a 1988 essay Chris Anderson concedes the postmodern position that stable meaning is impossible. In light of that, Anderson argues that

> the game that the essay wants us to play is just as valid as any other. It doesn't necessarily claim that the ontological questions aren't there. It simply says, for now they don't apply. For now join with me in assuming certain things and we can get a good deal of work done.
> ("Hearsay" 307)

I've considered his point a good deal recently and think Anderson is right to acknowledge the need to "get on with things," thereby escaping both paralysis and paralogy, acknowledging the need for purposeful action. And yet I do not comfortably embrace his Carlylean consolation that getting "a good deal of work done" is sufficient, especially when a consequence might be construed as the end of debate on the essay's status. We should continue to have students write "personal essays," but not because the genre is natural, organic, free, or inherently more empowering than other genres. We should recognize that as we colonize the genre, we seek to convert our students, too, as all teaching must inevitably. But we mustn't narrowly convert them to a literary aesthetic that focuses on the essay as object and casts its authors as unfettered individual voices. The power we hold out to students when we encourage them to essay is the power to be like other essayists, to write like authors their teachers read in serious leisure. If we read critically and self-critically, that does not seem a bad prospect.

Works Cited

Anderson, Chris, ed. *Literary Nonfiction: Theory, Criticism, Pedagogy*. Carbondale: Southern Illinois UP, 1989.

——. "Hearsay Evidence and Second-Class Citizenship." *College English* 50 (1988): 300-08.

Baldwin, Charles Sears. *College Manual of Rhetoric*. London: Longmans, Green, 1902.

Berlin, James A. *Rhetoric and Reality: Writing Instruction in American Colleges, 1900-1985*. Carbondale: Southern Illinois UP, 1987.

Bloom, Lynn, Z. "Why Don't We Write What We Teach? And Publish It?" *Journal of Advanced Composition* 10 (1990): 87-100.

Britton, James. "Spectator Role and the Beginnings of Writing." *Prospect and Retrospect: Selected Essays of James Britton*. Ed. Gordon M. Pradl. Upper Montclair: Boynton, 1982. 46-67.

Butrym, Alexander, ed. *Essays on the Essay*. Athens: U of Georgia P, 1989.

Clifford, John. "The Reader's Text: Responding to Loren Eiseley's '"The Running Man.'" Anderson 247-61.

Dillon, George L. "Fiction in Persuasion: Personal Experience as Evidence and as Art." Anderson 197-210.

Eagleton, Terry. *Literary Theory*. Minneapolis: U of Minnesota P, 1983.

Good, Graham. *The Observing Self: Rediscovering the Essay*. London: Routledge, 1988.

Hoy, Pat. "Students and Teachers Under the Influence: Image and Idea in the Essay." Anderson 287-300.

Lyotard, Jean-François. *The Postmodern Condition: A Report on Knowledge*. Trans. Geoff Bennington and Brian Massumi. Minneapolis: U of Minnesota P, 1984.

Miller, Susan. "Comment on 'A Common Ground: The Essay in Academe.'" *College English* 52 (1990): 330-34.

Newman, Samuel P. *A Practical System of Rhetoric*. 7th ed. Andover, MA: Gould, 1839.

Rygiel, Dennis. "On the Neglect of Twentieth-Century Nonfiction: A Writing Teacher's View." *College English* 47 (1984): 392-400.

Schilb, John. "Deconstructing Didion: Poststructuralist Rhetorical Theory in the Composition Class." Anderson 262-86.

Slevin, James. "Genre Theory, Academic Discourse, and Writing within Disciplines." *Audits of Meaning: A Festschrift in Honor of Anne E. Berthoff*. Ed. Louise Z. Smith. Portsmouth: Boynton, 1988. 3-16.

Spellmeyer, Kurt. "A Common Ground: The Essay in the Academy." *College English* 51 (1989): 262-76.

——. "Kurt Spellmeyer Responds." *College English* 52 (1990): 334-38.

Stewart, Donald C. "Collaborative Learning and Composition: Boon or Bane?" *Rhetoric Review* 7 (1988): 58-83.

Weber, Ronald. *The Literature of Fact: Literary Nonfiction in American Writing*. Athens: Ohio UP, 1980.

Wolfe, Thomas. "The New Journalism." *The New Journalism*. Ed. Thomas Wolfe and E.W. Johnson. New York: Harper, 1973. 3-52.

Winterowd, W. Ross. "Rediscovering the Essay." *Journal of Advanced Composition* 8 (1988): 146-57.

——. *The Rhetoric of the "Other" Literature*. Carbondale: Southern Illinois UP, 1990.

Wittgenstein, Ludwig. *Philosophical Investigations*. 3rd ed. Trans. G.E.M. Anscombe. New York: Macmillan, 1958.

Zeiger, William. "The Circular Journey and the Natural Authority of Form." *Rhetoric Review* 8 (1990): 208-19.

Why Don't We Write What We Teach? And Publish It?

LYNN Z. BLOOM

We teachers of writing should write literary nonfiction, assuming that that is what we teach, and we should publish what we write. That's the thesis of this article. That not enough of us do this is the subtext. Writing regularly should be as much a part of the teacher's activity as meeting class, and as unremarkable. If that were actually the case, I wouldn't need to write this article. Although what I advocate is appropriate for any teachers of writing, freshman English included, it is particularly important that teachers of advanced composition write and publish literary nonfiction. Teachers of advanced courses are more likely than freshman English instructors to be experienced full-time faculty members, and what we do should provide an exemplary model—really, a variety of models—for novice and junior colleagues. If we don't practice what we preach and teach what we practice, what credibility, what authority can we claim?

That creative writing teachers write poetry, plays, fiction, and short stories is a given, as it should be. In most places they're expected to publish, especially if they're teaching advanced students. So why not expect the same of teachers of parallel courses in nonfiction? Aren't the experienced academics who teach advanced composition already publishing? Many are, of course—most likely, academic articles in professional journals. Well and good if, for instance, the professor teaching a course in science writing is publishing in scientific journals. But advanced composition is not necessarily a course in academic writing. Indeed, advanced composition is like love: everybody knows what they mean by the term, few can define it to anyone else's satisfaction, and each practitioner has his or her own way of doing it. Recent surveys by Bernice Dicks and Priscilla Tate, for instance, indicate an extraordinarily wide range of writing in advanced composition courses, from the modes of discourse that populate freshman composition; to belletristic nonfiction; to fiction, poetry, and drama; to business, technical, legal, or medical writing in specialized courses on those subjects.

Diverse though they are, these courses nevertheless expect student writers to write and revise a great deal, to be able to write with proficiency in the modes of their discipline, and to become conscious stylists who regard style as integral to the work. In fact, the most commonly used textbooks in advanced composition courses, whose texts range from Homer's *Odyssey* (in translation) to Lewis Thomas's *The Lives of a Cell*, are books on style, Strunk and White's *Elements of Style* and Zinsser's *On Writing Well* being the most commonly used.

And it is on belletristic nonfiction writing in which an author expresses a distinctive and individual style that I wish to focus the rest of this essay. We teach a lot of these essays in freshman English—essays by Bacon, Swift, Orwell, Woolf, Baldwin, Didion, E.B. White, McPhee, and a host of contemporary others. We also teach a lot of these essays (or longer books by the same writers) in advanced composition when it is not focused on specialized writing in a single discipline. But although we write articles in academic prose, too few of us write essays in other modes, other language. Too few of us write one or another forms of belletristic nonfiction in a persona, an individual and recognizable style (or combination of styles) that is our own. Too few of us write in ways that engage not only the mind but the heart, that not only teach but delight. Yet if more of us wrote and published belletristic essays, we could enliven and enhance the genre, our teaching, and our profession. And we'd have more fun.

On Writing Essays

In a country where an aspiring intellectual can still grow up wanting to be a novelist or, rarer still, a poet, nobody wants to be an essayist. Why, indeed, should anyone aspire to write in "this slithery form," as Elizabeth Hardwick describes it, "wearisomely vague and as chancy as trying to catch a fish in the open hand" (xv)—especially when academic life, where many frustrated writers end up, predicates promotion, tenure, and status on the publication of academic articles? Our academic journals, with rare exceptions, have no space, make no room, for belletristic nonfiction writing.[1] We put these constraints on ourselves; we have met the editors and they are us.

In his brilliant *Textual Power*, Robert Scholes points out that we English professors are terrible snobs. We divide the field into two categories, literature (good, important) and non-literature (trivial, beneath our notice). We can't produce real literature; only geniuses, working stiffs outside the academy, can do that, we claim. But, says Scholes, to link our academic activities to this "real" writing, we "privilege consumption over production." We call "the proper consumption of literature 'interpretation,' and the teaching of this skill, like the displaying of it in academic papers, articles, and books, is our greatest glory." We can teach students to read this writing, this utilitarian prose which Scholes calls "non-literature." And we teach students themselves to write "unreal versions" of it, which we call "composition." This "pseudo non-literature," produced in an "appalling volume," is at the bottom of the academic totem pole (or scrap heap). And why not? It isn't valued by those who write it, by those who teach it, or by those who employ those who teach it (5-6).[2]

Another way to improve the status of the currently lowly belletristic essay is to try to write it ourselves—though maybe we should wait until we're safely tenured and can afford to take the risk.[3] Literary nonfiction—the belletristic essay is essentially a short version of modes that could be book-length—is harder to write than it looks, because as with any other serious art form, there are no rules, no constraints except one: the work simply has to be true. That's the essential difference between literary nonfiction and fiction. As Annie Dillard explains,

> The essay can do everything a poem can do, and everything a short story can do—everything but fake it. The elements in any nonfiction should be true not only artistically, the connections must hold at base and must be veracious, for that is the convention and the covenant between the nonfiction writer and his reader. Veracity isn't much of a drawback to the writer; there's a lot of truth out there to work with. And veracity isn't much of a drawback to the reader. The real world arguably exerts a greater fascination on people than any fictional one. . . . The essayist does what we do with our lives; the essayist thinks about actual things. He can make sense of them analytically or artistically.
> ("Introduction" xvii)

Yet, literary nonfiction can use many of the same techniques that fiction does. It can present characters, flat or round, in action, in dialogue (even interior monologue), in context, and in costume. It can play with time, with language, with points of view and narrative persona. Literary nonfiction can take many forms, as illustrated by the variety in *Best American Essays*, and in much *New Yorker* nonfiction: memoir and partial autobiography; character sketch; travel narrative; natural, cultural, or social history or criticism; interpretation of a scientific, economic, or political phenomenon for non-specialists; interpretive reviews that comment at length on the work, the genre, or the performance. Although we know one when we see one, a belletristic essay is hard to define. It has no fixed length[4] and no predictable shape, and most essays, as Elizabeth Hardwick points out, "incline to a condition of unexpressed hyphenation: the critical essay, the autobiographical essay, the travel essay, the political—and so on and so on" (xiii). That's why collections of essays are hard to find in bookstores, which seldom have sections devoted to "Essays," but subdivide this amorphous genre into Travel, Biography—which invariably includes Autobiography, Social Commentary, and so on and so on.

William Gass, in a characteristically sparkling essay on Emerson as "an essayist destined from the cradle," points out important differences between the essay and "that awful object, the article." The essayist is "interested solely in the essay's special *art*," and is unconcerned with "scientific or philosophical rigor." The essay "is unhurried"; it "browses among books; it enjoys an idea like a fine wine; it thumbs through things." The essayist is more interested in the process of thinking about a subject than in having the last word, "exposing this aspect and then that; proposing possibilities, reciting opinions" (25). "The essay," says Hardwick summing up Gass, "is a great meadow of style and personal manner," illuminated by an "individual intelligence and sparkle. We consent to watch a mind at work, without agreement often, but only for pleasure" (xv).

In contrast, says Gass, the article "represents itself as the latest cleverness, a novel consequence of thought, skill, labor, and free enterprise; but never as an activity—the process, the working, the wondering." I quote his definition in full, a single sentence that could appear only in an essay, where the author is having fun with the language, but not in an article, for reasons that Gass makes apparent:

> As an article, it should be striking of course, original of course, important naturally, yet without possessing either grace or charm or elegance, since these qualities will interfere with the impression of seriousness which it wishes to maintain; rather its polish is like that of the scrubbed step; but it must appear complete and straightforward and footnoted and useful and certain and is very likely a veritable Michelin of misdirection; for the article pretends that everything is clear, that its argument is unassailable, that there are no soggy patches, no illicit inferences, no illegitimate connections; it furnishes seals of approval and underwriters' guarantees; its manners are starched, stuffy, it would wear a dress suit to a barbecue, silk pajamas to the shower; it knows, with respect to every subject and point of view it is ever likely to entertain, what words to use, what form to follow, what authorities to respect; it is the careful product of a professional, and therefore it is written as only writing can be written, even if, at various times, versions have been given a dry dull voice at a conference, because, spoken aloud, it still sounds like writing written down, writing born for its immediate burial in a Journal. (26-27)[5]

In case you missed the tone of that sentence, Gass drives home his point: "Articles are to be worn; they make up one's dossier the way uniforms make up a wardrobe, and it is not known—nor is it clear about uniforms either—whether the article has ever contained anything of lasting value" (26). Of course, Gass is being personal, provocative, deliberately outrageous. That's just the point; he's writing an essay, not an article.[6]

What's in It for Teachers?

Okay, so Gass has a gas in writing belletristic essays, and Emerson's prose was his power (Gass 34); what's in it for *us* as teachers? A lot. Sam Johnson said of biography, "Nobody can write the life of a man, but those who have eat and drunk and lived in social intercourse with him." Approaching a work in any literary genre from the outside, as a reader or critic, is very different from living in literary intercourse—Johnson's well-chosen word of intimacy—with it as a writer. We don't really understand an essay, or any other form of literature, until we've tried to write it.

The most important thing we learn about belletristic writing from doing it is to think like a writer, an essayist in Gass's sense, rather than as a critic, an article writer. If we think like writers, we will teach like writers rather than as critics.[7] Compare, for instance, how an autobiographer, Annie Dillard, explains what happens during the process of writing an autobiography, with what a critic, Mary Jane Dickerson, says about the same process. In "To

Fashion a Text," Dillard explains:

> My advice to memoir writers is to embark upon a memoir for the same reason that you
> would embark on any other book: to fashion a text. Don't hope in a memoir to preserve
> your memories. If you prize your memories as they are, by all means
> avoid—eschew—writing a memoir. Because it is a certain way to lose them. You can't
> put together a memoir without cannibalizing your own life for parts. The work battens
> on your memories. And it replaces them. . . . After you're written, you can no longer
> remember anything but the writing. (70-71)

In a subsection of "On Writing Autobiography" titled "Constructing Self Through the Dialogic Imagination," Dickerson says,

> Autobiography's origin as narrative that arises from a dialogue with the self and about
> the self in relation to others and a particular cultural landscape distinguishes autobiog-
> raphy and makes it especially appropriate for teaching advanced writing students about
> the subtle features inherent in the complex act of writing as social discourse. It is a
> dialogic system of speaking, writing, and reading in which the student writer addresses
> the self, others, texts, signs, and what goes on in the writer's culture. The element of
> performance pervades texts as writers voice themselves into being by speaking and
> behaving from varied perspectives. (137-38)

Although Dickerson is telling teachers of advanced composition what autobiographers do when they write autobiography, I have never in my reading of some three-thousand autobiographies in the past decade seen an autobiographer explain the process in either the critical jargon or the concepts that Dickerson uses. Autobiographers usually claim that they're telling the story of their lives, leaving out some things—Russell Baker says 99.5 percent—and shaping what remains artistically.[8] They talk about what they do in the natural language that Dillard and Baker use, the same language in which they write their narratives. This is the very language that teachers who have tried writing autobiography would use to explain the process to their students.[9] Teachers who write in the modes they're teaching become natural allies with their students writing in the same modes, rather than, as Scholes says in *Textual Power*, acting as "priests and priestesses in the service of secular scripture" and expecting students to worship in critical jargon at the altar of the "verbal icon" (12).

Among the belletristic writer's major concerns are form and style (those staples of advanced composition) and the endless possibilities of each in conveying the exact angle of vision, the precise nuance of meaning. Because belletristic writing is a more fluid medium than academic article writing, it is open to continuous experimentation with form. As Dillard says in "To Fashion a Text," "No subject matter is forbidden, no structure is proscribed. You get to make up your own form every time" (74).

So you experiment. Here's how a person, myself in this instance, might think about two writings—one academic, the other belletristic—on the same topic: the importance of friendship. In an academic article, I'd buttress an explicit thesis about the subject in general with references ranging, probably in chronological order, from Plato to Elizabeth Barrett Browning to George Bernard Shaw to Virginia Woolf, duly annotated. In pursuit of irrefutable logic, adequate development, credibility, balance, and fairness, I'd consult other published scholarly sources, too, from philosophy, psychology, sociology, women's studies. My own views, as exposition and argument, would emerge in juxtaposition with those of my sources, and I'd come to an explicit conclusion. Because the overall form of an academic article is fairly circumscribed—its shape accommodating norms of the discipline and even of specific journals—the experimentation would probably be on a micro rather than macro level. I would move, expand and delete paragraphs, sentences, and phrases for variety, emphasis, and elegance, but I would not alter the larger structure unless it were illogical or couldn't be supported.

I can see many more possibilities of form in a belletristic essay on friendship, which in fact I'm currently trying to write. My aim is to present an extended definition of friendship, illustrating general principles through specific details. The essay could contain a collage of vignettes, each illustrating a different aspect of a significant friendship I've had, long term and short, with women and men, with my husband and others, with children and grandparents. (Parents are tougher.) It could contain excerpts from personal letters, snatches of conversation (the remembered essence, not word-for-word), definitions formal and operational (perhaps from some of the same sources that I'd use in an academic article), brief analyses of others' friendships, real and literary, to juxtapose with my own, epigrams, fragments of biography, autobiography. I'll probably use all of the above and more that I haven't thought of yet, with the vignettes embedded in a matrix of the other materials, like plums in a pudding. I would be less concerned with logic than with the essential truth. A chronological organization of material wouldn't make much sense; maybe a psychological pattern would work best, from the least intense experience to the most profound. Or perhaps a framework that led from the more generally applicable to the most individual. Or some other way.[10] As E.M. Forster says, "How do I know what I think until I see what I say?"

What about style? Every writer, except a committee or a corporate author, has an identifiable style, even an "opaque" style celebrating "the joys of obfuscation," in Richard Lanham's term. I'd write any academic article in a style compatible with the one I'm using here, though less breezy for a very stuffy editorial board.[11] But that's because, unlike my professorial peers, I learned my literary style not from M. Derrida but from Dr. Spock, the Strunk and White of baby book authors.[12] I'd try for a persona that appears knowledgeable, intellectually sophisticated, honest, positive, witty, and likeable—and hope that it also seemed credible. To the extent that I could get away with conversational language, I'd use it, varying the length and structure of sentences and paragraphs. I'd write in the first person, where it sounded good. I'd use contractions, sometimes. Even fragments. I'd break the rules, as Orwell advises, "sooner than say anything outright barbarous." Unlike far too many academic writers and journal editors, I'd eschew critical jargon, especially trendy language, which I do not wish to valorize, whatever the pretext, in texts, subtexts, or intertexts. I am egotistical enough to want the readers of all my writing to wish they'd thought of saying it my way, and I'd use a similar style, perhaps a tad more casual, in a belletristic essay. There, given the subject of friendship and my first-person point of view, I'd worry about sentimentality. As Dillard says in defense of nonfiction prose,

> Like poetry, [it] can tolerate all sorts of figurative language, as well as alliteration and even rhyme. The range of rhythms in prose is larger and grander than it is in poetry, and it can handle discursive ideas and plain information as well as character and story. It can do everything. I feel as though I had switched from a single reed instrument [writing poetry] to a full orchestra. ("Fashion" 74-75)

Most of all, I'd listen to the sounds and the rhythm. If the writing didn't move, didn't read well, I'd do it over. And over again. (You are reading the twelfth draft.)

Finally, I'd have my husband, who is my best critic as well as best friend, read and critique it. Then a trusted colleague, or for a belletristic essay, a friend who is an avid and thoughtful reader. I'd revise the essay, let it sit quietly for awhile to ripen like a good camembert, then revise it again (would *peach* work better than *camembert*? *fine wine*? certainly not *banana*) and prepare to send it out for publication. But where? The *New Yorker*? John McPhee said he submitted everything he wrote to the *New Yorker* for over a dozen years before they finally accepted something. I know several superb writers who have been submitting their work in vain to the *New Yorker* for longer than that, and their lack of success scares me. Where else? *Harper's* or *The Atlantic*? Same story. Little magazines? Maybe. There appear to be enough to go around.

But I'd like to talk to my fellow teachers. I'd like to be able to pick up the *Journal of Advanced Composition* or *College Composition and Communication* or *Rhetoric Review* and find in them belletristic essays of the kind that we talk about in class and use as exemplary models. Would not the publication of literary nonfiction in the very journals devoted to academic articles on the same subject validate this kind of writing as no other sort of acknowledgment could do?[13] To exclude such writing is again to reinforce the inverted values Scholes takes to task in *Textual Power*, values that reinforce consumption at the expense of production.

Are the editors and review boards of composition journals competent to judge literary nonfiction? They'd better be. Such judgments are as sure as sin and error to teachers of composition (some of whom are journal editors), who make them all the time, in class and out, as they teach the published works of belletristic writers and respond to student essays. But wouldn't the publication of belletristic essays in our professional composition journals take up valuable space that should better be devoted to pedagogical theory and research? That's a matter of editorial judgment and policy. Every journal represents a competition for premium space. But it is equally true that journal editors are continually searching for high-quality submissions. It would be worth the risk for composition journal editors to solicit or encourage belletristic essays and see what they get, from teachers and their students. We ought to be speaking to each other through the witness of our writing.

The fact of publication not only validates the work, but professionalizes the writer as an author. Publishing authors learn what types of material editors of different publications are looking for, how the process of editing and revising for publication works and how rigorous it must be, and—eventually—when to accommodate an editor's suggestions and when to insist that their way is best. Through dealing with these concerns, over and over and over again, the publishing writer develops that self-critical facility so essential in enabling a novice, student or any writer, to move from amateur to professional status. Teachers who revise and submit their own work for publication have earned the right to expect their students to do the same.

What's in It for Students?

Isn't it our job, our mandate, as Bizzell (1982, but see also 1988), Bartholomae, and others have argued, to induct our students into the academy by teaching them to write academic papers in academic discourse? Isn't that why they have to take freshman English? And even upper level writing courses? If they can't write acceptable papers in their courses in other disciplines, won't it be our fault if we haven't taught them how to do it?

Yes and no. There is general agreement that we teach composition at any level to help students think, read, and write critically and well. We have an obligation, therefore, to fulfill this agreement, and if we don't we're at least partly responsible for the consequences. But there is considerable variation in what those terms mean to the authors of the plethora of existing composition textbooks, and those that sprout like daisies on the publishers' lists of newcomers every spring, attesting anew to the fact that there is no single right way to teach writing.

W. Ross Winterowd, who is "Rediscovering the Essay," says that "students should have the right *not* to be conclusive—as they must in formal essays—but rather to *explore* themselves and their worlds in informal essays" (146). Peter Elbow, among others, argues that it is undesirable to teach freshmen to write exclusively in academic discourse. "Life is long and college is short," he says in "Academic Discourse and Freshman Writing Courses." Students write academic prose only in college but very different kinds of writing on their jobs. Writing courses should encourage students to write what's meaningful to them, so they'll be "more likely to write by choice" outside of the courses, and able to do so. Chances are that voluntary writing won't be academic discourse. Rather, it will be writing, perhaps autobiographical—the kind that Winterowd is talking about, that enables students to *render* experience,[14] as most of the belletristic texts we teach in English courses do, rather than to *explain* it, the focus of nearly all other disciplines. Moreover, the ability to write good nonacademic discourse will help students translate the academic discourse of their textbooks "into everyday, experiential, anecdotal" language that they can understand and use (1-3).

Elbow expands his argument to say that it's impossible to teach academic discourse anyway, because "there's no *it* to teach. ... Academics simply don't discourse with the same discourse." Biologists don't write like historians, and even in English there is no single discourse community, but a variety ranging from "the bulldozer tradition of high Germanic scholarship" to the "genial slightly talky British tradition" (of belletristic essays) to "poststructuralist, continental discourse: allusive, gamesome—dark and deconstructive." Add to these the discourse of quantitative research, qualitative research, psychoanalytic and psychological interpretation. What is central to all kinds of academic discourse, says Elbow, is *"the giving of reasons and evidence rather than just opinions, feelings, experiences.* Being clear about claims or assertions rather than just implying or insinuating. Getting thinking to stand on its own two feet rather than depending on who says it or who hears it." And this is a major goal of schooling and literacy, "just *plain good discourse in general*—not good academic discourse" (4-9).

So we return to the possibility, as well as the desirability of teaching belletristic essay writing, "plain good discourse in general," as well as doing such writing ourselves. Such writing enables our students to find their own voices instead of ventriloquizing in an academic voice that lacks authority. We can see the results in the collections of Bedford prize student essays and other published student writing. Students take their writing seriously because they are invested in it; such investment makes them willing to write and rewrite and rewrite again. They become, with us, members of a community of writers.

In "Finding a Family, Finding a Voice," I explain how, as the consequence of an existential crisis—I believed my husband was dying of a malignant brain tumor—I decided to risk everything as a teacher, for I could not be more vulnerable, by writing and reading to my students the assignment I'd asked them to do, a personal essay on "Why I Write." Through seeing how much I cared about writing they, too, became committed to the hard work and continual rewriting that this demands. As they wrote in their writers' notebooks:

> All over [town] I run into Lynn Bloom's students moaning about their papers—they all want to put a lot into it.

Damn you, Lynn Bloom. Have you let me in for a life of writing, for a life of struggle to create, to express, to move from a state of knowing less to a state of knowing more or less what I want to say?

Here I am on a dismal rainy day, with my family life falling apart (and yes that makes me cranky, yes that makes it harder to get something done) and this class *cheers me up* and helps me believe I am a writer.

Having learned from Scholes how to teach literature and from my students, once again, how to teach writing, I taught last winter a graduate seminar called "Autobiography as a Literary Genre." Students could write either critical or autobiographical term papers.[15] When Ted, ordinarily articulate and self-possessed, had finished reading his, he began to sob—the first time such a thing had occurred in my thirty years of teaching. The rest of the class waited in respectful silence until our colleague had regained his composure. Then he led an engrossing discussion on his paper, which depicted his complex and painful relationship with his father. Instead of talking about belletristic writing, he had chosen to write it—and to understand it in his bones, and in his heart. As he did, so did we.

Notes

[1] One could argue that the plethora of little magazines, on campus and off, provide plenty of opportunity for publishing belletristic writing. That argument is beside the point unless we subscribe to these and read them regularly. C'mon now, fess up! How many little magazines do you read—regularly? How many have you read in the past five years? Have you ever submitted an essay to one? (Of course, one could ask the same questions about PMLA and expect the same dismal answers.)

[2] Scholes's solution to this problem is not to invert the hierarchy, but to deconstruct the binary oppositions between literature and non-literature, production and consumption, real world and academy. Ultimately this will result in teachers enabling students to respond to literary texts with texts of their own. We must, says Scholes,

> help our students unlock textual power and turn it to their own uses.... We must help them to see that every poem, play, and story is a text related to others, both verbal pre-texts and social sub-texts, and all manner of post-texts including their own responses, whether in speech, writing, or action. The response to a text is itself always a text. Our knowledge is itself only a dim text that brightens as we express it. That is why expression, the making of new texts by students, must play a major role [in freshman composition]. (20)

Scholes, Comley, and Ulmer's *Text Book* demonstrates the range of texts the students can write, empowered by this philosophy and creative latitude.

[3] Chris Anderson defends this position: "As someone struggling to gain professional accreditation, someone with a desire to write, someone trying to understand the important—and exciting—questions generated by contemporary criticism, someone who has published some scholarly articles and had others rejected, I find the essay an increasingly compelling model. The acceptance of second-class citizenship in exchange for freedom of movement is beginning to strike me as a pretty good bargain" (307). Anderson's ideas are first-rate; he shouldn't settle for "second-class citizenship."

[4] The five-paragraph theme is not an essay, except in the state of New Jersey, where the five-paragraph theme is required writing in mandated testing of senior high school students, whose scores are lowered if they do not follow its rigid format of an introductory paragraph, three body paragraphs, and a conclusion. In practice, this format is really a heuristic device, a formula to

elicit an allegedly linear thought pattern. Students (and teachers) who confuse format with form imperil their writing, as we know from reading formulaic, often inane, papers which use it. What's a "body paragraph," anyway?

[5]Of course, I could have summarized this in a phrase or two, but that would have defeated the purpose.

[6]The example from Gass's essay should, in that single sentence, dispel two objections faculty often voice against teaching (or allowing) students to write belletristic essays. Isn't all such writing personal narrative? Obviously, not narrative. Obviously not personal in the sense of autobiographical. Just as obviously, all writing, articles and essays alike, is personal inasmuch as it expresses the mind and passion of the writer. Isn't belletristic writing intellectually soft, much easier to do than intellectually rigorous academic writing? No more than figure skating is easier to do than hockey, impressionistic painting easier than hard-edge realism.

[7]That is one premise of Scholes's *Textual Power* and *Text Book*. It is also a major premise of Donald Murray's beloved book on how to teach writing, *A Writer Teaches Writing*. If Murray's book had been conceived as *A Teacher Teaches Writing* it would not, could not, have had the same impact. Other beloved books on writing and on teaching writing have been written by people whom Stephen North calls "practitioners," classroom writing teachers, themselves clearly expert writers, who "by virtue of some combination of eloquence and influence" have attracted "a considerable following" (22). Their "eloquence and influence" derive in large part from their engaging books: Walker Gibson's *Persona* and *Tough, Sweet, and Stuffy*; Ken Macrorie's *Telling Writing*; Nancie Atwell's *In the Middle*; Mike Rose's *Lives on the Boundary*; and the book that would seem the ultimate abdication of authority, Peter Elbow's *Writing Without Teachers*.

[8]In explaining how he wrote *Growing Up*, Russell Baker says:

> All the incidents are truthful. A book like that has certain things in common with fiction. Anything that is autobiographical is the opposite of biography. The biographer's problem is that he never knows enough. The autobiographer's problem is that he knows much too much.... He knows the whole iceberg, not just the tip.... So when you're writing about yourself, the problem is what to leave out. And I just left out almost everything—there's only about half a percent in that book. You wouldn't want everything; it would be like reading the *Congressional Record*. (49)

[9]Dickerson herself uses much clearer, simpler language in the questionnaires she gives to her students (144-46). Might she herself have written autobiography? Her article, with its strict focus on teaching, gives no clue.

[10]My friends and students who have read what used to be the ninth and final draft of the essay say that the most intriguing part is about my thirty-five-year friendship with a married man who is not my husband. They want to know more about how it's possible to have such a deep and enduring friendship without wrecking or even threatening my own marriage of thirty-one years, or his of equal longstanding. I'm reluctant to write more about this. To emphasize that friendship would throw the essay off balance. To analyze how Joe and I get along, and why, would make formal and deliberate what has been all these years casual and spontaneous. As Reynolds Price says of his memoir, *Clear Pictures*, I do not want to violate the trust of old friendships. I get uncomfortably self-conscious when I try to anatomize such a precious relationship. The public be damned. For now, anyway.

[11]In fact, I'm writing this article in a more casual, insouciant style, signalled by the two rhetorical questions in the very title, than I'd usually employ in academic writing because I want to make the point that it can be done. And that an academic journal will publish it. But that's risky—maybe they won't.

[12]Why Benjamin Spock? Because, "having written a doctoral dissertation on biographical method, I wanted to try practicing what I was preaching, and chose Dr. Spock because he was an interesting major figure accessible when I was at home rearing small children. Writing this biography knocked the dissertationese clean out of my style. Spock writes the way he talks, and since I included many quotations from interviews and from his writings, my own style had to be compatible with Spock's or the disparity would have been too disjunctive for readers. Spock himself is a conscious stylist.... He writes with absolute clarity, no ambiguity (especially when

a child's health and safety depend on it), careful but nontechnical explanations of terms, friendliness." ("Why I Write," 32-33.) My own writing departs from Spock's principles only to incorporate the intentional ambiguity of literary wit.

[13]This could have the same legislating effect on belletristic essays as would happen if *PMLA* were to publish an article on composition research. Likewise, every professional meeting devoted to composition, such as CCC, WPA, the Penn State conference, the national and regional conventions of NCTE, and the like, ought to have sessions devoted to the reading of belletristic writing, not just by literary superstars, but by members of the organizations.

[14]"To render experience is to convey what I see when I look out the window, what it feels like to walk down the street or fall down the street or fall in love—to tell what it's like to be me, what it's like living my life" (2).

[15]This alternative anticipated Spellmeyer's position in "A Common Ground: The Essay in the Academy," in which he argues that we as teachers should "permit our students to bring their extra-textual knowledge to bear upon every text we give them, and to provide them with strategies for using this knowledge to undertake a conversation which belongs to us all" (275). Exactly.

Works Cited

Anderson, Chris. "Hearsay Evidence and Second-Class Citizenship." *College English* 50 (1988): 300-08.

Baker, Russell. "Life With Mother." *Inventing the Truth: The Art and Craft of Memoir*. Ed. William Zinsser. Boston: Houghton, 1987. 33-51.

Bartholomae, David. "Inventing the University." *When a Writer Can't Write*. Ed. Mike Rose. New York: Guilford, 1985. 134-65.

Bizzell, Patricia. "Arguing About Literacy." *College English* 50 (1988): 141-53.

——. "Cognition, Convention, and Certainty: What We Need to Know about Writing." *Pre/Text* 3 (1982): 213-43.

Bloom, Lynn Z. "Finding a Family, Finding a Voice: A Writing Teacher Teaches Writing Teachers." *Writer's Craft, Teacher's Art: Teaching What We Know*. Ed. Mimi Schwartz. Portsmouth, N.H.: Boynton 1991. 55-67.

——. "How I Write." *Writers on Writing*. Ed. Tom Waldrep. New York: Random, 1985. 31-37.

Dickerson, Mary Jane. "'Shades of Deeper Meaning': On Writing Autobiography." *Journal of Advanced Composition* 9 (1989): 135-150.

Dicks, Bernice W. "State of the Art in Advanced Expository Writing: One Genus, Many Species." *Journal of Advanced Composition* 3 (1982): 172-91.

Dillard, Annie. "Introduction." *The Best American Essays 1988*. Ed. Annie Dillard and Robert Atwan. New York: Ticknor, 1988. xiii-xxii.

——. "To Fashion a Text." *Inventing the Truth: The Art and Craft of Memoir*. Ed. William Zinsser. Boston: Houghton, 1987. 55-76.

Elbow, Peter. "Academic Discourse and Freshman Writing Courses." CCCC Convention, Seattle, 17 Mar. 1989.

Gass, William H. "Emerson and the Essay." *Habitations of the Word: Essays*. New York: Simon, 1985. 9-49.

Hardwick, Elizabeth. "Introduction." *The Best American Essays 1986*. Ed. Elizabeth Hardwick and Robert Atwan. New York: Ticknor, 1986. xiii-xxi.

McPhee, John. Informal talk. Williamsburg, VA: William and Mary, April 1982.

North, Stephen M. *The Making of Knowledge in Composition: Portrait of an Emerging Field.* Upper Montclair, NJ: Boynton, 1987.

Scholes, Robert. *Textual Power: Literary Theory and the Teaching of English.* New Haven: Yale UP, 1985.

Scholes, Robert, Nancy R. Comley, and Gregory L. Ulmer. *Text Book: An Introduction to Literary Language.* New York: St. Martin's, 1988.

Spellmeyer, Kurt. "A Common Ground: The Essay in the Academy." *College English* 51 (1989): 262-76.

Tate, Priscilla. "Survey of Advanced Writing Programs." Unpublished report, 1985.

Winterowd, W. Ross. "Rediscovering the Essay." *Journal of Advanced Composition* 8 (1988): 146-57.

Gender, Culture, and Radical Pedagogy

Sexism in Academic Styles of Learning

DAVID BLEICH

In the fifth grade, I became empowered as a student. Until then, under the tutelage of Mrs. Kessler, Miss Sturgis, Miss Stout, Mrs. Montgomery, and Mrs. Levine, I had been a good student, but nevertheless a member of the "pack." In the fifth grade, I distinguished myself, became recognized as "the smartest kid in the class," played first base and batted third in the class softball lineup, and understood what it was to be singled out by the teacher for special privileges and class leadership. The teacher was Mr. Becker, a twenty-seven-year-old man who introduced sports and science into the curriculum«and for the first time in school, to me.

From then on, I paid attention to sports and science. I wanted to be a baseball player and then a physicist. Since I grew up to be skinny and weak, I gave up on joining Joe DiMaggio and decided that science was the place to be. In college, though, I began to feel that solving the conservation of momentum equations for ideal billiard balls moving on an ideal table was not interesting to me; but it still took a long time for me to admit that what I really wanted to do was read, write, talk, and teach. Over many years of earning a living as an English teacher, my sense of "real knowledge" also changed. My topic in this essay comes, in part, as a result of rethinking my having gone to an all-male "science" high school and to an all-male "science" college. It comes, in part, from trying to understand just what it was about science that seemed a little threatening to me. It also comes from my having identified this threat as something like the one posed by the gangs of male teenagers in motorcycle jackets who defined the territory in my childhood neighborhood in New York City. And it comes, finally, from learning that science is sustained by a society of men, for the disproportionate benefit of men, and at the disproportionate expense of women. In exploring this topic, I will try to say how and why the dominant styles of academic learning follow the traditions of scientific learning; to claim that discourse styles and classroom styles in the academy are affected, in far too great a degree, by values of classical sexism; and to suggest that these values are so deep—so ingrained in the general culture—that it is even difficult for well-meaning men and many women to detect that this is the case, much less lead us toward change.

The Ideology of Classical Sexism

In a book that is still being written, David F. Noble, a historian of technology at Drexel University, claims that academic culture, and science in particular, has been defined as a "world without women" at least since the twelfth century. His work concentrates on connections between the evolution of the academy and the development of the Roman Catholic Church. He shows that women in the first millennium were relatively prominent in religious monasteries, often founding them. These "coed" monasteries of the seventh and eighth centuries gave way in the eleventh century to the all-male cathedral schools, out of which came the universities as we now know them. Noble discusses the political battle in the Church throughout the first millennium, a battle between those advocating celibacy and the ascetic life for religious leaders and those advocating marriage. In about the eleventh century, the ascetic "party" gained ascendancy, and, in virulent campaigns against women, terrorized married clerics into giving up their wives and excluded all women from religious authority. Noble claims that, subsequently, the main home of science and all other intellectual life in Catholic Europe was in the celibate Church. In Protestant England of the seventeenth century, the situation was not that different. As Noble reminds us, Robert Boyle and Isaac Newton (from all the evidence available) never had female partners, and Boyle was given to practicing his science on Sunday, as a form of worship. Noble says similar attitudes about excluding women from science can be attributed to Galileo, Van Leeuwenhoek, and Gregor Mendel. In general, Noble thinks, most of the history of modern science shows that the exclusion of women and the hatred of women were defining elements of scientific culture and society.

Noble's narrative gives important support for what feminist thinkers today are coming to believe, namely, that science and intellectual life—all cultural activity, in fact, including the arts, even from classical antiquity and before—are marked not only by the exclusion of women but also by certain styles of thought, ways of reasoning, procedures for identifying problems, conventions of dealing with opposition, and prioritizing of subject matters, all of which have been appropriated by and have contributed back to the ideology of classical sexism: *the belief that men as a class are superior to women as a class, and the readiness to sustain this belief through violence against other people.* We probably will not find one man among those we know who agrees that this formulation represents *his* ideology, and I imagine that there is not one to whom it does not apply in one sense or another. I'm not saying this to be inflammatory, but to remember that even though we did not commit gang rape, participate in lynch mobs, or send people in freight trains to their deaths, we men have benefited from the sexist ideology of those who did commit these historic crimes.

Essentialization, Objectification, and Knowledge
One way to understand the emerging feminist critique of knowledge is to describe its use of language. The term *feminist*, for example, does not simply

mean "the women's point of view." It could mean this, but it also means "a point of view previously considered secondary." Even though *feminist* has a culturally implied reference to *masculine*, it has a *communally implied* reference to the idea that more than two genders exist and more than two genders *ought* to exist (communally implied within the feminist community through some feminists' opposition to the polarization of gender identity). This idea presents two challenges to speech conventions: that there are more than two genders and, simultaneously, that something exists *and* ought to exist. The view that only two genders exist derives from the traditional (masculine-endorsed) identity of sex and gender, from the traditional (masculine-endorsed) style of dichotomy and polarization, and from the related traditional convention of either/or thinking. This style of thinking has led (masculine) scholars to presuppose, and in some cases actually to claim, that "one gender must be dominant" and, thus, to justify retrospectively the history of masculine domination (as, for example, is done by the idea of the "great chain of being," a predominant idea of the Renaissance). This style also makes it seem absurd to claim that something is the case and ought to be the case at the same time. This absurdity is created by the axiomatic role of the traditional Aristotelian law of noncontradiction: "either A or not-A," which is one of the sources for both polarization and either/or thinking. From the very beginning, the feminist critique of knowledge challenges gender categories, the way categories in general are created, and the discourse styles that articulate these categories and practices.

The nonfeminist case of what light actually is also raised these and other questions about knowledge, particularly the issue of essentialization, the practice of settling on a single, unambiguous, "true" conception of phenomena and experience. At the beginning of this century, it was discovered that light could not be essentialized—that is, one could not decide that it was one and only one thing. Rather, it was either a wave or a particle. Scientists still are not happy with having to answer the question "What is light?" with "It depends," and most are still hoping for a "solution" to this problem. However, if either/or thinking were not the axiom, one might be happy with the "depends" character of light. Science has not stopped in its tracks because of this situation, and it is plausible that one could practice science quite well on a "depends" basis.

The logic of Plato, Aristotle, and Descartes necessarily essentializes the object of study, ideally through mathematical formulation. Many cognitive psychologists and artificial intelligence specialists also essentialize their object of study in this way, on the assumption that the "mind" is other than, separable from, and scientifically comprehensible independently of the body. For example, trying to conceive of a person without the categories "mind and body" or "soul and body"—perhaps thinking of someone as "could be many things in different contexts"—not only implies ethical hypocrisy but isn't "scientific." To be scientific is to essentialize the object of knowledge, to use language that indicates a strong boundary between the knower and the known and a strong boundary between knowledge of something and the thing "in itself." Even thinkers such as Husserl, who accepted the fact that science could no longer objectify the "known," nevertheless tried to subjectivize the "thing in itself" and, in this way, to establish utterly certain ground—an absolute, eternal foundation—for scientific knowledge.

Feminists adduce political grounds for rejecting the project of essentialization and objectification. In her essay, "Feminism and Science" (1982), Evelyn Fox Keller says that feminists often find "objectivity being linked with autonomy and masculinity, and in turn, the goals of science with power and domination" (238). To illustrate these links, she cites Francis Bacon, who thought that science is "leading you to Nature with all her children to bind her to your service and make her your slave" by means that do not "merely exert a gentle guidance over nature's course; they have the power to conquer and subdue her, to shake her to her foundations" (242). Historically, in the hands of men, objectification carried with it feelings and values of conquest and violence, particularly toward women. Thus, the feminist argument is this: because the ideology of male control of and violence toward females is already active and enacted in almost all social institutions—and has been for at least 8000 years, according to Gerda Lerner—the processes of knowing and the institutions of learning also reflect this ideology. Noble's historical perspective seems to make it clear that the practice of science (as we now know it) actually required the gathering of men together and, in a sense, "ganging up on" Nature, a female figure, to establish domination and control. What appears to be an epistemological approach—objectivity—is historically and culturally related to masculine domination of and violence toward women.

If this view seems overstated, consider this question: are there ways to talk about knowing that are not governed by the vocabulary of domination and control? Consider predictability, for example. A theory is not considered "scientific" if it does not predict the behavior of phenomena. Is there any doubt that the need to predict is governed by the need to control? In biology and the social sciences, it is the "control group" that finally authorizes the "experimental group," and those who reject psychoanalysis as a science do so because there cannot be "control groups" in the usual sense. Hierarchical thinking provides another example. Is there any doubt that knowledge hierarchies (such as the great chain of being or the Darwinian taxonomy) are sought in order to control new phenomena, and that often the hierarchies themselves are expected to "predict" the existence of new phenomena? (Like the search for the alleged "missing link" between simians and humans?) Although hierarchies have sometimes been benign (like the periodic table), is there any doubt that hierarchies we see daily in book ratings, university ratings, and hotel ratings, for example, are governed by considerations of wealth and power? We might each ask ourselves this question in regard to our respective gender identity: "How important are 'pecking orders' to me?"

Hierarchy in the Academic Disciplines

The question of hierarchy applies to the social organization of the sciences as well as to the task of conceptualizing data and experience. There are "hard" sciences, "soft" sciences, and the humanities. If you doubt that these disciplines are hierarchically arranged, consider which set of sciences gets the most funding and which the least. Sandra Harding takes up this question in her book, *The Science Question in Feminism* (1986):

> For the Vienna Circle, the [hierarchically arranged] sciences ... placed physics at its pinnacle, followed by the other physical sciences, then the more quantitative and "positive" social sciences (economics and behaviorist psychology were their models) leading the "softer" and qualitatively focused ones (anthropology, sociology, history). The feminist criticisms and reconstructive proposals appear also to assert a unity of science but to reverse the order of the continuum. And this thesis is asserted both as a description of what in fact is the case in the sciences and as a prescription for how the sciences should be ordered. It has been and should be moral and political beliefs that direct the development of both the intellectual and social structures of science. The problematics, concepts, theories, methodologies, interpretations of experiments, and uses have been and should be selected with moral and political goals in mind, not merely cognitive ones. (249-50)

Harding wants to see some reversals. Just as she reverses the traditional issue of "the woman question in science" to "the science question in feminism" in the title of her book, she advocates reversing today's hierarchy in academic subjects. None of these values in question (objectivity, mathematical formulation) are themselves necessarily masculine but have only been historically appropriated by a combined masculine ideology and social arrangement. Therefore, I will not dispute the value of hierarchical thinking by itself but concentrate on the newer and subtler strain in Harding's thought—her use of the "has been and should be" perspective on the social arrangement of the sciences (the same formulation I earlier applied to the question of the number of genders). I want to show not only that this is *not* an absurd principle but also that it is one *covertly* in use in the traditional practice of science, where it is suppressed in the service of other values.

Harding's point is that moral and political values have created the current hierarchical arrangement of the sciences. As Noble's work suggests, masculine interests produced the primacy of physics and other sciences most dependent on prediction, control, and detached objectivity. Harding substitutes *her* politics as the ground for a different objectification of things, an act that reverses the order of the hierarchy. What then is the net change in perspective that permits this "has been and should be" reasoning? It is the *announcement of values*—in contrast to the *declaration of facts*—that marks the difference between Harding and traditional thinkers. The same change describes the application of this kind of reasoning to the issues of how many genders there are. If gender is socially constructed and not biologically determined, then it would be correct to say that there have always been several genders—gay-male, lesbian, asexual, bisexual, variations of these, and the two traditional ones. To say that there "should be" these genders is really to say that the politics that recognizes and announces more than two genders "should be" our politics in the future. Here, too, the net change in perspective is the announcement of values, which comes as part of the change in values advocated by feminism. It is clear that the key substantive change in how things are done by feminists is one of *political disclosure*. But this disclosure changes almost everything—from the way money is spent, to the definition of problems, to the language used to present knowledge. Nothing in the feminist critique of science rejects mathematics, physics, or chemistry as valuable enterprises. What it does reject is the concealed sexism that has historically supported these enterprises. Sexism, either concealed or open, has censored the language and thought of women. In these instances where censorship has been removed, we can see how much other change must take place.

Feminist Revisions of Scientific Knowledge

Let me now describe one example from biology and one from physics to show how great such changes might be. Consider the biological concept of an autonomous system«like the circulatory system or the endocrine system, both isolated by the medical profession as "specialties" whose practitioners refuse to be any other sort of doctor than what is named by their specialty. In an essay published in 1989, Ruth Berman describes Barbara McClintock's early work in cell biology, for which McClintock was finally recognized as a Nobel laureate:

> In contrast to today's molecular biologists, far removed from living organisms other than bacteria and viruses and with little understanding of how they grow, McClintock's knowledge of the biological world is immense. She sees living systems not as linear progressions of molecular reactions enclosed in semipermeable sacs but as unique living beings in the process of constant development. Each genome, or hereditary system of the organism, is in continuous, organized interaction with the external stimuli and is itself changed in this process. The genome responds in an orderly, programmed sequence to the frequently encountered stimuli. Unanticipated shocks, however, induce a more profound and unpredictable genomic reaction, one that affects its structural organization as well as its action. But the process is not random, and the response, although complex, is incorporated and integrated with the development of the organism. (249)

Berman contrasts this conception of the "interactive" gene with the more current view of it as mechanical:

> The machine metaphor is, in fact, at the heart of present-day biological dualism and the gene-environment dichotomy, with the fixed-in-place-before-birth gene being given causal primacy. This biological determinist, or "hard-wired," rationale has been used

since the beginning of western civilization to blame the problems of the individual on her or his inherent nature and to absolve the social system from all responsibility, denying the need for change. It serves to justify the rule of a "naturally superior" power elite—and the science that serves it. (251)

As Keller explains, the usual conception of the cell hinges on a "master molecule" (the DNA in the gene) that governs or causes the behavior of the rest of the cell. This conception is generated by the "machine metaphor" that Berman describes, a metaphor casting the master molecule in the position of a "power elite" that determines what is then understood as caused, passive, or secondary cell behavior. In addition to the "master molecule" metaphor, there is the "hard-wired" figure, probably a contribution from today's hegemony of computer science (another male-dominated discipline) over other kinds of intellectual work. McClintock's conception is nonhierarchical in that she conceives the gene (and its DNA) as one part of an interactive system, each element of which is subject to change and development from unpredictable sources. Keller writes: "No longer is a master control to be found in a single component of the cell; rather, control resides in the complex interactions of the entire system" ("Feminism" 245). Although McClintock's idea is an authentic scientific alternative, it is not just that, according to Keller: it represents a whole different approach to nature and to thinking about it, one, perhaps, in which respect for its total integrity plays a key role, and where knowing about it means letting it be our teacher rather than our slave.

In *Reflections on Gender and Science* (1985), Keller discusses the epistemological problems raised by quantum mechanics:

Experience demonstrates the failure of the classical dichotomy; subject and object are inevitably, however subtly, intertwined. So far so good. The difficulties arise in the tendency to overestimate our capacity to describe that interaction. That is, if we are unwilling to acknowledge aspects of reality not contained in the theoretical description, it is the system itself, for example, the electron, which must bend, twist, or collapse in response to our observation. Such a system cannot be a classical particle; classical particles are not "spread out," nor do they "collapse." We give up the classical picture but impose on reality the picture of our theoretical description, saying, implicitly, that the system *is* this peculiar object, the wave function. In short, the subject-object dichotomy is relinquished, but the attachment to a one-to-one correspondence between reality and theory is not. In these interpretations, belief in the "knowability" of nature is retained at the expense of its "objectifiability." Reality then, of necessity, takes on rather bizarre properties in this effort to make it conform to theory, leaving very few content. (146-47)

Keller describes how quantum mechanics has forced scientists to abandon belief in the "classical particle"—an electron that has some essential being or character. But what scientists have done, she argues, is what Husserl also tried to do: retain the belief in "certain knowledge" by believing that the theoretical description *must* correspond to the reality—an absurdity if Keller's description is accepted. One can't give up a rigid boundary between subject and object without also giving up the exact correspondence between theory and experience. As Keller puts it, neither objectifiability nor knowability can any longer be absolute, axiomatic standards of scientific knowledge. They are not rejected, but they are no longer the only validation of the "scientifically" true.

If objectifiability and knowability are no longer rigid standards, then neither can predictability and control be considered so. All four principles come under the uncertain, unpredictable, variable regulation of affective, social, and political principles, which themselves exemplify the reduced rigidity of the first four principles. Admitting that affective, social, and political principles are and ought to be behind the initiatives of science means that human, collective choices are made about what to objectify, what to predict, what to control, and what to know. Reasons are given for such choices, and a logic of social benefits and dangers is attached to these reasons. For example, it is no longer unquestioned that gene-splicing should proceed because we should learn all we can; rather, *some* gene-splicing should be done because a particular constituency, say, AIDS victims, seems likely to benefit. Similarly, to proceed into space research just because it seems exciting may be quite objectionable given the needs of those that are not being met because of its costs. The desire to find an "ultimate" particle, or to determine just when the universe began, may be motivated by religious ideology and the masculine obsession with origins rather than by authentic scientific needs to know. (Would anyone like to present a gendered reading of scientists' search for the "Big Bang"?)

Sexism in the Social Sciences: A Case from Anthropology
In the social sciences, anthropology may seem exempt from this critique. Women have been prominent in this field for a long time, and its subject matter seems to be intrinsically egalitarian«the respectful disclosure of how other people live. But this exemption is historically not the case, and it is not the case today even in the most progressive contexts, including ethnography and ethnographic writing. A popular book in this area is James Clifford and George Marcus' *Writing Culture: The Poetics and Politics of Ethnography* (1986). Although this work explores social and political aspects of ethnography, only one of the nine contributors is female, and one of the editors (Clifford) writes in the introduction that "feminist ethnography . . . has not produced either unconventional forms of writing or a developed reflection on ethnographic textuality as such" (21). In a recent issue of *Signs*, two feminist anthropologists and one literary scholar answer Clifford and Marcus on this and several other, more far-ranging issues. Frances Mascia-Lees, Patricia Sharpe (the literary scholar), and Colleen Ballerino Cohen note that Clifford himself uses a feminist ethnography (Marjorie Shostak's *Nisa: The Life and Works of a !Kung Woman*) as the centerpiece of his own contribution

to the volume, and they observe that Clifford "prefers to write about feminists rather than inviting them to write for themselves" (13). Also, they cite several feminist anthropologists who took up issues addressed in *Writing Culture* long before the authors anthologized there took them up.

However, the main point of the critique by Mascia-Lees, Sharpe, and Cohen is to raise a key political issue about ethnographic research, an issue that the male editors and authors of *Writing Culture* do not see or do not seem to consider germane to their work: the view that the ethnographic researcher always occupies a position of political dominance over the subjects of the research. Citing Judith Stacey, another ethnographer, Mascia-Lees, Sharpe, and Cohen point out that subjects of ethnographies are "at grave risk of manipulation and betrayal by the ethnographer" and that "the research product is ultimately that of the researcher, however modified or influenced by the informants" (21). Furthermore, the use of this product—almost always a text—pertains more to the political community of anthropologists than to the communal welfare of those being studied. The authors cite P. Steven Sangren's observation that "whatever 'authority' is created in a text has its most direct social effect not in the world of political and economic domination of the Third World by colonial and neocolonial powers, but rather in the academic institutions in which such authors participate" (16).

Those who take the academic system for granted will find it hard to cope with this criticism. After all, how much are researchers and professors actually expected to do in the real world? This is the nub of the matter. The academy is socially and politically insulated from the subjects of its study—and this is true in every subject from science to literature. Academics are not finally expected to enact their work or even to produce work for whose social, political, and practical consequences they themselves are responsible. So rigid is the boundary that insulates academic research from everything else that most academics don't even consider themselves responsible for whether their research could or should be taught. In most universities, teaching and research are separate categories, as every tenure candidate well knows.

Mascia-Lees, Sharpe, and Cohen concentrate on the issue of postmodernism and the claims by many academic social scientists and humanists that postmodern attention to language, style, and textuality represents a move toward political enlightenment. They claim, however, that academic work done in the name of postmodernism shows no change in how academic business is conducted. They write (quoting cultural critic Craig Owens): "The absence of discussions of sexual difference in writings about postmodernism, as well as the fact that few women have engaged in the modernism/postmodernism debate, suggest that postmodernism may be another masculine invention engineered to exclude women" (17). As a case in point, Mascia-Lees, Sharpe, and Cohen examine Paul Rabinow's essay in the *Writing Culture* volume, an essay that "appears to deal seriously with feminism." They observe, however, that by creating a new ethical position for anthropologists—"critical cosmopolitanism"—and claiming that "we are all cosmopolitans," Rabinow concludes that "feminism is not an intellectual position he personally can hold" and thus "excludes himself from the feminist dialogue solely because he is male" (18). They then claim that Rabinow's choice of studying "elite French male colonial officials" puts him in the position of rendering "gender differences irrelevant" and of "reinforc[ing] the Western male as the norm." They point out that Rabinow's earlier work "relied exclusively on male informants, presenting women only marginally and as objects of his sexual desire, communicating through 'the unambiguity of gesture'" (19).

I think the point here is not that Rabinow's work is invalid, but that the elaborate verbal acrobatics he uses to justify his own work on male populations betray a concealed lack of political courage, a stubborn refusal to internalize and make his own his professed sympathy with the feminist program. His moves are characteristically academic: "I'm for the enfranchisement of women, but I won't accept their categories of thought—because of academic freedom." Mascia-Lees, Sharpe, and Cohen conclude with these thoughts:

> Ultimately, the postmodern focus on style and form, regardless of its sophistication, directs our attention away from the fact that ethnography is more than "writing it up" .... Politically sensitive anthropologists should not be satisfied with exposing power relations in the ethnographic text ... but rather should work to overcome these relations. ... Anthropologists may be better able to overcome these power relations by framing research questions according to the desires of the oppressed group, by choosing to do work that "others" want and need, by being clear for whom they are writing, and by adopting a feminist political framework that is suspicious of relationships with "others" that do not include a close and honest scrutiny of the motivations for research. (33)

Using the postmodernist interest in textuality as their jumping-off point, the authors here describe what it would be to change the axioms of academic work: to orient this work according to the needs of the (oppressed) group that is being studied. To extend this principle is to adopt the idea of socially generous research in all fields, that is, research that self-consciously contributes to a social constituency that it can help, enable, or empower. This means examining why we are doing research to begin with, who we are really writing for, and how we are going to learn from our students instead of enslaving them, just as scientists will learn from nature without enslaving it.

Competition and Individualism in the Humanities

These principles apply to us in the "English business" in the same way that they apply in the physical and social sciences. Some in language and literature disciplines (including, in part, history and philosophy) have celebrated the arrival of the "postmodern" textualist perspective as the key to liberating the subject of writing. Just as anthropologists have become self-conscious writers, so have historians and literary critics. The academic character of these fields, however, has not changed in the senses that Mascia-Lees, Sharpe, and Cohen advocate. Justifications for these authors' suspicions of postmodernist discourse can be found in the discourse styles of the humanities and the retrograde teaching styles in the great majority of humanities classrooms. For example, in the December 1989 issue of *College English*, James Reither and Douglas Vipond encouragingly describe a way to have students learn to work with one another«by normal measures, theirs is a progressive essay. In an early paragraph, they observe that one reason why collaborative work in classrooms has not succeeded more fully is that the term *social* is being used to describe language and literacy:

> Theorists have advanced so many competing notions of the social in writing and knowing that the term's ambiguity is perhaps unresolvable. . . . Calling writing a social process specifies too little about what kinds of social acts people are engaging in as they write. Saying that writing is a social process does not tell us much at all about what people do when they write or about what students might do to learn to write. Saying that writing is a social process does not specify what writers need to know in order to write. Thus, because the term social implicates too little by way of concrete activity, the generally theoretical discussion in the literature has not helped us see ways to overhaul our thinking about writing in practice or of teaching writing in practice.
>
> We find it more helpful to think of writing (and knowing) not as social but, more specifically, as collaborative. Instead of asking, "In what ways is writing a social process?" we ask, "In what ways are writers collaborating with others when they write?"
> (856)

I'm calling attention here to the habit of adversarial reasoning in scholarly work, and, also to Reither and Vipond's presupposition that the many theories about the social character of language must be "competing."

Will the history of science make as much or more sense if we do not assume that multiple theories are "competing" to become the main theory? According to Ludwik Fleck and Thomas Kuhn, we do not need the "competing theory" theory at all. Science has proceeded developmentally rather than dialectically. Both "new" scientific facts and new ways of understanding evolve through a combination of factors, including experimental data, the social arrangement of scientists, religious and political values, historical accident, and immediate needs. Why then is there both the historical illusion of competition as well as routine assumption of it in an essay about classroom writing published in 1989? Why don't Reither and Vipond just say that they would like to reflect on social views of language by considering its implication of collaboration?

Clearly, they use the idea of "competing notions" for the same reason that they present their "collaborative writing" experience in oppositional vocabulary: that is the way scholarly work is done. In order to justify new work on a topic, graduate students are trained—some would say "forced"—to review the literature and say why it is inadequate; new work can only be done if others have "failed to note" it. Alternatively, new work is done assuming that there is one whole truth and that various scholars are busy assembling all the pieces. Therefore, scholarship in the humanities assumes either that one worker will "win" the truth competition or that several workers will assemble the one whole truth. What is hard to find is scholarship that is clearly responsive to socially and politically grounded needs for understanding, scholarship that does not seem to be participating in either the truth or power sweepstakes. The ethics of competition and individualism are the guiding ideology of scholarship in the humanities, even work that many of us would consider politically progressive.

Where shall we look to understand why these values are so tenacious? And are we willing to say that these values, like objectivity and predictability, may be associated with the ideology of sexism?

Walter Ong is a "humanist's humanist," 1978 president of the Modern Language Association, erudite, gentle in tone and manner, and someone no one does not like. His scholarship does not read polemically, and most of those I know who have read his work, myself included, learn a great deal. Furthermore, Ong tends to look at the "big picture"; he seeks to understand language and literature both in a historical perspective and as part of people's daily experience. He is responsive to changes in society, particularly to technology, and he has been one of several leaders for those of us who have come to believe that writing (not just literature) is a deep and fascinating subject.

Just before *Orality and Literacy* was published in 1982, Ong brought out another book that is not as widely read, but one that helps to illuminate the issues I am now exploring, a book called *Fighting for Life: Contest, Sexuality, and Consciousness*. As well as anything in it, the opening paragraph of this work poses both its own problem and the problem in the academy and society that I think it represents:

> Contest is a part of human life everywhere that human life is found. In war and in games, in work and in play, physically, intellectually, and morally, human beings match themselves with or against one another. Struggle appears inseparable from human life, and contest is a particular focus or mode of interpersonal struggle, an opposition that can be hostile but need not be, for certain kinds of contest may serve to sublimate and dissolve hostilities and to build friendship and cooperation. (15)

This statement is the premise of Ong's work. Even though he allows that there may be either hostile or friendly contest, there is always some kind of contest. "Adversativeness," he explains, "has provided a paradigm for understanding our own existence: in order to know myself, I must know that something else is not me and is (in some measure) set against me, psychologically as well as physically" (15-16). Regardless of our own dispositions, and regardless of the moral and political features of history, contest and adversativeness are underlying facts, conditions, axioms of human existence.

In his second chapter, Ong discusses biological facts and sexual identity.

After allowing that "sex always works through and with a given culture" (52), he observes that "boisterousness is biologically determined . . . and we know that it is connected in some special way with masculinity." He continues: "However treated, it cannot be ignored. Boys will be boys. Sexually determined behavior is always mingled with other things. But it is still sexually determined behavior" (52). Here is a more revealing taste of Ong's reasoning and the direction of his thought. We begin to see here the almost exclusive emphasis on male psychology in this work and the invocation of the familiar justification of masculine excess and violence ("boys will be boys"). And we also find a clear statement of Ong's belief in biological, sexual determinism.

With these beliefs as a prologue, Ong then sets out to show that men are *biologically* more contest oriented than women. To this end, he cites sources that tell how male sexual definition of the fetus "depends on the excretion of androgens by the male embryo and fetus." From this fact, Ong draws the following conclusion:

> The male mammalian organism must from the start react against its environment. Thus masculinity has a certain resistance to being nurtured: for a male, being nurtured has special dangers. At its biological and historical source, the male's vocation is not acceptance but change. Again, masculinity means differentiation. (64-65)

It seems that this statement about male fetuses reacting "against" the environment is false. Why does the secretion of male hormones mean that the male fetus is reacting "against" the environment? Why doesn't Ong conclude that male embryos are developing in respect to *both* the female environment *and* the male genetic system and are being, in fact, nurtured by the female environment? Ong's biology seems no different in its politics than Aristotle's: for both, a prior ideological and social assumption about males produces the claimed biological "facts." Ong continues his biological reasoning to make what I think are other false judgments about sexual activity:

> The stress situation for the male, begun in the womb, comes to a peak in the mature male with sexual intercourse itself, in which the difference between the sexes reaches its maximum and which is always a test of the male's, not the female's physical ability to perform, to achieve intromission. (67)

There are several false judgments in this passage: that intercourse is naturally or necessarily a "stress situation" for the male; that there is a "maximum" of sexual difference during intercourse; and that sexual performance is a "test" for males and not for females. Viewed without a false biological premise and in a context we might call "conciliatory" or "cooperative" rather than "adversative," we might also reasonably judge that sex takes place when both parties are relaxed and not stressed; that intercourse follows from common desire and togetherness as much as, or more than, from difference; that either party's sexual performance is a function of the overall state of their relationship; and, in any event, that intromission is not necessarily the single goal or essential feature of sexual activity. The judgments that Ong reaches in this and in the previous cases stem from an underlying acceptance of the ideology of sexism, as well as the ideology of heterosexism.

This ideology is partially concealed by this language of "contest." But there is no doubt that the underlying biological contest that forms the basis for Ong's cultural claims about the necessity of contest is the alleged contest between men and women. Because men are "naturally" adversative, this contest can't be avoided: in the next-to-last paragraph of his treatise, Ong observes, "The entire history of consciousness can be plotted in relation to the always ongoing male-female dialectic" (208).

One of the main reasons for Ong's investigation of sexuality is his wish to illuminate the history of academic life. He is well aware that the Roman Catholic Church is one of the defining influences of today's academy and that "the Church has from the beginning been very much at home in the agonistic male world, and nowhere more than when engaged in intellectual activity" (169). Ong believes that technology—through electronic amplification, for example—has helped to put the female voice volume on a more equal footing with the male. He notes that the greater role of women in today's academy has begun to change its historically agonistic style. But not very much thought is given to these changes in his book. He is openly concerned, however, with "Christian life and worship." It is clear that he requires the biological thoughts reviewed above for his view of religious life: he needs the essentialized categories of male and female because "the Church is sexually defined" (172): Holy Mother Church and God the Father. He requires the idea of a highly differentiated male because of the masculine identity of God: "We are distanced from God as from a father.... God is male. He is not nature, Nature is feminine, Mother Nature" (175).

I think we are back to the story told by David Noble. In spite of Ong's scholarship and thoughtfulness, he remains an advocate of a way of life in the academy that depends on the privileging of men. If Ong were female, and not by vocation an advocate of the Church and its history, I very much doubt that he could possibly construe thousands of years of the masculine oppression of women as related to a biological necessity for contest. I very much expect that he would mention rape and male violence toward women at least a few times while alluding to the achievements of disputation in Church-run academies. Yes, I am consciously presenting this *ad hominem* argument. I assume that every person is a political figure (especially those of us who speak and write in public), and so my argument is also trying to say what problems appear when political self-disclosure and announced political purpose are not part of the research agenda.

The way language and literature are studied today is still deeply dependent on competition between individuals. Unfortunately, Ong spells out attitudes that do inform academic work as much in the liberal humanities as in the sciences and social sciences. The "critical exchange" section of *Critical Inquiry* and the letter section in the *New York Review of Books* show some honest-to-goodness mutual hacking. Universities have been grudging to admit that there is more undiscovered and unread literature produced by disenfranchised people than there now exists in the so-called canon. In Washington at the MLA meeting in 1989, an old white man and an unctuous university president defended the "great books," while women, black people, and political risk-takers asked, "Who is to decide what books are 'great'?"

Hierarchy and Competition in the Classroom

A related, less discussed, but ultimately just as consequential issue is the competitive character of schooling from the fourth grade on. The tests and grades that contaminate each person's contact with texts and with other students derive from the masculine interest in games, rules, and winning. In composition studies, perhaps the most progressive of all academic disciplines in its desire to be politically responsive and responsible, only a small minority has challenged the obsession with grading and has begun to reflect on the problem of making all review processes«of students' and of teachers' work«into occasions for collective and mutual learning; only very few have raised the problem of taking the fear and "performance anxiety" (described by Ong in regard to male sexuality) out of speaking one's mind and telling the truth. Only a small minority is paying attention to language use more than to technical proficiency. And only a minuscule group«compared to the total population of writing teachers«is forcefully and selfconsciously teaching the political character of language and writing, or teaching writing, speaking, and collaborative language study as part of an agenda of socially generous research.

On this point, consider Carol Stanger's essay, "The Sexual Politics of the One-to-One Tutorial Approach and Collaborative Learning." In almost every classroom, there is what we may euphemistically call the "tutorial" assumption, in which the hierarchical relation of the teacher to the individual student is the one and only relationship in which writing is meaningful. Stanger observes that the "instructor doesn't consider his or her thirty students as a group, a class; instead they are only thirty individuals." There is no "subjective collaboration" here (a term used by Adrienne Rich eighteen years ago to say what teaching ought to be) but, rather, the compliance of the student with the instructions of the teacher. Even if the teacher is female, Stanger points out, the hierarchical structure of the relationship continues to keep the student in a compliant position, while the female teacher has unintentionally gone along with a socially masculine style.

Furthermore, as long as the teacher retains a remedial approach, her or his own subjectivity is not part of the relationship and, thus, there is no subjective collaboration in this approach either. Stanger observes that the hierarchical relation requires the use of models. The editing instructor has at his or her disposal many models that can be overtaken by the student. But she emphasizes that the models themselves are a problem: "Models express the male value of the ideal text; the ideal text is a male value because it expresses hierarchical thinking and absolute external values" (36). Models are like mathematical and physical abstractions: they either may or may not be thought of as "ideal." But as I suggested earlier, the masculine handling of science has always privileged the abstract as ideal, and this is what Stanger is referring to in writing pedagogy: either the teacher's style or writing by "experts" plays the role for the "item to be imitated" in order to reach that other ideal, "excellence." Thus, if a paper is judged disorganized because it does not seem to fit any of the models the instructor has in mind, the instructor will not entertain the possibility that the paper "was organized in a more organic, female form." Stanger reasons:

> So, in the one-to-one tutorial, the instructor judges the paper against an ideal text, a composite of the male canon, and bestows authority on the essay as well as controlling its interpretation. Sensing this political reality, how would [a female student] feel empowered to revise on her own? (36)

In the majority of classrooms that presuppose the one-to-one relation, she goes on, "members of the class are not encouraged to read one another's work; all work on their own writing while they wait to see the teacher" (35). In recommending the peer group as an audience for each writer, Stanger presents collaborative learning as a solution that, at first, is to benefit female students who do not feel empowered to be independent. Ultimately, however, student collaboration becomes a classroom structure that contributes to the independence of all students.

Conclusion
From a feminist perspective, the teaching of language and literacy is always the teaching of language to the disenfranchised. The privileged are themselves disenfranchised insofar as they can speak only to themselves and understand few others; the middle class is disenfranchised by the narrow discourse of how to get ahead; the poor are disenfranchised because others will not listen or hear. Black English is "substandard"; Spanish is "not our language"; women's journals are "emotional" and "disorganized"; slave narratives are not "great literature"; children's and young people's language are "naive and undisciplined." It is nothing other than sexism when only the language of masculine interests is considered the proper subject in the study of literacy«the language of academic discourse and expository prose; the language of corporate and military science and technology; the words, the names, the ideas, and the priorities of the male hegemony in almost all public contexts. Feminism has shown that all of us, privileged and unprivileged,

women and men alike, are implicated in the discourse of sexism, and that the total scene of teaching and learning language must finally be responsive to these political claims.

Works Cited

Berman, Ruth. "From Aristotle's Dualism to Materialist Dialectics: Feminist Transformation of Science and Society." *Gender/Body/Knowledge: Feminist Reconstructions of Being and Knowing.* Ed. Alison M. Jaggar and Susan R. Bordo. New Brunswick: Rutgers UP, 1989. 224-55.

Clifford, James, and George Marcus, eds. *Writing Culture: The Poetics and Politics of Ethnography.* Berkeley: U of California P, 1986.

Harding, Sandra. *The Science Question in Feminism.* Ithaca, NY: Cornell UP, 1986.

Keller, Evelyn Fox. "Feminism and Science." *Signs: Journal of Women in Culture and Society* 7 (1982): 589-602. Rpt. in *Sex and Scientific Inquiry.* Ed. Sandra Harding and Jean F. O'Barr. Chicago: U of Chicago P, 1987. 233-46.

———. *Reflections on Gender and Science.* New Haven, CT: Yale UP, 1985.

Mascia-Lees, Frances E., Patricia Sharpe, and Colleen Ballerino Cohen. "The Postmodernist Turn in Anthropology: Cautions from a Feminist Perspective." *Signs: Journal of Women in Culture and Society* 15 (1989): 7-33.

Ong, Walter. *Fighting for Life: Contest, Sexuality, and Consciousness.* Ithaca, NY: Cornell UP, 1981.

Reither, James A., and Douglas Vipond. "Writing as Collaboration." *College English* 51 (1989): 855-67.

Stanger, Carol A. "The Sexual Politics of the One-to-One Tutorial Approach and Collaborative Learning." *Teaching Writing: Pedagogy, Gender, and Equity.* Ed. Cynthia L. Caywood and Gillian R. Overing. Albany: SUNY P, 1987. 31-44.

The Dialectic Suppression of Feminist Thought in Radical Pedagogy

Robert G. Wood

Undoubtedly, the dialectic process articulated in Hegel's *Phenomenology of Spirit* has had major influences on some of composition's more notable theorists of radical or liberatory pedagogy. Theorists like Paulo Freire and Henry Giroux, although different from each other in a number of ways, seem to agree that the goal of liberatory pedagogy should be to bring about some kind of dialectic change. That is, students and their teachers should be able to enter into a relationship similar to the master-slave relationship described by Hegel, thus aiding them both in achieving what Freire calls a "critical consciousness." My aim, though, will be to challenge assumptions that the dialectic process works toward the benefit of all students; rather, I want to show that the dialectic search for critical consciousness contains an androcentric bias which can work to suppress the development of feminist thought in female students.

In recent years, a number of feminist theorists have argued that the dominant conception of the dialectic denies women the opportunity for transcendence. It is precisely this breakdown of the dialectic, I will argue, that suppresses feminist thought in the classroom. My ultimate goal here, however, is to show that the dialectical structure through which radical pedagogy presently operates does not have to be a totalizing construction. Instead, I will argue that the dialectic of radical pedagogy is merely inadequate for an increasingly pluralistic culture and that through feminist deconstruction of the phallogocentrism of the dialectic, a reconstruction can take place which allows feminist thought to engage fully in a multiplicity of dialectics which will ultimately bring about positive social change.

The Dialectic of Radical Pedagogy

Although some say that the seeds of the dialectic can be found well before his *Phenomenology of Spirit* (Butler 174), it is Hegel's fully articulated dialectic that perhaps has had the most profound influence on modern critical thought. Hegel's dialectic process explains, among other things, how men and women come to acquire an awareness or consciousness of themselves, others, and, more importantly for the theorists of liberatory pedagogy, their social situations within a dominant cultural system. It should be no surprise then that the theories of radical pedagogues like Freire and Giroux have been heavily influenced by the Marxist version of the dialectic, which locates the possibilities for social change in the confrontation between the proletariat and the bourgeoisie, since the nature of their roles as educators often forces them to confront the problems that affect the performance of students belonging to socio-economically oppressed cultures. For these theorists, the dialectic presents a praxis that will ultimately bring about a sense of self-consciousness, which they view as the impetus for social change.

It would be prudent then to begin by noting briefly that the dialectics of radical pedagogy do not correlate fully with the dialectics of Marx and Hegel. There are, however, certain consistencies between the three dialectics where we can clearly see the influence of Hegel on the theories of Marxism and radical pedagogy. In the broadest sense, the dialectics of radical pedagogy, Hegel, and Marx are concerned with transforming a human condition, whether it be through perfecting philosophical knowledge or through attaining social agency. And it is in the latter where the dialectics of Marxism and radical pedagogy are perhaps most closely tied to Hegel.

For example, the position of the illiterate student in liberatory pedagogical theory closely mirrors the positions of both Hegel's slave and Marx's proletariat, for in all three instances we find a negated being, or that which is oppressed by that which holds power. In his master-slave narrative, Hegel writes: "But the [master] is the power over this thing [the slave], for he proved in the struggle that it is something merely negative; since he is the power over this thing and this again is the power over the other" (115). Although the slave here represents a number of philosophical concepts for Hegel, the slave also may stand as a metaphor for those students who have been mystified by an illiteracy resulting from oppressive socio-economic structures. Like Hegel's slave, the students of liberatory theory are initially powerless. They have been marginalized by their lack of access to the dominant literacy, but it is here that liberatory theory seeks the dialectical transformation of the mystified students into socially conscious citizens with empowered voices. Thus, liberatory theory seeks to create a new literacy that is both democratic and non-oppressive.

The dialectic, then, is crucial to liberatory theory because, by definition, radical theorists are unhappy with the current state of things and, by definition, the dialectic represents a process for change. In *Literacy: Reading the Word and the World*, Freire and Macedo explain that the emphasis of liberatory literacy is on change:

> In our analysis, literacy becomes a meaningful construct to the degree that it is viewed as a set of practices that functions to either empower or disempower people. In the larger sense, literacy is analyzed according to whether it serves to reproduce existing social formation or to whether it serves as a set of cultural practices that promotes democratic and emancipatory change. (viii)

We see here that merely reproducing the literacies of a dominant culture is unacceptable to the aims of liberatory praxis since this reproduction involves no transformation of the structures that oppress the marginalized students to begin with. Liberatory theory, according to Freire and Macedo, must somehow change social practices.

Working initially with Brazilian peasants, Paulo Freire evolved a theory for education based on the dialogic interaction between student and teacher which focuses on those who were deemed hopelessly ignorant or incapable of learning as a result of their economic deprivation and lack of access to the educational systems of the wealthy. According to Aronowitz and Giroux, the student in Freire's dialectic process, like Hegel's slave, seeks a legitimate voice to reclaim that which has been taken away:

> [Freire's] overriding goal of empowerment for oppressed Brazilian peasants entailed distinct but closely related steps: the validation of the "voices" of the people who are traditionally deprived of legitimate participation in political as well as civil society. Thus, Freire's pedagogy is dialogic: learning occurs within conversation, and not as top-to-down instruction between the teacher and student. (12)

As Hegel's dialectic is mainly a reaction to the linear rationality of Kantian thought, so too is Freire's dialectic a response to the linear inscription of what he calls the "banking concept" of education, the method that he claims is most practiced in today's educational institutions (*Pedagogy* 57). Freire's model eschews the banking concept because in this system knowledge is deposited by the teacher into students who act as docile receptacles. Conversely, an interactive dialogue is central to Freire's dialectic process, but with the banking concept of education, there is no dialectic. In *Pedagogy of the Oppressed*, Freire notes that "Dialogue with the people is radically necessary to every authentic revolution. This is what makes it a revolution, as distinguished from a military *coup*" (122). We find in Freire, therefore, a continuous process of dialogic interactions between teacher and student, between scholar and reader, between dominant culture and the oppressed.

Giroux reminds us that not only does liberatory theory utilize the dialectic in its approaches to teaching, but by nature it is itself dynamic, thus continually inventing and reinventing itself:

> [Pedagogical theory] is a discursive practice, an unfinished language, replete with possibilities, that grows out of particular engagements and dialogues. It offers up new categories, examples, and insights for teachers and others to engage and rethink everything from the purpose and meaning of schooling to the role that educators might play as cultural workers. Its specificity and value lie in its success in providing a language that ruptures the business-as-usual relationship between theory and practice, pedagogy and teaching, and schools and critical public cultures. (4)

Perhaps unique to the dialectic of radical pedagogy is the role that the teacher plays in the educational transformation of both herself and the student. Ira Shor explains that "The crux of liberatory theory rests in the empowering animation of critical consciousness, through the students' object-subject switch, in an egalitarian, experience-based dialogue, initiated by a teacher functioning in a mobile complex of roles" (122-23). Even though the teacher in liberatory theory does not occupy exactly the same position as the master in Hegel nor the bourgeoisie in Marx, the teacher is ultimately transformed, along with the student, by the dialectic in a similar way that Hegel's and Marx's binary opposites are transformed in each of their dialectics. In *Education for Critical Consciousness*, Freire maintains that liberatory theory "frees the educator no less than the educated from the twin thralldom of silence and monologue. Both partners are liberated as they begin to learn, the one to know self as a being of worth...and the other as capable of dialogue in spite of the strait jacket imposed by the role of educator as one who knows" (vii-ix). Thus, we see that liberatory pedagogy is equally necessary for the teacher as it is for the student.

Although a number of connections exist between the dialectics of Hegel and radical pedagogy, the final connection I wish to make here concerns the concept of work and its relation to self-consciousness. Drawing from the theological implications found in the *New Testament* book of *James*, Hegel notes that it is through putting theory into practice that one achieves self-consciousness:

> the [slave], *qua* self-consciousness in general, also relates himself negatively to the thing [the master], and takes away its independence; but at the same time the thing is independent vis-à-vis the bondsman, whose negating of it, therefore cannot go the length of being altogether done with it to the point of annihilation; in other words, he only *works* on it. (115-16)

Hegel's concept of *work* here is complex and difficult to summarize, but it appears that Marxist theorists and, hence, radical pedagogues have interpreted this idea to mean that by working on the problem of their own material condition, those who are oppressed can come to a self- or critical consciousness which can ultimately transform their condition—what Freire calls *conscientizaçao* (*Pedagogy* 19). That is, by working on that which is the subject of one's domination, one not only sees the need for transformation, but enacts in the subject of oppression the need for self-reflection, which causes the subject to enter into the dialectic with its object. Perhaps we can understand this interaction better in terms of actual classroom practice. For example, by focusing writing assignments on, say, the lack of economic opportunities for African Americans, or the immigration policies of the United States, teachers, in theory, can help students come to an awareness, through their work, of their own situations of deprivation. Furthermore, through their work, which might come in the form of letters of protests or essays demanding social change, the conditions of their oppression will at least be brought to the attention of the oppressors.

As we have seen, Hegel's dialectic is fundamental to the process of liberatory pedagogy, for according to theorists like Marx, Freire, and Giroux the dialectic is the process through which social transformation occurs. Through their engagement in a dialogic relationship—which entails the active exchange involved in dialogue—both teachers and students become liberated by the transformation of their consciousness. Thus, liberatory theorists tend to view the dialectic as an all-encompassing process, that is, as equally transformative for all oppressed student groups whether they be Brazilian peasants or African Americans, males or females.

What is important to note is that in Hegel's dialectic, the agent for change is located within the one who is oppressed. For example, in the master-slave narrative, it is the slave who provides the force for change. And for the liberatory theorist, it is the student who acts as the agent for change. In the dialectic, then, any student suffering from the domination of another gains the power to transform his or her own situation. A number of theorists, however, have critiqued the dialectic, arguing that within certain oppressive structures the dialectic merely reproduces the dominant hegemony by producing passive beings who cannot bring about change. For members of the Frankfurt School, however, it is not that the dialectic is incapable of achieving the fully synthesized transformation that we find in Hegel; rather, the problem is that the dialectic has broken down in such a way that neither the oppressed nor the oppressors are able to change their situations.

The Breakdown of the Dialectic

Having explored the connections between Hegel's dialectic and the dialectic of radical pedagogy, I'd like to look at the ways in which the dialectic process can malfunction, exploring first how Hegel's/Marx's dialectic breaks down, and then how the dialectic of radical pedagogy suppresses the development of feminist thought.

In the *Dialectic of Enlightenment*, Max Horkheimer and Theodor Adorno present an argument that serves as an example of just how fragile the dialectic process is and how easily it can turn into a system of domination for the subaltern. They begin their critique of the dialectic by asserting, "In the most general sense of progressive thought, the Enlightenment has always aimed at liberating men from fear and establishing their sovereignty. Yet the fully enlightened earth radiates disaster triumphant" (3). In fact, it is not so much Hegel's dialectic that Horkheimer and Adorno are criticizing here; it is that, in their view, there is no true dialectic at work in Enlightenment philosophy. Humankind's *hubris* and desire to dominate nature—concepts that permeate Enlightenment thought—have negated and therefore suppressed the element of fear or self-reflection that we find in Hegel. As mentioned earlier, self-reflection is crucial to achieving transcendence in both Hegelian and liberatory theory. It is the single element that convicts the oppressor, and without it neither the student nor the teacher can achieve a critical consciousness.

How, then, can the dialectic break down in pedagogical practice? According to Horkheimer and Adorno, the dialectic breaks down when the subject of oppression mystifies its objects through labor. We have already seen how students can come to a critical consciousness through their work, but Horkheimer and Adorno suggest that oppressed people can become further oppressed through the wrong kind of work—that is, through work that hides their condition. Once again, we see this kind of work rooted in the banking concept of education. Even the most well-intentioned teachers can at times engage in banking concept practices, focusing students' attention on the formal elements of writing to such a degree that there is little room left for critical content. Thus, the teacher regresses to the position of the oppressive master and the students regress to *passive* slaves. Horkheimer and Adorno make it clear that such a dialectic utilized by the banking-concept teacher will always break down.

We can use Horkheimer and Adorno's discussion of Odysseus' encounter with the Sirens to serve as an analogy for the way in which the banking-concept teacher truncates the dialectic. For Odysseus, it is the fear of succumbing to the Sirens' song—which in the Marxist dialectic represents the call for a proletariat revolution—that prompts him to fill his crew members' ears with wax and to have himself tied to the mast of his ship. But to Horkheimer and Adorno, "The dread of losing the self and of abrogating together with the self the barrier between oneself and other life, the fear of death and destruction, is intimately associated with a promise of happiness which threatened civilization in every moment" (33). Thus, Odysseus resists the Sirens' song in order to maintain his mastery over himself and over nature, which Odysseus clearly sees as his rightful place. But in doing so, he has separated himself from his crew, who continue to labor undistracted by neither the song of the Sirens nor the commands of Odysseus:

> Odysseus is represented in labor. Just as he cannot yield to the temptation to self-abandonment, so, as proprietor, he finally renounces even participation in labor, and ultimately even its management, whereas his men—despite their closeness to things—cannot enjoy their labor because it is performed under pressure, in desperation, with senses stopped by force. (35)

To extend this analogy, then, the banking-concept teacher similarly refuses to relinquish his or her domination over nature, and thus over students, for to do so would result in a loss of his or her classroom authority. Likewise, whereas in liberatory theory the students come to discover the need for critical consciousness through their work (praxis), in the banking concept students are oppressed by the work itself to the point where they do not become aware of the necessity for critical consciousness. Consequently, they continue to work, harder and harder, the way Odysseus' men worked when their ears were filled with wax, completely unaware of their own oppression. And because the students, now thoroughly mystified and disabled, cannot see the need for critical consciousness and thus cannot enact change, the teacher too is relegated to his or her role as oppressor.

Again, it is important to note that what is key to the destruction of the dialectic in the Enlightenment according to Horkheimer and Adorno is humankind's desire for mastery over self and nature, which always includes a certain amount of arrogance. And such arrogance in any dialectic results in the perpetuation of the dominant hegemony, for it is arrogance that denies the need for self-criticism. Even though radical pedagogy does not intend to function like the banking concept of teaching, it, too, being a product of masculine Enlightenment philosophy, sometimes functions within a reductionist view of oppression which assumes that all oppressed people are equally oppressed and that all oppressed people are in an equal situation to enact social change (Weiler 451). For a number of feminist theorists, however, the dialectic itself is an oppressive process, a male construct formed on androcentric principles, which presumes to include women but, like the dialectic of Horkheimer and Adorno, merely reproduces the same hegemonic structures. Perhaps the important question to ask now is: How can women achieve a dialectical transformation when the subject of the dialectic is always male? In other words, can women achieve a critical consciousness through the dialectic of radical pedagogy or will the dialectic further repress their situation?

This appearance that radical pedagogy works from the position that there is some sort of universality in oppression has proved to be highly problematic for a number of feminist theorists, particularly those concerned with the construction of gender. According to theorists like Simone de Beauvoir, for example, the notion of universality can only be represented by the masculine. Consequently, any dialectic that assumes the commonality of the subaltern will never fail to reproduce masculine domination. In *The Second Sex*, de Beauvoir argues that asymmetrical gender relationships have caused the dialectic to fail because women have been socially constructed into roles that subjugate them to the position of other, whereas men are always the subject and, hence, control the entire dialectic process.

In *Gender and Knowledge*, Susan J. Heckman notes that central to de Beauvoir's analysis of gender prescriptions is that the "fundamental distinction between the Self and Other is not symmetrical" (74). De Beauvoir argues that the social relationship between men and women is represented fully in the master-slave dialectic of Hegel. In Enlightenment thought in particular, man is always defined as the master of nature; he is "both positive and neutral" (Heckman 74). Woman on the other hand, is *not man*; she is his antithesis. Thus, according to de Beauvoir, the engendered categories of man and woman predispose woman to a position where she is always already the subaltern to man's universal. In *Gender Trouble*, Judith Butler explains de Beauvoir's notion of how the universal is masculine and how it ultimately excludes and subjugates women:

For Beauvoir, the "subject" within the existential analytic of misogyny is always already masculine, conflated within the universal, differentiating itself from a feminine "Other" outside the universalizing norms of personhood, hopelessly "particular," embodied, condemned to immanence. Although Beauvoir is often understood to be calling for the right of women, in effect, to become existential subjects and, hence, for inclusion within the terms of an abstract universality, her position also implies a fundamental critique of the very disembodiment of the abstract masculine epistemological subject. That subject is abstract to the extent that it disavows its socially marked embodiment and, further, projects that disavowed and disparaged embodiment on to the feminine sphere, effectively renaming the body as female. (11)

Because women are always already objects of the masculine order, they have become "locked into an Otherness that is central to human life" (Heckman 74). If through Enlightenment philosophy men have achieved mastery over nature, women have themselves become not only equated with nature—through the maternal activities of giving birth to and raising children—but are, according to de Beauvoir, a nature dominated by men.

Women, as objects of the masculine order, therefore, serve the purpose of reproducing that order, a role from which it appears they cannot escape. Heckman notes that "women, according to de Beauvoir, are more prey to the species because of their connection to reproduction, are more limited by nature than are men" (74). In other words, the biological *sex* of women has placed them in the role of giving birth to and nursing children, activities that do not necessarily demand that women be taken out of the work force entirely or for an extensive length of time, especially if child care responsibilities can be shared with men. It is the *gender* of women, however, which has produced a hegemonic system that essentially relegates women to full-time child care providers, which, in turn, strips them of nearly all economic and political power. Furthermore, the engendering system is such that it causes both men and women to believe that it really is natural for women to be the primary child-care providers and that men are indeed the ones who should rule the economic and, thus, the political world. Judith Butler calls this hegemonic system of gender reproduction a *literalizing fantasy* (70). Within this literalizing fantasy, then, women are so closely bound to nature, that they are at a loss to rise above it. They, therefore, become passive objects; that is, they come to believe that their gender prescriptions are natural and that any attempt to change them would be futile. Consequently, women *become* passive objects that cannot achieve transcendence.

De Beauvoir's discussion of gender reproduction is important to the situation of women in liberatory pedagogy. As I have already mentioned, one of the criticisms of liberatory theory by some feminists is that it assumes a kind of universality of oppression. In de Beauvoir's theory, then, liberatory theory is always already masculine and, therefore, it too situates female students as the objects of domination. In radical theory, all students begin as the objects of oppression, but according to de Beauvoir, female students cannot achieve the kind of critical consciousness that males can because women have been constructed not only as objects, but as passive objects as well. Like Odysseus' crew, they are mystified, cut off from the knowledge of the purpose of their work. Hence, passive female students, like Odysseus' crew, engage in their work without the power to enact the dialectic which brings them to critical consciousness. In this way, liberatory pedagogy merely reproduces a masculine system where feminist thought is repressed.

Heckman notes that in some ways Luce Irigaray agrees with de Beauvoir's critique of the male-dominated dialectic, for she too argues that "any epistemology that is rooted in the subject is inherently phallocratic" (82). Irigaray, however, differs significantly from de Beauvoir in that she believes that women are not merely the objects of the androcentric dialectic, but that they are outside the dialectic altogether. In her discussion of Irigaray, Heckman notes that "since women cannot be subjects, they cannot be the active, autonomous agents that, men have claimed, make history" (83). According to both Irigaray and de Beauvoir, women have been powerless to create their own history and thus their own epistemologies. What differentiates de Beauvoir from Irigaray, however, is that de Beauvoir sees a place for women within the Enlightenment epistemology of the androcentric dialectic, whereas Irigaray believes that the inability for women to create their own epistemology ostracizes them from patriarchal epistemology. Irigaray, thus, begins with de Beauvoir's critique of the dialectic, but ultimately moves to a critique of de Beauvoir. Judith Butler notes that for Irigaray, "both the subject and the Other are masculine mainstays of a closed phallocratic signifying economy that achieves its totalizing goal through the exclusion of the feminine altogether" (9).

In *This Sex Which is not One*, Irigaray argues that, unlike the binary structures of androcentric signifying systems, women represent a multiplicity of positions, languages, and desires. However, because the dominant androcentric structures do not allow space for the multiplicity of women, feminine signifying systems are therefore marginalized:

> Must this multiplicity of female desire and female language be understood as shards, scattered remnants of a violated sexuality? A sexuality denied? The question has no simple answer. The rejection, the exclusion of a female imaginary certainly puts woman in the position of experiencing herself only fragmentarily, in the little-structured margins of a dominant ideology, as waste, or excess, what is left of a mirror invested by the (masculine) "subject" to reflect himself, to copy himself. Moreover, the role of "femininity" is prescribed by this masculine specula(riza)tion and corresponds scarcely at all to woman's desire, which may be recovered only in secret, in hiding, with anxiety and guilt. (30)

Returning to de Beauvoir's argument, Irigaray asserts that "this domination of the philosophic logos stems in part from its power to *reduce all others to the economy of the Same*" and "from its power to *eradicate the difference between the sexes* in systems that are self-representative of a masculine subject" (74). Again, we find that the masculine reduction to universality or sameness is at the heart of the breakdown of dialectic for women. Through this reduction, the difference and multiplicity that women bring to a signifying system like the dialectic is repressed. And if woman's difference and multiplicity is repressed, then she is essentially negated. She therefore becomes *unrepresentable*.

We know from theorists like Mikhail Bakhtin and Jacques Lacan that language itself is dynamic, that it works dialectically. If, as Irigaray argues, women are left out of the dialectic process, are they not also absent from language? Irigaray's theory of women as the unrepresentable is also seen clearly in the phallocratic theories of language espoused by Lacan. Heckman argues that "Lacan represents the most extreme statement of phallogocentrism" (84). In Lacanian theory, the universal signifier is the phallus. That is, everything meaningful is represented by the masculine, whereas everything that is non-masculine, hence feminine, is according to natural law lacking and thus exists outside the signifying system. Lacan says,

> There is no such thing as *The* woman, where the definite article stands for the universal. There is no such thing as *The* woman since of her essence—having already risked the term, why think twice about it? Of her essence, she is not all. (qtd. in Heckman 84)

Although Lacan himself recognized that the nature of the phallus is indeed socially constructed, it remains that the symbolic order is masculine and thus women are both subjugated and ostracized by it. In "The Laugh of the Medusa," Hélène Cixous takes this a step further by arguing that phallocratic language is a locus for the reproduction of feminine oppression:

> I meant it when I speak of male writing. I maintain unequivocally that there is such a thing as *marked* writing; that, until now, far more extensively and repressively than is ever suspected or admitted, writing has been run by a libidinal and cultural—hence political, typically masculine—economy; that this is a locus where the oppression of women has been perpetuated, over and over, more or less consciously, and in a manner that's frightening since it's often hidden or adorned with the mystifying charms of fiction; that this locus has greatly exaggerated all the signs of sexual opposition (and not sexual difference), where woman has never her turn to speak—this being all the more serious and unpardonable in that writing is precisely *the very possibility of change*, the space that can serve as a springboard for subversive thought, the precursory movement of a transformation of social and cultural structures. (249)

We therefore find, according to French feminists like de Beauvoir, Irigaray, and Cixous, that women are indeed placed in an *impossible* situation when it comes to the dialectic. Whether woman is merely the Other of the dialectic or whether she is unrepresented by the dialectic altogether leaves us with a situation where women are incapable of transcendence; that is, the dialectic has broken down for and has suppressed women. It follows then that the female student in radical pedagogy is also placed in a difficult situation. Even if the liberatory teacher is female, the epistemologies that govern the linguistic and dialogic systems in which transcendence is supposed to take place are totalizing in their male dominance. Furthermore, through this dialectic, women are constructed as passive beings.

Transcending the Dialectic

We are left, then, with what appears to be an irreconcilable problem presented to women students by the androcentric dialectic of radical pedagogy. We have seen how, in seeking to liberate all oppressed students, the dialectic of radical pedagogy breaks down and feminist thought is thus suppressed. This suppression is accomplished, first, by radical pedagogy's tendency to reduce all oppressed objects to a universal subaltern; and, second, feminist thought is suppressed by women's impossible situation of being always already constructed by the dominant discourse of our society into the role of Other, a role from which it seems they cannot escape, a role that shapes them into passive beings who are unable to enact dialectical change.

As teachers who are truly committed to feminist concerns, we must, at this point, ask ourselves some pertinent questions regarding the future of our pedagogical practices: Are women doomed to totalizing masculine pedagogical systems for which there is no hope for transcendence, and, thus, no hope for a social change that includes the empowerment of women? Is there anything in radical pedagogy worth redeeming or should we discard it altogether? Feminist theorists are divided on these issue. Theorists like Irigaray and Cixous, one the one hand, believe that since women exist outside the dialectic to begin with, they should create their own dialectic epistemology based on purely feminine perspectives. On the other hand, theorists like Judith Butler, Teresa de Lauretis, and Kathleen Weiler believe that feminists should work from within the androcentric dialectic, to deconstruct and transform it.

Luce Irigaray, having already argued that women are excluded from the male dialectic, sees the effort for reconciliation between the androcentric and the gynocentric as futile. Instead, Irigaray argues that women need to separate themselves in opposition to men in order to escape the constraints of male domination:

> For women to undertake tactical strikes, to keep themselves apart from men long enough to learn to defend their desire, especially through speech, to discover the love of other women while sheltered from men's imperious choices that put them in the positions of rival commodities, to forge for themselves a social status that compels recognition, to earn their living in order to escape from their condition of prostitute . . . these are certainly indispensable stages in the escape from their proletarization on the exchange market. But if their aim was simply to reverse the order of things, even supposing this to be possible, history would repeat itself in the long run, would revert to sameness: to phallocraticism. It would leave room neither for women's sexuality, nor for women's imaginary, nor for women's language to take (their) place. (33)

By rejecting the male dialectic, according to Irigaray, women become freed from the negation by the universal and thus find space to create their own existence, to create a stable feminine subject. For Cixous, what is central to creating women's own existence is having the uninterrupted time and space to develop women's writing. Like Irigaray, Cixous believes that women should resist the phallocratic dialectic, that they should "break out of the snare of silence" (251). Cixous notes, "It is by writing, from and toward women, and by taking up the challenge of speech which has been governed by the phallus, that women will confirm women in a place other than that which is confirmed in and by the symbolic, that is, in a place other than silence" (33).

For some feminists, this rejection translates into the call for a separatist education. In her essay, "The Soul of a Woman's College," delivered at Scrips College in Claremont, California in 1984, Adrienne Rich explains why she too believes that women should separate from the masculine order to gain their own identity. According to Rich, a gynocentric education produces in women a sense of confidence and self-esteem that would otherwise be repressed in a phallocratic education. Rich notes that her reason for desiring the proliferation of women's colleges stems from the exclusion of feminine participation in co-educational colleges. "I wanted a place which women would feel was theirs," says Rich: "That most of the world is not a women's place, but a women-negating place, and that women need a sense of what a women's place can be. . . . That's *my* word—I think today you feminists call it 'consciousness'" (195-96).

Although some feminists see complete separation from male economy as the only alternative to domination, a number of other feminist theorists believe that the creation of the thoroughly gynocentric order that Irigaray and Cixous argue for can become equally oppressive as an androcentric one. In *Gender Trouble*, Judith Butler argues that by seeking an identity that is exclusively female, one essentially constructs a "stable" subject which in turn works to suppress feminine difference in the same way that liberatory pedagogy does:

> Indeed, the premature insistence on a stable subject of feminism, understood as a seamless category of women, inevitably generates multiple refusals to accept the category. These domains of exclusion reveal the coercive and regulatory consequences of that construction, even when the construction has been elaborated for emancipatory purposes. (4)

In *Thinking Fragments*, Jane Flax takes a slightly different view than Butler as to why women should not seek complete separation from male systems. Flax says, "By conceptualizing woman as the problem, we repeat rather than deconstruct or analyze the social relations that construct or represent us as a problem in the first place. If the problem is defined in this way, woman retains her traditional position: the 'guilty one,' the deviant, the other" (138). For Flax, then, a women's paradigm that excludes the male merely reduces both paradigms to a male/female binary structure where the male economy is dominant.

Once again, we find women placed into a seemingly impossible situation. If the possibility for women to achieve a social transcendence does not exist through the dialectic of traditional liberatory pedagogical practices, and if women cannot achieve liberation by creating a dialectic that is wholly gynocentric, then what can women do to break the cultural hegemony? The answer for some, and the answer for which I am arguing in this essay, is for feminists to begin by resisting totalizing structures—thus deconstructing the androcentric dialectic—then reconstructing a dialectic based on a plurality of subject/object positions.

In *Alice Doesn't*, Teresa de Lauretis suggests that feminist resistance from within androcentric culture is not only entirely possible but perhaps most profitable for women as well. Unlike Cixous, who see feminist writing as tool to create an identity for women outside the boundaries men, de Lauretis believes that feminist (re)reading and writing are themselves the beginning for deconstructing androcentric dominance:

> Strategies of writing *and* of reading are forms of cultural resistance. Not only can they work to turn dominant discourses inside out (and show that it can be done), to undercut their enunciation and address, to unearth the archaeological stratifications on which they are built; but in affirming the historical existence of irreducible contradictions for women in discourse, they also challenge the theory in its own terms, the terms of semiotic space constructed in language, its power based on social validation and well-established modes of enunciation and address. So well-established that, paradoxically, the only way to position oneself outside that discourse is to position oneself within it—to refuse the question as formulated, or to answer deviously (though in its own words), even to quote (but against the grain). (7)

Even though Lacanian theory essentially negates women's place in language, de Lauretis argues that women can indeed find voices by using androcentric language as a means of resistance. De Lauretis attacks the dialectic by attacking its power to reduce to the universal binary. By foregrounding the numerous contradictions of totalizing masculine theories, de Lauretis effectively creates a space for women to position themselves, not merely as the *Other* or the *unrepresentable*, but as viable voices of opposition to phallocratic dominance. In fact, *Alice Doesn't* serves as one example of feminist resistance to and thus recreation of male dominated cinema through its deconstruction of it. De Lauretis remarks that her book "may be seen as an eccentric reading, a confrontation with theoretical discourses and expressive practices... which construct and effect a certain representation of 'woman'" (5). Thus, for de Lauretis, the mere recognition that the dialectic breaks down in its masculine form is itself enough *conscientization* for women to begin to enact change.

Judith Butler likewise agrees that women can gain power and thus enact social change by deconstructing masculine signifying structures. Butler, like de Lauretis, begins by challenging the totality of the "unrepresentable" in Lacanian theory (147). Drawing on the works of Jacqueline Rose and Jane Gallop, Butler argues that the many contradictions involved in the construction of gender provide women discursive space to challenge the phallocratic order. For Butler, the task of feminist theory is to utilize this discursive space, "to disrupt the foundations that cover over alternative cultural configurations of gender . . . to destabilize and render in their phantasmic dimension the 'premises' of identity politics" (147).

We find, then, that it is de Lauretis' and Butler's insistence on the *plurality* or *multiplicity* among women—that women truly are the "sex which is not one"—which effectively deconstructs the masculine dialectic. And it is here, moreover, that as teachers of writing we can raise our own consciousness about the limitations of the present condition of liberatory pedagogy. The problem isn't so much that the dialectic of radical pedagogy cannot work for the development of feminist thought; rather, the problem, as Kathleen Weiler argues in "Freire and a Feminist Pedagogy of Difference," is that traditional liberatory theory is too limiting. Weiler begins her essay by noting that liberatory pedagogical theory and most feminist theories have a number of things in common. She suggests first that the two kinds of theories tend to acknowledge that people are oppressed by their material conditions; second, that consciousness must contain with it a critical capacity; and, third, that both theories "hold strong commitment to justice and a vision for a better world and of the potential for liberation" (450). Weiler, however, notes that these goals alone do not provide an adequate foundation for a liberatory pedagogy that includes women:

> As universal goals, these ideals do not address the specificity of people's lives; they do not directly analyze the contradictions between conflicting oppressed groups or the ways in which a single individual can experience oppression in one sphere while being privileged or oppressed in another. (450)

Perhaps, then, the problem with the relationship between radical pedagogy and feminist students is that radical pedagogy's own internal dialectic, the process that keeps it dynamic and thus pertinent to its social purpose, has, contrary to Giroux, failed to keep up with the rapidly changing social climate of American education. As Weiler argues, liberatory theory grew out of real-life situations of poverty and oppression. For example, Freire's theory grew out of the very real oppression of Brazilian peasants. His theory is specific to that situation (although clearly commonalities exist in oppressive situations elsewhere), a situation which was not so much concerned with liberating women from androcentric political structures as it was with helping an entire class of people to survive.

Reconstructing Liberatory Pedagogy

Throughout this paper, I have argued that the dialectic of radical pedagogy in its present form can suppress the development of feminist thought in at least two ways: the first is by effectively reproducing gender prescriptions that always already construct women into the role of *Other*, which, in turn, create passive objects that cannot transform their condition. The second way that the dialectic of radical pedagogy suppresses feminist thought is through its tendency to reduce all oppressed people into a category of *sameness*. That is, liberatory theory tends not to distinguish between, say, the oppressed condition of a male migrant farm worker and the oppressed condition of a white, middle-class female. Both indeed may be oppressed, but their oppressions and, hence, the solutions to their oppressions will be very different. The problem with this kind of reductionist view of oppression is that it silences *difference*, which, therefore, as a number of feminists have argued, silences women, thus essentially leaving them out of the dialectic altogether.

We are left wondering, then, if the dialectic is so destructive to the development of feminist thought, what beneficial role, if any, can the dialectic play in the writing classroom? Although it would be impossible for me to answer this question adequately at this point, I would like to suggest that the feminist critiques of the dialectic can provide us with a starting point for reconstructing a liberatory pedagogy that includes women. Perhaps one of the implications of these feminist critiques of the dialectic is not a new concept in pedagogical practice but one that bears repeating: that we as writing teachers must consciously work toward deconstructing the always already otherness of female students. We must first be aware that by the time both male and female students get to our classrooms, they have been thoroughly engendered into roles that to many appear to be *natural*; for female students, unfortunately, this usually means their subjection to the passive role of *object*. And part of the reason why these gender roles are so powerful is that they are rarely challenged openly, especially in legitimating institutions like the university. In our teaching practice, then, we can help female students to become conscious of the oppression brought on by their gender constraints by foregrounding feminist issues and concerns. The obvious benefit of doing this is that both male and female students become aware that their genders are not entirely natural but that they have been constructed into certain sexual, and, thus, social and political roles. The important thing, though, is that by deconstructing the female student as object, we provide a space for an active student, and an active female student, even within an androcentric dialectic, is capable of creating social change.

The second implication that feminist critiques of the dialectic provide for writing teachers comes from their insistence on plurality in the classroom. What we need is a pedagogy that rejects the universalization of the dialectic. That is, we need to be aware that a number of shifting and competing dialectics can occur simultaneously, and that the teacher must be conscious of his or her shifting roles within these dialectics. These shifting and competing dialectics become very clear when we consider issues of race and economic status as areas that complicate the binary master/slave dichotomy of the dialectic, for it is possible to be both oppressor and oppressed at the same time. In fact, one recent criticism of some feminist theories is that the theorists themselves—mostly white, middle-class Europeans and Americans—work from positions of privilege and that they neglect issues concerning women of color and women who are physically oppressed, such as those politically imprisoned in South America. Kathleen Weiler notes that "Recognizing the standpoints of subjects as shaped by their experience of class, race, gender, or other socially defined identities has powerful implications for pedagogy, in that it emphasizes the need to make conscious the subject positions not only of students but of teachers as well" (470). Thus, by foregrounding our own positions as subjects and objects of oppression, we can encourage students to explore their own often ambiguous positions. The foregrounding of such ambiguities can only lead to a better understanding, a better *consciousness* of *difference* among both students and teachers.

Finally, it is important for us to keep in mind that the dialectic is only a story, albeit a very powerful one, a story that explains a masculine view of the Western world. And as a story, it explains certain things accurately, but as an androcentric story, it leaves out a host of alternative world views. What we can do as writing instructors, however, is help our students see the limitations of this story and to help them take control of it, to augment it, to create a place for themselves within it, and to respect and engage with the stories of others.[1]

Notes

[1] I'd like to thank Marilyn M. Cooper for her inspiration and support in writing this essay.

Works Cited

Aronowitz, Stanley, and Henry A. Giroux. *Education Under Siege*. New York: Bergin, 1985.

Butler, Clark. *G.W.F. Hegel*. Boston: Twayne, 1977.

Butler, Judith. *Gender Trouble*. New York: Routledge, 1990.

Cixous, Hélène. "The Laugh of the Medusa." *New French Feminisms*. Ed. Elaine Marks and Isabelle De Courtivron. Amherst, MA: U of Massachusetts P, 1980.

De Beauvoir, Simone. *The Second Sex*. Hammondsworth, England: Penguin, 1972.

De Lauretis, Teresa. *Alice Doesn't: Feminism, Semiotics, Cinema*. Bloomington: U of Indiana P, 1984.

Flax, Jane. *Thinking Fragments: Psychoanalysis, Feminism, and Postmodernism in the Contemporary West*. Berkeley: U of California P, 1990.

Freire, Paulo. *Education for Critical Consciousness*. New York: Continuum, 1990.

———. *Pedagogy of the Oppressed*. New York: Continuum, 1970.

Freire, Paulo, and Donaldo Macedo. *Literacy: Reading the Word and the World*. Amherst: Bergin, 1987.

Giroux, Henry. *Border Crossings: Cultural Workers and the Politics of Education*. New York: Routledge, 1990.

Heckman, Susan J. *Gender and Knowledge*. Boston: Northeastern UP, 1990.

Hegel, G.W.F. *Phenomenology of Spirit*. Trans. A.V. Miller. London: Oxford UP, 1977.

Horkheimer, Max, and Theodor W. Adorno. *Dialectic of Enlightenment*. New York: Continuum, 1990.

Irigaray, Luce. *This Sex Which is not One*. Trans. Catherine Porter and Carolyn Burke. Ithaca, NY: Cornell UP, 1985.

Rich, Adrienne. *Blood, Bread, and Poetry*. New York: Norton, 1986.

Shor, Ira. *Critical Teaching and Everyday Life*. Chicago: U of Chicago P, 1980.

Weiler, Kathleen. "Freire and a Feminist Pedagogy of Difference." *Harvard Educational Review* 61 (1991): 449-73.

Paulo Freire and the Politics of Postcolonialism

HENRY A. GIROUX

> Yet we have different privileges and different compensations for our positions in the field of power relations. My caution is against a form of theoretical tourism on the part of the first world critic, where the margin becomes a linguistic or critical vacation, a new poetics of the exotic.
>
> Caren Kaplan

The work of Paulo Freire continues to exercise a strong influence on a variety of liberal and radical educators. In some quarters his name has become synonymous with the very concept and practice of critical pedagogy. Increasingly, Freire's work has become the standard reference for engaging in what is often referred to as teaching for critical thinking, dialogical pedagogy, or critical literacy. As Freire's work has passed from the origins of its production in Brazil, through Latin America and Africa to the hybrid borderlands of North America, it has been frequently appropriated by academics, adult educators, and others who inhabit the ideology of the West in ways that often reduce it to a pedagogical technique or method. Of course, the requisite descriptions generally invoke terms like "politically charged," "problem-posing," or the mandatory "education for critical consciousness" and often contradict the use of Freire's work as a revolutionary pedagogical practice.[1] But in such a context, these are terms that speak less to a political project constructed amidst concrete struggles than they do to the insipid and dreary demands for pedagogical recipes dressed up in the jargon of abstracted progressive labels. What has been increasingly lost in the North American and Western appropriation of Freire's work is the profound and radical nature of its theory and practice as an anti-colonial and postcolonial discourse. More specifically, Freire's work is often appropriated and taught "without any consideration of imperialism and its cultural representation. This lacuna itself suggests the continuing ideological dissimulation of imperialism today" (Young 158). This suggests that Freire's work has been appropriated in ways that denude it of some of its most important political insights. Similarly, it testifies to how a politics of location works in the interest of privilege and power to cross cultural, political, and textual borders so as to deny the specificity of the other and to reimpose the discourse and practice of colonial hegemony.

I want to argue that Paulo Freire's work must be read as a postcolonial text and that North Americans, in particular, must engage in a radical form of border crossing in order to reconstruct Freire's work in the specificity of its historical and political construction. Specifically, this means making problematic a politics of location situated in the privilege and power of the West and how engaging the question of the ideological weight of such a position constructs one's specific reading of Freire's work. At the same time, becoming a border crosser engaged in a productive dialogue with others means producing a space in which those dominant social relations, ideologies, and practices that erase the specificity of the voice of the other must be challenged and overcome.

Homelessness and the Border Intellectual

In order to understand Freire's work in terms of its historical and political importance, cultural workers have to become border crossers. This means that teachers and other intellectuals have to take leave of the cultural, theoretical, and ideological borders that enclose them within the safety of "those places and spaces we inherit and occupy, which frame our lives in very specific and concrete ways" (Borsa 36). Being a border crosser suggests that one has to reinvent traditions not within the discourse of submission, reverence, and repetition, but "as transformation and critique." That is, "One must construct one's discourse as difference in relation to that tradition and this implies at the same time continuities and discontinuities" (Laclau 12). At the same time, border crossing engages intellectual work not only in its specificity and partiality, but also in terms of the intellectual function itself as part of the discourse of invention and construction, rather than a discourse of recognition whose aim is reduced to revealing and transmitting universal truths. In this case, it is important to highlight intellectual work as being forged in the intersection of contingency and history arising not from the "exclusive hunting grounds of an elite [but] from all points of the social fabric" (Laclau 27).

This task becomes all the more difficult with Freire because the borders that define his work have shifted over time in ways that parallel his own exile and movement from Brazil to Chile, Mexico, the United States, Geneva, and back to Brazil. Freire's work not only draws heavily upon European discourses, but also upon the thought and language of theorists in Latin America, Africa, and North America. Freire's ongoing political project raises enormous difficulties for educators who situate Freire's work in the reified language of methodologies and in empty calls that enshrine the practical at the expense of the theoretical and political.

Freire is an exile for whom being home is often tantamount to being "homeless" and for whom his own identity and the identities of others are viewed as sites of struggle over the politics of representation, the exercise of power, and the function of social memory.[2] It is important to note that the concept of "home" being used here does not refer exclusively to those places in which one sleeps, eats, raises children, and sustains a certain level of comfort. For some, this particular notion of "home" is too mythic, especially for those who literally have no home in this sense; it also becomes a reification when it signifies a place of safety which excludes the lives, identities, and experiences of the other, that is, when it becomes synonymous with the cultural capital of white, middle-class subjects.

"Home," in the sense I am using it, refers to the cultural, social, and political boundaries that demarcate varying spaces of comfort, suffering, abuse, and security that define an individual's or group's location and positionality. To move away from "home" is to question in historical, semiotic, and structural terms how the boundaries and meanings of "home" are constructed in self-evident ways often outside of criticism. "Home" is about those cultural spaces and social formations which work hegemonically and as sites of resistance. In the first instance, "home" is safe by virtue of its repressive exclusions and hegemonic location of individuals and groups outside of history. In the second case, home becomes a form of "homelessness," a shifting site of identity, resistance, and opposition that enables conditions of self and social formation. JanMohamed captures this distinction quite lucidly:

> "Home" comes to be associated with "culture" as an environment, process, and hegemony that determine individuals through complicated mechanisms. Culture is productive of the necessary sense of belonging, of "home"; it attempts to suture . . . collective and individual subjectivity. But culture is also divisive, producing boundaries that distinguish the collectivity and what lies outside it and that define hierarchic organizations within the collectivity. "Homelessness," on the other hand, is . . . an enabling concept . . . associated with . . . the civil and political space that hegemony cannot suture, a space in which alternative acts and alternative intentions which are not yet articulated as a social institution or even project can survive. "Homelessness," then, is a situation wherein utopian potentiality can endure. ("Worldliness" 27)

For Freire, the task of being an intellectual has always been forged within the trope of homelessness: between different zones of theoretical and cultural difference; between the borders of non-European and European cultures. In effect, Freire is a border intellectual,[3] whose allegiance has not been to a specific class and culture as in Gramsci's notion of the organic intellectual; instead, Freire's writings embody a mode of discursive struggle and opposition that not only challenges the oppressive machinery of the State but is also sympathetic to the formation of new cultural subjects and movements engaged in the struggle over the modernist values of freedom, equality, and justice. In part, this explains Freire's interest for educators, feminists, and revolutionaries in Africa, Latin America, and South Africa.

As a border intellectual, Freire ruptures the relationship between individual identity and collective subjectivity. He makes visible a politics that links human suffering with a project of possibility, not as a static plunge into a textuality disembodied from human struggles, but as a politics of literacy forged in the political and material dislocations of regimes that exploit, oppress, expel, maim and ruin human life. As a border intellectual, Freire occupies a terrain of "homelessness" in the postmodern sense that suggests there is little possibility of ideological and hegemonic closure, no relief from the incessant tensions and contradictions that inform one's own identity, ideological struggles, and project of possibility. It is this sense of "homelessness," this constant crossing over into terrains of otherness, that characterizes both Freire's life and work. It is as an exile, a border being, an intellectual posed between different cultural, epistemological, and spatial borders that Freire has undertaken to situate his own politics of location as a border crosser.

Freire as Border Crosser
It is to Freire's credit as a critical educator and cultural worker that he has always been extremely conscious about the intentions, goals, and effects of crossing borders and how such movements offer the opportunity for new subject positions, identities, and social relations that can produce resistance to and relief from the structures of domination and oppression. While such an insight has continuously invested his work with a healthy "restlessness," it has not meant that Freire's work has developed unproblematically. For example, in his earlier work, Freire attempted to reconcile an emancipatory politics of literacy and a struggle over identity and difference with certain problematic elements of modernism. Freire's incessant attempts to construct a new language, produce new spaces of resistance, imagine new ends and opportunities to reach them were sometimes constrained in totalizing narratives and binarisms that de-emphasized the mutually contradictory and multiple character of domination and struggle. In this sense, Freire's earlier reliance on emancipation as one and the same with class struggle sometimes erased how women were subjected differently to patriarchal structures; similarly, his call for members of the dominating groups to commit class suicide downplayed the complex, multiple, and contradictory nature of human subjectivity. Finally, Freire's reference to the "masses" or oppressed as being inscribed in a culture of silence appeared to be at odds with both the varied forms of domination these groups labored under and Freire's own belief in the diverse ways in which the oppressed struggle and manifest elements of practical and political agency. While it is crucial to acknowledge the theoretical and political brilliance that informed much of this work, it is also necessary to recognize that it bore slight traces of vanguardism. This is evident not only in the binarisms that inform *Pedagogy of the Oppressed* but also in *Pedagogy in Process: The Letters to Guinea-Bissau*, particularly in

those sections in which Freire argues that the culture of the masses must develop on the basis of science and that emancipatory pedagogy must be aligned with the struggle for national reconstruction.

Without adequately addressing the contradictions these issues raise between the objectives of the state, the discourse of everyday life, and the potential for pedagogical violence being done in the name of political correctness, Freire's work is open to the charge made by some leftist theorists of being overly totalizing. But this can be read less as a reductive critique of Freire's work than as an indication of the need to subject it and all forms of social criticism to analyses that engage its strengths and limitations as part of a wider dialogue in the service of an emancipatory politics. The contradictions raised in Freire's work offer a number of questions that need to be addressed by critical educators about not only Freire's earlier work but also about their own. For instance, what happens when the language of the educator is not the same as that of the oppressed? How is it possible to be vigilant against taking up a notion of language, politics, and rationality that undermines recognizing one's own partiality and the voices and experiences of others? How does one explore the contradiction between validating certain forms of "correct" thinking and the pedagogical task of helping students assume rather than simply follow the dictates of authority, regardless of how radical the project informed by such authority. Of course, it cannot be forgotten that the strength of Freire's early discourse rests, in part, with its making visible not merely the ideological struggle against domination and colonialism but also the material substance of human suffering, pain, and imperialism. Forged in the heat of life-and-death struggles, Freire's recourse to binarisms such as the oppressed vs. the oppressor, problem-solving vs. problem-posing, science vs. magic, raged bravely against dominant languages and configurations of power that refused to address their own politics by appealing to the imperatives of politeness, objectivity, and neutrality. Here Freire strides the boundary between modernist and anti-colonialist discourse; he struggles against colonialism, but in doing so he often reverses rather than ruptures its basic problematic. Benita Parry locates a similar problem in the work of Frantz Fanon: "What happens is that heterogeneity is repressed in the monolithic figures and stereotypes of colonialist representations.... [But] the founding concepts of the problematic must be refused" (28).

In his later work, particularly in his work with Donaldo Macedo, in his numerous interviews, and in his talking books with authors such as Ira Shor, Antonio Faundez, and Myles Horton, Freire undertakes a form of social criticism and cultural politics that pushes against those boundaries that invoke the discourse of the unified, humanist subject, universal historical agents, and Enlightenment rationality. Refusing the privilege of home as a border intellectual situated in the shifting and ever-changing universe of struggle, Freire invokes and constructs elements of a social criticism that shares an affinity with emancipatory strands of postmodern discourse. That is, in his refusal of a transcendent ethics, epistemological foundationalism, and political teleology, he further develops a provisional ethical and political discourse subject to the play of history, culture, and power. As a border intellectual, he constantly reexamines and raises questions about what kind of borders are being crossed and revisited, what kind of identities are being remade and refigured within new historical, social, and political borderlands, and what effects such crossings have for redefining pedagogical practice. For Freire, pedagogy is seen as a cultural practice and politics that takes place not only in schools but in all cultural spheres. In this instance, all cultural work is pedagogical, and cultural workers inhabit a number of sites that include but are not limited to schools. Most recently in a dialogue with Antonio Faundez, Freire talks about his own self-formation as an exile and border crosser. He writes,

> It was by travelling all over the world, it was by travelling through Africa, it was by travelling through Asia, through Australia and New Zealand, and through the islands of the South Pacific, it was by travelling through the whole of Latin America, the Caribbean, North America and Europe—it was by passing through all these different parts of the world as an exile that I came to understand my own country better. It was by seeing it from a distance, it was by standing back from it, that I came to understand myself better. It was by being confronted with another self that I discovered more easily my own identity. And thus I overcame the risk which exiles sometimes run of being too remote in their work as intellectuals from the most real, most concrete experiences, and of being somewhat lost, and even somewhat contented, because they are lost in a game of words, what I usually rather humorously call "specializing in the ballet of concepts." (13)

It is here that we get further indications of some of the principles that inform Freire as a revolutionary. It is in this work and his work with Donaldo Macedo, Ira Shor and others that we see traces, images, and representations of a political project inextricably linked to Freire's own self-formation. It is here that Freire is at his most prescient in unraveling and dismantling ideologies and structures of domination as they emerge in his confrontation with the ongoing exigencies of daily life as manifested differently in the tensions, suffering, and hope between the diverse margins and centers of power that have come to characterize a postmodern/postcolonial world.

Reading Freire's work for the last fifteen years has drawn me closer to Adorno's insight that, "It is part of morality not to be at home in one's home" (qtd. in Said, "Reflections" 365). Adorno was also an exile, raging against the horror and evil of another era, but he was also insistent that it was the role of intellectuals, in part, to challenge those places bounded by terror, exploitation, and human suffering. He also called for intellectuals to refuse and transgress those systems of standardization, commodification, and administration pressed into the service of an ideology and language of "home" that occupied or were complicitous with oppressive centers of power. Freire differs from Adorno in that there is a more profound sense of rupture, transgression, and hope, intellectually and politically, in his work. This is evident in his call for educators, social critics, and cultural workers to fashion a notion of politics and pedagogy outside of established disciplinary borders; outside of the division between high and popular culture; outside of "stable notions of self and identity . . . based on exclusion and secured by terror" (Martin and Mohanty 197); outside of homogeneous public spheres; and outside of boundaries that separate desire from rationality, body from mind.

Of course, this is not to suggest that intellectuals have to go into exile to take up Freire's work, but it does suggest that in becoming border crossers it is not uncommon for many of them to engage his work as an act of bad faith. Refusing to negotiate or deconstruct the borders that define their own politics of location, they have little sense of moving into an "imagined space," a positionality from which they can unsettle, disrupt, and "illuminate that which is no longer home-like, *heimlich*, about one's home" (Becker 1). From the comforting perspective of the colonizing gaze, such theorists often appropriate Freire's work without engaging its historical specificity and ongoing political project. The gaze in this case becomes self-serving and self-referential, its principles shaped by technical and methodological consider-ations. Its perspective, in spite of itself, is largely "panoptic and thus dominating" (JanMohamed, "Worldliness" 10). To be sure, such intellectu-als cross borders less as exiles than as colonialists. Hence, they often refuse to hold up to critical scrutiny their own complicity in producing and main-taining specific injustices, practices, and forms of oppression that deeply inscribe the legacy and heritage of colonialism. Edward Said captures the tension between exile and critic, home and "homelessness" in his comment on Adorno, though it is just as applicable to Paulo Freire:

> To follow Adorno is to stand away from "home" in order to look at it with the exile's detachment. For there is considerable merit in the practice of noting the discrepancies between various concepts and ideas and what they actually produce. We take home and language for granted; they become nature and their underlying assumptions recede into dogma and orthodoxy. The exile knows that in a secular and contingent world, homes are always provisional. Borders and barriers, which enclose us within the safety of familiar territory can also become prisons, and are often defended beyond reason or necessity. Exiles cross borders, break barriers of thought and experience. ("Reflections" 365)

Of course, intellectuals from the First World, especially white academ-ics, run the risk of acting in bad faith when they appropriate the work of a Third World intellectual such as Freire without "mapping the politics of their forays into other cultures," theoretical discourses, and historical expe-riences (JanMohamed, "Worldliness" 3). It is truly disconcerting that First World educators rarely articulate the politics and privileges of their own location, in this case, so at the very least to be self-conscious about not repeating the type of appropriations that inform the legacy of what Said calls "Orientialist" scholarship (*Orientalism*).

Freire and Postcolonial Discourse

I want to conclude by raising some issues regarding what it might mean for cultural workers to resist the recuperation of Freire's work as an academic commodity, a recipe for all times and places. Similarly, I want to offer some broad considerations for reinventing the radicality of Freire's work within the emergence of a postcolonial discourse informed by what Cornel West terms the "decolonization of the Third World," and characterized by "the exercise of . . . agency and the [production of] new . . . subjectivities and identities put forward by those persons who had been degraded, devalued, hunted, and harassed, exploited and oppressed by the European maritime empires" (4). The challenge presented by Freire and other postcolonial critics offers new theoretical possibilities to address the authority and discourses of those practices wedded to the legacy of a colonialism that either directly constructs or is implicated in social relations that keep privilege and oppression alive as active constituting forces of daily life within the centers and margins of power.

Postcolonial discourses have made clear that the old legacies of the political left, center, and right can no longer be so easily defined. Indeed, postcolonial critics have gone further and provided important theoretical insights into how such discourses either actively construct colonial relations or are implicated in their construction. From this perspective, Robert Young argues that postcolonialism is a dislocating discourse that raises theoretical questions regarding how dominant and radical theories "have themselves been implicated in the long history of European colonialism—and, above all, the extent to which [they] continue to determine both the institutional conditions of knowledge as well as the terms of contemporary institutional practices—practices which extend beyond the limits of the academic institution" (viii). This is especially true for many of the theorists in a variety of social movements who have taken up the language of difference and a concern for the politics of the other. In many instances, theorists within these new social movements have addressed political and pedagogical issues through the construction of binary oppositions that not only contain traces of racism and theoretical vanguardism but also fall into the trap of simply reversing the old colonial legacy and problematic of oppressed vs. oppressor. In doing so, they have often unwittingly imitated the colonial model of erasing the complexity, complicity, diverse agents, and multiple situations that constitute the enclaves of colonial/hegemonic discourse and practice.[4]

Postcolonial discourses have both extended and moved beyond the parameters of this debate in a number of ways. First, postcolonial critics have argued that the history and politics of difference are often informed by a legacy of colonialism that warrants analyzing the exclusions and repressions that allow specific forms of privilege to remain unacknowledged in the language of Western educators and cultural workers. At stake here is the task of demystifying and deconstructing forms of privilege that benefit maleness, whiteness, and property as well as those conditions that have disabled others to speak in places where those who are privileged by virtue of the legacy of colonial power assume authority and the conditions for human agency. This suggests, as Gayatri Spivak has pointed out, that more is at stake than problematizing discourse. More importantly, educators and cultural workers must be engaged in "the unlearning of one's own privilege. So that, not only does one become able to listen to that other constituency, but one learns to speak in such a way that one will be taken seriously by that other constituency" (42). In this instance, postcolonial discourse extends the radical implications of difference and location by making such concepts attentive to providing the grounds for forms of self-representation and collective knowledge in which the subject *and* object of European culture are problematized.[5]

Second, postcolonial discourse rewrites the relationship between the margin and the center by deconstructing the colonialist and imperialist ideologies that structure Western knowledge, texts, and social practices. In this case, there is an attempt to demonstrate how European culture and colonialism "are deeply implicated in each other" (Young 119). This suggests more that rewriting or recovering the repressed stories and social memories of the other; it means understanding and rendering visible how Western knowledge is encased in historical and institutional structures that both privilege and exclude particular readings, particular voices, certain aesthetics, forms of authority, specific representations, and modes of sociality. The West and otherness relate not as polarities or binarisms in postcolonial discourse but in ways in which both are complicitous and resistant, victim and accomplice. In this instance, criticism of the dominating other returns as a form of self criticism. Linda Hutcheon captures the importance of this issue with her question: "How do we construct a discourse which displaces the effects of the colonizing gaze while we are still under its influence" (176).

While it cannot be forgotten that the legacy of colonialism has meant large-scale death and destruction as well as cultural imperialism for the other, the other is not merely the opposite of Western colonialism, nor is the West a homogeneous trope of imperialism. This suggests a third rupture provided by postcolonial discourses. The current concern with the "death of the subject" cannot be confused with the necessity of affirming the complex and contradictory character of human agency. Postcolonial discourse reminds us that it is ideologically convenient and politically suspect for Western intellectuals to talk about the disappearance of the speaking subject from within institutions of privilege and power. This is not to suggest that postcolonial theorists accept the humanist notion of the subject as a unified and static identity. On the contrary, postcolonial discourse agrees that the speaking subject must be decentered, but this does not mean that all notions of human agency and social change must be dismissed. Understood in these terms, the postmodernist notion of the subject must be accepted and modified in order to extend rather than erase the possibility for creating the enabling conditions for human agency. At the very least, this would mean coming to understand the strengths and limits of practical reason, the importance of affective investments, the discourse of ethics as a resource for social vision, and the availability of multiple discourses and cultural resources that provide the very grounds and necessity for agency.[6]

Of course, while the burden of engaging these postcolonial concerns must be taken up by those who appropriate Freire's work, it is also necessary for Freire to be more specific about the politics of his own location and what the emerging discourses of postmodernism and postcolonialism mean for self-reflectively engaging both his own work and his current location as an intellectual aligned with the State (Brazil). If Freire has the right to draw upon his own experiences, how do these get reinvented so as to prevent their incorporation by First World theorists within colonialist rather than decolonizing terms and practices? But in raising that question, I want to emphasize that what makes Freire's work important is that it doesn't stand still. It is not a text for but against cultural monumentalism, one that offers itself up to different readings, audiences, and contexts. Moreover, Freire's work has to be read in its totality to gain a sense of how it has engaged the postcolonial age. Freire's work cannot be separated from either its history or its author, but it also cannot be reduced to the specificity of intentions or historical location.

Maybe the power and forcefulness of Freire's works are to be found in the tension, poetry, and politics that make it a project for border crossers, those who read history as a way of reclaiming power and identity by rewriting the space and practice of cultural and political resistance. Freire's work represents a textual borderland where poetry slips into politics, and solidarity becomes a song for the present begun in the past while waiting to be heard in the future.[7]

Notes

[1] See Stygall for an excellent analysis of this problem among Freire's followers.

[2] My use of the terms "exile" and "homelessness" have been deeply influenced by essays by Becker, JanMohamed ("Worldliness"), Said, Martin and Mohanty, and Kaplan. See also selected essays in Bell Hooks' *Talking Back* and *Yearning*.

[3] I have taken this term from JanMohamed, "Worldliness."

[4] For an excellent discussion of these issues as they specifically relate to postcolonial theory, see Parry, JanMohamed (*Manichean*), Spivak, Young, and Bhabha. The ways in which binary oppositions can trap a particular author into the most essentialist arguments can be seen in a recent work by Patti Lather. What is so unusual about this text is that its call for openness, partiality, and multiple perspectives is badly undermined by the binarisms which structure around a simple gendered relation of truth to illusion.

[5] This position is explored in Tiffin.

[6] I explore this issue in *Border Crossings*.

[7] This essay will appear in revised form in McLaren and Leonard.

Works Cited

Becker, Carol. "Imaginative Geography." School of the Art Institute of Chicago. Unpublished essay, 1991.

Bhabha, Homi K., ed. *Nation and Narration*. New York: Routledge, 1990.

Borsa, Joan. "Towards a Politics of Location: Rethinking Marginality." *Canadian Women Studies* 11 (1990): 36-39.

Freire, Paulo. *The Politics of Education: Culture, Power, and Liberation*. Trans. Donaldo Macedo. South Hadley, MA: Bergin, 1985.

Freire, Paulo, and Antonio Faundez. *Learning to Question: A Pedagogy of Liberation*. New York: Continuum, 1989.

Freire, Paulo, and Donaldo Macedo. *Literacy: Reading the Word and the World*. South Hadley, MA: Bergin, 1987.

Giroux, Henry A. *Border Crossings: Cultural Workers and the Politics of Education*. New York: Routledge, 1992.

Giroux, Henry A., and Donaldo Macedo. *Paulo Freire: History, Pedagogy, and Struggle*. U of Minnesota P, forthcoming.

Hooks, Bell. *Talking Back: Thinking Feminist, Thinking Black*. Boston: South End, 1989.

——. *Yearning: Race and Gender in the Cultural Marketplace*. Boston: South End, 1990.

Horton, Myles, and Paulo Freire. *We Make the Road by Walking: Conversations on Education and Social Change*. Ed. Brenda Bell, et al. Philadelphia: Temple UP, 1990.

Hutcheon, Linda. "Circling the Downspout of Empire." *Past the Last Post*. Ed. Ian Adam and Helen Tiffin. Calgary, Canada: U of Calgary P, 1990.

JanMohamed, Abdul R. *Manichean Aesthetics: The Politics of Literature in Colonial Africa*. Amherst: U of Massachusetts P, 1983.

——. "Worldliness-Without-World, Homelessness-as-Home: Toward a Definition of Border Intellectual." U of California, Berkeley. Unpublished essay.

Kaplan, Caren. "Deterritorializations: The Rewriting of Home and Exile in Western Feminist Discourse." *Cultural Critique* 6 (1987): 187-98.

Laclau, Ernesto. "Building a New Left: An Interview with Ernesto Laclau." *Strategies* 1 (1988): 10-28.

Lather, Patti. *Getting Smart: Feminist Research and Pedagogy within the Postmodern*. New York: Routledge, 1991.

Martin, Biddy, and Chandra Talpade Mohanty. "Feminist Politics: What's Home Got to Do With It?" *Feminist Studies/Critical Studies*. Ed. Teresa de Lauretis. Bloomington: Indiana UP, 1986.

McLaren, Peter, and Peter Leonard, eds. *Paulo Freire: A Critical Encounter*. New York: Routledge, 1993.

Parry, Benita. "Problems in Current Theories of Colonial Discourse." *The Oxford Literary Review* 9 (1987): 27-58.

Said, Edward W. *Orientalism*. New York: Vantage, 1979.

——. "Reflections on Exile." *Out There: Marginalization and Contemporary Cultures*. Ed. Russell Ferguson, Martha Gever, Trinh T. Minh-ha, Cornel West. New York: New Museum of Contemporary Art and MIT P, 1990.

Shor, Ira, and Paulo Freire. *A Pedagogy for Liberation: Dialogues on Transforming Education.* South Hadley, MA: Bergen, 1987.

Spivak, Gayatri C. *The Post-Colonial Critic: Interviews, Strategies, Dialogues.* Ed. Sarah Harasym. New York: Routledge, 1990.

Stygall, Gail. "Teaching Freire in North America." *Journal of Teaching Writing* 8 (1989): 113-25.

Tiffin, Helen. "Post-Colonial Literatures and Counter-Discourse." *Kunapipi* 9:3 (1987): 17-34.

——. "Post-Colonialism, Post-Modernism, and the Rehabilitation of Post-Colonial History." *Journal of Commonwealth Literature* 23:1 (1988): 169-81.

Young, Robert. *White Mythologies: Writing History and the West.* New York: Routledge, 1990.

West, Cornel. "Decentering Europe: A Memorial Lecture for James Snead." *Critical Quarterly* 33 (1991): 1-19.

After Progressivism: Modern Composition, Institutional Service, and Cultural Studies

MICHAEL MURPHY

Education in America, especially literacy education, has always been marked by a peculiar faith in social progress. From the establishment of the first universities in the New World with the mission to build an American New Jerusalem, to the Whitmanian determination to create a wholly literate and enlightened populace to oversee the functioning of an idealized democracy of intellectual and social equals, to the technocratic dream behind the founding of the "new university" at the turn of the century which looked toward the erection of a self-evidently fair and rational "meritocracy" administered by benign Science, to (especially important for modern composition as a university discipline) the Cold War imperative for "Space Age" national "advancement" in education, Americans have regarded the schools as perhaps the most important agents in fulfilling a whole host of manifest destinies. In *The Composing Process of Twelfth Graders*, Janet Emig bears witness to the implication of English teachers in this sense of mission when she quips of the five-paragraph theme—which she identifies as a kind of pedagogical monolith of the American secondary-school, "so indigenously American that it might be called the Fifty-Star Theme"—that its very discussion should invoke echoes of "Kate Smith singing 'God Bless America' or the piccolo obligato from 'The Stars and Stripes Forever'" (97). Indeed, it is hard to overestimate the power and regularity with which such echoes have informed generations of dutifully committed teachers of that formula and a host of other similar formulas—teachers placed by proverb in the very "trenches" of the "fight" for progress, whose work needed always (and still needs, it seems) to be underwritten by just such a compelling sense of purpose in order to alleviate its well-documented laboriousness.[1] In the light of such purpose, service in the institution—a vocation, we should note, clearly inscribed in and reinforced by composition's powerful institutional gendering as something like housewife/schoolmarm in the male-dominated English department—by simple immediate extension works to represent service in the progress of the social organism as a whole.

And yet as composition struggled to begin to come of age as a self-conscious academic discipline in the late 1960s and early 1970s, it seemed anxious to mark itself a certain distance, even if sometimes somewhat tentatively, from this still largely intact sense of the educational institution as enrolled in some greater mission of social progress, and especially from the sense of its own institutional service as part of that mission. And since then, in fact, as the first waves of exhilaration over modern composition's then newfound, Sputnik-inspired institutional legitimacy finally began to flatten out, it has been fashionable for self-conscious teachers of writing to show a "healthy" cynicism about, sometimes even disdain for, composition's role as an institutional servant, or at least about the ends toward which that service has typically been directed.[2] Even, say, since James Britton and the "growth model" theorists began in the middle and late sixties to challenge the traditional American grammarian's emphasis on propriety—along, at least implicitly, with its corollary ethic of good citizenship (an ethic which served to ally that tradition of grammatical propriety powerfully to the new institutional forces of cognitivism and classical rhetoric through their respective associations with technocratic first-citizen science on the one hand and the very roots of Western civicism on the other)—it seems to me that it has been part of the discipline's set of implicit agreements, only seldom expressed openly, that "compositionists" need to qualify their presumed complicity with the goals of the general university community in order to take themselves seriously as practicing intellectuals.[3] Those goals, that is, were coming to be implicated more and more frequently, and on occasion even quite explicitly, in what Richard Ohmann, for example, began calling "the military-industrial complex" in an indictment of conventional writing instruction as crudely transparent "rhetoric for the meritocracy" (93, 97).

Of course, the exercise of this sort of obligatory qualification has not been taken up monolithically in every disciplinary quarter. One need look no further than Carnegie-Mellon's continued success conducting federally-funded empirical research in cognitive psychology—as well as the number of dissertations and published papers invested each year in Carnegie-Mellon-style scientism—to see that the matrix of power relations behind modern composition's original institutional legitimation which had begun to crystal-lize even in the early 1960s still exists and still generates a network of negotiable institutional currencies.[4] But it seems to me that a clearly recognizable strain of composition scholarship, growing in the 1970s and 1980s all the time more definitive of the disciplinary mainstream, trades much on the signs of its often only partially articulated opposition to this matrix. Literacy-for-the-war-effort-style social utility has long since been confronted by a competing disciplinary currency, so that by and large institutional legitimacy has been defined increasingly in the last twenty years in very different terms, even when unconsciously or half-consciously. That is, the traditional American progressivist sense of education in the service of highly generalized social goals—through which, as I have suggested, the American academy has traditionally drawn its cultural power—can be seen to have reached a certain frenzied apogee in the defense department's attempted commandeering of the literary academy in the 1960s.[5] But after the waning of general enthusiasm over this recognition and embrace by the educational and social establishment sometime in the late sixties and early seventies, it became increasingly difficult, and remains difficult, to mark one's professional seriousness in composition studies without demonstrating some form of antagonism to one or another of those ostensibly universal social goals, or at the very least without cultivating a certain cynical self-consciousness about enlistment in their service.

In fact, it seems to me that this impulse can be seen to have manifested itself to some degree or another in a remarkable share of the different agendas brought to composition studies over the last twenty-five years (after the formative big three scientisms, that is, of cognitive psychology, classical rhetoric, and post-Chomskyan linguistics)—though this is a manifestation easily overlooked, from within the climate of recent composition scholarship. Such scholarship, that is, has often been anxious in its admirable enthusiasm for a heightened intellectual rigor in composition to dismiss much of this work (which admittedly can now be seen as significantly reactionary) without, nonetheless, having sufficiently acknowledged its contexts and purposes. It should not be difficult to recognize the brashly anti-grammar-and-style "vitalists" of the early 1970s, for instance, as significantly formed by radical anti-service and anti-establishment inclinations, such vitalism's now potentially offensive and much-critiqued romance of the autonomous creative individual notwithstanding. As spirited proponents of an "authentic voice," such vitalists saw literacy as the key much rather to a heightened humanity than to any sort of conventional civic propriety and complained that the mechanized bureaucracy of the university and the stifling conventionality of traditional prescriptive "English" instruction stunted their students' real intellectual development. Ken Macrorie's notorious comma-splice-eliminating, five-paragraph-theme-manufacturing composition monster, "Engfish," a sort of a Nurse Ratchett for the academy, effectively blanched and regularized its healthily spirited and idiosyncratic university students into proper and insipid automatons exactly suitable for the purposes of domination by the boorish and sometimes brutally exploitive powers that be (like the anti-Civil-Rights racists Macrorie continually chides, or the university president who ruthlessly squashes a student protest in the book's prologue). In this way, Macrorie clearly connects service in the traditional academy with the larger goals of a repressive culture, effectively implicating them both, in fact, in a "conspiracy of silence" carried out simultaneously against both pre-Civil-Rights "blacks" and the "slaves in my classes" (54). Expressivist-affiliated scholars like Anne Berthoff and James Miller, whose work had influence not only on the process, revision, and group-work movements but also on the imperative for connecting writing to "critical thinking," either ignored or openly disavowed the set of sciences (cognitivism, empirical research, transformational grammar, structuralist linguistics) that had been used to authenticate composition's practical usefulness in something like "the real world." And this was true even when the expressivists would embrace science as an "abstract" principle, separate as much as possible from the smack of such real-world pragmatism carried by science's association with technology (as Berthoff herself does with her unswerving faith in the composing process as a sort of holistic manifestation of a scientistic natural order[6]). In "The Problem of Problem-Solving," her much-cited attack on Janice Lauer's call for the use of cognitive psychology in composition research, Berthoff openly berates those she calls "the technologists of learning" for pedagogical and scholarly "approaches which are politically not above suspicion," pointing with great censure to the traditional "alliance between the needs of commercial interests and what the American public schools offer" (237, 239). And old-guard literary-trained compositionists like W. Ross Winterowd, whose orientation in rhetoric served as a kind of home base from which to write on composition impulses as diverse as speech-act theory, discourse analysis, and invention heuristics—while still convinced of composition's social utility in a conventional way ("all of my somber . . . moralizing about commitment, authority, and service" [335])—could still be seen to rail (both openly and implicitly by way of a self-consciously elegant, literary prose style) against the simplicity and theoretical naivete of the volumes of practical advice on writing and teaching writing that served to demonstrate that utility: "an endless string of pedagogical tips: teaching without teachers; teaching with tape recorders; teaching writing with or without writing; teaching writing through immersion in TV game shows; teaching games through an immersion in writing; infinite variations on the touchy-smelly-looky-listeny-writey model" 329). Even if composition could still perform an indispensable service to the university community, such scholars decided, nearsighted allegiance to the performance of that service had resulted in a shameless anti-intellectualism.

So by the middle seventies (though it's easily forgotten lately) vanguard composition scholarship had settled into an orthodoxy of what might be called controlled institutional dissent—or at least a measured rejection of the old earmarks of composition's institutional function—clear enough, though often only indirectly expressed: an at least vague sense of dissatisfaction with the writing teacher's traditional role in the institution became an important badge of pedagogical and scholarly purposefulness. Even a book as soberly scientistic in tone and as invested in the utility of training in all the old institutional proprieties that defined "acceptable" prose as Mina Shaughnessy's *Errors and Expectations* had by 1977 developed a sophisticated squeamishness about the suggestion carried by such proprieties of an uncritical alliance with the implied goals of the institution. Shaughnessy carefully marks her reservations about those goals, conceding almost obligatorily:

> When one considers the damage that has been done to students in the name of correct writing, this effort to redefine error so as to exclude most of the forms that give students trouble in school and to assert the legitimacy of other kinds of English is understandable. Doubtless it is part of a much vaster thrust within this society not only to reduce the penalties for being culturally different but to be enriched by that diversity. (9)

Without question, then, a certain smack of unholiness began to pervade the original founding alliance—powerfully seductive to the new compositionist struggling to take him or herself seriously in the 1960s—between composition as an independent discipline and its surrounding academic and social institutions.

And of course, more recent expressions of composition's frustration with and uneasiness about this alliance, like perhaps most notably Patricia Bizzell's groundbreaking work in such essays as "Cognition, Convention, and Certainty" and "What Happens When Basic Writers Come to College?" or James Berlin's now almost standard "Rhetoric and Ideology in the Writing Class"—fueled by the explosion of structuralism and sign theory into the contemporary radicalisms of knowledge/power relations and ideological critique—are the direct heirs to this general anti-service impulse, though they are clearly far more explicit, emphatic, and incisive about the dangers of composition's traditional role as institutional and social servant, as well as about the insidious process by which composition has been interpellated as such a servant. They worry openly about the indoctrination of students into the socially oppressive terms of traditional academic discourse, about how to enable students to become "resisting, negotiating subjects within positions of power in the dominant culture" (Berlin, "Contemporary" 50) and about "the school's function as an agent of cultural hegemony" (Bizzell, "Cognition" 237). And of course they have even been—quite rightly, if on occasion somewhat nearsightedly—vocal in their insistent dissatisfaction with the limits of the work of their anti-service predecessors, whose pedagogies, they point out, were always ultimately disabled by an insufficient understanding of the ideological constructedness of language and the writing subject. The battle-lines, then, have emerged even more clearly under the influence of "cultural studies": there is nothing indirect about the way this new generation of compositionists has announced its rejection of old-style institutional service, in which (in its crudest form) teaching students clarity and grammatical correctness would, it was supposed, somehow manifest itself unproblematically in the good of the social organism as a whole. Berlin and Bizzell—along now to some degree or other with a whole range of different figures from John Schilb to Henry Giroux to Victor Vitanza to Linda Brodkey to Charles Schuster—have taken up composition's post-Sputnik-era tradition of submerged anti-establishmentarianism and made its active, self-conscious articulation the cornerstone of new cultural-studies-informed pedagogies.

Indeed, it is difficult at this moment in the development of the discipline not to read the history of modern composition as the story, carried out across all composition's major phases in the last twenty years, of a continual evolution ever closer to a refined and effective critical rejection of the institutional and social role concretized for it in the 1960s, a narrative having come to its conclusion in some sense with cultural studies' recent foregrounding of politics in the academy. Composition, it seems, has finally begun to throw off the oppressive yoke of its tangled institutional archaeology (through which, as we have seen, it always rooted and rerooted itself in the grand American myth of progress and service) and has become an autonomous, self-conscious field of inquiry on its own terms, now fully the equal of (and no longer the ostensibly insipid housewife to) that centered in the "English" department, at the same time empowering its students similarly in the classroom. Never has the imperative for composition to renounce its traditional role as a "service" discipline, then—which as we have seen ended in producing (among other things) uncritical pragmatism, science-as-totem, and blind participation in the often oppressive project of the institution—seemed so pressing or so nearly fulfilled.

Progress, "Expressionism," and Disempowerment in the Institution

And yet it is difficult at the same time—in the crudest possible terms, for example, when ostensibly professionalized "compositionists" typically still teach four courses a semester—not to wonder if all these attempts to mark a distance between composition as an intellectual project and the overwhelming smack of institutional and social enlistment implied by composition's formative keeping-up-with-the-Russians impulse haven't themselves all ultimately been coopted by the residue of that impulse in a way that renders them largely harmless.[7] Avant-gardes of all sorts, especially academic ones, have a long history of disappointingly partial successes. Even if the categories set up by composition's latest coming-of-age narrative (institutional service and intellectual independence) seem powerfully convincing, it is still easy to imagine that the sense of disciplinary arrival they imply may seem suspect. At least implicitly, composition, even at its avant-garde fringes, by and large still conceives its project in the same service-oriented terms that it has staked so much of its own sense of intellectual legitimacy on rebelling against.

And of course the persistence of these terms is especially clear in the earlier manifestations of what I have called the anti-service impulse, which have been under fairly constant attack for different, though parallel, reasons recently by that impulse's more contemporary representatives. As I have already suggested, we have been reminded often in the last ten years or so of the politically disabling effect of the "humanist" cult of art and the autonomous creative individual in the academy, as well as of the overwhelming humanist orientation of the bulk of the earliest composition pedagogies implicated in what I have tried to identify as a generalized implicit resistance to composition's traditional designation as a service discipline.[8] What it seems to me hasn't been adequately considered, though, is that this often-noted political disability, normally articulated simply as the artist's general withdrawal from the social, worked not only (as we have so often heard) to de-politicize the humanist-aestheticist English classroom in a larger ideological sense, but also in a much more local sense to effectively disable composition's own attempts in the 1970s to rebel against the politics of institutional service.

Probably the most notable of these now familiar critiques of the humanist-aestheticist tradition within the field of composition itself have been James Berlin's, made public for an especially wide disciplinary audience in *College English*.[9] Berlin perceptively summarizes the reasons for the social and political ineffectuality of what he calls "expressionism" (while acknowledging its intention of political committedness)[10] by explicating the epistemological assumptions on which it is founded:

> The underlying conviction of expressionists is that when individuals are spared the distorting effects of a repressive social order, their privately determined truths will correspond to the privately determined truths of all others; my best and deepest vision supports the same universal and external laws as everyone else's best and deepest vision.
> ("Ideology" 486)

Hence, of course, the function of the expressionist composition classroom as a social sedative by which knowledge in general is rendered politically neutral through the elision of cultural difference and ideological constructedness.

But as I have suggested, such an epistemology can also be seen—less obviously, perhaps, but just as powerfully—to accomplish the resurrection of composition's service ethic, even from within expressionism's often explicitly anti-service position (just as its explicit claims to "empower" students through "personal growth" and "self-discovery" can be seen ultimately to disable them with its implication of "universal and external laws"): universally recognizable social goals and duties still exist for "expressionist" teachers as they did in the traditional service model, even though one must now be able to see through "the distorting effects of a repressive social order" in order to recognize them. While "expressionist" writing teachers are no longer enlisted (as in the old Sputnik-era model) in the service of a standing institution which was taken unproblematically to reflect a body of universally recognizable truths, they nonetheless come to be enlisted in a similarly compelling (and coopting) service—this time, the service of a set of nobler and more cryptic truths which are accessible only through the cultivation of "personal" literacy and which have by and large eluded that institution. In this way, Berlin's "expressionists" establish a sense of professional order that corresponds perfectly to the theoretical assumptions behind their pedagogical order, even though it fulfills their "anti-service" impulse only quite problematically. That is, the social goals of the enlightened teacher in this model (usually somewhat contrary to those of the institution) are still, like the work of their students, validated by reference to an unchanging and universal if somewhat mysterious internal reality in something like artistic truth (even if instead of to a simple consensus in common sense, as the scientism of the traditional service model would have it). "Expressionist" composition, then, has no better chance of achieving an effective critical position in the arena of institutional politics than its students do of seeing, as Berlin says, that the expressionist vision "in fact represents the interests of a particular class, not all classes" (487). Ideological constructedness, including the constructedness of the terms of the academic enterprise itself, are cloaked under a deified essentiality, figured ultimately as "art."

Indeed, then, vanguard composition scholarship's strategy of institutional resistance in the 1970s was clearly compromised—as Linda Brodkey has also suggested provocatively in "Modernism and the Scene(s) of Writing" (though again at the level of the individual student in the classroom and not at the level of the discipline in the institution)—by its intuitive adaptation of the high modernist strategy of cultural resistance, played out in its cult of the individual artistic genius. And this intuition is not surprising given that the literary training of most second-generation compositionists asked them to see the appreciation of enactments of this strategy as their primary professional vocation. That the New Criticism was invented as a technology of consumption for the products of high modernist culture is hardly a new idea, and that New Critically-trained "compositionists" brought the baggage of the high aestheticist's withdrawal from a compromised culture into the Self with them as they confronted the problems of professional legitimation in an emerging discipline is understandable.[11] They would resist an institutional alliance they found problematic in the terms they knew best, the same terms in which the modernist artist (as it is so often explained) resisted the industrialized culture that alienated him or her.[12] So it is not without significance to note the connection here to how powerfully and how often teaching came to be figured as high art in composition scholarship in the 1970s:[13] like the noble modernist alone in a garret, the enlightened compositionist would cultivate truth and beauty as a form of resistance in the cloister of the classroom.

And yet the ultimate political effectivity of such a gesture of resistance, as critiques like Berlin's and Brodkey's have made clear at the student level, should not be overestimated. For both the modernist aesthete withdrawing as a mode of resistance into high art and what James Berlin calls the "expressionist" teacher of composition to whom modernism eventually gave indirect intellectual animation, the epistemological commitment to essentialized ideals, at any level of accessibility, implied a faith in progress easily more powerful than their respective senses that their work was implicated in a "politics" that needed critical engaging: even if it were only for the enlightened literate, there was still illumination above ideology and discourse to move toward. The attempted replacement of science by art as twentieth century high culture's animating discourse has done little to achieve the sort of liberatory radicalism it seemed to promise.[14] Beyond the momentary, though not altogether inconsiderable, sobering effect provided by their respective shock values, the rebellion against the politics of progressivist institutional service implied by Ken Macrorie's attempted reinvigoration of the mechanical and anti-intellectual "Engfish" monster seems in the end little more effectively subversive than the more general revolt, say, against the politics of progressivist technological "advancement" taken up explicitly by T.S. Eliot's intensive *l'art-pour-l'art* cultivation of aesthetic form, both of which ultimately get reenlisted in progressivist service on another *merely somewhat less conventional* level. In the end, then, composition's wide reaction in the 1970s against the mindless assumption about social progress embodied by the traditional service ethic, a reaction launched under the banner of high aesthetic anti-institutionalism largely at the residual impetus of the abating New Criticism, could be only a decidedly partial success.[15] Clearly, its implied sense of social progress was entirely as real as the traditional and explicit allegiance to the sort of old-fashioned, for-the-good-of-all progress it defined itself largely against; and its ultimate effect, in fact, was the invocation of what it seems to me hard not to recognize precisely as modern composition's golden age of "progressive" thinking.

Progress, Cultural Studies, and Disempowerment
If the disabling effect of this implicit recuperation of the progress ethic seems striking, the degree to which its residue quite openly marks composition's most significant contemporary expression of resistance to institutional service is perhaps shocking. Indeed, it could well be argued that composition's cultural studies movement is itself largely coopted by the same progressivist discourse that we have seen embodied in the expressionist pedagogy that cultural studies seems most self-consciously poised against: even while it has articulated an effective alternative to the compromising epistemology it critiques so thoroughly, the progressivist trappings of that epistemology often remain disturbingly uninterrogated in the new orthodoxy of radical composition scholarship. In the earliest, most tepid articulations of the new epistemology for composition, these trappings were sometimes painfully obvious: Richard Young, Alan Becker, and Kenneth Pike—peculiarly situated between a cautious theory of anti-foundationalist rhetoric and various affiliations with the positivist establishment—argued for a kind of happily enlightened scientism in tagmemics, a system of cognitive principles designed as a kind of exhaustive science of language use and yet based on the conviction that knowledge is shaped by arbitrary distinctions embedded in different languages.[16] And later, even in an institutional climate generally more agreeable to the aims and methods of critical theory, composition

scholars as serious and as intellectually energetic as C.H. Knoblauch and Lil Brannon proposed their own "New" rhetoric largely as a way of giving new urgency to all the now traditional 1970s progressivist pedagogical themes which had by then crystallized into an easily recognizable cluster: process-over-product, grammatical relativism, group work, non-quantitative evaluation, freedom from generic and formal constraints, exhaustive revision, decentered classroom authority, writing-across-the curriculum, and so on.[17]

But more startling is the sort of casual obliviousness with which recent cultural-studies-oriented critiques of progressivist pedagogy (by all accounts considerably more self-conscious and militant) seem prone to fall into progressivist discourse themselves, threatening in this way to coopt cultural studies as simply the latest in composition's long line of ultimately moderationist liberalisms. We have seen, for example, the committedness of James Berlin's critique of "expressionism." Invoking Louis Althusser and Michel Foucault by way of Swedish Marxist sociologist Goran Therborn, Berlin argues that "Ideology is . . . inscribed in language practices, entering all features of our experience" ("Ideology" 479) in order to press still-expressionist-invested composition scholarship "to place the question of ideology at the center of the teaching of writing" (492). He goes on from this first principle toward such an objective by claiming that "A rhetoric can never be innocent, can never be a disinterested arbiter of the ideological claims of others because it is always already serving certain ideological claims" (477), and then by attacking what he sees as composition's two main rhetorics on this basis: the rhetoric of cognitivism for "claiming for itself the transcendent neutrality of science" and the rhetoric of "expressionism" (as we have seen) for obscuring ideology with a "creative realization of the self, [which] exploit[s] the material, social, and political conditions of the world in order to assert a private vision" (478, 487). Instead, he offers what he calls "social-epistemic" rhetoric, which, "self-consciously aware of its ideological stand" (478), eliminates "arguments from transcendent truth since all arguments arise in ideology" (489). So he is scrupulous in his anti-foundationalism and insists that only such scrupulosity can effectively empower the reading and writing subject.

Nevertheless, it seems to me as if in a kind of unconscious mouthing of composition's apparently immanent progressivist heritage, Berlin goes on to take "democracy" as just such a transcendent truth, as an absolute value (here an "ethical" one) which requires no justification or explanation. And his anti-foundationalism starts sounding strangely compromised in order to accommodate the unblinkingness of this value.[18] Though knowledge-as-ideology is inescapably a matter of "linguistically-circumscribed" possibilities, it nonetheless turns out, it seems, also to have certain features which are somehow inherently democratizing: "ideology is always pluralistic, a given historical moment displaying a variety of competing ideologies and a given individual reflecting one or another permutation of these conflicts" (489,

479). That "all arguments arise in ideology," he continues with newfound tautological verve, "thus inevitably supports... democracy.... Because there are no 'natural laws' or 'universal truths' that indicate what exists, what is good, what is possible, and how power is to be distributed" (489-90). That particular ideologies are culturally dominant and that subjectivity is ideologically constructed, then (the ostensible basis of "social-epistemic" rhetoric and its accompanying pedagogy), is apparently no longer important: knowledge is no longer a "never innocent" matter of "ideological conflict," but an unproblematic manifestation of something like "free competition" in which all positions of subjectivity have equal dialectical chances (492, 489). Democracy bubbles up from nowhere, erupting in the progressivist rhetoric of pluralism and egalitarianism, which of course sits more than a bit unevenly with Berlin's stated concern over "the interpellations of subjects" which "are always already ideological" (490). He speaks of promoting "self-fulfilling behavior" which would serve to flesh out one's "full humanity," even though "There is no universal, eternal, and authentic self," and "selves" are "social construct[s]," the ideological "creation[s] of a particular historical and cultural moment" (490, 489). He invokes "the greater good of all" (490) with similar fervor—even though knowledge of such ostensibly universal good is attained only by way of highly subjective and suspect "socially-devised definitions" (489)—just as he vigorously holds onto the idealist orthodoxy of "false consciousness" (490) while his "social-epistemic" rhetoric is said to be founded immovably on "the inherently ideological nature of rhetoric" (489) and thus the unavoidable "falseness" of *all* consciousness. And he argues passionately for "the liberatory classroom," as if it were somehow above ideology and indoctrination, even though "a way of teaching is never innocent" (491, 492).

All that is potentially radical about Berlin's deployment of "social-epistemic rhetoric," then, seems to me in this way quickly coopted by its implicit association with composition's progressivist baggage. The progressivist discourse of educational democracy—along with its allied senses of duty ("our responsibilities as teachers and citizens" [493]) and social welfare ("the greater good of all" [490])—is so fundamental a part of the language of composition scholarship that it can effectively underwrite the work of even as guarded an anti-foundationalist as Berlin.[19] Very much, in fact, as in the "expressionist" model Berlin critiques so thoroughly, both student and teacher are pressed into the service of an absolute which works to represent the establishment, in this case the apparently self-evident value of "democracy." The goals of the classroom and the goals of the social organism at large, it seems, are once more essentially the same, just as the progressivist ethos insists they must be.

Not surprisingly, this leads Berlin back to an espousal of a kind of happy Freireanism (the circle-up-the-desks progressivist idyll), in which the classroom serves as the ultimate enactment of the birthright democracy in which the committed pedagogue hopes to empower students to participate. In the same way, then, that Berlin's discourse of essentialized democracy reenlists composition in the service of the institution by ignoring differences between contesting social interests in favor of some "greater good of all," his corresponding vision of classroom practice also serves, I think, largely to make students impotent in the larger economy of cultural politics: when we pretend that the institutionally inherent differences between teachers and students don't exist (even though teachers write syllabi, choose readings, assign grades), students are both deceived about the politics of the classroom and encouraged to ignore such differences between cultural affiliations outside the classroom in favor of a happy faith in the inherent cultural authority and personal integrity of their own free "opinions." Patricia Bizzell gets at the problem perceptively in another context:

> Ultimately, I am calling for the inspection of what some curriculum theorists have called the "hidden curriculum": the project of initiating students into a particular world view that gives rise to the daily classroom tasks without being consciously examined by teacher or students. If we call what we are teaching "universal" structures or processes, we bury the hidden curriculum even deeper by claiming that our choice of material owes nothing to historical circumstances. To do this is to deny the school's function as an agent of cultural hegemony, or the selective valuation and transmission of world views.
>
> ("Cognition" 237)

In his establishment of democracy as a transparent value, a matter of political "ethics," then, Berlin ignores the problematics of discourse and ideology he theorizes so finely and insists on so stubbornly. Freireanism not only "hides" but positively *denies* that such implicit curricula exist: a course's focus is to be created by equal participation inside the classroom, just as meanings, one must assume, are to be generated outside it somehow "freely" in culture at large. Indeed, as Bizzell suggests, the institution's "function as an agent of cultural hegemony" must be taken responsibility for—and not be made even more insidious than such cultural functions already are through any pretense of "natural" democracy—if students will be saved paying a crippling cultural price for it. Once more, even for as focused a critic of the establishment as James Berlin, the compositionist is enlisted in the service of a transcendent good embodied in the proper function of the institution, and the composition student is left, once again like the discipline itself, inadvertently but undeniably disabled.

Progress, Disciplinary Archaeology, Critical Literacy, Politics-as-Ethics
It seems to me fundamentally important for those interested in radicalizing composition as a cultural force, then, to recognize the powerful disciplinary heritage in the context of which the cultural studies movement in composition must make its play for disciplinary authority, a heritage from which that movement characteristically sees itself as having effected a fairly breathtaking secession. In this context, I should make clear that I do not wish by any means to single out James Berlin for critique, to suggest that he has been less

than one of the most important and clearly committed voices in the struggle to bring cultural studies meaningfully to composition, or to diminish his obvious contribution to composition's development as a critical intellectual project. But I do hope to make the presence of the latent and largely disabling residue of progressivist libertarianism in Berlin's work suggest the difficulties inherent in any attempted radicalizing of composition. If even Berlin's very deliberate, self-conscious, and carefully theorized assault on the cultural orientation of traditional composition pedagogy can be in some way implicitly shaped by the spirit of that orientation, then it is clear that we need to develop and maintain a special fastidiousness about the discourses that enable our own critical formations as participants in such a dialogue. All that we can speak in our attempts to contribute to the development of the project that composition has become must necessarily be framed by an extraordinarily complicated institutional archaeology, one out to enlist us in projects of its own from the start.

What this paper amounts to, then, is a call to composition's cultural studies contingent to maintain a diligent self-consciousness about the ways in which the shape of the discipline itself implicitly but powerfully asks that contingent to construct its commitment to the social. And such a self-consciousness, I think, should begin with a recognition of the peculiar power that the discourse of progress has been made to wield for composition, a power consolidated by a narrative in which all new disciplinary developments become stages in an evolution toward something like a discipline effectively engaged in the service of the essentialized general good of the social organism. First science, then art (and now social justice) have been made to serve as the essentialized goal—in Saussurian terms, the transcendental signified—that makes that narrative meaningful, the absolute toward which progress is taken to be directed. But if we have come to accept the deployment of some theory of anti-foundationalist rhetoric as the single useful mode of contemporary resistance—and I think such acceptance is definitive of all serious manifestations of the cultural studies/ideological critique impulse in the academy—then models of making composition a site for meaningful cultural engagement simply cannot allow themselves to be underwritten by any such transcendental signified even as "ethics." If all knowledge is, as Berlin says so eloquently, "an arena of ideological conflict" (489), then "progress's" implication of a finally useful goal—even if a mysterious and ultimately unattainable goal, as in aesthetic fulfillment, or an ostensibly enlightened goal, as in social justice—can only serve to perform a dangerous effacement of that conflict. It is vital, then, to recognize the monumental historical significance of the ongoing play for power made by progress as a concept: meaning is always a matter of problematic, contestatory difference; never simple reference, as progress would have it.

So the real urgency of cultural studies' commitment to the social is animated not by the invocation of any timeless code of democracy or even ethics—as so much of the cultural studies contingent in composition, like Berlin, have had it, and as composition's traditional urge to justify itself as an academic discipline by making some sort of contribution to the general project of the social organism would suggest—but simply because the production and distribution of knowledge is *inherently* a matter of social contest, one in which we are always already positioned at the moment we consider opening our mouths to speak. Indeed, the contemporary theoretical fetishization of ethics (only the latest in a long line of powerful essentialist mystifications) is what the example of Berlin suggests most graphically as we begin to think in the early 1990s about the sorts of effects cultural studies can have on academic practice: politics-as-ethics is only the dangerously moderationist pseudo-radicalism to which contemporary cultural studies has been propelled by the academy's progressivist residues, which we need to remember wield special power in composition.[20] We do not need to invoke the moral to speak of power/knowledge relations and of participation in the "ideological arena" of knowledge: as readers and writers we simply have no other choice. If we accept that meaning is always cultural and ideological, then textual action *is* political action, so our insistence on the importance of intervening in the production and distribution of cultural meanings needs no justification by way of moral right; such intervention happens unavoidably whenever we open our mouths to speak. As makers of and traffickers in knowledge, that is, we necessarily find ourselves always already engaged (and *positioned*) in the ideological contest of culture at large, and not propelled into the fray by some innate sense of any timeless principle of "justice" or "fairness." In fact, to recognize the promotion of, say, democracy as this sort of unconditional, *unconstructed* "ethical" imperative is actually to effectively tame all that is potentially radical about cultural studies' anti-foundationalism, no matter what smack of political "involvement" it may carry; simply, it amounts to the restoration of the essentialized referent. As Victor Vitanza has insisted, the great "narratives of emancipation" clung to by "social-consensual theory-hopeful rationalists, who through social reengineering and instrumental reason . . . want to cure society and make the world into a great, good place," ultimately "only further remystif[y] and disempower students and us all" (143, 142). Such categories as the scientific, the aesthetic or the politically ethical cannot be left uninterrogated. Instead, we need to ask tirelessly what cultural forces provide the imperative behind the constitution of those categories, and what the effects of such constitution are, especially when the categories in question serve as the grounds for other knowledge. And the progress ethic in which composition has been steeped for at least thirty years refers us constantly, as we have seen, to such ostensibly self-evident grounds for knowledge, replacing one for another ingeniously as each outlives its rhetorical utility.

This, the deft and constant deferral of serious critical engagement behind reference to apparently self-evident absolutes which defy interrogation, is progress' great insidiousness. It also suggests the challenge presented by the composition studies tradition to the critical integrity of cultural studies's commitment to the social. Progress has a vital interest in seeing cultural studies represent this commitment as a matter of "ethics": even if invoked to provide an imperative for investigating knowledge as an "ideological contest," ethics posits the same sort of final, universal ground for knowledge—the greater good of all—that is at the center of progress' cultural powerplay *precisely by serving to obscure that contest.* If as I argued earlier, then, the political disability of much of traditional composition pedagogy has to do with its implication in "modernist" strategies of resistance, then this essay can also be understood as a call for composition to become a cannily *"post*modern" discipline—that is, to carefully interrogate and disclaim the effects of the essentialist epistemology on which modernism—and modern composition, in turn—was largely founded.

It is only in this way, I argue, that composition can accomplish either of the imperatives which were beginning to be set for it at least implicitly as early as 1965 by what might meaningfully be called its first avant-garde: the liberation of the discipline itself from uncritical service in the academic institution and the liberation of the student from uncritical service in the arena of culture at large. As I have suggested, it seems to me vital to recognize that both depend on the assumption of the same critical posture and that neither can be achieved successfully without the other: composition studies cannot become politically effective, either as a discipline within the academic institution or a pedagogical technology for its students within their larger cultural spheres, without stubbornly resisting the urge to defer critical interrogation by positing an essentialized reality of some sort or other, an urge made frighteningly manifest in the great American (and modernist) fantasy of "progress." The mindless institutional service effected by such deferral on one front—in the hierarchy of disciplines within the academy—is destined to replay the larger mindless cultural service effected by that same deferral on the other—in the classroom. And the recent movement to bring cultural studies to composition has only partially succeeded in establishing the resistance to such service that it seemed to promise. We can only stop being a "service" discipline when we begin taking intelligent, self-conscious account of the ideological conditions that have enabled us. Indeed, effectively renouncing blind institutional and cultural service means sensitively and assiduously sorting out, delineating, and critiquing composition's complicated intellectual heritage—carefully accounting for the ideological forces that have enabled its erection as a discipline—exactly what essentialist allegiance to the idea of "progress" makes impossible. Critical intellectual work, literacy even—both inside and outside the classroom—can mean nothing else.

Notes

[1]It is difficult, for example, for any teacher of college composition, struggling to think through the implications and presuppositions of his or her practice critically—while teaching, say, four sections of first-year composition—not to take as emblematic Berlin's report of "four teachers and two graduate assistants" at Michigan in 1894 who "were responsible for 1,198 students" in a day when convention dictated the writing of daily or near daily themes ("Reality" 22), or in turn not to rally around Stephen North's observation of the tendency in English departments to write composition off as "academic dirty work" (13).

[2]See Chapter 1 of North for a thorough discussion of Cold War nationalism's crucial role in shaping modern composition as an academic discipline. Albert Kitzhaber's 1966 call for "a 'New English' to take its place alongside the 'New Mathematics' and the 'New Science' now being taught in many United States schools," though, pointed out recently by Harris, serves to suggest the contours of that role pretty plainly (635). See also note 5 of this paper.

[3]There are notable exceptions—like W. Ross Winterowd and Louise Phelps, who self-consciously combine a high theoretical seriousness (largely unallied to the disciplinary forces of science and classicism which would capitalize most clearly on the Cold War sense of educational crisis) with a willingness to understand—sometimes even with a profound commitment to—the cultivation of literacy as a public service performed in a spirit of republican, even classically modeled civic responsibility. But such scholars seem to me decisively outnumbered by those who would lay claim to such seriousness by way of an at least partial (or even implicit and unarticulated) repudiation of the role of institutional servant. In fact, theorists like Winterowd and Phelps, despite their allegiance to some form of the service ideal, are typically most troubled by those composition scholars who embrace institutional service least problematically.

It is worth noting, too, that Phelps has pointed out a potentially serious problem with my enterprise in this paper on a related score: she reminds me that academic work (and work in general) is necessarily *always already* implicated in a context and is thus unavoidably enlisted in the "service" of certain interests. I do not at all mean by calling attention to the ways in which it seems to me that composition has been intellectually and institutionally disabled by "service" in such projects that "service" in the abstract can be escaped. Much to the contrary, my project is fundamentally based on this very problematic, and I do not intend to give the impression that I endorse disciplinary "liberation" in any naively Romantic way. Instead, I argue only that critical engagement, literate intellectual work, means being as self-conscious and savvy about this process of enlistment as possible—only that service, that is, should at all costs never be blind, and that such blindness makes for the crudest kind of ideological indoctrination.

[4]See Lauer and Asher for a sense of the still formidable marketability of different forms of empirical research in contemporary composition studies.

[5]If this language seems extreme, witness for example the almost rabid rhetoric of civic duty that marks documents like the NCTE's 1961 *The National Interest and the Teaching of English* ("Only a quality education will prepare our youth for the test" [136]) and the Commission on English's 1965 *Freedom and Discipline in English* ("The commission was fully aware of the importance of [its] objective for the students who will be the future citizens of a great democracy" [viii])—documents which were clearly direct responses to establishment culture's new eagerness to embrace English studies as something like a "national priority," a matter even of national security (an eagerness manifested materially in the advent of "Project English"). Or see the barely submerged us-and-them nationalist sensibility so important to a book like Corbett's omnipresent 1965 *Classical Rhetoric and the Modern Student*, which is rife with Cold War language and categories and which from the perspective of 1990 often seems even crudely and frighteningly propagandistic, especially in the simple casualness with which its ostensibly arbitrary and innocent examples of logical forms and moves invoke the terms of Cold War conflict as generic content. In this way, the book works powerfully to legitimize the apparent importance of those terms even when applying them to examples of specious argument. It includes, for example, exercises in the logical evaluation of such syllogisms as "No Russians are democratic. All Americans are democratic. [Therefore] All Americans are Russians" and

"Since only radicals want to subvert the duly constituted government of a country, this man can't be a radical because he wants to preserve the government of the country" (60, 61).

[6]See, for instance, Berthoff's suggestion that "Interpretation is a branch of biology" (*Making* v).

[7]Slevin outlines the managerial practices by which compositionists are effectively de-professionalized, denied, for example, the time and job security needed to participate in professional development as a scholar given as a matter of course to faculty in other disciplines.

[8]Most notably, see one of the introductions to teaching critical theory published in the last ten years, such as Catherine Belsey's *Critical Practice*. More incisively, see recent articulations of the problematics of radical Marxism in the Humanities in the work of such figures as Stanley Aronowitz, Henry Giroux, and Peter McLaren, or on a somewhat different radical left, Mas'ud Zavarzadeh and Donald Morton (see especially "Theory Pedagogy Politics: The Crisis of the 'Subject' in the Humanities" and the recent collection of the same name).

[9]Here I will quote from "Rhetoric and Ideology in the Writing Class"; see also "Contemporary Composition: The Major Pedagogical Theories." For a significantly more thorough treatment of the same ideas, see Berlin's *Rhetoric and Reality*.

[10]Berlin concedes, "Most proponents of expressionistic rhetoric during the sixties and seventies were unsparingly critical of the dominant social, political, and cultural practices of the time," and he even offers Peter Elbow as an example of this sort of outspoken though ultimately impotent political consciousness (485). Also, it's worth noting the other less strictly theoretical grounds on which Berlin makes his critique of "expressionism": the disabling effect of its suggestion that "effective resistance can only be offered by individuals, each acting alone," its reification of "entrepreneurial virtues" like "private initiative" and "risk taking," and the way it promotes "a variety of forms of consumer behavior" by making leisure (and never work) the only possible site of "self-discovery and fulfillment" (487). Though these are astute and useful readings of expressionism's various social utilities, I have confined myself to Berlin's sense of the theoretical limits of expressionist epistemology (even though it is perhaps less thoroughly articulated than the rest) since these theoretical limits will figure most prominently in what I will argue about composition and the progress ethic.

[11]See, for instance, Eagleton's *The Function of Criticism*, where he speaks of "the liberal humanist consensus which was, in effect, criticism's sole rationale" in the age of "New Criticism's cloistered aestheticism" (86, 85).

[12]Of course, it is something of an over-simplification (and a popular one) to reduce as undeniably varied and complicated a cultural impulse as "modernism" to a single aesthetic-epistemological tenet in this way, just as it smacks of over-simplification to explain New Criticism in turn wholly as a manifestation of such an impulse. And even though one might name a good number of writers, artists, intellectuals, and so on commonly identified as "modernist" who neither advocated nor enacted any withdrawal from the social into high art—what Andreas Huyssen has called an aestheticist "anxiety of contamination" (vii)—it is not without value to see the phenomenon of "modernism" *more generally* as born significantly out of the need for just this kind of withdrawal. I do not intend to suggest that there were either no modernist aesthetes (consider Pound) or no New Critics (remember New Criticism's self-consciously political roots in Agrarianism) who had political preoccupations or who were willing to see their aesthetic positions as politically conditioned and implicated. I argue only that the general modernist impulse for aesthetic cultivation can be seen ultimately to represent a strategic shrinking from what modernism conceived as "administered" culture through the cultivation of a profound and compelling (though ultimately disabling) individuality.

[13]For a sense of this conjunction (of writing and teaching writing behind art in humanist-aestheticist circles) see the work of William Coles.

[14]It is useful to consider, for example, how vigorously a voice as steeped in modernist discourse as, say, I.A. Richards' in *Science and Poetry* (1926) can be seen to have insisted on conceiving its modernity as a manifestation of the early twentieth-century assertion of idealist art against empiricist science. For a sense of the failures of modernism as this sort of project, Jameson's observations on Wyndham Lewis are typical of similar critiques articulated from various lefts:

The most influential formal impulses of canonical modernism have been *strategies of inwardness*, which set out to reappropriate an alienated universe by transforming it into personal styles and private languages [and which] have seemed in retrospect to reconfirm the very privatization and fragmentation of social life against which they meant to protest (2; emphasis added). Also see Huyssen, Krauss, Eagleton (*Against*), Lyotard, and Foster.

[15]It would be a grave over-simplification, of course, to understand all the 1970s composition scholarship that I have called "progressivist" as animated wholly by New Critical aestheticism. I claim only that progressivism's strategy of institutional resistance devolved mainly from a sense of the culturally liberating effects of art, played out most importantly in the academy for composition scholars like Britton, Macrorie, and Coles by the grand institutional specter of the New Criticism. This does not mean that the theoretical implications of this strategy of resistance were played out with any kind of consistency in the other aspects of progressivist practice. Very general disciplinary impulses like the ones I have named aestheticism and scientism are seldom manifested in categorically distinct ways. Science, for instance, once allied very powerfully to classicism and what I see as the first generation of modern composition "progressivism" in the post-Sputnik era via the Aristotelian sense of rhetoric as a descriptively exhaustive and perfectly logical taxonomy (as in, say, Lauer's determination to use empirical research in order to arrive at a finally prescriptive and exactly *correct* cognitive model of composing), quickly becomes a convenient ally for the second-generation "progressivist" fixation on process, despite the same group's celebration of art (see, for example, Britton's commitment to painstaking empirical research in order to demonstrate the pedagogical urgency of teaching "expressive" writing). composition's discourse of development is invested with a similarly curious and complicated disciplinary currency as is writing-across-the curriculum. This, in fact, is why I will come to insist later in this essay on the vital importance of acute theoretical self-consciousness for meaningful composition scholarship.

[16]See especially Chapters 1 and 2, where the authors argue that reality is "a creation that reflects the peculiarities of the perceiver" and that a language is "a theory of the universe, a way of selecting and grouping experiences" (25, 27).

[17]For a fairly detailed explication of the intellectual archaeology behind the alliance of these themes, see Bizzell's reading of what she calls "personal-style pedagogy" ("Composing").

[18]I will focus here on Berlin's attempts to provide a theoretical justification for his sense of democracy as a natural right, but I should note that he seems aware of the essentialist implications of such a sense in as much as he is tempted at times to avoid it by simply begging the question and claiming his embrace of democratic idealism as something like a frank admission of his own ideological orientation. The real issue for a social-epistemic rhetorician, of course, would be to account for the cultural reasons behind such an orientation. Anything less amounts to what I find my students doing all too often: deferring serious discussion by claiming what they call "a right to my own opinion."

[19]It's worth noting that the pattern suggested by "Rhetoric and Ideology in the Writing Class" is representative of almost all Berlin's other work as well, though admittedly a bit less plainly so in more recent essays. It is characteristic, that is, for Berlin to invoke anti-foundationalist rhetoric in order to argue in strikingly dutiful, sometimes even baldly patriotic terms for "democracy, [which] ordinarily provides political and social supports for open discussion, allowing for the free play of possibilities in the rhetorics that appear" (*Reality* 5) and for a politically interested pedagogy as "an effort to prepare students for critical citizenship in a democracy"—or even to appeal without irony to the ostensible authority of "leaders in government, business, and industry" ("Composition 51, 53) as reliable evaluators of this capacity for "critical citizenship" in students. That his more recent work represents what seems a self-conscious (if only partially successful) attempt to suppress this rhetoric of democratic fervor is similarly suggestive: the movement from pronouncements of "the greater good of all" promised by democracy ("Ideology" 490) to the somewhat less energized and more theoretically careful "rigor and promise of a dialogic rhetoric in a democracy" ("Composition" 54) does a good deal to indicate the palpability of this contradiction between cultural studies' radical anti-foundationalist imperative and composition's residual progressivist discourse.

[20]I hope in disavowing "ethics" in this way that I do not seem to prudishly assume what Bizzell has recently so eloquently denounced as the "posture of frozen horror at the operations of the ethical binary" typical of "American intellectuals" ("Marxist" 68). I certainly do not mean this paper to be a call to inaction, and I am in fact not ultimately unwilling to reunderstand "ethics" in an aggressively post-foundational, "dialectical" manner like the one Bizzell hints at. But then ultimately, I would argue, why bother? I have to wonder, that is, not only about the philosophical problems but even about the simple practical *utility* of salvaging "ethics" as a key animating principle for "political" intervention (even if it serves to make certain social issues raised by ideological critique more, say, popularly compellingly and thus broadly accepted, what can ethics do in the end to make critique and the deployment of such sentiment finally more *incisive and useful*?). And I worry significantly, on the other hand, about what seem to me the likeliest effects such a salvaging might have on the possibilities for cultivating what I think of as *a more truly enabling critical self-consciousness*, at both individual and institutional levels.

Works Cited

Belsey, Catherine. *Critical Practice*. London: Metheun, 1980.

Berlin, James A. "Composition and Cultural Studies." *Composition and Resistance*. Ed. Mark Hurlbert and Michael Blitz. Portsmouth, NH: Boynton, 1991. 47-57.

——. "Contemporary Composition: The Major Pedagogical Theories." *College English* 44 (1982): 765-77.

——. "Rhetoric and Ideology in the Writing Class." *College English* 50 (1988): 477-94.

——. *Rhetoric and Reality: Writing Instruction in American Colleges, 1900-1985*. Carbondale: Southern Illinois UP, 1987.

Berthoff, Anne E. *The Making of Meaning: Metaphors, Models, and Maxims for Writing Teachers*. Upper Montclair, NJ: Boynton, 1983.

——. "The Problem of Problem-Solving." *College Composition and Communication* 22 (1971): 237-42.

Bizzell, Patricia. "Cognition, Convention, Certainty: What We Need to Know about Writing." *Pre/Text* 3 (1982): 213-43.

——. "Composing Processes: An Overview." *The Teaching of Writing*. Ed. Anthony R. Petrosky and David Bartholomae. Chicago: U of Chicago P, 1986. 49-70.

——. "Marxist Ideas in Composition Studies." *Contending with Words: Composition and Rhetoric in a Postmodern Age*. Ed. Patricia Harkin and John Schilb. New York: MLA, 1991. 52-68.

——. "What Happens When Basic Writers Come to College?" *College Composition and Communication* 37 (1986): 294-301.

Britton, James, et al. *The Development of Writing Abilities (11-18)*. London: MacMillan, 1975.

Corbett, Edward P.J. *Classical Rhetoric for the Modern Student*. New York: Oxford UP, 1965.

Eagleton, Terry. *Against the Grain*. London: Verso, 1986.

——. *The Function of Criticism: From the Spectator to Post-Structuralism*. London: Verso, 1984.

Emig, Janet. *The Composing Process of Twelfth Graders*. NCTE Research Report No. 13, 1971.

Foster, Hal. *Recodings: Art, Spectacle, Cultural Politics*. Seattle: Bay, 1985.

Freedom and Discipline in English: Report on the Commission on English. New York: CEEB, 1965.

Harris, Joseph. "After Dartmouth: Growth and Conflict in English." *College English* 53 (1991): 631-46.

Huyssen, Andreas. *After the Great Divide: Modernism, Mass Culture, Postmodernism*. Bloomington: Indiana UP, 1986.

Jameson, Fredric. *Fables of Aggression: Wyndham Lewis, the Modernist as Fascist*. Berkeley: U of California P, 1979.

Knoblauch, C.H., and Lil Brannon. *Rhetorical Traditions and the Teaching of Writing*. Upper Montclair: Boynton, 1984.

Krauss, Rosalind E. *The Originality of the Avant-Garde and Other Modernist Myths*. Cambridge: MIT P, 1985.

Lauer, Janice M., and J. William Asher. *Composition Research: Empirical Designs*. New York: Oxford UP, 1988.

Lyotard, Jean-François. *The Post-Modern Condition: A Report on Knowledge*. Trans. Geoff Bennington and Brian Massumi. Minneapolis: U of Minnesota P, 1981.

Macrorie, Ken. *Uptaught (A Professor Discovers His Students on the way to a New University)*. Rochelle, NJ: Hayden, 1970.

The National Interest and the Teaching of English: A Report on the Status of the Profession. Urbana: NCTE, 1961.

Ohmann, Richard. *English in America: A Radical View of the Profession*. New York: Oxford UP, 1976.

Richards, I.A. *Science and Poetry*. London: Kegan, 1926.

Slevin, James F. "The Politics of the Profession." *An Introduction to Composition Studies*. Ed. Erika Lindemann and Gary Tate. New York: Oxford UP, 1991. 135-59.

Shaughnessy, Mina P. *Errors and Expectations: A Guide for the Teacher of Basic Writing*. New York: Oxford UP, 1977.

Vitanza, Victor J. "Three Countertheses: Or, A Critical In(ter)vention into Composition Theories and Pedagogies." *Contending with Words: Composition and Rhetoric in a Postmodern Age*. Ed. Patricia Harkin and John Schilb. New York: MLA, 1991. 139-72.

Winterowd, W. Ross. "Getting It Together in the English Department." *ADE Bulletin* 55 (November 1977): 28-32.

Young, Richard E., Alan L. Becker, and Kenneth L. Pike. *Rhetoric: Discovery and Change*. New York: Harcourt, 1970.

Zavarzadeh, Mas'ud, and Donald Morton. "Theory Pedagogy Politics: The Crisis of 'The Subject' in the Humanities." *boundary 2* 1986: 1-22.

The Other Reader

JOSEPH HARRIS

Let me begin with two readings of advertisements. The first is by a student in a university writing course:

> The DuraSoft's commercial opens with a man's voiceover, similar to the Calvin's voice, which is slightly feminine and artistic sounding. The man is reciting his own prose about the woman of his dreams as she is shown floating down to earth: "... like an angel dropped down from heaven ... with eyes as brown as ... bark." Then he pauses, "No, that's not it." The sound of a film rewinding is heard as she re-ascends back up into the clouds, all in a choppy fashion. He then says: "... with eyes as violet as the colors of a child's imagination." The beautiful dream woman then stares directly into the camera with very unnatural, almost glowing blue-violet-colored eyes.
>
> While the overall look and sound of this commercial is very pleasing to the senses, an educated and aware person sees it on a deeper level. The purpose of the DuraSoft commercial is to sell colored soft contacts to women. The way the commercial achieves this is by making the viewer (read woman) want to be as beautiful and desirable as the dream woman seen and described in the ad.
>
> While this ad is soothing to the eyes and ears, and, to a degree, fires the imagination, it is actually propaganda specifically aimed at impressionable young women and insecure women, who have become that way with the "help" of the same medium.... At the end of this ad, the man's voice says, "DuraSoft Colors Contact Lenses. Gives Brown Eyes a Second Look." How sad that is. According to this ad, those of us not "blessed" with blue eyes must now change our eye color to be considered attractive. And the saddest part of all is that most people aren't even aware of it.

And here is Leslie Savan writing in the *Village Voice* on another DuraSoft ad, this one targeted more directly at black women:

> In one TV spot, three pretty women—two white, one black—frown into mirrors. The black woman is ethnically correct ("good hair," looks like Lisa Bonet), but she's as sad as her eyes are deep brown. "There's someone special inside you, and DuraSoft Colors contact lenses can change your eye color to hers," a female voice-over says. Now bejeweled and glowing with emerald eyes, our black lady is ogled by a guy—as she gazes off into the sunset, savoring her ($200-$300) secret....
>
> Women of all races seem eager to unleash that special someone imprisoned by their irises.... The light ooh-la-la, purchasable fun of henna, fake eyelashes, or dotted nail polish that women can reimagine themselves with has always been a little burst of wildness, a temporary freedom from the physical self. That's fashion and fad. But it's hard to distinguish the difference between remodeling the self out of boredom and remodeling out of desire to become another. (56)

In one sense, there's not much to argue with in either of these readings. As both writers are quick to point out, the aim of advertisements is indeed to sell things, and they usually try to do so by suggesting that you will somehow be happier or prettier if you buy what they have to offer. The writing in both pieces is lively, fun, and accurate. And each does a nice job of showing how the DuraSoft ads play on (and add to) the ways women in our culture are made to feel anxious about how they look. (Though, I'd argue that this sort of criticism has become so easy and familiar that most of us can do it pretty well without giving it much thought, which is perhaps one reason why the writings here of a college student and a professional critic seem so much alike.) What troubles me, though, is how each writer seems to describe not her own response to the ad but that of some *other viewer*. And so while my student speaks indignantly and eloquently in the name of those "impressionable young women and insecure women" who are taken in by the DuraSoft spot, she also hints that she is among those "educated and aware" viewers who see it "on a deeper level." Similarly, Savan notes the eagerness of "women of all races . . . to unleash that special someone imprisoned by their irises," while at the same time implying that there are still a few of us left who can make that hard distinction between "remodeling the self out of boredom and remodeling out of desire to become another." In short, neither is fooled, though both think that others are.

The problem, of course, is finding those other dumber viewers. Our society is saturated with ads. Everyone sees through them; no one is immune from their appeal. If we want to understand anything about how they work, we need to unravel this paradox. Instead, most writing on advertising treats the viewer as either a skeptic or a shill. And so, for instance, John Berger writes that advertising "is always about the future buyer. It offers him an image of himself made glamorous by the product or opportunity it is trying to sell. The image then makes him envious of himself as he might be" (132). But it's hard to imagine Berger himself falling for such a scam. And, similarly, when Mark Miller writes of a TV spot for Shield soap that its "strategy is not meant to be noticed," we know immediately that here is one viewer who has not been taken in (48). But who has?

A Discourse of Alarm

I don't mean to side here with advertisers like Hal Riney who argue that since "people today are adwise," there's nothing really to worry about (qtd. in Miller 49). My point is that before we can have effective criticism of advertising, or of any other part of popular culture, we need to admit that all of us respond to it in ways that are often at once both pleased and skeptical, amused and doubting, open and resisting. What won't help is speaking in the name of someone who fails to see what we do, or who falls for things that we don't.

And yet this is often precisely what happens. For instance, a few years ago, I asked a group of university students to come up with a magazine ad they found interesting or compelling and to write a piece that told why. A week or so later we sat in class and talked about two of their responses: one poked fun at the macho Americanism of an ad for Hero cologne; the other mocked the tacky fantasy of a layout for Forever Krystal perfume. The students were happy, this was easy stuff, they felt in the know. To a person, they had decoded my assignment as meaning: show me how you see through this ad. I looked around the room and counted eighteen pairs of jeans and eighteen pairs of running shoes. (I was the only exception, with my proper academic penny loafers and baggy corduroys.) How is it, I asked, that nobody here is taken in by advertising and yet we all dress alike? Can we find a way of talking about the effects ads have not on other people but on ourselves? And then our conversation, which had been going so well, began to falter.

We have few models of what such talk or writing might look like. What we have instead is a long tradition of speaking, usually in tones of consternation and dismay, about the effects popular texts could have on some other reader. We can trace this discourse of alarm back to the worries of Socrates and Plato that many of the Homeric verses they themselves are able to quote by heart might have a corrupting influence on lesser men, could in fact turn them into cowards or religious skeptics, and thus that all but the most "austere and less pleasure-giving" poets would need to be banned from their ideal city (*Republic* 398b). Similarly, a central aim of modern literary studies has been to get students to resist the (supposedly) coarse pleasures of popular culture in favor of the more refined ones offered by art—as can be seen in Matthew Arnold's concern with domesticating the tastes of the "bawling, hustling, and smashing" populace of his day (451), and later in the worries of F.R. Leavis about the threats posed to "culture" by "mass civilization." Since then there has been no lack of critics from Theodor Adorno and Dwight MacDonald to Laura Mulvey and Guy Debord to talk about how the mass media continue to fix the spectator (that is, other spectators) in a state of critical apathy and listlessness. And many current postmodern or leftist critics are just as presumptuous. A salient case in point is E. Ann Kaplan, who claims in *Rocking Around the Clock* to account for how "the institutional practices [of MTV] construct subjects to the tune of 28 million" (29), without feeling a need to talk with any one of these "subjects" personally, or to explain how she alone among them escaped the hegemonic clutches of music television.

One response to such moralizing has been to argue that the actual readers of popular texts are in fact far more active and resistant than they are often assumed to be. While this is in many ways an appealing stance, it still places the critic in the odd position of describing how someone else reads a text with the result that it is often not clear how *the critic* reads it. My hunch is that the responses of such "other readers," however well or sympathetically described, will almost always turn out to be less complex and interesting than those of the critic him or herself—so that, even at its best, such criticism is apt to run into the kind of problem faced by Janice Radway, whose *Reading the Romance* is a rare attempt to document some of the ways popular texts actually get read by "ordinary" people.

To do so, Radway interviewed some frequent readers of romance novels (or Harlequins) about "their own working definition of the genre...and their preferences for particular kinds of romances, heroines, and heroes" (13). Radway has been criticized for relying too heavily on the responses of a single master reader, a bookstore employee who also puts out a newsletter about romances; but that's not my worry here, since even if this charge is accurate, her lone informant is still one more than most critics have ever consulted. My concern is with what Radway *does* with the responses of her informants, with the relation she sets up between their ways of reading and her own. The troubling thing is that, after showing how the women in her study see their reading of romance novels as a way of contesting and escaping the demands placed on them as wives and mothers, Radway still feels compelled to note that

> while the act of reading is used by women as a means of partial protest against the role prescribed for them by the culture, the discourse [of the romance] itself actively insists on the desirability, naturalness, and benefits of that role by portraying it not as the imposed necessity that it is but as a freely designed, personally controlled, individual choice. (208)

In other words, they've missed something. And so Radway's stance is perhaps not so different from my student's or Savan's, for like them she sees dangers lurking in popular texts that the readers she speaks for do not. It is little surprise, then, that she ends her study of the romance with the pious hope that there will someday be "a world where the vicarious pleasure supplied by its reading would be unnecessary" (222).

In their own texts, each of these writers, from Plato and Arnold to my student and Radway, presents a figure of the critic who can read (and often even enjoy) popular works without being injured or seduced by them. Yet each doubts that others can do the same, and so ends up arguing for a kind of censorship, or at least for a better world where the pleasures such texts offer are no longer needed (like sexless views of heaven). A deep anti-democratic impulse, a kind of fear of the mob, runs through such writings. Those other readers can't be trusted. Their responses need to be trained, domesticated, disciplined. And, in the meantime, they need to be guarded against the influences of popular and thus suspect texts—from things like imitative poetry in Plato's time, or serial novels in Arnold's, or television in our own.

In "Cultural Studies: Two Paradigms," Stuart Hall distinguishes between a kind of scholarship that looks at the particular ways a culture is lived and experienced by the individuals in it, and another whose aim is to uncover the ideological forces that structure and determine those experiences. While the first approach tries to see how the forms of a culture are taken up and revised by the people in it, the second looks instead for those ways in which that culture might be said to be "speaking through" the voices of such individuals (42). As teachers and critics, we clearly need to keep both emphases in mind. We need, that is, not only to listen closely to what "ordinary" people tell us about what they read and watch and listen to, but also to push against their usual modes of interpreting, to look with them for alternative ways of understanding our common culture. The problem, though, as I see it, has once again to do with the relations between these two kinds of work. Bringing the voices of ordinary readers and scholars, or of students and teachers, into anything like a reciprocal exchange (in which both sides of the conversation are able to affect the views of the other) proves something easier said than done. What often happens instead is that the structural or ideological analysis of the scholar subsumes the views of the ordinary reader, so that while the concerns of certain groups do get "spoken for" in some kinds of criticism, the actual words of non-academics rarely find their way into the writings of even the most political critics. And even on those odd moments that they do, they are usually positioned in ways that give them little power or authority.

And so, once again, the problem with *Reading the Romance* is not so much that Radway fails to listen to her informants, but that her own closing analysis discounts what they have to say, reduces their ways of reading to merely a "partial protest." The comments of her informants, that is, don't seem to have much influenced *her* view of the romance, and the reading she offers of it in her last chapter—in which she argues in solid if predictable academic fashion that such novels reproduce the values of patriarchy—often seems less to respond to their concerns than to correct them (209-22). But what if Radway had begun with her own ideological reading, and then tried to show the sorts of pressures these other non-academic readers brought to bear upon it, the ways their views of the romance forced her to revise her own? That is, can we imagine a kind of criticism in which the comments of ordinary readers (or students) function not only as material for the writer to work with and explain—as examples of what she herself has to say, perhaps, or as illustrations of the problem she wants to address—but also as checks against the bias of her own reading, as statements of views she must in some way respond to?

Listening to the Other Reader

It is here that work in composition can powerfully inform that in cultural studies. Teachers and scholars like Mina Shaughnessy, Shirley Brice Heath, Mike Rose, and David Bartholomae have begun to offer us ways of reading student writings not simply for the errors or gaps they may reveal but also for the logic of the positions they are struggling to develop—a sense that is often hard to discern due both to the inexperience of many student writers and to the set of expectations that guide our readings of their texts. One of the projects of composition has been to revise those expectations, to find new ways of reading texts that are still in early or formative stages, or that seem written in odd or unfamiliar idioms. To put it another way, the comments of the "other reader," however unformed or clichéd these may sometimes seem, have long been given a kind of serious attention in composition that they have rarely been offered elsewhere. (Indeed composition is the only field I know of where student writings are regularly the focus of scholarly articles.) This habit of attention can be of some real help, I think, in trying to understand how non-academics read popular texts.

Let me give an example. One of the recurring themes of much writing about soap operas is that such shows vicariously fill needs that are otherwise left unmet in the lives of their viewers, and thus serve to "reconcile her," as Tania Modleski argues, "to the meaningless, repetitive nature of much of her life and work in the home" (97). Such phrasings reveal a common image of the soap viewer as a housewife or woman with a low-status job, who, unlike us, often finds it hard to distinguish clearly between reality and the "mass-produced fantasies" of TV. Consider this exchange between soap critic and fan, which appears near the start of Ruth Rosen's "Search for Yesterday":

> For some viewers, the world of the soap and their own daily lives begins to blur. Early in my research, I encountered one such fan. At a local supermarket, I picked up *Soap Opera Digest*, a magazine that offers weekly synopses of soap plots and articles about the stars. The cashier, in her late teens, quickly spotted the magazine that I had hidden between the detergent and the broccoli. Its cover featured a couple from ABC's popular soap, *General Hospital*. As she rang up the items, the cashier commented, "I think Grant and Celia will work it out, don't you?" Stunned, I nodded. She bagged my groceries and continued her monologue on Grant and Celia's marital problems, offering suggestions and advice. Imperceptibly, I had slipped into the curious world of the soap opera. The cashier simply assumed that I too was a "resident" of *General Hospital*'s fictional Port Charles. (43)

Rosen goes on to explain that she can "understand the feelings" of such viewers because once, some fifteen years back, she had been confined to a hospital bed (that is, temporarily an invalid), and had found some solace herself in watching *General Hospital*—though she has of course since then recovered (both physically and intellectually, it would seem) and is now at most only "an occasional abuser, not a confirmed addict" of soaps (43). But far stronger than her empathy for those still hooked on soaps, though, is a set of class antagonisms that separate her from such fans. Note how Rosen describes the cashier first as "quickly spotting" the magazine she has so discretely "hidden," which the young woman then "assumes" might give the two of them something to talk about—a faux pas that leaves the critic "stunned" as the cashier launches obliviously into a "monologue" while bagging her groceries. Note too how Rosen persistently reads everything this young fan says or does as a sign of her lack of sophistication. But isn't it at least possible that she might have meant "I think Grant and Celia will work it out, don't you?" in a kind of laughing or knowing way, as an ironic comment on the inevitable progress of such TV romances? If Tania Modleski had said the same thing to Rosen, how would she have interpreted it? And why is reading *Soap Opera Digest* so very different from reading literary criticism or biography? Would Rosen have been stunned in quite the same way if it had been a Viking Critical Edition the cashier had noticed, and if she had used that as a pretext to talk about, say, the marital problems of Vrosnky and Anna as if they were all "residents" of nineteenth century Moscow? And even if we were to accept her unflattering sketch of this young woman, wouldn't this still raise the question of why Rosen picks as her prototypic viewer of soaps someone who seems so foolish and naive? (My own experience is that many academics, professionals, and college students also watch and talk about soaps regularly and that about half of these viewers are men.)

What most strikes me here, though, is how little Rosen feels she needs to say about this woman. We are told her age and class ("the cashier in her late teens"), and quoted *one sentence* of her remarks, from which we are then expected to derive the tone and gist of the rest of her "monologue on Grant and Celia's marital problems." Rosen seems to assume, that is, that we already pretty much know what this young woman is able to say before she even begins to speak—and thus that there is little need for us to attend to her actual remarks. But what if we refused to suppose this? What if we assumed instead that fans of soaps are likely to know things about them that we don't, and that our job, both as teachers and critics, is to find out what these are, to help them articulate these sorts of alternative knowledges? And what if instead of representing these "other viewers" of pop culture with a single sentence, a casual comment in a supermarket line, we listened to their remarks at length and with some real care? Here, for instance, is an excerpt from an essay written by a first-year student at the University of Pittsburgh that shows her taking what seems to me a rather sophisticated sort of pleasure from the soaps. After beginning her piece by talking about her commitment to various soaps—taping them, talking about them with friends and family, reading *Soap Opera Digest*, watching the annual soap awards—she goes on to say:

> I do not believe that soaps are very realistic. It is very difficult to try to take them seriously. For example, don't you just love it when the women wake up in the morning with hair and make-up perfect. Not even a smudge on their face and not a piece of hair out of place. What beauty queens! But you have to admit it is always interesting to see which man they will be sleeping with this time. I do not think it could be the same man two nights consecutively. Almost impossible!
>
> I find it amazing how the characters get around so fast. One minute they will be at a business meeting, and the next they will be at dinner. Soaps always seem to take place inside, it is very rare to see the outside world. What kind of transportation do they use to get around?

> I think that time is important, and you would not believe how fast the children grow up. One day they are born, and three months later they are five years old. Wow, how time flies! And at Christmas time, Christmas day always seems to last for four days. Yes, how nice, but so strange.
>
> Another thing I find humorous and hard to believe is that everyone on soap operas knows each other. Is the town that small that it only consists of those thirty or forty people? I bet if you sat down and figured it out, every one of them could be related in some way or another. It is so hard to keep track of who used to be married to whom and who had an affair with whom, etc. . . .

So here is a fan who, far from experiencing some sort of blurring between her own world and that of the soaps, actually seems to delight in their *conventionality*, in the ways they distort and exaggerate the events of everyday life. From this point in her piece, she goes on to detail the twists of some particularly bizarre plot lines (a special pleasure of many soap fans), and then concludes by saying:

> Most of the time when I am sitting there watching my soap, I find myself laughing because it is so unrealistic. I feel relieved that I do not have their overwhelming problems. Maybe other viewers feel the same way. I am just glad that life is not a soap opera.

While one could perhaps read this ending as evidence of the power of soaps to "reconcile" their viewers to the status quo, I think it very hard to read the piece as a whole as coming from someone who has taken up fantasy residence in another world. This writer is not Rosen's young cashier. If anything, she is something of a formalist, whose main pleasure in the soaps seems to stem from observing their (often absurd) narrative ploys. Whether many "other viewers feel the same way" as her, I don't know. But I am inclined to put more stock in her account than in the supposed responses of the "housewives" that other critics claim to speak for. And, in any case, my aim is not to determine if her views are somehow more authentic or typical than those of Rosen's cashier, but to suggest that, if we bother to look for them, we are likely to find that the responses of actual viewers to soaps are not as easy to predict as many critics seem to think.

Cultural Criticism in the Composition Class
The college writing class is only one of many places where we might look for such accounts of how ordinary readers deal with popular texts. The sort of ethnographic work done by Radway is another useful source, as are newsletters, fanzines, club materials, letters columns, and the like. But as I've tried to point out in talking about Radway, there is still always the question of what to do with such accounts once you have them. As writing teachers, we are trained to read the comments of ordinary readers with more generosity and care than they are perhaps usually given. Also, we are well-placed to get more accounts of how such readers deal with popular texts, since we can ask our students to write about them. But the request needs to be made in the right way, since if it's not, we're likely to get yet more pieces on the supposed

responses of "impressionable young women" and the like. You have to articulate a reaction before you can either celebrate or criticize it. We need then to set up classrooms where students can talk about their responses to popular texts as mixed rather than simple, where they can write as people who are at once rock fans *and* intellectuals, who watch old sitcoms *and* read criticism, who wear levis *and* look skeptically at advertising.

One way I've tried to do so is through having students look at the uses they make of popular texts in forming their own self-images or identities. The idea driving this work is that identity rises out of identification, that we define who we are by whom we choose to stand with and against, and thus that in an electronic culture much of our sense of self is shaped by (or set against) the voices and images of television, radio, movies, pop music, fashion, advertising, and the like. For such a course to work, it is vital that students don't get the sense that there is some sort of party line to be either mimicked or resisted, and especially that they don't feel required to adopt an adversarial stance towards their own culture, to side somehow with the university and against the media, but rather that they can write of the pleasures as well as the problems they find in popular texts.

Thus instead of asking students to interpret a series of pop texts that I have selected beforehand, I usually ask them to read the work of various critics and to test their ideas against the evidence of texts—ads, cars, buildings, clothes, celebrities—that they themselves choose to write on. The goal of such work is not simply to have them "apply" a certain interpretive method, but to point out its uses and limits, to extend or revise or argue against what a particular critic has to say. And so, for instance, I've asked students to offer a reading of a television show that either adds to or causes problems for Alexander Nehamas's claim that "television rewards serious watching" (158). At other times I've had them draw on the method and vocabulary of Judith Williamson in analyzing the workings of an advertisement, not in order to determine what the ad "really means," but to see what her approach might be said both to reveal and to obscure. I've had them send away for and analyze fan club materials in order to respond to what John Caughey has argued about the "imaginary relationships" people create between themselves and celebrities. And I've asked them to pick a text—a magazine, a television show, a rock song—and then define the sort of viewer or reader it seems to address, at first using Barbara Ehrenreich's critique of *Playboy* as a model for their work, and then doubling back to assess what the strengths and limits of such an approach are. The specific assignments and readings change from term to term. Their point stays the same: to offer students some chances to work with and through a number of ways of reading our culture, and, in doing so, to begin to define their own places in it.

In the process, they may also learn something about the sorts of power and insight that study at a university can offer them, much as we can learn, if we care to, from the alternative practices of reading they bring to the classroom. Nina Schwartz has argued that we need to help students draw on the various sorts of "inappropriate knowledge" they have all acquired, to make use of the things they know about the workings of schools, fraternities, families, workplaces, pop culture, and the like, but which they often are unable to talk about because we offer them no place or occasion to do so. We can all gain much when they do, for when students start to tell us what they know about our culture, it means they are no longer the sort of "other readers" whose responses critics must worry about and speak for—but people we can listen to and learn from.[1]

Notes

[1]Since one of my points here is that classroom work can and ought to inform our work as critics much more fully than it often does, I'd especially like to thank my colleagues in the English department at the University of Pittsburgh, where teaching regularly gets talked about in ways I find extraordinarily exciting and useful. In particular, as I was writing this, I also had the good luck to be working with Richard Miller on his Ph.D. project on the relations between cultural criticism and pedagogy, and I know his take on Radway, Kaplan, and Modleski has strongly shaped mine. At the same time, I was also cowriting an essay on "The Classroom in Theory" with Jean Ferguson Carr and Stephen L. Carr, and I am sure that many of their ideas and phrasings have found their way into this piece as well. Again, my thanks go to them all.

Works Cited

Arnold, Matthew. *Poetry and Criticism*. Ed. A. Dwight Culler. Boston: Houghton, 1961.

Berger, John J. *Ways of Seeing*. New York: Penguin, 1972.

Caughey, John L. *Imaginary Social Worlds*. Lincoln: U of Nebraska P, 1984.

Ehrenreich, Barbara. *The Hearts of Men: American Dreams and the Flight from Commitment*. New York: Anchor, 1983.

Hall, Stuart. "Cultural Studies: Two Paradigms." *Media, Culture and Society* 2 (1980): 33-48.

Kaplan, E. Ann. *Rocking Around the Clock: Music Television, Postmodernism, and Consumer Culture*. New York: Methuen, 1987.

Leavis, Frank Raymond. "Mass Civilization and Minority Culture." *Education and the University*. 2nd ed. London: Chatto, 1948. 141-71.

Miller, Mark Crispin. *Boxed In: The Culture of TV*. Evanston: Northwestern UP, 1988.

Modleski, Tania. *Loving with a Vengeance: Mass-Produced Fantasies for Women*. New York: Routledge, 1988.

Nehamas, Alexander. "Serious Watching." *South Atlantic Quarterly* 89.1 (1990): 157-80.

Plato. *The Republic*. Trans. G.M.A. Grube. Indianapolis: Hackett, 1974.

Radway, Janice A. *Reading the Romance: Women, Patriarchy, and Popular Literature*. Chapel Hill: U of North Carolina P, 1984.

Rosen, Ruth. "Search for Yesterday." *Watching Television*. Ed. Todd Gitlin. New York: Pantheon, 1986. 42-67.

Savan, Leslie. "The Color Blue." *Village Voice* (3 Nov. 1987): 56.

Schwartz, Nina. "Conversations with the Social Text." *Reclaiming Pedagogy: The Rhetoric of the Classroom*. Ed. Patricia Donahue and Ellen Quandahl. Carbondale: Southern Illinois UP, 1989. 60-71.

Williamson, Judith. "Woman is an Island." *Studies in Entertainment*. Ed. Tania Modleski. Bloomington: Indiana UP, 1986. 99-118.

Articulation Theory and the Problem of Determination: A Reading of *Lives on the Boundary*

JOHN TRIMBUR

The narrativity of an individual life is a literary trope that figures across a range of genres. From memoirs, biography, the journalistic profile, and the celebrity story to the autobiographical novel and *bildungsroman*, the narrativity of a life is a familiar and apparently altogether consumable literary convention, turning up in bestsellers such as *Iacocca: An Autobiography* and popular magazines such as *People*. Other forms of writing, too—popular psychology books such as Gail Sheehy's *Passages* and the gamut of self-help and popular advice tracts that line bookstore shelves—seem to take it for granted that an individual life not only can be narrated but that such narration can make a life intelligible and thereby subject to control and change.

Harvey Kail suggests that composition theory and textbooks likewise rely on the narrativity of a Student Writer's life by projecting mythic quests for students to take on their road to advanced literacy. In "Narratives of Knowledge: Story and Pedagogy in Four Composition Texts," Kail argues that we can read out the plots of standard textbooks such as Becker, Young, and Pike's *Rhetoric: Discovery and Change*, Ann Berthoff's *Forming/Thinking/Writing*, William E. Coles, Jr.'s *Teaching Composition*, and Kenneth A. Bruffee's *A Short Course in Writing* in order to identify their underlying narratives and the tales they tell of the formation of a personality through emergence into literacy. According to Kail, these narratives are familiar ones, based on Christian and social traditions deeply rooted in American culture, such as the search for identity, salvation, self-improvement, and knowledge. By paying attention to these narratives, moreover, Kail suggests an alternative way to represent composition studies, not just as a series of discrete theoretical positions on a taxonomic grid (Becker, Young, and Pike are "cognitivists," Berthoff a "neo-Cassirerean," Coles an "expressivist," Bruffee a "social constructionist") but as a series of conjunctures that link scholarly and pedagogical discourses and practices to culturally sanctioned narratives, to the interests, institutions, and identities these narratives call up, and to the way these narratives make the meanings of reading and writing intelligible to students and teachers alike.

By and large, however, composition studies has paid relatively little attention to its own narrativity, to the way in which composition theory and practice are articulated to the master narratives that charter belief and action in American culture. This may appear to be surprising because the notion that knowledge is invariably authorized by its narrativity has become something of a commonplace in postmodern thought. Richard Rorty, Jean-François Lyotard, and others, for whatever differences may otherwise divide them, seem to agree that what we have traditionally called knowledge is in fact a "fiction," a manufactured account that legitimizes itself precisely to the extent it holds its readers in the thrall of persistent and unexamined metaphors and metanarratives.

There has, of course, been a recent turn toward narrative in composition studies, in part following Jane Tompkins' call to "unlearn" the critical essay and write in a more personal and autobiographical style. In the work of Donald McQuade, Nancy Sommers, and others, however, narrative remains separate from "thesis-driven" exposition. It figures as an academically devalued genre capable, its advocates hold, of redeeming prose by replacing the authoritarian, masculinist, and hierarchical strategies of arguing for a position with the immediacy and authenticity of lived experience rendered narratively. This turn to narrative, thus, has largely limited itself to counterposing narrativity as a way of knowing to argumentative strategies, instead of probing for the connections between narratives and other discursive forms and cultural practices—or, as Kail might put it, how the discourse of composition studies joins together with available culturally authorized narratives and the social contexts in which these narratives arise.

In this essay, I want to suggest, in the broadest sense, the usefulness of investigating the conjunctures at which discourses and practices in the field of composition studies are linked to discourses and practices outside of it. I will be looking in particular at how the narrativity of an individual life in Mike Rose's *Lives on the Boundary* is articulated to wider cultural narratives. I have chosen to focus on *Lives on the Boundary* in part because it makes its own narrativity so explicit by relying on autobiography to tell the story of what the book's subtitle calls the "struggles and achievements of America's educational underclass." But I am also interested in *Lives on the Boundary* because its use of such a popular genre to narrate its concerns makes the book more problematical than has usually been acknowledged.

The Problem of Narrativity in *Lives on the Boundary*
Since *Lives on the Boundary* appeared in 1989, it has been hailed as the book composition studies was waiting for. Addressed to the general public, as well as to education and composition specialists, *Lives on the Boundary* seemed to do the kind of cultural and ideological work needed in the Reagan/Bush era of educational retrenchment by providing an eloquent and moving case for

expanded educational opportunity, multicultural curricula, enlightened pedagogy, and the educability of all Americans. At last, it appeared that someone had succeeded in translating the hard-won experience and expertise of writing teachers, and especially of basic writing teachers in open admissions programs, into a popular idiom capable of affecting public opinion. *Lives on the Boundary* was greeted as the book to give composition studies a public voice and visibility to counter bestsellers such as E.D. Hirsch's *Cultural Literacy* and Allan Bloom's *The Closing of the American Mind* and commission reports from William Bennett, Diane Ravitch and Chester Finn, and Lynne J. Cheney.

To bring his case to a broad audience, Rose has chosen to devote a substantial part of the book to his own life. Rose tells the story of his "passage from South Vermont [the working-class neighborhood where he grew up] to Loyola," where Rose was an undergraduate and, as he puts it, "entered the conversation" (67). We follow Rose on a kind of pilgrim's progress, from his struggles as a high-school student who arises, miraculously, from the slough of Voc-Ed despond, through college and the temptations of literary studies in graduate school to his redemptive work as a teacher of the neglected and underprepared. This narrative, of course, possesses enormous cultural resonance, recalling such autobiographies as Richard Wright's *Black Boy* and Richard Rodriquez's *Hunger of Memory*. But because the tale of a poor or working-class youth's rising from his humble origins is such a familiar one, it also contains some political risks I think have not been adequately accounted for. To put it as directly as I can, the risk is that readers will take *Lives on the Boundary* to be another comforting American success story of an individual who, through the power of education and the guidance of more experienced teacher-mentors, takes the predictable road to self-improvement and upward mobility, from the mean streets of Los Angeles to the halls of UCLA. Such a narrative, furthermore, would seem to fit right in to what Harvey Graff calls the "literacy myth": the moral consensus that has dominated the meanings of literacy since the mid-nineteenth century by representing the ability to read and write as a social explanation of success and failure in class society, a token of middle-class propriety, and a measure to divide the worthy from the unworthy poor.

The issue I am concerned with here is whether Rose's decision to use the narrativity of a life backfires on him. Despite Rose's obvious intentions to argue for fundamental reforms in American education, the question needs to be asked whether the autobiographical impulse in *Lives on the Boundary* inevitably locates the book for its readers within what Kristin Ross calls the "exemplary bourgeois cultural project" of narrating a life, individualizing a person's fate, and positioning readers as witnesses to an edifying tale of individual initiative and the transformative powers of education and literacy. But before I consider whether Rose's life history is absorbed, inadvertently or not, by the cultural narrative it articulates, I want first to define more precisely the notions of conjuncture and articulation I will be using to read *Lives on the Boundary*.

Taxonomies and Conjunctures

For the most part, literature reviews and histories of writing instruction have used a taxonomic strategy to order composition by dividing and classifying its various pedagogies, rhetorics, and research programs into categories, with perhaps the discontinuity of a Kuhnian paradigm shift to demarcate one approach from another. Like any rhetorical strategy, taxonomies both enable and constrain their users, bringing some things to light while suppressing others. Taxonomies, in other words, need to be seen not so much in terms of their truth value as their uses and what they make possible.

The standard taxonomies in the field, such as James A. Berlin's expressionistic, cognitivist, and social-epistemic rhetorics, Lester Faigley's expressive, cognitive, and social views of composing, and Stephen North's division of the field into researchers, historians, scholars, and practitioners are useful for the ordering functions they perform and the differences, both practical and theoretical, they bring to the surface. Particularly for a young and emerging field such as composition studies, taxonomies can codify positions that might appear otherwise to arise spontaneously from the pressures of practice. In this regard, Berlin's and Faigley's taxonomies especially have contributed to the professionalization of the field by giving it a shape, by identifying central issues, and by lifting the study and teaching of writing from the shared activity of a few like-minded individuals at the margins of English departments into the realm of scholarly controversy where a set of standard positions defines the context of issues and establishes the terms of ongoing discussion. From this perspective, we might say that without taxonomies it would be difficult to think and speak composition studies at all. By dividing and classifying, taxonomies create a unity of differences as the terrain of composition studies.

At the same time, such division and classification tends to make instances of intellectual work into synechdoches or labels for trends and currents in the field. The work of David Bartholomae, for example, and in particular his essay "Inventing the University," is often cited as a founding statement of a social constructionist, academic discourse approach to writing instruction. Although, as Carolyn C. Ball argues, this conventionalized view may actually ignore or suppress expressionist or cognitivist currents in Bartholomae's writing, the treatment of "Inventing the University" as a kind of shorthand token seems virtually to be called for by the generic function of the literature review and the scholarly convention of locating one's work in relation to prior work, as the ground to validate new inquiries or a foil to establish counter-tendencies.

However, as Susan Miller says of North's division of composition studies into humanistic "scholars" and empiricist "researchers," taxonomies are based not on "logical, but political, differences" (37). Taxonomic categories need to be seen not just as the formal defining terms of a field of study but as the result of particular conjunctures that ascribe certain cultural meanings and political valences to ideas and practices. Unlike the categories of a taxonomy, which reside in the space of logic, conjunctures are located in actual historical time. A conjuncture designates those moments when ideas (whether in the form of theories or narratives or other genres) are joined to other ideas, practices, institutions, interests, and subjectivities. Conjunctures constitute the temporal and temporary moments at which ideas take on particular social weight, cultural meaning, and rhetorical effect not because of their intrinsic or essential identities (as specified categorically) but because of the way these ideas are articulated concretely by specific men and women and take on specific identities in specific historical settings and social contexts.

To give a brief example: from a conjunctural perspective, the emphasis on the value of personal voice and individual sincerity in the work of Peter Elbow cannot be reduced simply to a category of expressionistic rhetoric that distinguishes it, say, from the emphasis on academic discourse and the kind of imitative ventriloquy Bartholomae notes in students' efforts to appropriate the institutional voices of the university. The sincerity of self-revelation that Elbow struggled to teach young men writing statements of conscientious objection during the Vietnam War carries a quite different political meaning from the usual practice of sincerity in expressionistic rhetorics. Berlin, correctly I think, sees these rhetorics as critical of "the dehumanizing effects of industrial capitalism" but at the same time indebted to "the entrepreneurial values capitalism most admires: individualism, private initiative, the confidence for risk taking, the right to be contentious with authority (especially the state)" (487). The point here is that apparently identical ideas and practices can take on quite different cultural meanings and political valences depending on the conjuncture at which (and to which) they are articulated. The rhetorical effect of ideas and practices is produced not only by reference to their logical features but also by the practical joining together of discourse, institutions, and interests that social utterances and performances inevitably enact. When sincerity of expression is linked to mass movements against war, as occurred during the Vietnam War, or invoked as a means to give voice to those who have been systematically silenced, as during the Black Expressionist movement of the 1960s (see Leroi Jones/Amiri Baraka's classic essay "Expressive Language"), an expressionistic rhetoric can indeed be oppositional in effect. At other times, however, in "normal" classrooms of middle-class students, expressionistic rhetoric may well serve simply as a form of personal protest that, as Berlin notes, is "easily coopted by the very capitalist forces it opposes" or, at best, a limited means of "creative realization of the self" (487).

What I am suggesting is that there is no way to tell on the basis of a taxonomic categorization, to predict with certainty the effects. Unlike the categories in a taxonomy, which are meant to have a predictive value, the notion of a conjuncture suggests that nothing can be guaranteed ahead of time strictly according to formal or textual qualities alone. Rather effective meaning is a matter of what happens: practice takes place in historical time and social space.

Stuart Hall's Theory of Articulation

The notion of a "conjuncturalist" approach to the relationship between ideas, practices, and social formations might be seen as an attempt to formulate a neo-Marxist model of determination. As Raymond Williams notes, "No problem in Marxist cultural theory is more difficult than that of 'determination'" (83). Part of the difficulty may be attributed in the first place to the writings of Marx and Engels, which seem at times to presuppose a fixed correspondence among the existing stage of material production, social relations, and consciousness. In *The German Ideology*, for example, Marx states quite clearly that the "mass of productive forces accessible to men determines the conditions of society" (18). There is a tendency in Marx's writings to see human activity and historical development as governed by scientific laws of determination, a tendency that objectifies the social process and, as Engels indicates in a letter to Bloch in 1890, reads human will and agency out of history. "The historical event," Engels writes, may "be viewed as the product of a power which works as a whole unconsciously and without volition. For what each individual wants is obstructed by everyone else, and what emerges is something that no one willed" (476). At the same time, of course, one can also find equally authoritative passages that seem to affirm the creativity of human agency, even if it operates within particular constraints. Probably the best-known statement of this view is Marx's famous remark that "people make history but in conditions not of their making."

According to Williams, the confusion surrounding the problem of determination results in part from the "extraordinary linguistic complexity" of the term "determine" (84). While the term has certainly been colored in its uses within the Marxist tradition by scientistic biases and a typically nineteenth-century postivist quest for certainty, the root sense of "determine," Williams says, refers not only to an external force or authority—whether history or God—that decides or controls the outcome of an action but also to the way limits are set and pressures exerted by the momentum of the social process itself. According to the latter sense of the term, Williams says, "'Society' is then never only the 'dead husk' which *limits* social and individual fulfillment"—as it sometimes appears in orthodox Marxisms that hold to an abstract determinism based on isolated and autonomous forces acting upon the social formation from outside. Instead, for Williams, society "is always also a constitutive process with very powerful *pressures* which are both expressed in political, economic, and cultural formations and, to take the full weight of 'constitutive,' are internalized and become 'individual wills'" (87; emphasis added).

Perhaps the fullest exploration of the problem of determination in contemporary Marxist thought occurs in Stuart Hall's theory of articulation. Like Williams, Hall wants to develop a model of determination based not upon the implacable and predictable laws of history but upon the limits and pressures of specific historical, social, and cultural conjunctures. Situating his theory of articulation within past and current critical discourses, Hall has attempted to formulate a model of determination that avoids, on the one hand, the traditional Marxist view of a fixed and necessary correspondence between cultural practices and social structures and, on the other, more recent poststructuralist views of the indeterminacy or necessary non-correspondence and incommensurability of discourses, practices, and structures. By looking at how particular ideas, discourses, and practices are linked—or articulated—to particular conjunctures in the social formation, Hall has sought to define a "Marxism without guarantees," a guide to action that relies not on the predictive certainties of classical Marxist theory but on a reading of those linkages and how they articulate, at specific times and places, interests, subjectivities, and social forces.

Hall's theory of articulation was developed as part of a larger project to define the meaning of cultural studies in relation to what Hall calls "culturalist" and "structuralist" paradigms of critical thought. Cultural studies is often seen as the effort of the Birmingham (UK) Center for Contemporary Cultural Studies, under Hall's directorship, to balance the culturalist work of Williams, Richard Hoggart, and E.P. Thompson from the late 1950s and early 1960s (the period of the emergence of the British New Left) against the impact of more recent poststructuralist and postmodernist trends on Marxist thought in the 1970s and 1980s, as embodied above all in the influence of Althusser's structuralist Marxism. The usual version holds that a balancing act between the two paradigms was achieved by turning to Gramsci and his notions of hegemony and a war of positions in civil society—to account, on the one hand, for the empirical specificity characteristic of Williams and, on the other, the importance of difference that emerges from Althusser. This is a fair portrayal in a general sense but somewhat unnuanced. Cultural studies, at least in Hall's representation of it, is not so much an effort to locate a middle ground between the two paradigms as to use the two paradigms themselves as limits and pressures on each other—to hold them in dynamic tension as forms of reciprocal interrogation. To see how Hall's theory of articulation derives from this dynamic tension, we need now to look more closely at the way Hall reads the two paradigms against each other and the effect of this reading on Hall's model of determination.

First of all, the culturalist work of Williams, Hoggart, and Thompson registers a break from the reductionist economic determinism of orthodox

Marxism in the direction of a Marxist or socialist humanism that emphasizes the creativity of cultural practices and the authenticity of working-class experience. In various ways, Williams, Hoggart, and Thompson argued that the popular culture of the working class is not simply a form of false consciousness imposed from above in the interest of ruling elites but rather is a way of life and shared subjectivity that resists as much as it accommodates the dominant order. According to this view, precisely because the formation of subjectivities is linked to class position, the lived experience of the working and subordinate classes offers a grounds to measure the distorting effects of ideology against reality. The culturalist paradigm, in other words, severs the ties of the left to the mechanical materialism of traditional Marxism but preserves a necessary correspondence among class position, cultural practices, and forms of consciousness as the framework of determination.

In contrast, the structuralist paradigm argues that there is no essential subjectivity at the center of experience but that experience of the "real" is itself made available and intelligible only as an effect of ideology, already preshaped by the categories, classifications, and frameworks of culture. In this sense, the structuralist paradigm loosens the ties in culturalism between cultural practice and social position by thinking of the social formation as a unity which is constructed through the differences of relatively autonomous practices rather than an expressive totality of corresponding practices. In Hall's view, Althusser's notion of the social formation as a structure in dominance of relatively autonomous practices and institutions that cannot be reduced to a system of homologous correspondences typifies the structuralist paradigm. These structures, as Althusser has it, "hail" or "interpellate" subjects by creating subject positions which speak and place individuals in capitalist social relations. Subjects, as Hall says, are by this account "bearers of structures" rather than "active agents" in making their own history.

Hall's strategy is to use these two paradigms as limits and pressures on each other. Hall takes Althusser and the structuralist paradigm as a way to reread Williams and the culturalists, to retain the creative subject by turning it into a subject positioned not by an essential class location but by mediating social and cultural forces, a subject in ideology who lives, as Althusser puts it, in and through imaginary relations to the real and contradictory conditions of existence. Althusser's understanding of the social formation as a complexly overdetermined structure instead of a simple or monolithic one allowed Hall, as he says, "to live in and with difference," to imagine a social formation determined by a totality of relatively autonomous institutions and practices (in, say, education, culture, mass media, the rituals of everyday life, and so on) which can be reduced neither to forms of each other nor to reflexes of the economic order but which still cohere as a unity in difference. For Hall, there is no necessary correspondence between cultural practices and social structures that can be referred to the determinations of class position or authentic experience.

At the same time, Hall also wants to put a break on certain poststructualist tendencies, arising in part from Althusser but certainly exceeding him, to think that there is not only no necessary correspondence but rather that there is a necessary non-correspondence that makes it analytically impossible to relate practices, beliefs, discourses, identities, and institutions to each other in determinate ways. According to Hall, Foucault and other post-Althusserians take the emphasis on difference in Althusser's relative autonomy of overdetermined practices in the direction of a radical heterogeneity, incommensurability, and the absolute autonomy of practices that refuses to think of determination as anything other than local and specific contingencies. In other words, Hall is prepared to follow the poststructuralists by thinking that cultural and social practices can be read as if they were textual or linguistic events. But by reaching back to the culturalist emphasis on lived experience, Hall also wants to resist what he sees as the typically postmodern abandonment of any appeal to the "real" or to experience outside of discourse. Hall holds on to the Marxist project of theorizing a complex unity of the social formation—but not by relating base to superstructure or latent to manifest content in a structure of necessary correspondence. Instead, Hall is proposing a fractured or articulated totality in which people make their own history, only under conditions not of their making.

Hall's theory of articulation conceptualizes the conjunctures at which people knit together disparate and apparently contradictory practices, beliefs, and discourses in order to give their world some semblance of meaning and coherence. Articulation theory, in other words, describes how people make a unity which is neither necessary nor previously determined. So, if Hall uses Althusser to set limits on the essentialism of class identity in the culturalist paradigm, by the same token he uses Williams and draws upon Gramsci to put pressure on what he calls the "creeping functionalism" in Althusser's structuralism, the tendency to see ideology as performing the function required of it by reproducing the social relations of production without countertendencies. In Hall's view, Althusser's "ideological state apparatus," the famous ISA, collapses the state and civil society, precisely the gap through which Hall sees the pressures of ideology from below running, in the tensions and conflict between the people and the ruling bloc. This domain of the popular is not strictly imposed from above but rather is negotiated in a contested arena where the struggle for hegemony and consent takes place. By using Gramsci's theory of hegemony and Ernesto Laclau's argument that the political connotation of ideological elements has no necessary belongingness to class or social location, articulation theory, Hall says, "enabled us to think how an ideology empowers people, enabling them to make some sense or intelligibility of their historical situation, without reducing those forms of intelligibility to their socio-economic or class location or social position" (53). The point for Hall is that one can connect cultural practices to the social formation—only not in advance. Articulation is always a matter of struggle in a war of positions where nothing is certain ahead of time but rather a matter of practice. No outcome can be guaranteed, as it is in orthodox Marxism, by the laws of history but must be determined concretely at specific conjunctures of history.

By refusing the scientistic metanarrative of orthodox Marxism and denying the necessary correspondence between practice and class location, Hall poses instead the quite practical yet crucial analytical question: "under what circumstances can a connection be forged or made" among particular ideologies, political subjects, cultural practices, and social movements and institutions? The double meaning of articulation—to put into words and to yoke together physically—offers both "a way of understanding how ideological elements come, under certain conditions, to cohere together within a discourse, and a way of asking how they do or do not become articulated, at specific conjunctures, to certain political subjects" (53). The workings of articulation, as Hall describe them, are simultaneously discursive and social: articulation names those historical moments at which certain ideas are uttered and combined (sometimes by severing ideological elements from their conventional uses and recombining them with other elements) into material forces capable of binding subjects together in social identities and movements.

Articulating *Lives on the Boundary*

From the perspective of articulation theory, the question to ask of *Lives on the Boundary* is how Rose puts into words the narrativity of his own life and how this articulation is thereby linked to other discourses, practices, subjectivities, and institutions. Rose has chosen to narrate his life history, as a student and a teacher, both to indict an educational system that wastes the intellectual curiosity of young people and adults and to demonstrate the possibilities of individual growth and development within America's educational underclass. Rose wants readers to see, and to feel, how such class-based educational practices as testing and tracking produce the desire of poor and working-class students not to excell and get ahead but to be "average," to distance themselves emotionally from a reward system that neglects their talents and potential. And he wants readers to understand how the intervention of caring teachers can mobilize and cultivate the intellectual resources of non-mainstream students. This is a story worth telling, especially at a moment in our collective history when "reform" movements in education are calling for higher standards, national testing, teacher accountability, discipline, and a return to a canonical curriculum. It is a story to break the prevailing silence in public discourse about education by speaking of democratic aspirations to increase access, to open opportunity, and to remove educational barriers to the poor and working class.

The problem, though, is whether the narrativity of a life in *Lives on the Boundary* is adequate to Rose's purposes, whether it can adequately represent the social processes of illiteracy and school failure in contemporary America and project a compelling vision of needed change. As I have already suggested, as a coming of age narrative, *Lives on the Boundary* might be read as an instance of the "exemplary bourgeois cultural project" of narrating a life. What makes the narrativity of a life so "exemplary" as a class-based tale is the fact that just to have a life—to experience oneself as possessing a life that can be narrated in the first place—is itself a particular historical development, inseparable from the emergence of individualism and the authority and autonomy ascribed to the bourgeois subject in class society. The narrativity of a life, in other words, is not something that is naturally given but rather is a strategic trope for what C.B. Macpherson calls the ideology of "possessive individualism," in which the individual emerges as a social subject by taking on a proprietary relationship to his or her own life. The autobiographical impulse to narrate a life, therefore, is not a straightforward one but rather the result of a particularly bourgeois cultural project of making and owning a sovereign and inalienable life, free from the ascriptions of birth, status, and social obligation in traditional society.

The classic coming of age narrative, however, tends to naturalize this struggle to fashion a self-created life and an individual personality by representing the passage from youth to maturity not as the formation of a particular kind of subjectivity in class society but as a timeless biological and psychological process. The rhetorical effect is an ostensibly universal subject whose life is narratable because its meanings transcend historical circumstance by expressing general laws of development and human nature. What is disguised or mistaken to be a natural desire to tell one's own story is, in fact, a critical moment in the bourgeoisie's growing self-consciousness and cultural self-confidence, as it entitles its members to author their own life histories and to inscribe the formation of the bourgeois personality in literature and popular culture as the normative story of growing up.

Such a coming of age narrative has a fairly predictable and formulaic narrative pattern. The plot typically recounts the adventures and crises of an alienated youth and how these youthful exploits and the wisdom of older and more experienced adults enable the youth to reconcile his or her identity to the constraints of class society. Readers are often offered a vicarious experience of the transgressions and marginality of youth, but only so that such disruptions of adult order and common sense will enable readers more surely than ever to define the boundaries of the normal. In this sense, what we call the coming of age narrative enacts not only a rite of passage from youth to maturity but also a ritual of inversion that permits formulaic moments of violation in order to contain their subversive force within the hierarchical patterns of mature order and authority.

According to Marxist critics such as Georg Lukács and Jean-Paul Sartre, the classic coming of age narrative tells how the disruptive desires and the turbulence of youth are contained by class society as the central character achieves maturity by taking on a professional calling and joining the adult world of full-fledged citizens. An atmosphere of calm typically pervades the narrative, the result of what Lukács sees as the social optimism of the rising bourgeoisie and the narrative transformation of a troubled youth into a well-adjusted and idealized bourgeois subject. For Sartre, this calm is a matter of the distanced lucidity of the narrator who represents the desires of youth as an "adventure" and a "brief distraction which is over with" (134). As the turbulent events of youth are situated narratively at the remove of time, they are relieved of their convulsive energies by the narrator's achieved stability and maturity. For this reason, the formation of a personality, as Sartre says, "is told from the viewpoint of experience and wisdom; it is listened to from the viewpoint of order" (134).

For Lukács and Sartre, the subject is shaped not only archetypally by the passage from youth to maturity and innocence to experience, but also practically by reconciling his or her youthful desires to the alienated adult world of work. In a typical coming of age narrative, a youth will wander through bohemia, want to be a writer or a painter, experiment with drugs and sexuality, travel to exotic places—and then settle down by choosing a profession, a calling, a *metier*. In other words, in the classic tale of the formation of a bourgeois personality, a youth comes into maturity by internalizing the necessity of work in the capitalist division of labor as a matter of personal choice, and the narrative represents this choice as a moral lesson learned from the errors and enthusiasms of youth. As Sartre says, "Neither the general nor the doctor impart their memories in a raw state: they are experiences that have been distilled, and we are warned as soon as they begin to speak that their story has a moral" (134).

Readers will recognize the classic features of the coming of age narrative in *Lives on the Boundary*. The book does indeed narrate a rite of passage, from a turbulent adolescence in South Los Angeles through a youthful flirtation with Beat culture and a brief literary romance with graduate studies in English to Rose's mastery of the secrets of the academy brought about by his acquisition of an identity and professional expertise as teacher and researcher. Rose's struggle, for himself and his students, to crack the code of the university appears in this narrative both as an affirmation of the (adult) authority of academic discourse and its institutions and as an act of benevolence toward the underprepared, from whose ranks Rose has risen. The question then is whether, or to what extent, *Lives on the Boundary* enacts the kind of reconciliation to the party of order and maturity that Lukács and Sartre find characteristic of the classic coming of age narrative.

The question of the social allegiances of *Lives on the Boundary*, I believe, hinges on the problem of determination I have been concerned with in earlier sections of this essay. Lukács and Sartre link the coming of age narrative, historically and culturally, to the formation of the bourgeois subject as the owner and operator of an exemplary life, an act of self-creation that culminates in the moralization of professional work as an explanation of success and failure in class society. From this perspective, the cultural practice of narrating a life seems to fit neatly with class location, and one might therefore postulate a necessary correspondence between the genre and the reproduction of capitalist social relations. There are, of course, other ways of narrating a life, as Sartre's admiration for Jean Genet in *St. Genet* indicates, that hold on to a position of marginality, criminality, and transgression that will not be reconciled to the dominant order. Mike Rose's book, however, is not written from such an outsider's perspective. But it is not written from the inside, either. Rather, as the title tells us, the book is located at the boundary of the dominant culture, at the points of intersection where the lives of the dispossessed encounter an educational system that sorts individuals into a capitalist division of labor, allotting life chances by separating mental from manual labor, the upwardly mobile from those stuck in place.

Lives on the Boundary is more than just an account of how Rose slips through the system, more than a tribute to the initiative (and luck) of the few who make it. What allows Rose to evade the class-bound limits of the self-made coming of age narrative—and what distinguishes his book from Wright's and Rodriquez's autobiographies—is his refusal to separate himself from the lives on the boundary and to take on the kind of distanced lucidity that Sartre finds characteristic of the genre. For Wright and Rodriquez, the cultural trajectory of personal development alienates them from their indigenous communities. In a very real sense, each confirms the adage that you can't go home again, that you can only look back. Wright and Rodriquez become professional writers, men of letters, and take on cosmopolitan identities that lead them to view their places of origin in terms of a cultural deficit, a lack of sustaining social and intellectual resources. Rose, however, despite his journeys into the wider world and his standing as a successful professional, never quite leaves his neighborhood or his youth behind. He remains open to the pressures of the milieu in which he grew up—the frustrated aspirations and ambitions of the people he knew along the way. As Rose discovers through his interactions with underprepared students and adult learners, the narrativity of his own life is articulated in terms of other lives. The veterans Rose teaches in a special program at UCLA figure as his "Voc-Ed comrades reincarnated" (137), and his work with Concepcion Baca (a student who drops out of UCLA, goes to work, and then returns to complete her degree and go on to graduate studies) causes him to register "how much of myself I saw in her" (204). Rather than calling attention to the distance between himself and America's educational underclass, as Wright and Rodriquez do, Rose repeatedly uses the story of his own personal success as a sign of the educability of all those others who have fallen through the systemic cracks in American schools.

The point is that Rose does indeed use a conventionalized and formulaic coming of age narrative, but he diverts it from the usual pattern of the self-made success story and the edifying tale of maturity to articulate another set of social, cultural, and educational interests that offer a democratic vision of education for all. In this sense, Rose rearticulates one of the most basic of American myths by severing the cultural meaning of personal success and professional achievement from its usual conservative functions. Rose's own professional expertise appears in *Lives on the Boundary* not as a reconciliation to work in class society or an exemplary lesson in maturity but as a practice that links his own labors to those of students and adult learners at the margins of the educational system and to the popular pressures from below that have struggled to extend educational opportunity. Like Mina Shaughnnessey and Kenneth A. Bruffee in the days of open admissions at CUNY and David Bartholomae and Patricia Bizzell, Rose re-makes himself as a teacher and researcher, joining his expertise in close reading to the social force of protest movements of the late 1960s and early 1970s that fought to open higher education to those who had been excluded and, in effect, created the historical conjuncture from which the figure of the basic writer arises in composition studies.

By the account I offer here, Rose's professional expertise is not just the result of individual initiative, the accumulation of credentials, and the creation of a career. Instead, professional expertise is articulated with and to political subjectivities and social movements. Expertise is certainly coded by the cultural narratives of maturity and distanced lucidity as a particular determination of consciousness and class position. If professional practices and discourses typically represent the dispossessed as a client population in need of the intervention of expert benefactors, the political valence and cultural meaning of professional work nonetheless cannot be guaranteed in advance as an accommodation to the dominant culture and its division of specialists and laypersons. Professional expertise, as I believe *Lives on the Boundary* demonstrates, can also articulate a sense of solidarity with the aspirations and purposes of the dispossessed. It all depends on practice.

Rearticulating Literacy

But if the effects of professional work depend on practice, it is not the case that professional practices are themselves offered freely; nor can they be enacted simply by an act of will. While the conditions of professional work are not predetermined in a final and fixed sense, they are determinate—the result of how they are joined together with other practices in an ensemble of overdetermined social relations and cultural realities. This point is worth mentioning because one of the dangers of professionalism is its tendency to generalize the conditions of its own work into causal factors that determine success and failure in class society. On one hand, the relative autonomy of professional work—what professionals experience daily as a series of individual decisions and responsibilities—can lead them to cast success and failure as a matter of volition and individual effort. On the other hand, professionals, especially in education, often make the forms of literacy they have mastered into causal factors that explain the fate of individuals and social formations.

Rose comes close to this occupational hazard of professionalism when he claims that his work with veterans made him realize that "education has the power to equalize things" (137). One might justifiably worry that Rose has slipped into the peculiarly American view of education as a social panacea—the great American literacy myth that the ability to read and write determines the outcome of people's lives. At least according to revisionist currents in literacy studies, this might well appear to be exactly what Rose has done.

From Lévi Strauss in *Tristes Tropiques* to J. Elspeth Stuckey's recent and provocatively titled *The Violence of Literacy*, revisionist critics have held that literacy is not primarily a means of intellectual development and upward mobility. Instead, as Lévi Strauss says, the "only phenomenon with which writing has always been concomitant is the creation of cities and empires, that is the integration of large numbers of individuals into a political system, and their grading into castes or classes" (337). Stuckey is even more direct when she says that "literacy is a system of oppression that works against entire societies as well as against certain groups within given populations and against individual people" (64). From this perspective, to speak of the transformative powers of literacy for the individual, as Rose does, at best is naive and at worst reproduces a discourse of equal opportunity and predictably unequal results, thereby turning systematic inequality into the result of differences in individual effort and talent, not of social determinations.

Stuckey is right to emphasize the connections between literacy and the way individuals are ranked in an unequal social order. At the same time, however, she seems to argue that there is a necessary correspondence between the cultural practices of literacy and social structures. According to Stuckey, people like Rose fail to see how the "violence of literacy is the violence of the milieu it comes from, promises, recapitulates. It is attached inextricably to the world of food, shelter, and human equality" (94). Literacy, for Stuckey, is determined by—or "attached inextricably" to—the reproduction of class relations in advanced capitalist society. Literacy has a locked-in, guaranteed-in-advance class character.

In contrast, Rose avoids the mechanical determinism in Stuckey's account by offering a sense of how literacy is articulated in variable and sometimes unpredictable ways to the social formation. In *Lives on the Boundary*, we do see the violence of literacy Stuckey describes. Rose's profile of the adult learner Millie and her struggle with a multiple-choice reading comprehension test demonstrates how schooled literacy disconnects underprepared students from their practical knowledge of the world and leads educators thereby to label them as cognitively deficient (216-20). Literacy does indeed function, as Rose shows, as an instrument to pathologize subjects. But, for Rose, literacy can also function in a variety of other ways that evade the surveillance of a class-based educational apparatus. "Consider the sources of literacy," Rose says, "among the children of El Monte: shopkeeper's signs, song lyrics, auto manuals, the conventions of the Western, family stories and tales, and more" (236). What Rose sees here is how literacy is not only a tool of a class-based ranking system but also a cultural resource embedded in and persistently available through the "pop cultural flotsam" that pervades the American landscape—"television and *People* magazine," "the Bible and . . . American media illusion" (237). For Rose, literacy is a matter not simply of the limits of an oppressive social order. It is also a quite concrete pressure and sensuous activity that surrounds all Americans and can be tapped for the purposes of human development and liberation. Whether that happens or not, I have tried to suggest throughout this essay, depends not on a fixed or necessary correspondence between literate practices and the social formation but rather on how individuals and groups articulate literate practices to institutions and subjectivities.

In this regard, Rose's sense of how "education has the power to equalize things" can be useful precisely to the extent it is detached from its usual political meaning of giving everyone an equal chance (when unequal class-based outcomes can be predicted in advance) and rearticulated as a political pressure to change the standards and practices that are used to evaluate and rank students in the first place. Investing education with "the power to equalize things" can avoid being simply another version of the literacy myth to the extent it articulates redefined standards and practices of literacy that are capable of promoting a more equal social order. Rose's account of the popular and everyday sources of literacy begins imagining such a redefinition and thereby contests not only the traditional view of what makes a person literate but also the current neoconservative monopoly of the public discourse on educational standards. What Rose suggests is that it is not enough just to change or expand our sense of literacy to include non-canonical and unauthorized forms of writing—and then continue to evaluate and rank students in the same old ways. Rose also wants to appropriate the "literacy crisis" from the Reagan/Bush camp, to rearticulate it as a matter not of whether standards are high enough but rather of how standards can be reconceived to serve popular aspirations and democratic goals.

Lives on the Boundary takes a lot of risks. To recount his life, Rose turns to the familiar coming of age narrative that has historically and culturally been encoded with the entrepreneurial values of individual initiative, professional maturity, and personal success. Rather than presenting a critical analysis to demystify the genre (as radical theorists typically do), Rose has sought to rearticulate the narrative from the inside—to disconnect its cultural meanings and political valence from its usual ideological function of reproducing capitalist social relations and instead to join together the narrativity of his own life to the ongoing struggle for democracy and social justice. In this regard, Rose's use of such a popular genre as autobiography not only allows him to speak to the public as well as to specialists; it also allows him, strategically, to locate *Lives on the Boundary* in the current cultural wars of position to secure popular consent and social allegiance. In *Lives on the Boundary*, Rose has chosen to speak in the idiom of what Gramsci calls the "national-popular," the constellation of common sense, ideological elements, and everyday practices that shape the subjectivities of civil society. What Rose thereby seems to suggest is that the task of radical democracy is not just to speak as critics against the master narratives of American culture but to speak as rhetors through them—to rearticulate the social and ideological force of the American *mythos* in the name, the voices, and the interests of the many.

Works Cited

Ball, Carolyn C. "The Politics of Citation." CCCC Convention. Cincinnati, 19 Mar. 1992.

Bartholomae, David. "Inventing the University." *When A Writer Can't Write: Research on Writer's Block and Other Writing Process Problems*. Ed. Mike Rose. New York: Guilford, 1985. 134-65.

Berlin, James. "Rhetoric and Ideology in the Writing Class." *College English* 50 (1988): 477-94.

Elbow, Peter. "A Method for Teaching Writing." *College English* 30 (1968): 115-25.

Engels, Friedrich. Letter to J. Bloch, 1890. *Marx and Engels: Selected Correspondence*. New York: International, 1935. 476.

Faigley, Lester. "Competing Theories of Process: A Critique and a Proposal." *College English* 48 (1986): 527-42.

Hall, Stuart. "On Postmodernism and Articulation: An Interview with Stuart Hall." Ed. Lawrence Grossberg. *Journal of Communication Inquiry* 10.2 (1986): 45-60.

Jones, Leroi (Amiri Baraka). "Expressive Language." *Home*. New York: William Morrow, 1966. 166-72.

Kail, Harvey. "Narratives of Knowledge: Story and Pedagogy in Four Composition Texts." *Rhetoric Review* 6 (1988): 179-89.

Lévi Strauss, Claude. *Tristes Tropiques*. Trans. John and Doreen Weightman. New York: Pocket Books, 1977.

Lukács, Georg. *The Theory of the Novel*. Trans. Anya Bostock. Cambridge: MIT P, 1971.

Macpherson, C.B. *The Political Theory of Possessive Individualism*. New York: Oxford UP, 1962.

Marx, Karl, and Friedrich Engels. *The German Ideology*. New York: International, 1970.

McQuade, Donald. "Living In—and On—the Margins." *College Composition and Communication* 43 (1992): 11-22.

Miller, Susan. *Rescuing the Subject: A Critical Introduction to Rhetoric and the Writer*. Carbondale: Southern Illinois UP, 1989.

North, Stephen. *The Making of Knowledge in Composition: Portrait of an Emerging Field*. Upper Montclair, NJ: Boynton, 1987.

Rose, Mike. *Lives on the Boundary*. New York: Penguin, 1990.

Ross, Kristin. *The Emergence of Social Space: Rimbaud and the Paris Commune.* Minneapolis: U of Minnesota P, 1988.

Sartre, Jean Paul. *What Is Literature?* Trans. Bernard Frechtman. New York: Harper, 1965.

Sommers, Nancy. "Between the Drafts." *College Composition and Communication* 43 (1992): 23-31.

Stuckey, J. Elspeth. *The Violence of Literacy*. Portsmouth, NH: Boynton, 1991.

Tompkins, Jane. "Fighting Words: Unlearning to Write the Critical Essay." *Georgia Review* 42 (1988): 585-90.

Williams, Raymond. *Marxism and Literature*. New York: Oxford UP, 1977.

Peer Response in the Multicultural Composition Classroom: Dissensus–A Dream (Deferred)

Carrie Shively Leverenz

The use of peer response in writing classes has long been touted as a means of granting students increased authority over their reading and writing. By instituting peer responding, the theory goes, the teacher gives up his or her place as the *only* authority in the classroom, allowing students to share authority in the evaluation of their own and their peers' writing. As such, peer response has often been seen as an integral part of a liberal, sometimes even a radical, pedagogy. Early proponents of peer response, particularly Kenneth Bruffee, have argued that asking students to work collaboratively on their writing eases their initiation into academic ways of thinking and writing and gives them some power over that initiation. Operating from an epistemology that sees knowledge as socially constructed by members of established knowledge-making communities who "share the same paradigms and the same code of values," Bruffee reasons that in order for students to become knowers, they need to learn to "converse better" using the "normal discourse" of these communities (643).[1] To become "knowers" within the university, then, students must learn to use the university's recognized language.

As Bruffee has acknowledged, his commitment to collaborative learning grew out of his experience teaching writing during the 1970s in the Open Admissions program at the City University of New York, a program based on the ideal of extending higher education to students once excluded from the university. And on the surface, peer response as a form of collaborative learning does seem to advance the aims of a liberal pedagogy by treating students who were once outsiders as insiders, as apprentice members of the academic community. But as Greg Myers and John Trimbur have argued, Bruffee's model of peer response might not be as beneficial to students as he imagines. Although Bruffee's pedagogy does give students practice in how to become members of established knowledge-making communities, it does not give them a mechanism for critiquing those communities. Basing their views on a Marxist critique of knowledge production in a capitalist culture,

Myers and Trimbur find particular fault with Bruffee's valorization of community consensus. As Myers and Trimbur see it, a theory of collaboration that emphasizes consensus downplays the existence of conflict or dissent and ignores the role that existing power relations play in the collaborative group and in the larger culture. As a result, Bruffee's pedagogy fails to address adequately the issues of cultural difference that have become an increasingly important focus in composition courses, especially those that seek to be "multicultural."

Both Myers and Trimbur argue for an approach to collaborative learning that attends to the nature of difference and dissent that exists within groups. Such an approach would enable teachers and students to go beyond a mere replication of established knowledge-making communities to a critique of those communities' practices, practices that inevitably include the silencing of difference and the maintenance of the status quo. Myers admits that he does not have specific suggestions for how to implement this collaboration-as-critique in the classroom. Instead, he recommends that teachers adopt a new stance toward their teaching, "an awareness that one's course is part of an ideological structure that keeps people from thinking about their situation, but also a belief that one can resist this structure and help students to criticize it" (169). Trimbur sees collaborative learning as the means by which students can learn to do this kind of questioning. According to Trimbur, "Students' experience of non-domination in the collaborative classroom can offer them a critical measure to understand the distortions of communication and the plays of power in normal discourse." For Trimbur, replacing an emphasis on consensus in the classroom with "a rhetoric of dissensus"—a way of talking productively about difference—can help students "demystify the normal workings of discourse communities," workings that typically include the erasure or silencing of difference (615).

Because of this emphasis on dissensus, the view of collaborative learning espoused by Myers and Trimbur seems particularly relevant to writing courses that seek to recognize multiculturalism by validating the cultural differences that exist both inside and outside the classroom. If, by working in groups, students can learn to recognize and value their own and others' differences, then perhaps they will be equipped to critique the ways in which established knowledge-making communities ignore or erase difference in order to maintain a single, authoritative, "normal discourse."

Or perhaps not. While both Myers and Trimbur note the ways in which institutionalized groups work to normalize themselves, they hold out hope that student groups within progressive classrooms can somehow escape from, or at least step outside of, this normalizing function. Unfortunately, they can give only theoretical answers to questions regarding how collaboration might play itself out in concrete classroom settings. Important as their work has been, it has not told us what really happens when groups of students work together in writing classes that explicitly value difference. When we look at real classrooms, the way dissensus works becomes complicated. Despite the efforts of teachers to create the critical stance toward academic discourse that Myers and Trimbur advocate, the normalizing function of the institution does not always allow for such idealized dissensus to occur. In this article, I offer a small but detailed picture of how a dissensus pedagogy can be constrained by the institutional context in which it is taught. In particular, I focus on one peer response group in a class designed to be multicultural and to value difference. While I realize this one group does not allow me to generalize about all dissensus or consensus pedagogy, I believe that such microanalyses of real students are a necessary part of the dialectic between our theories and the reality of practice.

Collaboration in the Multicultural Writing Class: Institutional Contexts
In order to explore the role that difference might play in collaborative groups in a multicultural composition class, I conducted an ethnographic study of peer response in a second-level writing course entitled, "African-American Voices in Literature: Intermediate Essay Writing." Taught at a large state university in the midwest, this course was designed as part of the University's new General Education Curriculum which requires students to take three writing-intensive courses. According to the university's guidelines, the second-level writing course should emphasize the skills of expository writing and oral presentation, with the ultimate goal of extending students' ability to read carefully and express ideas effectively. The guidelines also state that the second-level writing course should focus on cultural diversity in America with special attention given to issues of race, class, gender, and ethnicity. Like many multicultural courses lodged in an institutional context, this course seems to embody an irreconcilable tension between the institution's goals for teaching writing as "preparation" and the goals of valuing difference within the academy.

While the institutional goals of the course pose a subtle challenge to the normal workings of the academic community, the local context made these goals more explicit. Even the racial make-up of the class let students know that this course was somehow "different" from most of their classes. At this university, a majority of the students are white; in a typical class of twenty-five, it is unusual to find more than one or two students of color. "African American Voices," however, enrolled eleven African American women, five African American men, two white women, and one Asian American woman. For many students, this was the first class they had ever taken in which African Americans were so clearly the majority. Another important "difference" in this class was that the instructor, MJ, was one of the few female African-Americans on the faculty.[2] MJ, a specialist in rhetoric and composition who had written the original proposal for this course, was committed to giving students access to literature not normally taught in the English department. In the specific class I observed, the reading list included only works by African American authors, ranging from *Incidents in the Life of a Slave Girl* to the film *Straight out of Brooklyn*. By asking students to read texts exclusively by African Americans, MJ implicitly challenged the norms of the academy.

MJ also challenged the established standards of the institution in the kind of writing she asked students to do. On the first day of class, MJ made it clear that although they would be reading literature, this would not be a traditional literature class focused on the interpretation of texts. Instead, students would be writing about the *issues* raised in the texts, and they would be permitted to use their own experience, in addition to the texts, as support for their ideas. MJ intended this dual validation of authority to be both liberating and challenging for students. She explained,

> As we got started talking about the issues, I realized many of the people in the class don't have a lot of experience talking about texts so to get them to move from [talking about their experience to talking about texts] might be harder. Or all their experience would be outside of texts and the whole idea of using texts as support for your position would be something that we would have to learn over time.... I'm one of those people who actually thinks that in the academy lived experiences always get pushed aside as invalid, and I am not the kind of scholar who likes to call on texts all the time. I think lived experiences have to find a place in the academy or you just exclude a whole group of people.... As far as I'm concerned, though, the goal is to bring the two together.

MJ was committed to giving her students, and especially her African American students, the opportunity to feel that their experience counted, an opportunity she thought rarely happened in "normal" academic practice. But MJ did not want students to reject academic ways of thinking and writing altogether. MJ commented, "I'm really trying to affirm their own experience while at the same time trying to move them to a more balanced view of academic ways of thinking." For example, she felt obligated to teach them to use textual authority in ways that were deemed acceptable by the academy and that were mandated by the university's guidelines for the second-level writing course. Thus, while MJ wanted to complicate and extend notions of academic authority, she did not discount that authority. In this sense, MJ took exactly the stance that Myers recommends. She saw herself as obligated by virtue of her employment in the institution to pass on the institution's values. But she also sought to teach students to question those values. While class discussion often focused on analyzing literary texts, for example, MJ encouraged students to draw on their experience in understanding those texts. In one class discussion, MJ was particularly pleased when a student compared Langston Hughes' folk philosopher Semple to Mr. Gaines, a character from the television show "A Different World," remarking that in most English classes students don't dare admit that they watch television.

We can also see MJ's dual stance toward the norms of the institution in one of the prompts she gave students for their second critical essay:

Many people believe that one criterion of good literature is that it is timeless (i.e. has universal appeal across time and audience). Pick two poems from our selection of readings which, though written many decades ago, speak to (or articulate) a contemporary issue(s). Explain the issue(s) and how the poems illustrate this universality.

This prompt reveals MJ's careful attempt to validate both the textual authority that is normally valued by the university and the authority of lived experience that is typically devalued. The notion that good literature is timeless or universal, that it can *articulate* an enduring truth, is a traditional literary one that grants certain texts a kind of transcendent power. However, by asking students to discuss the ways in which a poem might *speak to* (as distinguished from *articulate*) a contemporary issue, she is asking them to use their own sense of relevance in determining what makes a text "timeless" or "universal." In other words, she is suggesting that texts are not universal in and of themselves but have relevance to contemporary readers only because those readers designate them as relevant. By extending academic authority to include the authority of lived experience, MJ implicitly allowed multiple grounds of authority to coexist in her classroom. Such a move challenges the rules of "normal" academic discourse that require there to be *one* source of authority: the authority of texts.

Through her course goals, assignments, and the nature of class discussions, then, MJ validated the use of at least two different kinds of authority on which to base a claim: lived experiences and textual authority. By continually validating both types of authority, MJ ensured that her students would feel free to argue from both. However, when these students were left on their own, in peer response groups, their responses to texts did not mirror MJ's goals of accepting multiple levels of authority. Instead, in the group I examined, the strength of the normalizing discourse of the academy made itself present. In particular, I will show how one student's alliance with established academic standards, especially the emphasis on textual authority, led to a forced consensus by group members that silenced the very kind of differences being validated by the class.

Peer Response in "African American Voices in Literature"
MJ assigned students to peer response groups early in the quarter and asked them to respond to each of the four essays they were required to write. In putting the groups together, MJ tried to be sure that each group had at least one strong writer or leader and that there were no apparent conflicts among group members. Because I was particularly interested in the role that "difference" would play in students' responses to their peers' texts, I chose to study closely the peer response group that seemed the most diverse. The group had four members: Beth, a white woman who was a senior majoring in English; Carol, an African American woman and sophomore honors student; Patricia, a Korean American woman and senior history major; and

Robert, an African American man who was a well-known college athlete majoring in business.

For the peer responding session that is my focus here, Beth, Carol, and Patricia were present.[3] Of three writing prompts, each had chosen to respond to the one that invited students to consider the universality or timelessness of the poems they had read. They did so, however, in strikingly different ways. Beth wrote a fairly traditional literary essay, one based on a close reading of the texts and organized around a single thesis. In this essay, entitled "Feminist Interpretations," she argues that Jean Toomer's "Karintha" and Langston Hughes' "Harlem (A Dream Deferred)" are universal in that they deal with what she calls "the keeping down of women." Beth makes her case for the universality of these texts by comparing them to Sylvia Plath's *The Bell Jar* and Doris Lessing's "To Room Nineteen," two more-or-less canonical literary works by white women. This essay was fairly characteristic of Beth's approach to all of the reading and writing assigned in the class. For Beth, what makes a piece of literature "good" is not its relevance to her personal experience (as a white woman, none of the literature read in class spoke directly to her experience) but its appeal to what she called "universal human emotion." As an English major, Beth has been trained to read and value literature for its transcendent qualities; and as a writer of fiction, Beth tries to create literature that she imagines will have universal appeal. Because Beth values the power of literary texts, it is not surprising that she uses her knowledge of literature to construct herself as an authority in her writing, providing as support for her arguments textual evidence gleaned not only from the texts assigned in class, but from texts she has read elsewhere, texts that are often unfamiliar to her classmates. Significantly, she did not seem to see her approach as one option among many, but as the "right" way to write about texts.

Carol took a much more experience-based approach in her essay about the universality of literature. In "Going Out With a Bang," Carol wrote in response to the poems "If We Must Die" by Claude McKay and "We Wear the Mask" by Paul Dunbar. For Carol, what makes these poems universal is not their appeal across audiences but their relevance across time. Specifically, Carol argues that McKay's call for African Americans to struggle to their deaths for freedom is as compelling today as it was when the poem was written, citing the Rodney King case as support for her claim. While Beth relies on texts by white women as her source of authority, Carol relies on examples from contemporary African American experience; and while for Beth, "universal" necessarily implies an erasure of race-specific appeals, for Carol there can be no such erasure. In an interview, Carol admitted that even in her introductory writing course where she was the only African American student and where the only text they read by an African American was a poem by Langston Hughes, she still managed to write exclusively about racial issues.

Patricia's essay was different from Beth's and Carol's, most notably in its multiple focuses. In Patricia's paper, titled simply "Toomer and Cullen," Patricia asserts two unrelated theses, each with a different kind of support. In the first part of her essay, Patricia argues that Toomer's "Karintha" is universal because it illustrates the devastating consequences of sexual abuse. This part of her paper is composed largely of generalizations: Patricia cited neither textual support nor personal experience to lend authority to her assertions. In the second half, Patricia argues that what makes Countee Cullen's poem "Heritage" universal is that it describes the problem of being torn between two cultures, which Patricia sees as a continuing problem for minorities in the U.S. Here, Patricia supports her discussion of the problem of double consciousness by referring to her experience as a Korean American who came to the U.S. when she was ten years old. This essay is typical of much of Patricia's writing in the class. While Beth relied on the authority of literary texts and Carol relied on the authority of her perspective as an African American, Patricia struggled throughout the quarter to find a way to speak authoritatively. In her "Toomer and Cullen" essay, Patricia took what came to be a characteristically dual stance toward the issue of African American experience. On the one hand, like Beth, Patricia wants to erase or downplay an emphasis on racial difference. According to Patricia, one of the problems with these "culture classes" as she called them (and here she included the one she had taken on Korean American experience) is that there is too much emphasis on difference and not enough on commonalities. On the other hand, Patricia is sympathetic with the special problems faced by minorities in the U.S., often comparing the problems of African Americans to the problems of Asian Americans. In this sense, she is like Carol, who relied on her lived experience as a source of authority in her reading and writing about texts. But, of course, she is also *not* like Carol: she is not an African American whose perspective is especially validated by the course content, or by the class dynamics, or by the instructor. In this class, perhaps as much as or more than in a class dominated by members of the majority culture; Patricia felt herself to be an outsider.

By MJ's standards, all three writers based their arguments on acceptable types of authority. However, Beth, in assuming that she knows the correct way to write about texts, tried to convince her group members that these multiple authorities are inadequate. Because Beth's group members acknowledge her experience with texts, they allow her to subvert the local contexts MJ set up in the class, and grant authority to what they intuit as her more authoritative voice.

Reading A Peer Response Session
Beth, who easily asserted a text-based authority in class discussion and in her writing, assumed a similarly authoritative stance in her peer response group. From the moment peer response began, Beth seemed completely comfort-

able acting as an authoritative reader of her peers' writing. Beth opened the peer response session (the group's second but her first) by telling Carol and Patricia, "Before we start this, I do a lot of workshopping and used to tutor writing students, okay? So I'm not being harsh when I'm saying stuff on your papers. I don't mean it that way." In response to Beth's announcement, Patricia said, "I think that's kind of good," and Carol added, "Yeah." Since both Carol and Patricia had described the first peer response session as difficult primarily because they were inexperienced as responders, it seems likely they found Beth's authoritative stance comforting: certainly *she* would know what they were supposed to do. After all, Beth's claim to authority in peer responding was based on her certification by the institution; she had taken the university's peer tutoring course and had been authorized by the institution to advise other students about their writing.

Beth's statement also reveals that she is accustomed not just to responding but to issuing criticism in response to others' writing, criticism that is sometimes considered "harsh." By assuring Carol and Patricia that she doesn't intend her remarks to hurt their feelings, she is setting them up to expect negative comments while also warning them not to take those comments personally and to see her criticism as in their best interest. She is thus putting them in a position of having to *take* whatever she says without questioning it. Given her remarks, it seems likely that Beth does not think of Carol and Patricia as peers who share her values. In an interview, Beth told me that one of the reasons she disliked peer response was that, as a creative writing major, she was used to workshops in which everyone took their peers' writing seriously and people felt free to criticize each other's writing without fear of hurting people's feelings. In this class she felt she had to control her criticism, depending on how much a person could handle. While her sensitivity might be seen as a good thing, it was, by her own admission, a product of her sense that her classmates were not up to her standards of critiquing. Beth commented, "Maybe it's just because I'm impatient, I don't know, but being older than most of these students I'm in class with, and having much more writing experience than they do, really gets frustrating."

After these introductory remarks from Beth, the group agreed to read and then discuss one paper at a time, writing comments directly on the draft. They started with Patricia's paper. As might be expected, Beth found it easy to act as an authority in response to Patricia's draft, both in her written comments and in group discussion. For example, Beth asserted her authority in the sheer number of marks that she made on Patricia's text, marks that included crossing out sentences, correcting verb tenses, changing words, and underlining and circling words and phrases that Beth then commented on. In addition, Beth's discursive comments on Patricia's draft were written in an explicitly authoritative tone. Beth often gave instructions for revision, for example, "This needs clarifying!" By using the imperative voice, Beth further established herself as an authority whose advice must be *obeyed*. More important than Beth's tone, however, was the nature of the commentary she uttered so forcibly: in both her written comments and discussion of Patricia's draft, she constantly searched for the textual authority the institution values. For example, Beth questioned Patricia's assertion that "Cullens had become an example for the black people," asking if she had gotten this information from the poem.

In the group's discussion of Patricia's draft, Beth continued playing the role of the authority. She initiated and controlled the discussion, the bulk of which was devoted to Beth's explanation of her written comments. Although Beth began her critique of Patricia's paper by commenting on what she called "superficial things" like inconsistent verb tenses, she quickly extended her criticism to the content of Patricia's paper, questioning Patricia's interpretations of "Karintha" and "We Wear the Mask." For example, Beth asked Patricia if she really meant to say that Karintha felt worthless, adding that she had not interpreted Karintha that way. She then told Patricia, "You have to quote directly from the text to back up your idea." In this exchange, Beth took the position of the skeptical academic reader who requires textual evidence in order to be convinced. But she also represented the "teacher" who has the "right" interpretation confronting the student who is "wrong." Beth took on a similar stance when she asked Patricia, "In Dunbar's 'We Wear the Mask,' remember? Who do you say wears the mask?" Recognizing by Beth's tone that she may have made an interpretive error, Patricia responded not by looking at her draft to see what she had written, but by declaring that she doesn't know and will have to reread the poem. Even though Patricia acknowledged a need to reconsider what she has written, Beth went on to correct her reading of the poem, saying directly to Patricia: "It is 'we' who are wearing the mask. 'They' may be wearing the mask but that's not the issue. That's not what the poem was about; that's not what the poet was talking about. So, you are forced to deal with what the poet is talking about. . . . You've got to stick with the text." Beth did not seem to trust Patricia to "get it right" even on a second reading and thus felt compelled to give her the "right" answer and to remind her that "right" answers can only be found through a correct reading of the text.

In addition to presenting herself as an authority in the interpretation of literature, Beth also presented herself as an experienced member of the academic discourse community, at least the one that values textual evidence above all. Beth told Patricia, "I wrote this everywhere [on your paper]. The text is your authority. The text is always your starting point." Commenting on one of Patricia's unsupported generalizations, Beth warned, "You have to get that out of the text. If you don't you're not allowed to put that in. It's against the rules, whatever rules there are." Near the end of the response session, Beth advised Patricia to draw more explicit parallels between her experience as an Asian American and the double consciousness Dunbar describes in "We Wear the Mask." Said Beth,

> All the time, I wrote this all over the place, you need comparable parallels to the text. The text is your authority and you're reaching from the text out to find examples from what you are to bring back to the text and compare it. The text is always your starting point. The text is your authority. Either you have it from the media or literature or everyday life but you need something to prove it, okay, and that's what the text is. That's why you have to stay with it.

Here, Beth seemed on the verge of allowing that something other than literature could stand as support for Patricia's ideas—media or everyday life, she suggested. But such a suggestion was buried in the middle of a long comment that began and ended with an assertion of the text's authority.

It is not particularly surprising that Beth was able to act as an authority in response to Patricia's writing. During whole class discussions of the readings, Patricia's comments were often tentative, exhibiting neither the authority of experience with literary interpretation nor the authority of personal experience with African American issues. As a consequence, Beth might have easily felt herself to be a more authoritative reader than Patricia, even before she read her writing. And because English was Patricia's second language, her writing contained many surface errors not common in the writing of native speakers—problems with word endings, prepositions, verb tenses—that might have reinforced Beth's sense that she was a more authoritative writer as well. Further, Patricia acknowledged Beth's authority, commenting, "[Beth] knows what she's doing, she's very qualified, I think. She just tells me a lot of things that I can do better."

What is somewhat surprising is the ease with which Beth asserted authority over Carol's writing. Given that "African American Voices" focused exclusively on literature by African Americans, was taught by an African American instructor, and enrolled a clear majority of African American students, one might expect Beth to grant Carol some authority as an African American, an authority that Beth herself could not presume to assert. But Beth proceeded to judge Carol's writing according to the same standards she used to judge Patricia, and presumably herself: the established standards of "normal" academic writing that privilege textual authority and devalue the authority of lived experience.

In her written comments on Carol's draft, Beth assumed her characteristic authoritative stance, circling and underlining questionable words and phrases and using the imperative voice to warn Carol against making unsupported generalizations: "These are vague references to the text. You've got something here, make it concrete." A careful reading of Beth's comments, however, suggests that she may have expected Carol to resist her authoritative stance. For example, in response to Carol's sentence "Also, these white people have purposely planned to continuously enslave African Americans economically," Beth circled "purposely" and wrote, "might try 'seemingly.' Makes the sentence less generalized. Quote from MJ: 'Don't make generalizations for which you have no evidence.'" Here, Beth bolstered her authority by explicitly aligning herself with the teacher. By doing so, she is less likely to be seen as personally objecting to Carol's statement and more likely to have her advice accepted as representing the institution's standards.

Beth did seem on the verge of validating some of the differences in Carol's writing when she praised what she called Carol's "rhetoric," comparing it to that of Martin Luther King, Jr. In addition to making positive comments next to particular words and phrases on Carol's draft, Beth wrote at the end of Carol's paper:

> Your opening and closing are simply close to brilliant. There's a lot of rhetoric working here, and you must use the text to back up that rhetoric. Make your text as powerful as you want by basing it in the poem! You have a touch for some of this—explore it! Watch generalizations. If you dare use them, back them up with concrete evidence.

In these remarks, Beth seemed to validate qualities of Carol's writing that would not necessarily have been validated by the academy. Her praise of Carol is undercut, however, by her continued insistence that rhetoric cannot stand alone, that it must be backed up not just by examples but by *textual* evidence. Note in this regard Beth's instruction to Carol that she make her text as powerful as *she* wants by "basing it in the poem." Here Beth conflated Carol's standards with her own and with those of the academy, assuming that there was only one way to construct a powerful argument.

The group discussion of Carol's draft proceeded in much the same way as the discussion of Patricia's writing. Beth initiated and dominated the discussion, explaining her comments paragraph by paragraph. Although Beth complimented Carol more than she did Patricia, she still emphasized Carol's need to provide textual support for her assertions. For example, after pointing out an effective generalization, Beth told Carol, "Keep parts like that so that you can compare them with the text. Compare it to the text constantly." And again, she explicitly aligned herself with the instructor when she reminded Carol that MJ had said, "You cannot make generalizations without having [support]."

Of course, it is one thing for Beth to assert herself as an authority; it is another thing for her to be considered one by her peers. But for a number of reasons, Beth's authority went more or less unquestioned in this peer response session. Throughout Beth's lengthy and detailed discussion of their papers, Patricia and Carol listened quietly, occasionally rephrasing one of Beth's suggestions to be sure they understood what she wanted them to do. And although Carol and Patricia had read and written comments on each other's drafts, Beth's analysis of their work left them with little to add but agreement. At the end of Beth's discussion of Patricia's draft, for example, Carol simply added, "That's the same thing I got out of it. You need an introduction, and after some of the things you were saying, it was, like, how do you know? Then when you were saying your problems as an Asian American, it's, like, well, how does that relate to the poem?"

Similarly, Beth's extensive response to Carol's paper seemed to leave Patricia with little to say. Patricia more or less reiterated Beth's caution against overgeneralizing and agreed with her recommendation that Carol provide more examples. But unlike Beth, who positioned herself as more knowledgeable than her peers, Patricia addressed Carol *as* a peer: "You're a lot like me. I try to get my feelings in there so hard and then you forget that other people reading this are not going to get the same ideas I am. Like she's saying, use a lot of examples, because you do generalize a lot—and so do I." Although Patricia saw Carol's writing as similar to her own, she defined that similarity primarily in terms of their failure to measure up to existing standards for academic writing, standards that include a narrow focus, emotional distance, and extensive textual support. In separate interviews, Patricia and Carol both claimed they had a problem with wanting to make their papers "too big" by going beyond the texts discussed in class. Patricia admitted that one important lesson she had learned from Beth was that writing had to be based on the texts as "the facts" because "If you start with your own opinion, you can get into trouble."

I have discussed Beth's responding strategies at length because her responses dominated the peer response session. One reason Beth might have felt the need to explain her comments in such detail was that her handwriting was almost unreadable. But given the nature of her explanations—asking Patricia if she knew what a colloquialism was and asking Carol if she knew what "rhetoric" meant, for example—it is also likely that Beth saw her peer group members as incapable of understanding her comments. What is perhaps most distressing about Beth's domination of her peer response group is that her assumption of an unquestionable authority seems to be a product of her institutional position as a successful writer (an English major and a creative writer) and responder to writing (a peer tutor).

When it came time to discuss Beth's draft, Beth managed to control that discussion as well. Because Beth had brought to class only one handwritten copy of a partial draft that consisted of an outline of her ideas and a list of possible examples, Carol and Patricia, in effect, had no writing to respond to. While Beth was out of the room, Carol and Patricia conferred about what their response to Beth should be. Both expressed their frustration with being unable to respond:

> Carol: It's very, very rough.
> Patricia: That's why, I'm like, I don't know what to say. I have no idea what to say.
> Carol: It's just like fragments of what she wants.
> Patricia: Cause she's going to elaborate on all this. So, it's kind of like, should I even say anything about it?
> Carol: She knows what she's gonna do, but the thing is, she shouldn't have brought it in like this.

When Beth returned, she asked her peers what they thought. Before they could respond, Beth explained at length what she wanted to do in the paper, something that she hadn't invited either Carol or Patricia to do. Perhaps the most striking part of her explanation was her reflection on the kind of evidence she would provide in support of her ideas. She began by asking Carol and Patricia if they had read the book *Backlash*. When they admitted they hadn't, Beth explained that "it has examples *galore* in it of what I'm talking about in my paper." Beth then pointed out that "[MJ] is very interested in our own personal experiences which is very interesting, and it's a good idea for a class like this." Reading aloud from the prompt that all three group members had chosen, Beth concluded, "So she wants text and personal [experience], so I made it a point to do that. I mean, you can do one or the other, but I made it a point to do both, to get the point across better." Here Beth showed her awareness of the instructor's desire to extend what will count as authority in this class and revealed her intention to use multiple kinds of authority to make her writing more effective. Unfortunately, Beth did not encourage Patricia and Carol to rely on their own experience as valid evidence, perhaps because she felt they needed to master a facility with textual evidence first before they could earn the right to go outside of the text. It is also possible that Beth felt less qualified to judge the effectiveness of her peers' personal testimony: put in the position of having to judge their writing in an institutional context, she relied on the established standards of the institution. But a final explanation also seems possible: namely, that even Beth's "nontextual" evidence was really "textual"; her references to women's lived experience did, after all, come from *Backlash*, a *text*. So her claim to be validating personal experience as evidence, even in her writing, proved false.

In the end, Carol and Patricia's only response to Beth's draft was to say that because it was incomplete, they couldn't really respond. Patricia closed the discussion by joking, "You really do your own criticism. You don't really need us."

Beth and the Institution

Although, inevitably, a multitude of factors contributed to what happened here, it seems important to highlight the authoritative stance Beth took in response to her peers' writing and to look closely at the kind of authority she was asserting. Two important sources of Beth's authority seem to be her confidence in her reading and writing ability and her unstated belief in a single standard for judging writing. As a consequence, Beth approached the "differences" in her peers' writing as weaknesses or problems that needed to be corrected and that she felt in a position to correct. While Beth's voice does reflect what many of us have heard (and said) about writing and texts, constructing her as the embodiment of the institution's normalizing discourse, as I have done here, is a strong statement. In order to better understand how Beth speaks for the institution (and how Patricia and Carol recognize that voice), we need to look at Beth's position within the class itself.

Despite MJ's validation of multiple authorities, Beth never came into line with MJ's view. Throughout the class, Beth seemed to contrast "universal" literature with "issue-oriented" literature that, in Beth's opinion, appealed only to special interests or groups. Note that Beth acknowledges that the use of personal experience makes sense "in a class like this." Beth seems to have relied on her experience in other classes to presuppose that "literature in general" did not follow the rules of response MJ was advocating. In an early class discussion, MJ asked students to talk about books they particularly liked or disliked. When a number of African American students complained about the irrelevance of a book like *The Great Gatsby*, Beth adamantly defended it, arguing that Fitzgerald wasn't interested in "surface things" like the signs of wealth in the book, but in "human emotion." Later in the same discussion, MJ asked students if they had special expectations when they read books by African Americans. Beth responded that blacks tend to write about issues whereas whites don't. When several African American students said that they expected African American literature to express the "truth" and to teach them something, arguing that white writers can't write about what it means to be black and that white readers can't understand black literature in the same way that black readers can, Beth insisted that good writing transcends differences, that it is about "universal human experience." In an interview, Beth remarked, "I tend to shy away from issue-like things, issue-like books and literature and focus more on what I was talking about the very first day, you know, universal things and human emotion. That's what I try to write, and that's what I enjoy reading." It should not be surprising that Beth's position was different from the position of most of the other students in the class. And it is exactly this kind of difference that teachers of multicultural courses seek to highlight. Unfortunately, Beth was unable to see that her position was *a* position, just one among many. Of course, Beth's position is *not* just one among many: it represents the dominant paradigm in most English departments, at least those where a large number of faculty were trained under the doctrine of New Criticism. As a result, it is likely that Beth's belief in the superiority of literature that dealt with "universal human experience" was one passed on by her professors and one that she was rewarded for adopting. Even in this class context, Beth's "traditionalism," although challenged, was subtly rewarded: Beth received "A's" on all her papers and received a "+" for her peer response.

Although one of the goals of a course like "African American Voices" is to complicate the notion that there is such a thing as "universal human experience," Beth was perplexed to find her views called into question by others in the class, going so far as to complain in private to MJ about her classmates' insistence on discussing literature exclusively in terms of African American experience and their hostility toward her views. Ideally, having one's established views called into question results in self-reflection and perhaps a modification or a qualification of those views, but Beth showed no sign of budging from her position. Even when MJ warned her against telling people that they were wrong, Beth said only that she knew she needed to learn to be patient.

Perhaps Beth's distress over the loss of her authority in the class as a whole contributed to the strength with which she asserted her authority in her peer response group. As we can see in the peer response session described above, Beth adhered to a New Critical approach in her discussion of literature and imposed that approach on her peers by emphasizing that texts, not one's interpretation of them, should serve as the foundation for writing in this class. In her criticism of her peers' interpretations, she also implied that there was only one "correct" reading of a text, and given Beth's years of training in reading and writing about texts, she was able to imply, fairly confidently, that hers was the correct reading.

Similarly, Beth seemed in full confidence that her approach to writing about texts was *the* correct approach. And the fact that all three group members had chosen to write about the universality or timelessness of literature (Beth's specialty) probably gave her even more confidence. If Beth's view of literature seems dominated by a New Critical paradigm, her view of writing—with its emphasis on a single thesis, textual support, and some matters of style—seems equally dominated by current-traditional rhetoric. Although "New Criticism" and "Current Traditional Rhetoric" are umbrella terms for a complex of ideas, they share in common a valorization of texts and a devaluing of personal experience, a belief in a single approach to the reading and writing of texts and a dismissal of other approaches, and a claim to be above the politics of individual and cultural differences. Perhaps most importantly, they once shared enormous power as normalizing forces in the field of English studies. And although on a theoretical level, the tenets of New Criticism and Current Traditional Rhetoric have been thoroughly disputed, their legacy lives on in many literature and composition classrooms as well as in students like Beth. Read in this way, the power that Beth asserted in the peer response group was a power granted her by virtue of her alliance with a very powerful institution.

This explanation of why Beth was able to position herself as an unassailable authority in the peer response group also explains to some extent why Patricia and Carol were unable or unwilling to resist her power. In the larger classroom setting, Beth's view was a minority view and one loudly opposed by many of the other students, but in her peer response group, Beth was able to assert her view without the opposition of a half dozen students and without the intervention of the teacher. Neither Patricia nor Carol had the experience or success with reading and writing about texts that might have given them the confidence to oppose Beth—Patricia was a second language user and Carol had received the lowest grade in the class on her first essay. In fact, they both responded positively to her authoritative reading of their work; in separate interviews, both reported that this peer response session had been helpful. Patricia, who felt insecure about her reading and writing abilities and was uncertain how to do the kind of writing required in "African American Voices," found Beth's corrections of her text particularly helpful. Patricia seemed to want a clear statement of what an acceptable essay should be, and Beth was able to issue that statement. Patricia was also sympathetic to Beth's view of literature. It was Patricia who on the first day of class said that she had enjoyed reading *The Great Gatsby*, thus provoking the hostility of some of the African American students and the support of Beth. And Patricia's view that these "culture classes" overemphasize people's differences is not unlike Beth's view that good literature is universal.

In "African American Voices," where neither Beth nor Patricia could claim special insight into the literature based on their experience, an emphasis on universality or commonality gave them access to the texts they were reading. It also gave them a way of deflecting whatever discomfort they might have felt about their racial positions in relation to the class. Patricia, whose parents owned a grocery in a predominantly black neighborhood in Los Angeles, seemed especially uncomfortable writing or talking about African American experience. Admitting that among the Koreans she knew there was a great deal of prejudice against African Americans, Patricia explained that she had enrolled in "African American Voices" in order to overcome her limited perspective and to gain insight into African American culture. In spite of her desire to understand African American experience on its own terms, however, Patricia seemed unable to confront directly that experience and was made especially uncomfortable by the rage and hostility that some of the literature and some of the students expressed. Although Beth never referred to herself as "white," her frustration with the African American students' emphasis on their experience may also have been a product of her anxiety about racial difference and her desire to be free of accusations of prejudice or feelings of collective white guilt. Any discussion of the oppression of African Americans potentially implicated her, and she actively resisted such an implication. For example, by aligning herself with her African American instructor in her criticism of Carol's generalization about the economic oppression of African Americans, Beth lessened the chance that her criticism would be seen as racist. Similarly, Beth's retreat into claims of universality can be seen as an attempt to avoid dealing further with the problem of how to talk about African American experience without implicating herself as a white person. Unfortunately, her claims of universality served to mark her further as a member of the majority culture who had the luxury to choose not to deal with the messy matter of racism in America. Beth and Patricia's difficulty in dealing with racism was perhaps best illustrated during a class discussion that took place the day after the LA riots broke out. MJ opened the discussion by allowing students to express their anger and pain over the outcome of the first Rodney King trial. She then moved the discussion to a more general consideration of racism in America. When she raised the issue of racism against African American women, Beth questioned whether such a thing existed, admitting that although she frequently witnessed racism against African American men, she did not believe there was racism against African American women. By making racism a male problem, she once again removed herself from racial guilt. Patricia avoided implications of racism by saying nothing during the discussion of the Rodney King verdict and the LA riots. In fact, Patricia told only me that she was from Los Angeles and that her father's grocery had miraculously remained untouched while most of the other Korean businesses in the neighborhood were destroyed.

Because Patricia was sympathetic to Beth's views and seemed comfortable with Beth's authoritative stance and because Robert was frequently absent from the peer response group, Carol would have been alone if she had chosen to oppose Beth. Although a number of African American students felt powerful enough to oppose Beth in class, they also knew they could rely on their peers for support. In the peer response group, Carol could not count on that support. Although Carol's writing indicated that she did not share Beth's approach to literature, Carol chose to voice her dissent only in the private space of her final draft. In spite of Beth's attempts to fit Carol's writing to the established mold of academic writing, Carol managed to resist Beth's authoritative voice in her revision and to continue writing "differently." This difference emerges in Carol's choice to support her generalizations not with more textual references to the poems but with additional references to Rodney King and to her own experience as an African American university student. And while in some cases she chose to tone down her assertions about the oppression of African Americans, in other cases she did not. Perhaps one of the most interesting ways in which Carol resisted Beth's advice was by borrowing and extending Patricia's misreading of Cullen's "We Wear the Mask." Beth had explicitly told Patricia that she was *wrong* to say that it was the oppressors who were wearing a mask, when according to Beth's reading the poet was clearly describing how the oppressed must wear a mask if they want to fit in with the majority culture. In Carol's revised essay about the continuing effects of racism, she wrote, "In the poem, the oppressed group of people are wearing the mask. However, the poem can be interpreted to read as the oppressor wearing the mask. Racism can cover itself from being seen as it really is and can dodge confrontation, by wearing a mask." In the margin next to this sentence, MJ wrote, "Good point," and at the end of the essay commented, "This essay is much better than the first one. Your tone is more confident. I love your use of masks as worn by the oppressors. That is quite innovative."

In spite of enormous pressure to conform to traditional conventions of academic discourse, in her revised draft, Carol clearly produced a different kind of discourse, one that challenged the narrow standards of text-based academic writing by relying on African American experience and by openly interpreting a piece of literature in ways that served her larger purposes. But Carol was able to make these challenges only outside the classroom, allowing Beth and Patricia to continue believing that the rules for academic writing that Beth asserted were not open to question. In the public arena of her group and her class, the dissensus represented by Carol's writing went unarticulated and unheard.

Dissensus—A Dream (Deferred)

If, as Myers and Trimbur have proposed, collaboration in the classroom can give students opportunities to understand and to criticize the normalizing function of established knowledge-making communities, "African American Voices in Literature" seemed a perfect site for such a critique. The content of the class, the racial make-up of the class, the teacher's explicit validation of differences in the class, and the important role that collaboration played all seemed likely to yield the "rhetoric of dissensus" that Trimbur has argued is necessary. But, as this discussion has attempted to demonstrate, such was not the case. Rather, the peer response group that I studied functioned in ways eerily similar to the established knowledge-making communities that Myers and Trimbur attack. This group was not made up of knowledgeable peers who share the same paradigms and the same set of values but, instead, replicated an uneven distribution of power. And the member who had the greatest power was the one best able to articulate the authoritative and exclusionary rules of the "normal" discourse of the community and to use those rules to reject and hence silence the "abnormal" discourse of her group members. As a result, no "rhetoric of dissensus" made it possible for the group to talk productively about their differences because the rules of "normal" discourse had already determined that differences must be treated hierarchically. Although students recognized that their reading and writing were different, they could think about those differences only in terms of what was right and wrong.

I have, of course, presented here only one reading of one peer response session involving just three students, a sample too small to invite generalizations. But I believe by looking closely at one episode in these students' lives, we can bring into focus the power of the institution to silence difference. Beth's voice, after all, is the voice of the institution. It is the voice of every teacher who had ever given her an "A" for abiding by the established conventions and norms of academic writing. More to the point, perhaps, Beth's voice is our voice. Hearing Beth speak in that voice proved especially unsettling for me, for she was a flesh-and-blood embodiment of institutional power, one who acted consistently to maintain the status quo and to silence difference. Even more troubling is the fact that Beth, a bright and thoughtful student, had been taught to maintain the status quo without what many teachers see as an equally crucial lesson: the capacity for self-reflection that would have enabled her to see the consequences of her behavior for herself, her peers, and ultimately her society.

Those of us who would answer the call of Myers and Trimbur for collaboration-as-critique must recognize that students' experience in the classroom is not one of "non-domination," as Trimbur has suggested. Clearly, students like Beth, Carol, and Patricia *are* dominated by the institutionalized context of the classroom. Critiques of the normalizing function of institutionalized discourse communities must begin, therefore, by challenging the assumption that any setting within the academy represents one of "non-domination," and thus with a critique of the peer response group, of the classroom, and of the established knowledge-making community known as school.

For teachers and students alike, such a critique requires us to listen closely to our own voices, to hear in ourselves the voice of the institution reifying the status quo and silencing difference over and over again. It is only through this kind of intense listening that a space can be created for a rhetoric of dissensus that would allow us to talk productively about the normalizing function of the university, of writing classrooms, and particularly of institutionalized courses on diversity. What this study reveals, in concrete and vivid detail, is the enormous difficulty of that task. In spite of this difficulty, or perhaps more accurately because of it, we will need a good deal of luck as well as tenacity and courage in meeting the challenge to create a rhetoric of dissensus that would animate not only our scholarly discussions but also the classrooms where students like Carol, Patricia, and Beth meet systems of discursive power.

Notes

[1] According to Bruffee, "normal discourse" is "pointed: it is explanatory and argumentative. Its purpose is to justify belief to the satisfaction of other people within the author's community of knowledgeable peers" (643). Although Bruffee allows for the emergence of "abnormal discourse"—discourse that occurs when "consensus no longer exists with regard to rules, assumptions, goals, values and mores"—this "abnormal discourse" is not the community's valued discourse (648).

[2] Although any research project is inevitably collaborative, ethnographic research is especially so. I would, thus, like to acknowledge my special indebtedness to the instructor of "African American Voices" for giving me access to her classroom. I would also like to thank the students in that course, especially the students described in this essay, for allowing me to observe their learning. The names of the instructor and students are pseudonyms.

[3] It is important to note that although MJ made peer response an important part of the course, requiring it for each of the four essays students wrote and deducting one-half of a letter grade from an essay turned in by a student who did not attend peer response, students' participation was fairly irregular. For example, Beth missed the first peer response session. Robert, who is described as a member of this group, missed the first two responding sessions and failed to bring any writing to either of the two sessions that he attended. Although Robert's absence may have influenced how the group worked, it is difficult to imagine what difference his presence would have made since he played a fairly passive role in the group and in class.

Works Cited

Bruffee, Kenneth A. "Collaborative Learning and the `Conversation of Mankind.'" *College English* 46 (1984): 635-52.

Myers, Greg. "Reality, Consensus, and Reform in the Rhetoric of Composition Teaching." *College English* 48 (1986): 154-74.

Trimbur, John. "Consensus and Difference in Collaborative Learning." *College English* 51 (1989): 602-16.

Rhetoric, Philosophy, and Discourse

Nietzsche in Basel: Writing Reading

J. Hillis Miller

> Nietzsche in Basel studied the deep pool
> Of these discolorations, mastering
> The moving and the moving of their forms
> In the much-mottled motion of blank time.
>> Wallace Stevens

> Reading and writing and 'rithmetic,
> Taught to the tune of a hickory stick.

> Truth-content is only to be grasped through immersion
> in the most minute details of subject-matter.
>> Walter Benjamin

In an interview soon to be published in the *Journal of Advanced Composition*, Gary Olson responded to a claim I made about the close relation between the teaching of reading and the teaching of writing by pointing out that making such a claim might diminish the independent role of programs in composition. I suppose he meant that if everyone assumes students already learn to write in classes in reading, then specialized courses in composition might be unnecessary. This was the attitude of some colleagues of mine at both Johns Hopkins and Yale back in the sixties and early seventies. So I am aware that arguing for a tight bond between reading and writing has important implications for the power structures of departments within universities and colleges. My exploration of this topic is made within that context. I claim, however, that far from weakening the role of programs in composition, my position would greatly strengthen it by recognizing that the teaching of composition is not just an instrumental sideline in higher education. It is not just the teaching of correct grammar, spelling, paragraph structure, and so on that should have been mastered already in high school. On the contrary, learning to write teaches habits of reading that are fundamental in any course or discipline, not to speak of political or social life outside the university. In a democracy, bad readers are in great danger. You might elect the wrong leaders or buy bad merchandise. As you write, so you read. As you read, so you write. Writing is a reflection and testimony to the habits of reading in the writer. A paradigmatic example of that is the way translating something you think you can read perfectly well in the original language shows you places where you do not understand. The standard way of testing in college classes what you have assimilated from required reading is to ask you to write something about it. Learning to write well is at the same time learning to read well. The two always go inextricably together. Let me explain this further.

Reading, Writing, and Ideology

Reading and writing, along with the rudiments of arithmetic, are, or used to be, the first things taught small children in grade school. Speaking is taught in the family, primarily by the mother, hence "mother tongue." If speaking one's mother tongue seems almost "natural"—taken in with mother's milk, so to speak—reading and writing are cultural and social, unnatural. If someone does not teach you, you will never learn to read and write. Though some parents teach their children reading and writing, the school system assumes it starts from scratch. Reading and writing are imposed by the first extra-familial authority the child encounters. The schoolroom is a scene of instruction reinforced by the hickory stick that is the synecdochic representative of all the power of the state. If you do not learn to read and write, you will be beaten. Today, beating of grade school children happens less often, but the imposition of a culture's ideology by teaching reading and writing is no less puissantly enforced in all sorts of ways. These are no less violent for not involving physical punishment. The imposition of this socializing force continues even into required undergraduate courses in writing. It may be that students resist these courses so much because they unconsciously see them as a continuation of those first awful weeks away from mother with Dick, Jane, and the alphabet in the first grade.

What do I mean by "ideology" when I say the teaching of reading and writing from grade school through graduate school is one of the most powerful ways a culture's ideology is imposed? I mean by ideology the confusion of linguistic with natural reality. We are led to think it is natural whereas it is actually linguistic. Louis Althusser, in a celebrated essay, speaks of the way what he calls "state apparatuses," including schools, enforce an ideology, defined by him as the imaginary version of our real relations to our fellows and to material reality. These apparatuses do this enforcing by hailing or interpellating someone to be the person the state wants him to be. A police officer says, "Hey You!" and I instinctively respond, "Who, me?"[1] The teaching of both writing and reading is a splendid example of that interpellation: "Hey you! You have split an infinitive and spliced with a comma!" "I'm sorry. I'll never do it again."

Reading and writing are always closely associated in this process of appropriation, accommodation, or socialization, that shapes the illiterate child into a citizen. The two go together from the beginning. The child in the first grade is taught to read in order to be able to write and taught to write in order to be able to read. In one way or another, that goes on being the case even in college courses in composition, even though the student's ability to "read" in the literal sense may be (falsely) taken for granted in courses in composition. Of course, much teaching of reading goes on in composition courses. What the student is learning in other courses about how to read also affects in important ways how he or she writes. Thus, composition teachers have every reason to be deeply interested in how reading is taught or in what is assumed about reading in other courses or in the culture generally.

What ideology is it that learning to read and write in our culture imposes? And how does such learning instill it in children? It is now widely recognized that grade school textbook readers are not ideologically neutral, though some people of course would still want to claim they are. An interlocked system of assumptions about race, class, gender, and family relations is implied in those little stories about Dick and Jane. That this assertion is controversial is demonstrated by the recent hullabaloo about the inclusion of several grade school readers that presented gay and lesbian families among a multitude of other possibilities from which the teacher might choose.[2] William Bennett in a television talk show vigorously opposed even making it possible to choose to use such a reader. "Grade school teachers," I am told he said, "should just teach reading." But there is no such thing as an ideologically neutral reader. The one showing a gay family is just as ideological as the one presuming the proper family consists of a mother, a father, and two children, a boy who plays with trucks and a girl who plays with dolls.

But however important this ideological reinforcement is, I am less interested here in the thematic content of grade school readers or in the writing exercises the children are given than in the complex system of assumptions presupposed in prescriptions for correct writing and reading that are imposed in our culture from the first grade through graduate school and beyond. Whenever I correct a split infinitive or a run-on sentence in the draft of a graduate student's dissertation chapter, I am continuing the work of policing begun in the first grade. Whenever one of my copyeditors goes through a book manuscript of mine and makes changes in the name of correctness, clarity, or "the house style," that policing continues. In my rewriting of the manuscript of this essay to make it clearer and more correct—for example, by eliminating sequences of "of clauses"—I am showing that such policing, as Foucault predicts, has been internalized. Finally I do not need the composition police at all. That might be the measure of a successful program of instruction in composition. A set of rules and habits in both reading and writing becomes so thoroughly internalized and instinctive that it no longer needs to be externally enforced. Though, of course, what I write is not "literature," it is nevertheless instructive to imagine what would happen to Shakespeare, Faulkner, Joyce, Woolf (or, for that matter, Derrida) if they were "copyedited" in the same way. If they needed to defy standards of correctness in order to say what they wanted to say, that suggests that there may be some things worth saying that cannot be said in a "correct" style.[3]

Just as the thematic content of grade school readers is not neutral, so also the standards of correctness and clarity in writing are not natural or universal. They too are ideological. Their ideological content is all the more powerful for being surreptitious, for being disguised as universal and natural. What system of assumptions is it that all this teaching and correcting imposes? It is just that assemblage of concepts that make up what is called "logocentrism" or "Western metaphysics." It is not for nothing that the first stage of the medieval trivium, the first thing students were taught, was grammar. Medieval grammar, as Gary Olson reminds me, was much wider in scope than our modern notion of grammar as parts of speech and correct usage. Grammar was exegesis as the bringing out of the meaning of a text. Nevertheless, exegesis probably meant then something much closer to a process of correct parsing than anything like modern critical commentary. Grammar, followed by logic and rhetoric, was the foundation on which the whole airy edifice of the quadrivium, the sciences of the external world—arithmetic, geometry, astronomy, and music—was built.

Assumptions that go back to the Greeks, especially to Aristotle, underlie the teaching of grammar and composition. Grammar itself, as everyone knows, was a codification by scholars of the practice of Greek and Latin writers. Grammar was an empirical and reductive description of actual practice, in all its heterogeneity, that then became prescriptive. As we say they did, so should you do. This notion was ultimately transferred along with its terminology to vernacular languages, where it fits more or less well, but by no means perfectly. The oddnesses of Milton's language in *Paradise Lost* are a sign of this. Nothing quite like an ablative absolute exists in English. No process could be more artificial, nor more an act of cultural power, than this development of standards of grammatical correctness. (Note the double "of clause.")

Grammar, logic, and rhetoric, the interwoven sequence of the trivium that has now been combined in our single modern discipline of composition, presume definite standards of coherence. A shapely discourse should have a beginning, middle, and end, like a good Aristotelian plot. Everything should hang together. Nothing extraneous should be included. All should be governed by a single idea or ground that might be called the "logos" of the whole discourse. The distinction between literal and figurative language is assumed, along with the priority of the former over the latter. Figurative language is an adornment added through metaphorical transfers to a literal base whose meaning is guaranteed by its referentiality. The literal language of a good composition refers, truthfully, either to the external world or to the subjectivity of the one who composes the discourse. That subjectivity remains as a sovereign, separate, paradigmatically masculine, ego in control of word choices determined by what "he" wants to say. The word "composition" suggests a consciously controlled act of putting together.

Perfect translatability between one language and another is assumed. Those copyeditors I have mentioned show an extreme reluctance to allow the inclusion of citations in a foreign language. What will happen to this present essay will be a test of that. It is assumed that everything can be said and can be said in English. This everything that can be said can always be said clearly, correctly, and coherently, that is, by following the rules of good writing. This is the version within the discipline of composition of that basic principle of the modern university: the principle of sufficient reason. That principle assumes that everything has its "reason." This reason can and should be given. That is what the university is for, to account for everything.

Suppose a teacher of composition were to want to put this millennial ideology in question, at least to show that it is an ideology, a linguistic fiction not a natural fact? How would he or she go about doing that? The danger is that teachers of composition may assume that the reading chosen for the course can be liberating while the formal instruction in the rules of correct composition remains the same. This does not work. It does not work because the formal aspect of composition is even more powerful in imposing an ideology than is the thematic content of what is read. This is parallel to the way those in women's studies, minority discourse, or multiculturalism are in danger of falling into the hands of those they challenge if their language repeats in symmetrical mirror image the modes of language of the hegemonic discourse they would contest. Real change will come only through changes that go all the way down to the ground, so to speak, changes in language that challenge all that system of assumptions about language I have described.

I am aware that changes of this sort in the teaching of composition are taking place here and there. Nevertheless, a major frontier for teachers of composition today still remains devising ways to avoid inadvertently reinforcing in teaching rules of correct composition the things they are in the thematic side of their teaching trying to put in question. I am also aware that what I am advocating will seem scandalous to some. These will be those people for whom standards of clarity, unity, and correctness seem universal and natural, not local, ideological, and historically conditioned. Or these may be people who think English, taught in the traditional way, should be a model for the world. To such people the only alternative to this model is anarchy and chaos. They imagine teachers of composition urging their students to write wildly or to persist in "expressing themselves" without regard for any rules. In fact, the alternative ways of writing I am imagining would require as severe a discipline to acquire and master as traditional standards of correctness. This is partly because the traditional standards would also have to be mastered. Those authors I mentioned—Joyce, Derrida, and the rest—conspicuously did that.

I am also aware that it is difficult to conceive just what an alternative way of writing might be like, an anti-logocentric way, a way based on difference and radical heterogeneity rather than on models of sameness and unity. But

many models are already available of what such writing might be like, not only
in those authors I have mentioned but, for example, in certain feminist or so-
called minority writers active today. The writing I shall now discuss is another
example of prose that is stylistically as well as thematically against the grain
of the assumptions about good writing we have inherited as a crucial part of
our hegemonic culture.

Nietzsche and Rhetoric

My example is Friedrich Nietzsche's early writings on rhetoric. Or rather I
take Nietzsche in Basel not so much as an example as a parable or allegory of
the connection between reading and writing for which I have been arguing.
By "early writings on rhetoric" I mean primarily the lectures on rhetoric,
"Darstellung der Antiken Rhetorik," a course delivered in the winter semester (1872-73) at the University of Basel to two students, and the incomplete
essay of summer, 1873, "Über Wahrheit und Lüge im Außermoralischen
Sinne."[4] In these early works, Nietzsche, as Wallace Stevens puts it, "studied
the deep pool/Of these discolorations . . . In the much-mottled motion of
blank time"—that is, he studied the colors of rhetoric as they (and our
understanding of them) have evolved through Western history.

Why did Nietzsche have only two students and those from the institutes
of Germanistic and Jurisprudence? Because in the aftermath of the controversy over *The Birth of Tragedy* all the students in classical philology were
boycotting his course.[5] Those who consider acting practically on the suggestions made in this essay should keep Nietzsche's fate in mind. Nietzsche had
been appointed an ordinarius professor of classics at Basel in 1869, at the
extraordinarily young age of twenty-four. He resigned his post in 1879 for
reasons of ill health. Thereafter, he published the series of great works for
which he is known. Though Nietzsche is a master of German style, though
his works are an admirable exploitation of the resources of the German
language, they hardly conform to normal standards of correctness. My
hardworked hypothetical copyeditor, agent of the style police, would have
had as much trouble with his work as with Joyce, Woolf, or Faulkner. Even
The Birth of Tragedy, published in 1872 while Nietzsche was still a professor
and prior to the lectures on rhetoric, is more a parody of an academic treatise
than a solemn fulfillment of its requirements.

Why did Nietzsche write the way he did? The early works on rhetoric may
suggest an answer. They may also hint at a deeper reason why Nietzsche left
the university. How could he fulfill the terms of his contract to teach and
write in a certain way and at the same time say what he wanted to say, or what
he found himself saying? On the one hand, the lectures on ancient rhetoric
follow the norms of an academic course. On the other hand, when they are
read carefully, with that attention to minute detail for which Benjamin calls,
they turn out to be strangely complex and heterogeneous.

These early works are inhabited by a contradiction. As scholars have shown, Nietzsche borrowed freely for his account of ancient rhetoric from books by Friedrich Blass, Gustav Gerber, and Richard Volkmann. The contradiction is present in these sources. On the one hand, the lectures on rhetoric present a traditional and derivative typology of tropes. Even the examples he uses often come from those sources. Except for an occasional qualification, nothing, for example, could be more conventional than Nietzsche's account of "Der Tropische Ausdruck (The Tropical Expression)" in the seventh lecture and of "Die Rhetorischen Figuren (The Rhetorical Figures)" in the eighth lecture. His descriptions of tropes ("metaphor, synecdoche, metonymy, antonomasia, onomatopoeia, catachresis, metalepsis, epithet, allegory, irony, periphrasis, hyperbaton, anastrophe, parenthesis, and hyperbole" [53-55]) depend on the traditional distinction between the literal use of a word and its transferred uses: "Bei den Tropen handelt es sich um Übertragungen: Wörter statt anderer Wörter gesetzt: an Stelle des Eigentlichen das Uneigentliche. (Tropes deal with transferences: words are used instead of other words: the figurative is used instead of the literal" (64, 65). (A more literal translation of the last phrase would be: "in place of the proper the improper.")

Such formulations depend on an unambiguous concept of literal or proper language. They presuppose that literal meanings are prior to figurative meanings: "Die eigentlichen Bedeutungen erscheinen so als die älteren, schmucklosen. (The proper meanings, therefore, seem to be the older, plainer ones)" (52, 53). First there is the literal word that calls a ship's prow a prow. Such words are authorized, made proper, by their direct relation to the thing they name. There, before our eyes, is the front of the boat. We properly or with propriety call that the prow. The truth value of such language is a truth of correspondence or *adequatio*. The complex Aristotelian epistemology connecting the seeing and naming of a thing with access to its essential form lies behind and supports the notion of proper language.[6] With the literal or proper name firmly in place, the tropical expression is then brought in, or carried over, from its own literal meaning to substitute for that proper name. Now the transferred literal term is used figuratively in place of the literal expression. The improper displaces the proper. We say, "The ship plows the waves." Tropes, it can be seen, are a matter of transference or changing places. The figurative word takes the place of the literal word, the improper the place of the proper. Tropes are usurping placeholders.

Along with this quite traditional theory of tropes is present even in Nietzsche's early works a quite different concept of figurative language. This too comes from Nietzsche's sources, especially Gustav Gerber's *Die Sprache als Kunst*.[7] Gerber, in turn, served as a conduit to Nietzsche for the theories of language in German Romanticism, in Friedrich Schegel, Novalis, Jean Paul Richter, and others. But Nietzsche would already have known these authors through his training in German literature and idealist philosophy at Schulpforte and the University of Leipzig. The copresence and mutual interference of two ideas about tropes constitutes the originality and interest of Nietzsche's early writings on rhetoric. According to the alternative theory, interwoven inextricably with the other, all words are aboriginally metaphorical transferences. No proper language exists. The "proper" is already "improper." "Truth" is therefore not grounded in access through the senses to the essence of the thing. Truth is rather a conventionally agreed upon set of lies. Truth is lie not in the sense that it can be measured as false against some attainable correct naming. Truth is lie in the sense that it claims a false grounding in things as they are, when in fact it is constitutive, not constative. Here is the crucial paragraph in "Über Wahrheit und Lüge":

> Was ist also Wahrheit? Ein bewegliches Heer von Metaphern, Metonymien, Anthropomorphismen kurz eine Summe von menschlichen Relationen, die, poetisch und rhetorisch gesteigert, übertragen, geschmückt wurden, und die nach langem Gebrauche einem Volke fest, canonisch und verbindlich dünken: die Wahrheiten sind Illusionen, von denen man vergessen hat, daß sie welche sind, Metaphern, die abgenutzt und sinnlich kraftlos geworden sind, Münzen, die ihr Bild verloren haben und nun als Metall, nicht mehr als Münzen in Betracht kommen. (182)

> What is truth? a mobile army of metaphors, metonyms, anthropomorphisms, in short, a sum of human relations which were poetically and rhetorically heightened, transferred, and adorned, and after long use seem solid, canonical, and binding to a nation. Truths are illusions about which it has been forgotten that they *are* illusions, worn-out metaphors without sensory impact, coins which have lost their image and now can be used only as metal, and no longer as coins. (250)

This passage has been frequently interpreted, explicitly or implicitly.[8] Nevertheless, it needs to be read carefully again here in the context of the particular questions I am raising now. One obvious feature of the paragraph is the way Nietzsche uses figures to talk about a truth that exists only as a fabric of figures. This already contradicts Nietzsche's apparent goal: to give clear conceptual knowledge of what truth is. Along with being told that truths are illusions, we are told that truth is a mobile army and that truth is a worn coin. Each figure Nietzsche uses has its own implications. To call truth a "mobile army" is to ascribe to that swarm of figures a martial function. Those metaphors, metonymies, and anthropomorphisms are engaged in a *Blitzkrieg*. A *Blitzkrieg* against what? Presumably against the knowledge that these illusions *are* illusions. This army of tropes has force. It is a force irresistibly bringing about a forgetting. Ultimately a whole nation, ein Volk, using that language is bewitched by the figures into forgetting the figures are figures, the illusions illusions. As Nietzsche puts this in "Über Wahrheit und Lüge," the human situation is to be "clinging to a tiger's back in dreams" (247). The image of the army and the image of the tiger join a long series of violent figures in the essay. These figures suggest that the human condition is one of extreme danger. We forget the figures are figures and take them as truthtelling concepts, solid, canonical, and binding. To make this aboriginal error of taking a figure literally is not a benign or noble illusion. Rather, it is like living in danger of being eaten by a tiger we do not even know is there because we are sound asleep on its back.

The concluding metaphor saying truths are coins which have lost their image seems clear enough until you begin to think about it. Then it can be seen to be an example of what it talks about. It is a figure whose conceptual value is too easy to take at face value, as we use a coin without bothering about what it is made of. Figurative language is to the illusory literal or conceptual language derived from it as a coin stamped with the image that makes it a coin worth so much in a given currency is to that same coin when its image has been worn away to invisibility and the coin has become a mere piece of metal. I conflate literal and conceptual language because Nietzsche does so, for example in his account of the way the word "leaf" falsely subsumes all the variety of leaves, no two of which are alike, under the general concept of "leaf." Truth (in the sense of the conventional, illusory truth a "folk" accepts) is like a coin that no longer has its image. A little reflection will show that something is wrong with this figure. The functioning of the figure depends on the traditional Aristotelian definition of a figure as a substitution for a literal word. But Nietzsche is putting just that hierarchy into question. When the image is worn from the coin, the bare metal beneath is revealed. This is supposed to correspond to the figure when it is taken literally as a concept or a literal term. But the bare metal is rather the underlying meaningless matter, substratum of the image. The image gives the metal meaning, makes it a coin. A bare piece of metal is hardly an appropriate image for the columbarium of concepts Nietzsche describes later in the essay as a figure for a fully established canonical language. The image makes the metal something that passes current as a value among the folk of a particular nation, just as it is the figure taken literally that is solid, canonical, and binding. The crisscross of substitutions put in play by the figure does not correspond to the concept. The figure rather obscures or reverses the putative concept. The image on the coin is more like the concept that gives the coin value, while the underlying metal is more like the sensible figure that sustains it. Nietzsche seems to have got his lines crossed in making the crisscross of substitutions.

Far from untangling or reversing the play of substitutions that has made us take illusion as truth, far from putting real truth in place of the illusory truth of figure, as Nietzsche's formulations promise to do, his figure of the coin worn bare reasserts the illusion it would demystify. This occurs another way in what happens to the figure of force in the passage. If the mobile army of tropes has military force, the kind of force brute physical nature has, the return of the coin to bare metal, that is to brute physical nature, deprives the coin of sensible force and renders it "kraftlos," powerless. The two attributions of force are not congruent or logically coherent. Nietzsche's attempt to use figure to demystify the power of figures has reasserted that power in a way giving only an illusory clarity. Rather than substituting a tropical expression for a literal one, an improper expression for a clear and distinct proper one, Nietzsche has substituted one trope for another and has remained always within the same domain of tropical language. The figure of the coin substitutes for the initial conceptual formulation about the way truth is a mobile army of metaphors, metonymies, and anthropomorphisms. The figure "illustrates" the concept in a sensible figure, making it easier to understand, though nevertheless still subservient to it. But the original conceptual formulation was already a figure, the figure of an army. The new figure of the coin displaces the initial figure of the army. The operation of Nietzsche's language gives an example of what he is claiming to talk about in clear conceptual language, but that fact prevents his language from being conceptual, clear, or literal. It does not and cannot give the knowledge it promises, since no metalanguage exists taking us outside the illusions of ordinary language, its taking of figurative language as literal, the improper as proper. This should come as no surprise, since by Nietzsche's own account no proper language exists for which the army of figures he presents is the displacement.[9]

Literal and Figurative Language

Is this erasure of the traditional relation between literal and figurative language anticipated at all in the lectures on classical rhetoric, given just a few months before "On Truth and Lying" was written? The evidence given so far would suggest that it is not. This would lead to a plausible scenario, even though the publication already in 1872 of *The Birth of Tragedy* shows that "On Truth and Lying" did not spring from nowhere. Nevertheless, it might be argued that Nietzsche presented to his students during the school year a conventional and derivative account of ancient rhetoric. Then in the summer of 1873 he developed his own rhetorical theory, something that anticipates or contains in germ the ideas about morality, language, and rhetoric of the "mature Nietzsche," the Nietzsche of *The Genealogy of Morals* or of the so-called *Will to Power*. A little more reading in the lectures on rhetoric shows that this teleological scenario is false. The ideas about tropes, language, and rhetoric in "Über Wahrheit und Lüge" are already fully sketched out in the third lecture of "Darsetellung der Antiken Rhetorik," "Verhältniss des Rhetrorischen zur Sprache (The Relation of the Rhetorical to Language)." This lecture systematically undoes the presuppositions about language, rhetoric, and tropes that are the basis of ancient rhetoric. Formulations almost identical to those in "On Truth and Lie" already occur. The latter might be defined as an expansion of the third lecture in the course. That third lecture was taken chiefly from Gerber, often word for word, as the concordance prepared by Anthonie Meijers and Martin Stingelin shows.[10]

That third lecture develops a series of interrelated propositions. All language is figurative from the beginning. It is tropological because it is based on a sequence of displacements from a forever unknowable reality.

Therefore, the distinction between literal and figurative language is false. No literal language exists. This means that the distinction between rhetoric as knowledge of tropes and rhetoric as knowledge of various persuasive techniques is also false, as is the distinction between rhetoric and ordinary language. Classical rhetoric employed tropes as one way to aid persuasion, as Nietzsche shows in detail in his account of the various forms of rhetoric: forensic, epideictic, deliberative. For Nietzsche, on the other hand, following Gerber, rhetoric as persuasion and rhetoric as tropes are the same, since all language is tropological and the tropes persuade. All language is persuasive rather than truth-telling. All language is primordially rhetorical. The means of this persuasion is the figurative displacements of all language. The latter is not a possible persuasive force in language freely manipulated by an orator to achieve a certain goal; it is an irresistible persuasive power built into a given language from the beginning. This force persuades the users of that language to take a pack of lies as the truth.

"Alle Wörter aber," says Nietzsche, "sind an sich und von Anfang an, in Bezug auf ihre Bedeutung, Tropen. (But, with respect to their meanings, all words are tropes in themselves, and from the beginning)" (22, 23). A little later: "Eigentlich ist alles Figuration, was man gewöhnlich Rede nennt. (What is usually called language is actually all figuration)" (24, 25). It follows from this that "die Tropen treten nicht dann und wann an die Wörter heran, sondern sind deren eigenst Natur. Von einer 'eigentlichen Bedeutung,' die nur in speziellen Fällen übertragen würde, kann gar nicht die Rede Sein. (The tropes are not just occasionally added to words but constitute their most proper nature. It makes no sense to speak of a 'proper meaning' which is carried over to something else only in special cases)" (24, 25).

It follows, "in turn," or by a further displacement, from this rejection of literal meaning that no separation can be made between "natural" language and rhetorical language. All language is already rhetorical through and through. It "desires" not to give true knowledge of the essence of things but to persuade its users to accept a set of illusions as true. Nietzsche's personification of language here as a being with desires not only uses one of the primary tropes, prosopopoeia, he identifies, it also displaces the orator's conscious desire to persuade—for example, the lawyer trying to persuade the court of his guilty client's innocence—to the unconscious workings of language:

> Es giebt gar keine unrhetorische "Natürlichkeit" der Sprache, an die man appelliren könnte: die Sprache selbst ist das Resultat von lauter rhetorischen Künsten. Die Kraft, welche Aristoteles Rhetorik nennt, an jedem Dinge das heraus zu finden und geltend zu machen, was wirkt und Eindruck macht, ist zugleich das Wesen der Sprache: diese bezieht sich ebensowenig wie die Rhetorik auf das Wahre, auf das *Wesen* der Dinge, sie will nicht belehren, sondern eine subjektive Erregung und Annahme auf Andere übertragen. (20)

> There is obviously no unrhetorical "naturalness" of language to which one could appeal; language itself is the result of purely rhetorical arts. The power to discover and to make

operative that which works and impresses, with respect to each thing, a power which Aristotle calls rhetoric, is, at the same time, the essence of language; the latter is based just as little as rhetoric is upon that which is true, upon the essence of things. Language does not desire to instruct, but to convey to others a subjective impulse and its acceptance. (21)

Nietzsche's theory of language, in particular his rejection of the traditional distinction between literal and figurative words, follows naturally and inevitably from his presuppositions about the human epistemological situation. This is an important point in my argument. Aristotle defines figurative language as a double displacement of literal language. The literal word is displaced by a figurative one that has itself been displaced from its literal meaning. We say, "The ship plows the waves." This account of figure, as I have said, is inextricably tied to the assumption that we have direct access, through our senses, to the true essence of things. Literal names record and take possession of the truth of things as they are. For Nietzsche, on the other hand, following again his sources, human beings are forever cut off from the truth about things by the mediated nature of their access to things through the senses and by way of the body. It follows from this situation, again as something inextricably tied to it, that all language is tropological displacement, figurative names for an unknown and forever unknowable "*x ignotum.*" The prow of that ship is *not* there before our eyes. We "see" only a nerve excitation; so "prow" is already a figure. To say "the ship plows the waves" substitutes one figure for another, not a figurative word for a literal one. This is argued first in the third lecture of "Darstellung der Antiken Rhetorik" and then in a similar way in "Über Wahrheit und Lüge." In both cases the claim is that so-called literal language is already the result of a whole series of figurative displacements:

Der sprachbildende Mensch fasst nicht Dinge oder Vorgänge auf, sondern *Reize*: er giebt nicht Empfindungen wieder, sondern sogar nur Abbildungen von Empfindungen. Die Empfindung, durch einen Nervenreiz hervorgerufen, nimmt das Ding nicht selbst auf: diese Empfindung wird nach aussen hin durch ein Bild dargestellt: es fragt sich aber überhaupt, wie ein Seelenakt durch ein Tonbild darstellbar ist? Müsste nicht, wenn vollkommen genaue Wiedergabe stattfinden sollte, vor allem das Material, in welchem wiedergegeben werden soll, dasselbe sein, wie dasjenige ist, in dem die Seele arbeitet? Da es nun aber ein Fremdes ist—der Laut—, wie kann da Genaueres herauskommen als ein *Bild*? Nicht die Dinge treten ins Bewusstsein, sondern die Art, wie wir zu ihnen stehen, das *pithanon*. Das volle Wesen der Dinge wird nie erfasst. (22, 23)

Man, who forms language, does not perceive things or events, but *impulses*: he does not communicate sensations, but merely copies of sensations. The sensation, evoked through a nerve impulse, does not take in the thing itself: this sensation is presented externally through an image. But the question of how an act of the soul can be presented through a sound image must be asked. If completely accurate representation is to take place, should the material in which it is to be represented, above all, not be the same as that in which the soul works? However, since it is something alien—the sound—how then can something come forth more accurately as an *image*? It is not the things that pass over into consciousness, but the manner in which we stand toward them, the *pithanon* [power of persuasion (plausibility; also a thing producing illusion)]. The full essence of things will never be grasped. (21, 23)

This short passage is a systematic dismantling of Aristotelian epistemology and its replacement by the claim that every human being is enclosed not only in the prison house of language but, outside that prison, by another: the prison of false nerve impulses that give us no direct access to the "essence of things." A given word naming some putative thing is the result not just of one, but of a whole series of displacements that can metaphorically all be called metaphors. The thing produces a nerve impulse. The nerve impulse produces a sensation, a mental image. The sensation is then expressed in a sound, the spoken word. This is another metaphorical displacement, since the spoken word is by no means of the same substance as the sensation-image but merely stands for it. It is in this sense that for Nietzsche "all words are tropes, in themselves, and from the beginning." They are tropes for that forever unavailable "mysterious *x*." It follows from this that what are ordinarily thought of as primary tropes, metaphor and metonymy, are no more than secondary displacements of the primary displacements producing language in the first place. This is what Nietzsche means when he says, "Die zweite Form des Tropus ist die *Metapher*. (The second form of the *tropus* is the metaphor)" (22, 23). In fact, metaphor "proper" would be the fourth degree of metaphorical displacement: from the nerve excitation to the sensation to the image of that sensation in a spoken word to the displacement of that word to a new use. Nietzsche says just this in a passage in "On Truth and Lying" that corresponds closely to the account of the origin of language in the third lecture:

Das "Ding an sich" (das würde eben die reine folgenlose Wahrheit sein) ist auch dem Sprachbildner ganz unfaßlich und ganz und gar nicht erstrebenswerth. Er bezeichnet nur die Relationen der Dinge zu den Menschen und nimmt zu deren Ausdrucke die kühnsten Metaphern zu Hülfe. Ein Nervenreiz zuerst übertragen in ein Bild! Erste Metapher. Das Bild wieder nachgeformt in einem Laut! Zweite Metapher. Und jedesmal vollständiges Ueberspringen der Sphäre, mitten hinein in eine ganz andre und neue.... Wir glauben etwas von den Dingen selbst zu wissen, wenn wir von Bäumen, Farben, Schnee und Blumen reden, und besitzen doch nichts als Metaphern der Dinge, die den ursprünglichen Wesenheiten ganz und gar nicht entsprechen ... nimmet sich das räthselhafte *x* des Dings an sich einmal als Nervenreiz, dann als Bild, endlich als Laut aus. (178)

The "thing-in-itself" (which would be pure, disinterested truth) is also absolutely incomprehensible to the creator of language and not worth seeking. He designates only the relations of things to men, and to express these relations he uses the boldest metaphors. First, he translates a nerve stimulus into an image! That is the first metaphor. Then, the image must be reshaped into a sound! The second metaphor. And each time there is a complete overleaping of spheres—from one sphere to the center of a completely different, new one.... When we speak of trees, colors, snow, and flowers, we believe we know something about the things themselves, although what we have are just metaphors of things, which do not correspond at all to the original entities.... [T]he mysterious *x* of the thing appears first as a nerve stimulus, then as an image, and finally as a sound. (248)

Nietzsche's assertion that all language is originally metaphorical must be distinguished from similar assertions by Rousseau and Condillac in the eighteenth century. Each has a different historical placement, a different location within the history of ideas. Rousseau and Condillac, in a different way in each case, hold to an empirical or Lockean epistemology. For Rousseau, for example, it is not some unhappy enclosure in a world of nerve excitations that leads his exemplary maker of the first metaphors to call a man a giant. It is a misinterpretation born of fear. Nietzsche's explanation of why all language is tropological, on the other hand, is rooted in nineteenth-century physiology and psychology. If you have a different conception of nerves, brain, body, senses, and consciousness, you will have a different notion of the origin of language and of the relation of language to reality. Nietzsche's ideas about nerve stimuli, sensations, the separation of what he calls "spheres," and our inability to confront the essence of things directly are essential to his theory of language, tropes, and rhetoric, not adventititious components of it. The same thing can be said of Aristotle. His ideas about *energeia, enargeia*, essence, being, form, and so on, are the presupposed background of the *Poetics* and the *Rhetoric*.

What then are we to make of the passages I cited earlier from the lectures on rhetoric in which Nietzsche appears to reaffirm the traditional formulation that makes figurative language a displacement of an original literal language? These passages must be a species of indirect discourse or erlerbte Rede. Nietzsche is repeating as a good pedagogue should what the authors he is telling his students about said and believed. Another way to put this is to say that the lectures on ancient rhetoric are, with the exception of the third lecture and a few touches here and there revealing what Nietzsche really thought, ironical through and through. They are the ironically solemn repetition of a colossal, centuries-long mistake, a mistake based on a false idea of language and epistemology that dominated both Greek and Roman ideas about rhetoric. Only rarely does Nietzsche allow his own opinions to break through the ironic deadpan miming of what Aristotle, Quintillian, and the rest had to say. An example is his comment on Quintilian's distinction between popular tropes and rhetorical tropes: "Thus, the popular tropes originated from embarrassment and stupidity (Verlegenheit und Dummheit), the rhetorical tropes from art and delight (Kunst und Wohlgefallen)." "This," says Nietzsche firmly, "is an entirely false contrast (ganz falscher Gegensatz)," as indeed it would be if he is right in refusing to distinguish between ordinary language and rhetorical language (52, 53). A moment earlier Nietzsche had quoted Jean Paul Richter as being right where the ancients were wrong when he said in the *Vorschule der Aesthetik* that "each language is a dictionary of faded metaphors (ein Wörterbuch erblasster Metaphern)" (52, 53). Though Nietzsche's early writings on rhetoric are an event, a decisive moment in the history of rhetoric, the ideas in them are by no means absolutely new. They have an immediate history in German

Romanticism and a much longer history going back to a counter tradition within Greek and Roman rhetoric. In the other direction, I have of course only begun to tell the story of Nietzsche and rhetoric. That story might culminate in an attempt to understand the reasons for the form of *Also Sprach Zarathustra* or for Nietzsche's dependence on the aphoristic fragment. That work must be deferred to another place.

A Counter-Mode of Composition

Nietzsche's early writings on rhetoric are a strong challenge to the authority of presuppositions about rhetoric within the long tradition of Western metaphysics. This tradition goes from Aristotle down to assumptions about English composition still of great force today. But Nietzsche's writing is also an example of the way this tradition cannot be successfully challenged in conceptual polemics. Through the anti-Aristotelian use of figure in the passages I have cited, through the use of fable in the opening paragraphs of "Über Wahrheit und Lüge,"[11] through the radical irony implicit in the inconsistencies of the course on rhetoric, Nietzsche sketches a counter-mode of composition that his later works more elaborately exemplify. It by no means goes without saying that everyone would wish to put in question the ideology underlying standard notions of correct writing. The great classicist Ulrich von Wilamowitz-Moellendorff,[12] Nietzsche's schoolfellow at the Schulpforte and his grand antagonist in the debate over *Der Gebürt der Trägodie*, might be taken as a representative defender of the Western tradition as it has been interpreted in later centuries. Much is at stake in a decision, such as Nietzsche took, to oppose that tradition. Moreover, some who want to challenge the ideology embodied in stylistic standards of clarity and coherence might not wish to follow just Nietzsche's alternative. Nevertheless, his work shows that a change in concepts about rhetoric and the intellectual tradition to which it belongs demands a change in style.

Nietzsche's early work, finally, also exemplifies the close tie between reading and writing for which I am arguing. Nietzsche's reading of ancient rhetoric and the best modern scholarship of his day on that rhetoric uncovered a contradiction within rhetoric and the commentary on it. His writing out of the lectures was a quietly ironic bringing into the open of that contradiction. "Über Wahrheit und Lüge," written just after the course, was an overt expression of Nietzsche's position and an exemplification of the style appropriate to it. In Nietzsche, reading and writing go together, as I have said they always do. My own essay in turn is an act of writing that is product of an act of reading, in this case a reading of Nietzsche. Though I have of course tried to be as clear, correct, and coherent as possible, to ward off beforehand the policing of the copyeditor, I too have found it necessary to use a somewhat oblique parable or fable to say what I have found myself saying. And who knows? There may even be some irony here and there in what I have said.

Notes

[1]See Althusser 127-86, especially pages 171-77.

[2]See Leo for a characteristically tendentious report. According to Leo, "The new multicultural ethic, shown clearly in doctrinal writings both inside and outside the school systems, is contemptuous of tolerance and 'information dominant' (i.e. neutral) teaching. The key words, 'positive teaching' and 'appreciating diversity,' mean that certain sets of ideas are about to be 'infused' as valuable, whether parents think so or not." But of course there is no such thing as neutral teaching, teaching that does not infuse certain sets of ideas. Why the furor? Quite a lot is at stake here. As Althusser says, "No class can hold State power over a long period without at the same time exercising its hegemony over and in the State Ideological Apparatuses" (146). Changes in grade school readers, not to speak of the many changes in the disciplines and programs in higher education, are signs that state power is shifting. Those in power are, not surprisingly, taking such steps as they can to keep that from happening. Their strength should not be underestimated. See, for example, Bennett.

[3]If on the one hand Jacques Derrida in the *JAC* interview defended from his own experience the rigorous discipline whereby French students learn to write correctly, his own practice stretches that standard of correctness to its limits and perhaps beyond (Olson). Following the normal rules of French composition would not teach you to write like Derrida. See, for example, what he says about a particularly exuberant passage of wordplay and syntax-twisting in "Fors": "Point de jeu, ici, sur les mots ou sur la syntaxe, pointe de contamination gratuite, seulement les contraintes de cette topique singuliére. Celle-ci produit la nécessité de ce langage avant d'être 'écrite en ses tournures bizarres, ses équivoques syntaxiques, ses dehors ressemblants" (21).

[4]For a bilingual version of the lectures on ancient rhetoric and an English translation of "On Truth and Lying," see Gilman et al. But readers should be aware that this edition must be used with circumspection. For a challenge to its accuracy and scholarship, see Bierl and Calder. For an annotated French version of Nietzsche's early writings on rhetoric, see Nietzsche "Rhetoric." For the German of "Über Wahrheit und Lüge," I have used the bilingual German and French edition: Nietzsche, *Das Philosophenbuch*. Page references are to these editions and are given in the text.

[5]See Bierl and Calder 364.

[6]For an account of Aristotelian epistemology, see a brilliant unpublished paper by Jonathan Cohen. Also see Lear.

[7]See Stingelin 346-49, and Meijers and Stingelin.

[8]See Derrida, "Mythologie" 247-324; de Man 239-43; Lacoue-Labarthe; Warminski; Miller 247-61. Lacoue-Labarthe's essay is a comprehensive discussion of Nietzsche's early writing on rhetoric.

[9]Another way to formulate this, as Steven Mailloux reminds me, would be to say that the initial distinction between literal and metaphorical language breaks down, leaving a single realm of language that is neither literal nor figurative. But that distinction underwrites the possibility of answering a question about what something *is*: "Was ist also Wahrheit?" In the disappearance of the distinction between literal and figurative language, the possibility of answering in literal language questions about what something is also vanishes. It is replaced by a potentially endless series of catachreses for an unknown x. Since that x remains forever unknown, it cannot ever be literally named. What is truth? Well, I cannot give you an answer to that in so many literal words. I can only answer in one or another catachresis. Truth is a mobile army. Truth is a worn coin.

[10]See Meijers and Stingelin 352-60.

[11]"Über Wahrheit und Lüge" begins as follows:

> In some remote corner of the universe that is poured out in countless flickering solar systems, there once was a star on which clever animals invented knowledge. That was the most arrogant and the most untruthful moment in "world history"—yet indeed only a moment. After nature had taken a few breaths, the star froze over and the clever animals had to die.

Someone could invent such a fable and still not have illustrated adequately how pitiful, how shadowy and fleeting, how purposeless and arbitrary the human intellect appears within nature. (246)

[12]For an excellent recent account of Wilamowitz-Moellendorff, see Calder.

Works Cited

Althusser, Louis. "Ideology and Ideological State Apparatuses (Notes towards an Investigation)." *Lenin and Philosophy and Other Essays*. Trans. Ben Brewster. New York: Monthly, 1972. 127-86.

Benjamin, Walter. *The Origin of German Tragic Drama*. Trans. John Osborne. London: NLB, 1977.

Bennett, William J. *The De-Valuing of America: The Fight for Our Culture and Our Children*. New York: Summit, 1992.

Bierl, Anton, and William M. Calder III. "Friedrich Nietzsche: 'Abriss der Geschichte der Beredsamkeit': A New Edition." *Nietzsche-Studien* 21 (1992): 363-89.

Calder, William M., III. "How Did Ulrich von Wilamowitz-Moellendorff Read a Text?" *The Classical Journal* 86 (1991): 344-52.

de Man, Paul. "Anthropomorphism and Trope in the Lyric." *The Rhetoric of Romanticism*. New York: Columbia UP, 1984. 239-63.

Derrida, Jacques. "Fors." Trans. Barbara Johnson. *Georgia Review* 31 (1977): 64-116.

———. "La mythologie blanche." *Marges de la Philosophie*. Paris: Minuit, 1972. 247-324.

Gilman, Sander L., et al., eds. and trans. *Friedrich Nietzsche on Rhetoric and Language*. New York: Oxford UP, 1989.

Lacoue-Labarthe, Phillipe. "Le détour," *Le Suject de la philosophie*. Paris: Flammarion, 1979.

Lear, Jonathan. *Aristotle: The Desire to Understand*. Cambridge: Cambridge UP, 1988.

Leo, John. "Heather Has a Message." *U.S. News & World Report* 17 Aug. 1992. 16.

Meijers, Anthonie, and Martin Stingelin. "Konkordanz zu den Wörtlichen Abschriften und Übernahmen von Beispielen und Zitaten aus Gustav Gerber: *Die Sprache als Kunst* (Bromberg 1871) in Nietzches Rhetorik-Vorlesung und in 'Ueber Wahrheit und Lüge im Aussermoralischen Sinne.'" *Nietzcsche-Studien* 17 (1988): 350-68.

Miller, J. Hillis. "The Disarticulation of the Self in Nietzsche." *Monist* 64 (1981): 247-61.

Nietzsche, Friedrich. *Das Philosophenbuch/Le Livre du philosophe*. Ed. and Trans. Angèle K. Marietti. Paris: Aubier-Flammarion, 1969.

———. "On Truth and Lying in an Extra-Moral Sense, 1983." Gilman, et al., 246-57.

———. "Description of Ancient Rhetoric, 1872-1873." Gilman et al., 3-206.

———. "Rhétorique et langage." Ed. and Trans. Phillippe Lacoue-Labarthe and Jean-Luc Nancy. *Poetique* 5 (1971): 99-142.

———. "Über Wahrheit und Lüge." *Das Philosophenbuch/Le Livre du philosophe*. Ed. and Trans. Angèle K. Marietti. Paris: Aubier-Flammarion, 1969.

Olson, Gary A. "Jacques Derrida on Rhetoric and Composition: A Conversation." *Journal of Advanced Composition* 10 (1990): 1-21.

Stevens, Wallace. "Description Without Place." *The Collected Poems of Wallace Stevens.* New York: Knopf, 1965. 339-46.

Stingelin, Martin. "Nietzches Wortspiel als Reflexion auf Poet(olog)ische Verfahren." *Nietzsche-Studien* 17 (1988): 336-49.

Warminski, Andrzej. "Towards a Fabulous Reading: Nietzsche's 'On Truth and Lie in an Extra-Moral Sense." *Graduate Faculty Philosophy Journal* 15 (1991): 93-120.

Externalism and the Production of Discourse

THOMAS KENT

Most current research in discourse production adheres to the Cartesian claim that a split exists between the human mind and the rest of the world. The primary evidence for this split comes from the common sense observation that each of us possesses a unique place in the world occupied by no one else: I have my mind; you have yours. According to this conception of our relation to the world, we have an "I"—or what we take to be an "I"—"in here" and reality existing somewhere "out there" waiting to be discovered. Connecting the "in here" and the "out there" is some sort of epistemological network that the "I" employs to know reality, a network sometimes called schemata, mental categories, modes of thought, signs, social norms, conventions, or just language. Richard Rorty describes the relationship among mind, mediating network, and reality this way: "We have a picture of the essential core of the self on one side of [a] network of beliefs and desires and reality on the other side. In this picture, the network is the product of an interaction between the two, alternately expressing the one and representing the other." (10). Donald Davidson calls the "network of beliefs and desires" that mediates between "the essential core of the self" and reality a *conceptual scheme*. Davidson explains that conceptual schemes are "ways of organizing experience; they are systems of categories that give form to the data of sensation; they are points of view from which individuals, cultures, or periods survey the passing scene" (*Inquiries* 183). For the Cartesian—someone who accepts the formulation of a subjective "in here" and an objective "out there" mediated by a discrete conceptual scheme—knowledge can be knowledge only of a conceptual scheme.

The Cartesian idea of a split between mind and world that I have crudely sketched here has come to be called "internalism." The internalist imagines that a conceptual scheme or internal realm of mental states—beliefs, desires, intentions, and so forth—exists anterior to an external realm of objects and events. In relation to meaning and language, the internalist thinks that we have ideas in our heads, a kind of private language, and then we find a public shared language to help us communicate these ideas. Because meaning and language are located within our conceptual schemes—within the wiring of our brains, or within the transcendental categories of our thought, or within our communal social conventions—human subjectivity becomes, for the internalist, the starting place for every investigation of meaning and language use.[1] Broadly speaking, I believe that internalism in one form or another controls our current thinking about the production of discourse, and I would like to suggest in the discussion to follow that we might now begin to disavow internalism in favor of a more useful way of talking about writing and about reading, too. First, however, I want to be clear about how I think internalism controls our current conceptions of discourse production.

Internalism in Current Composition Theory
Nowadays, we usually talk about discourse production by employing either an expressivist vocabulary, a cognitivist vocabulary, or a social-constructionist vocabulary (see Faigley; Berlin). We know, however, that these ways of talking about discourse production are not incommensurate; they may be mixed. For example, some cognitivists employ terms from the social-constructionist vocabulary, especially terms like "discourse community" and "paradigm," and both social constructionists and expressivists employ cognitivist terms like "protocol," "schema," "information processing," and "writing competence." So, I do not want to suggest that these vocabularies constitute autonomous and untranslatable languages, but I do want to suggest that, in general, these vocabularies incorporate quite different presuppositions and beliefs about the production of discourse and that employing one of these vocabularies usually means finding fault with another. For example, someone who employs an expressivist vocabulary, someone like Peter Elbow, will have a tough time swallowing the claims made by someone like Kenneth Bruffee who employs a social-constructionist vocabulary (see, for example, Elbow, "Closing My Eyes," 61-62).[2] Although clearly not incommensurate, these three different vocabularies nonetheless provide the means by which we can describe the different presuppositions that form the foundations for our most influential theories of discourse production. For the sake of our discussion here, I will not attempt to outline all of these presuppositions.[3] However, I do want to consider some of the more important assumptions that bind these seemingly disparate vocabularies to the internalist notion that a separation exists between a subjective "in here" and an objective "out there." This connection may be best revealed, I believe, by isolating the conceptual schemes embedded in these vocabularies, conceptual schemes that mediate between our internal mental states and the external world.

For the most part, expressivists claim that discourse production derives from innate categories that actually constitute the human mind. These categories go by different names; for example, Kinneavy, Cope, and Campbell call them "modes of discourse" (9) while Young, Becker, and Pike call them "repeatable units" (26).[4] Although different expressivists describe them in different ways, these innate mental categories perform fundamentally the same function in every expressivist theory of discourse production. For expressivists, innate mental categories function as a scheme either to represent reality or to frame reality. In the first view held by expressivists like Young, Becker, and Pike, mental categories constitute reality in the sense that reality, to be known at all, must show itself in one or another mental category. This formulation derives from Kantian idealism, and it argues that the world, in the sense of the thing-in-itself, cannot be known. We can only know the scheme—in the form of mental categories—that mediates between the subjective "I" and reality.

In the second view held by expressivists like Kinneavy, Cope, and Campbell, mental categories constitute frames (Kinneavy, Cope, and Campbell call them "windows on reality") through which we comprehend reality (9). Unlike the Kantianism of the first view, this second view makes a quasi-empirical claim: we observe that most people talk about the world by employing the same modes of discourse, so we assume that the modes must be generated by mental processes we all share. According to this line of thinking, our brains are wired in a way that allows us to get in touch with reality through the mediation of language. Although one view finds its home in Kantian idealism and the other in Cartesian empiricism, both views are very similar. The primary difference concerns only the nature of the conceptual scheme through which we come to know reality. According to the Kantian view, the scheme is innate mental categories which constitutes all that we may know of reality; according to the empirical view, the scheme is a mode of thought that allows us to know an objective reality that is independent of human consciousness. In both of these views, however, discourse production is reduced to getting in touch with one's internal subjectivity that is constituted by certain mental categories. In a sense, to write is to understand human subjectivity, for human subjectivity embodies all that we can know about the world. Stated differently, in order to say something about the world, we must accept the fact that a split exists between the subjective "in here" and the inscrutable "out there," and what mediates between this split are mental categories of one kind or another.

Closely related to expressivism, cognitivism—or "functionalism," as it is sometimes called—claims that the mind can be reduced to physical components or to psychological states that account for human action. For example, in the study of discourse production, cognitivists equate the activity of writing with mental activity, and they say things like "the process of writing is best understood as a set of distinctive thinking processes which writers orchestrate and organize during the act of composing" (Flower and Hayes 366). We discover the nature of these "distinctive thinking processes" through either the observation of human activity—the approach called qualitative research—or through the measurement of human activity by statistical means—the approach called quantitative research. Emulating what they imagine to be the activity of natural scientists, cognitivists construct from their observations or measurements a reductive model that explains the connection between mental states and human activity.[5] The connection between subjectivity, the "in here," and objectivity, the "out there," is always explained in terms of a cognitive theory—what goes on "in here"—and we get concepts like the category effect, top-down processing, the levels effect, activated semantic contexts, and schemas.[6] For cognitivists, an explanatory theory will always constitute a representation or a model of what the mind does in response to some sort of external stimuli.[7] As the functionalist philosopher C.I. Lewis puts it, "There are, in our cognitive experience, two elements: the immediate data, such as those of sense, which are presented or given to the mind, and a form, construction, or interpretation, which represents the activity of thought" (38). What cognitivist rhetoricians presuppose implicitly, Lewis states explicitly: a split exists between subjective experience, that which we can know through our theories of cognition, and objective reality, that which we can never know directly. Like expressivists, cognitivists define reality in terms of a state of mind. However, cognitivists do not claim that mental processes function the same as mental categories; unlike mental categories, mental processes do not constitute reality or shape reality. For cognitivists, descriptions of mental processes are representations of reality. These representations—I have been calling them "models"—make sense of the data emanating from "out there" that we can measure or observe, and like a CAT-scan or a mock-up of the nucleus of an atom, models supply snapshots of a reality existing outside our private subjectivity.

Unlike expressivists and cognitivists who talk about mental states, social constructionists talk about cultural norms. Social constructionists claim that subjectivity derives from conventionalized human behavior and not from innate mental categories or representations of mental processes. According to social constructionists, we manufacture our subjectivity through the social conventions we share with fellow human beings. We are who we are because of our position within a particular cultural domain or discourse community. People who inhabit different communities possess their own distinct vocabularies and their own reasons for behaving the way they do. In this account, subjectivity unfolds from the social norms that constitute everyday existence. The claim that subjectivity is socially constructed stems primarily from the influential work of Thomas Kuhn, although I do not think he now accepts most of the beliefs attributed to him regarding the social construction of knowledge. Kuhnian social construction is best represented by Stanley Fish and Kenneth Bruffee, rhetoricians who have done the most to promote Kuhnism in the areas of discourse production and discourse reception.[8] Both share the view that social norms shape our awareness of the world. For example, Bruffee argues that "to teach *King Lear* seems to involve creating contexts where students undergo a sort of cultural change. This change would be one in which they loosen ties to the knowledge communities they currently belong to and join another. These two communities would be seen as having quite different sets of values, mores, and goals, and above all quite different languages" (651). Bruffee contends that what we say about King Lear derives from the "knowledge community" to which we belong. Each community possesses its own conceptual scheme, its way of talking about the world, and everything we say or can say is relative to this conceptual scheme. In addition, different communities employ very different conceptual schemes, so when we move from community to community, we must learn "quite different languages." For the Kuhnian, then, different communities construct different and largely incommensurate languages, and these languages represent the world in entirely different ways. In this kind of epistemological system—like the expressivist and cognitivist systems—the objective world exists "out there" someplace, but we cannot get at it. For the social constructionist, we can only get at our communal conceptual schemes.

Although expressivists, cognitivists, and social constructionists differ in detail about the nature of discourse production, they nonetheless share the epistemological position that knowledge of the world and of other minds is relative to some sort of conceptual scheme, and, in turn, they presuppose that discourse production can be reduced to a process that represents, duplicates, or models these conceptual schemes. The internalism implicit in this epistemological position poses, however, two well-known and, I believe, insurmountable problems for expressivists, cognitivists, and social constructionists: the first concerns the problem of skepticism, and the second concerns the pubic nature of discourse production.

When we imagine that a separation exists between an inner subjective realm of meaning and thought, and an outer objective realm of objects and events, we obviously cannot explain how it is that we know anything at all about the world outside of our own subjectivity. In addition, we cannot explain how it is that we know the mind of another, since we only possess contact with our private minds or our internalized conceptual schemes. In the area of rhetoric, this problem shows itself when language is seen to organize or represent the world. For example, when expressivists and cognitivists claim that language mediates between the subject and the world, or when the social constructionist claims that language is relative to a discourse community, clearly a separation exists between an inner realm of mental states and an outer one of events and objects, a separation that creates doubt about the possibility of knowing with any certainty the world or the minds of others.

A related but more serious problem concerns the public nature of discourse. An account of discourse production or reception that presupposes an internalist view of language and meaning faces the difficulty of explaining how communication operates as a public phenomenon.[9] Without doubt, cognitivists have helped us understand the connections between discourse production and mental processes like brain physiology (Walker), modal perception (Kinneavy, Cope, and Campbell), thinking procedures (Flower and Hayes), logic (Young, Becker, Pike), and recall (Clark and Haviland); and social constructionists have helped us understand the value of empirical ethnographic studies (Brodkey), class and cultural analyses (Ritchie; Cooper and Holzman), and collaborative learning (Trimbur), just to cite a few examples where internalists have increased our awareness of the connections among discourse production, mental phenomena, and social conventions. However, none of these internalist models can tell us very much about the public nature of discourse or how it is that we can know the mind of another. I believe that this problem exists because internalism presupposes a Cartesian conception of mind that valorizes internal mental states to the detriment of communicative interaction, and, as I have suggested, this Cartesian valorization of mind leads directly to the construction of one epistemological system after another in an attempt to explain our linguistic ability in terms of a totalizing model. In addition, when internalists suppose that all we can ever know are the totalizing models that represent or correspond to reality, they can formulate no coherent response to the skeptic's complaint that we can never know with certainty anything at all.

An Alternative Vocabulary

Although internalism dominates current research in rhetoric, an alternative vocabulary is beginning to emerge that allows us to talk about the production of discourse without getting caught up in the old Cartesian dualisms and paradoxes. Referring to philosophy (although he just as easily could be referring to rhetoric) Davidson writes,

> It seems to me that the most promising and interesting change that is occurring in philosophy today is that these dualism are being questioned in new ways or are being radically reworked. There is a good chance they will be abandoned, at least in their present form. The change is just now becoming evident, and its consequences have barely been recognized, even by those who are bringing it about; and of course it is, and will be, strongly resisted by many. What we are about to see is the emergence of a radically revised view of the relation of mind and the world. ("Subjective" 163)

The "emergence of a radically revised view of the relation of mind and the world" predicted by Davidson is now upon us, and it has come to be called *externalism* in opposition to internalist Cartesian conceptions of mind and the world. Externalism defines itself within a philosophical tradition marked off roughly by Friedrich Nietzsche, John Dewey, Martin Heidegger, the later Wittgenstein, W.V. Quine, Rorty, and especially Jacques Derrida and Davidson. Broadly speaking, the externalist takes the position that no split exists between an inner and outer world and claims that our sense of an inner world actually derives from our rapport with other language users, people we interpret during the give and take of communicative interaction. Because language requires the existence of others, the public nature of language-in-use presupposes knowledge of other minds and of the world in which we operate. Although clear differences exist among externalists concerning the public nature of language and meaning, most externalists agree that the dualisms inherent in internalism cannot tell us much about how language enables us to understand others or how language enables us to get things done in the world. Among the language philosophers who have steadfastly advocated externalism and who have developed a clear response to Cartesianism, Davidson stands out.[10] His work represents a sustained attack on internalist conceptions of language and meaning, and I would like to suggest here some ramifications of his brand of externalism for a theory of discourse production.[11] I would like to consider first the general nature of Davidson's externalism by examining three key terms in the Davidsonian lexicon: the principle of charity, triangulation, and the passing theory.

In its most rudimentary form and as it is elaborated in Davidson's early essays, the principle of charity means that when we communicate, we have no choice but to minimize error and to maximize agreement concerning the meaning of another's utterances. As Davidson explains, "if we want to understand others, we must count them right in most matters" (*Inquiries* 197). The full impact of this seemingly self-evident claim may be appreciated only against the larger backdrop of meaning holism, a conception of meaning that directly attacks the internalist claim that meaning is a subjective and private matter.

When Hilary Putnam asserts that "meanings ain't in the head" (227), he means in part that we comprehend an utterance only through its holistic relation to other utterances; or, stated in a different way, we judge sentences to be true only because we can test them against other sentences that we already hold true. A sentence we believe to be true, therefore, does not correspond in some mysterious way to the world; rather, we hold sentences to be true because they cohere to other sentences we already believe to be true. From this externalist position, we no longer need to talk about language in terms of something that mediates between subjective mental states—thoughts, beliefs, intentions, or conceptual schemes—and a reality "out there," and, as Rorty explains, we no longer must assume that relations exist

> such as "fitting the world" or "being faithful to the true nature of the self" in which language might stand to nonlanguage. This assumption goes along with the assumption that "our language" . . . is somehow a unity, a third thing which stands in some determinate relation with two other unities—the self and reality. . . . Both assumptions enshrine the notion of language as medium. (13)

Davidson rejects these internalist assumptions, and in his principle of charity, he insists that language is not an internal matter by acknowledging the fact that in order to understand others we must know a great deal about what they already believe and hold true. Meaning holism emphasizes that something we call the world, or objective fact, or essential being does not make an utterance true; only other utterances make an utterance true.

The acceptance of meaning holism leads directly to what Davidson calls a "coherence theory of truth and knowledge."[12] Davidson writes,

> What distinguishes a coherence theory is simply the claim that nothing can count as a reason for holding a belief except another belief. Its partisan rejects as unintelligible the request for a ground or source of justification of another ilk. As Rorty has put it, "nothing counts as justification unless by reference to what we already accept, and there is no way to get outside our beliefs and our language so as to find some test other than coherence." About this I am . . . in agreement with Rorty. ("Coherence" 310)

A coherence theory rejects the claim that truth or knowledge represents reality or corresponds to something beyond the web of beliefs in which we are always situated. An assertion that we take to be true about the world makes sense only in relation to its ability to cohere to beliefs we already hold. Therefore, a coherence theory unites truth, knowledge, and meaning so that when we have one of these elements we also have the other two. Davidson explains that

> it is clear that speech requires a multitude of finely discriminated intentions and beliefs. A person who asserts that perseverance keeps honour bright must, for example, represent himself as believing that perseverance keeps honour bright, and he must intend to represent himself as believing it. On the other hand, it seems unlikely that we can intelligibly attribute attitudes as complex as these to a speaker unless we can translate his words into ours. (*Inquiries* 186)

According to Davidson, when we understand another's utterances—when "we can translate his words into ours"—we also understand the other's beliefs and intentions, and by accepting the fact that we cannot be completely wrong about the beliefs and intentions of others, we avoid the dualism of self and world as well as the kindred problem of universal skepticism. Of course, beliefs and intentions may change, but when they do, so must the meaning we attribute to the utterance that communicates these beliefs and intentions. Consequently, as Davidson points out, "Since knowledge of beliefs comes only with the ability to interpret words, the only possibility at the start is to assume general agreement on beliefs," and with this claim, we have come full circle back to the principle of charity ("Coherence" 196).

The principle of charity plainly constitutes more than the relatively commonplace dictum that we maximize agreement.[13] In an essay relating some of the connections between Davidson's philosophy and social science, Michael Root explains nicely the upshot of the principle of charity:

> Davidson's principle of charity does not recommend that in interpreting the thoughts of others we simply maximize agreement between ourselves and others. The principle is more subtle. It is primarily a norm that the interpreter employs in the initial stages of interpretation; it helps her to get a foot in the door. The principle counsels her to assume that a speaker's sentence is true when the speaker holds it true. If the interpreter assumes

that the sentence is an expression of what the speaker believes, this leads her to attribute beliefs to the speaker that agree with her own. (286)

Root refers here to the reception of discourse, the act of understanding another's utterance. However, the principle of charity works the same way when we produce discourse. When we produce discourse, we presuppose that an interpreter will assume that we intend him or her to hold our sentences true, and in a reciprocal manner, we will attribute beliefs to the interpreter that agree with our own. As Root points out, the principle of charity constitutes the opening move in all communicative interaction, and it asks us to think about communicative interaction as a public act and not as a subjective private act of the mind. When we regard communicative interaction as a public act, we can go along with Rorty who tells us that we no longer need to think of terms like meaning, language, belief, desire, intention, and truth

> as the name of a medium between self and reality but simply as a flag which signals the desirability of using a certain vocabulary when trying to cope with certain kinds of organisms. To say that a given organism—or, for that matter, a given machine—has a mind is just to say that, for some purposes, it will pay to think of it as having beliefs and desires. (15)

The kind of externalism promoted by Rorty and by Davidson in his principle of charity draws attention to the way we employ our vocabularies, and the way we employ our vocabularies cannot be separated from the way we interpret the meanings, languages, beliefs, desires, intentions (or the *minds*) of others. For Davidson, interpretation obviously holds center stage in his account of meaning and language, and interpretation depends on the communicative interaction he calls "triangulation."

Davidson argues that thoughts and mental states derive from the external world of communicative interaction and not from an internal realm of *a priori* mental processes, and he employs the term "triangulation" to describe the communicative interaction essential for thought and for our sense that we possess internal mental states. Because Davidson explains concisely what he means by triangulation, I will quote his explanation in full:

> Each of two people finds certain behavior of the other salient, and each finds the observed behavior of the other to be correlated with events and objects he finds salient in the world. This much can take place without developed thought, but it is the necessary basis for thought and for language learning. For until the triangle is completed connecting two creatures and each creature with common objects in the world there can be no answer to the question whether a creature, in discriminating between stimuli, is discriminating between stimuli at the sensory surfaces or somewhere further out, or further in. It takes two to triangulate. For each of us there are three sorts of knowledge corresponding to the three apices of the triangle: knowledge of our own minds, knowledge of other minds, and knowledge of the shared world. Contrary to traditional empiricism, the first of these is the least important, for if we have it we have the others, so the idea that knowledge could take it as a foundation is absurd. ("Measure" 7)

Davidson argues that knowledge of our own mind cannot be separated from knowledge of another's mind and knowledge of the world. Without the other, we can have no thoughts, no language, no cognizance of meaning, and no awareness that we possess something we call mental states. Public and external communicative interaction, through our ability to triangulate, forms the basis for internal mental states, and not the other way around. Internal cognitive processes, mental schemata, or conceptual schemes do not recreate an external world; instead, the external world creates our sense of an internal one.

From this Davidsonian perspective, solipsism—the skepticism inherent in internalism which results in our thinking that we create or help to create the external world—cannot be maintained. As Davidson points out,

> For if I am right, the kind of triangulation I have described, while not sufficient to establish that a creature has a concept of a particular object or kind of object, is necessary if there is to be any answer at all to the question what its concepts are concepts of. If we consider a single creature by itself, its responses, no matter how complex, cannot show that it is reacting to, or think about, events a certain distance away rather than, say, on its skin. The solipsist's world can be any size; which is to say, for the solipsist's point of view it has no size, it is not a world. ("Second Person" 7)

For our purposes, Davidson's point here concerns the skepticism inherent in internalist epistemologies: we can know our own minds but we can never be sure about the mind of another or about the nature of the world outside our minds. Externalists respond to this ersatz problem by reminding the skeptic that skepticism becomes a problem only when we posit a split between mind and world. Davidson argues correctly, I believe, that without an external world and other triangulating creatures in it, we could never say what internal concepts are concepts of. Clearly, when we communicate—when we employ language to get things done in the world—we always share concepts; if we did not share concepts, if we had no idea about the mind of another or about the world we share with others, communication would be impossible. Therefore, by asserting that mental states derive from our triangulation with an external world and with the utterances of others, Davidson's externalism avoids the skepticism innate in the claim that a split exists between our minds and the world.

For a theory of discourse production, the consequence of Davidson's conception of triangulation concerns the light it throws on the social and public nature of communicative interaction. With his insistence that we triangulate when we communicate, Davidson discloses another way to talk about discourse production. For example, when we think about writing as triangulation, we no longer need to talk about it as something we do primarily in our heads or in incommensurable discourse communities. From a Davidsonian perspective, writing becomes simply another species of communicative interaction that requires us to interpret continually and publicly the languages of others in an attempt to match our vocabularies with theirs. Triangulation directs us to think about the interpretations we give to the discourses of others, not the cognitive processes occurring inside our heads. As Davidson stresses, however, triangulation describes only the necessary but not wholly sufficient conditions for communicative interaction, so more than the act of triangulation is required to account for our ability to produce discourse. Davidson supplies this missing element with his notion of a passing theory.

Communicative interaction requires interpretation in the sense that we must come to a satisfactory understanding of another's utterances through the act of triangulation. When we triangulate, we always make what I have called "hermeneutic guesses" about the meaning of another's utterances. Davidson calls these guesses a "passing theory":

> I have distinguished what I have been calling the *prior theory* from what I shall henceforth call the *passing theory*. For the hearer, the prior theory expresses how he is prepared in advance to interpret an utterance of the speaker, while the passing theory is how he *does* interpret the utterance. For the speaker, the prior theory is what he *believes* the interpreter's prior theory to be, while his passing theory is the theory he intends the interpreter to use.... What must be shared for communication to succeed is the passing theory. For the passing theory is the one the interpreter actually uses to interpret an utterance, and it is the theory the speaker intends the interpreter to use.
>
> ("Derangement" 442)

For Davidson, communicative interaction requires on the spot interpretation that cannot be reduced to a schematic cognitive process or to any kind of epistemological system. As we communicate, we formulate passing theories—tenuous strategies for understanding the utterances of others—that cannot be formulated in advance of a communicative situation. Consequently, a passing theory should not be confused with something like linguistic competence, for no framework—something like a Chomskian grammar—established prior to communicative interaction can explain what happens during the act of communicative interaction. Davidson explains that "the passing theory cannot in general correspond to an interpreter's linguistic competence.... A passing theory is not a theory of what anyone (except perhaps a philosopher) would call an actual natural language. 'Mastery' of such a language would be useless, since knowing a passing theory is only knowing how to interpret a particular utterance on a particular occasion" ("Derangement" 442).

In his description of the passing theory, Davidson stresses the indeterminate nature of meaning and the thoroughly hermeneutic character of communicative interaction, and he champions a conception of language use which clearly rejects the internalist claim that communication consists in mastering a grammar, a set of behaviors, or a cognitive process.[14] Along with other strong externalists like Derrida, Lyotard, and Rorty, Davidson insists that no framework—no "learnable common core of consistent behavior, no shared grammar or rules, no portable interpreting machine set to grind out the meaning of an arbitrary utterance"—exists that will help us interpret the utterances of others ("Derangement" 445). Davidson tells us that, finally, linguistic ability coincides with our dexterity to converge "on a passing theory from time to time" ("Derangement" 445), and our dexterity, in turn, depends on our uncodifiable ability to "shift ground appropriately" (*Interpretation* 279). Because nothing exists to tell us how to shift ground appropriately, a passing theory, according to Davidson, "is derived by wit, luck, and wisdom," and no more chance exists "of regularizing, or teaching, this process than there is of regularizing or teaching the process of creating new theories to cope with new data in any field—for that is what this process involves" ("Derangement" 446).

Accepting the Davidsonian line of thinking about communicative interaction obviously requires us to relinquish many of our internalist presuppositions and intuitions about language. Davidson points out that when we take up externalism (or, at least, his brand of externalism) we abandon "not only the ordinary notion of language, but we have erased the boundary between knowing a language and knowing our way around in the world generally. For there are no rules for arriving at passing theories, no rules in any strict sense, as opposed to rough maxims and methodological generalities" ("Derangement" 446). As externalists, we give up the dream of totality held out by internalists who insist that discourse production and reception can be reduced to epistemological systems, cognitive processes, or paradigmatic social constructs. We are left with the awareness that, as Rorty explains, "If we ever succeed in communicating easily and happily, it will be because [your] guesses about what I am going to do next, including what noises I am going to make next, and my own expectations about what I shall do or say under certain circumstances, come more or less to coincide, and because the converse is also true" (14). Of course, externalists like Davidson and Rorty take the position that our guesses are always good enough and that the "rough maxims and methodological generalities" we employ to get things done in the world constitute all we need to know about the production of discourse. In the discipline of rhetoric, the ramifications of this kind of radical externalism have not been thoroughly traced out, and I cannot address here all of the myriad issues that should be discussed. However, I would like to take a stab at describing what I perceive to be one of the more important pedagogical ramifications of Davidsonian externalism for the discipline of rhetoric: the rejection of the dialectic method in the teaching of writing.

Beyond a Process-Oriented Vocabulary

If we take seriously Davidson's formulations of the principle of charity, triangulation, and the passing theory, we cannot escape the conclusion that in the area of discourse production no body of knowledge exists that can be taught. When we produce discourse, we engage in a kind of hermeneutic dance with other interpreters, and no grammar or theory of cognition can choreograph this dance in any meaningful way. On the other hand, the marks we make and the noises we utter may be choreographed, systematized, and taught, but these marks and noises should not be confused with communicative interaction. Machines, for example, can be programmed to generate words and sentences, but machines cannot write. Writing is communicative interaction, and until machines acquire the ability to get together socially and to construct cultural monuments—buildings, books, religions, political systems, and so forth—they can produce no public evidence of communicative interaction. From an externalist point of view, to say that machines cannot write is simply to say that writing is more than wiring and that no explanation of cognitive processes or brain function will explain the connection between language and human social life. Therefore, the systems formed by marks and noises can provide, at best, only very tenuous descriptions of the equipment (in the Heideggerian sense) employed by communicants.[15] Generating systematic marks and noises does not warrant communicative interaction.

If we accept the claim that writing is more than wiring and if we accept the admittedly more radical claim that writing cannot be reduced to a systemic process and then taught, our traditional views about the teaching of writing become exceedingly problematic. Traditional writing instruction employs what may be called the *dialectic method* modelled on the Platonic dialogues. The idea here is that students can be led to see the truth—or knowledge, facts, certainties, ideas, concepts, universals, timeless categories, systems of thought, or the like—through open-ended discussion that results in the discovery of new knowledge on the part of the students. Of course, behind this internalist conception of instruction lurks the claim that something exists "out there" (a body of knowledge or something similar to it) that students can learn and on which students may be tested and graded. When we stop talking about a body of knowledge or a set of well-defined skills that students should master, we obviously no longer possess anything to get at by employing the dialectic method. Clearly, however, we can employ the dialectic method to teach students a vocabulary that they may employ in order to talk about grammar, sentence construction, paragraph cohesion, modes of discourse, stylistic analysis, cognitive writing theory, ethnography, social construction theory, and so on, because every vocabulary can be reduced to a system and then taught. Learning a vocabulary, however, is not the same as *employing* a vocabulary. No process or system can explain, in any precise way, how we shift ground appropriately when we employ our vocabularies. Therefore, if we want to encourage students to think about writing as communicative interaction and not as a skill (like riding a bike) that can be mastered and internalized, I believe that we should become strong externalists and stop talking about writing in transcendental and internalist terms, and, consequently, stop employing a dialectic instructional methodology that presupposes essentialism and transcendence.

This shift from internalism to externalism would challenge us to drop our current process-oriented vocabulary, and begin talking about our concrete social and public uses of language. In fact, we are beginning already (albeit slowly) to talk differently about language, about the production and reception of discourse, and about rhetoric, too, although no one would deny that internalist vocabularies—in the forms of expressivism, cognitivism, and social construction—still dominate the discourse in our discipline. Such a shift toward an externalist vocabulary may not take a Davidsonian turn, and it may not resemble the brand of externalism that I have promoted here. However, I believe that the discipline is nonetheless moving steadfastly toward the rejection of a vocabulary that posits a split between the human subject and the world. With this move, we are now beginning to drop our efforts at reconciling ourselves with a world "out there," for as externalist philosophers like Nietzsche, Dewey, Heidegger, Wittgenstein, Quine, Foucault, Lyotard, Rorty, Derrida, and Davidson point out, we are always already reconciled.

Notes

[1]Historically, internalism, either of the Cartesian or the Platonist variety, has dominated the disciplines of rhetoric and literary criticism. In this century, internalism provides the foundation for practically all of the influential rhetorical and critical movements from Russian Formalism and Anglo-American New Criticism through Czech structuralism to more recent poststructuralist concerns.

[2]In his latest writings, Elbow maintains that his version of expressivist theory corresponds closely to social-constructionist thinking. For example, he writes,

> When people chant the doctrine, "all language is social, there is no such thing as private writing," they tend to mask or even deny this very concrete distinction between private and public writing. Of course language is a social construct and of course our private writing often responds to the discourse of others—but these obvious facts don't diminish the crucial pedagogical and political difference between helping people find occasions for private and safe reflection vs. not doing so. Helping them find those occasions tends to foster social interaction. ("Forward" 18)

If Elbow now endorses the social-constructionist claim that language is a social construct, his conversion represents, it seems to me, a radical departure from his earlier and very influential statements regarding the production of discourse. Take, for example, the following assertion in "The Truth About Meaning and Words" section of *Writing Without Teachers*:

> Meaning is like movies inside the head. I've got movies in my head. I want to put them inside yours. Only I can't do that because our heads are opaque. All I can do is try to be clever about sending you a sound track and hope I've done it in such a way as to make you construct the right movies in your head. (*Writing* 152)

Elbow goes on to say that this process of constructing the "right movies" is determined or at least guided by the speech community in which we live: "I can now give a clear picture of what I meant by speaking of the truth about the meaning of an utterance—the correct reading of a text: that interpretation is correct which the speech community builds into those words" (*Writing* 156). I gather from Elbow's formulation that some sort of shared mental framework exists which allows me to match my sound track with yours so that we finally "share" soundtracks. This idea sounds

Kantian to me, even if we grant that what is shared changes over time and from place to place. If Elbow now believes that language and, consequently, meaning is socially constructed, he cannot claim without serious contradiction that meaning is like movies inside the head. My understanding of Elbow's expressivist theory derives from what I take to be this Kantian position outlined in *Writing Without Teachers*.

[3]See Faigley for an excellent discussion of the general presuppositions inherent in expressivist, cognitivist, and social-constructionist vocabularies.

[4]On the surface, Young, Becker, and Pike's tagmemics would seem to share little in common with the expressivist theory of someone like Elbow. However, I believe that their conception of discourse production also posits the notion of innate mental categories that are shared by language users and that represent reality. For example, in *Rhetoric: Discovery and Change*, we are told:

> *People conceive of the world in terms of repeatable units.* In the continuously changing, dynamic flow of events, there are always recognizable, nameable, recurring "sames"—discrete units of experience. . . . Language provides a way of unitizing experience: a set of symbols that label recurring chunks of experience. . . . Language depends on our seeing certain experiences as constant or repeatable. And seeing the world as repeatable depends, in part at least, on language. (24-25)

These "repeatable units" constitute shared mental categories of perception that shape reality, so in order to express ourselves, we must employ these categories. Because I conceive of this approach to language as essentially Kantian, I include Young, Becker, and Pike (or at least their work in *Rhetoric: Discovery and Change*) as expressivist in nature.

[5]These cognitive models are always *reductive* in the sense that they explain a complex behavior like writing by reducing it to a set of easily understood principles.

[6]Cognitivists never claim that their theories about mental processes explain everything there is to know about discourse production; instead, they usually claim that their theories either (1) explain how the mind processes information so that writers will understand how to mold their discourse to help reader's process it, or (2) explain the writer's mental processes so that we know how to recognize and how to correct problems the writer might face during the composing act.

[7]Consider, for instance, the methodology employed by cognitivists in areas like schema theory and protocol theory. In these areas, cognitivists begin by observing or measuring behavior. From the data they gather from these techniques, they formulate conclusions such as, writers should make every effort "to activate schemata at high levels of the processing hierarchy" (Huckin 96), or writers "must find ways to create a reader-based structure of information in a text designed around its function" (Flower, Hayes, and Swarts).

[8]I stress the Kuhnian variety of social-constructionist theory because I believe it to be the most pervasive and influential version. Another important but secondary influence on social constructionist thought is the work of M.A.K. Halliday, whose social semiotic theory corresponds in some interesting fashions with Kuhn's.

[9]A significant part of Ludwig Wittgenstein's later philosophy constitutes an attack on internalist conceptions of language, especially the idea of a private language. For a good discussion of Wittgenstein's argument against the idea of a private language, see Kenny.

[10]For a comparison of externalist and internalist formulations of language and meaning, see Davidson, "Meaning, Truth and Evidence." For a further discussion of the connections between rhetoric and Davidson's philosophy of language, see Dasenbrock.

[11]In Davidson's analysis of communicative interaction, he takes speech to be the paradigmatic case of language use. Although Davidson clearly privileges spoken discourse (and I believe he is wrong to do so) his externalist description of communicative interaction still possesses significant consequence for written discourse.

[12]In an addendum to "A Coherence Theory of Truth and Knowledge," Davidson regrets "having called my view a 'coherence theory,'" for "my emphasis on coherence was misplaced; calling my view a 'theory' was a plain blunder" ("Afterthoughts" 135). By employing the terms "coherence" and "theory," Davidson fears, in part, that he may be seen to endorse a totalizing framework theory of truth, a view he clearly does not hold. For the purposes of the discussion here, however, I will continue to employ Davidson's original nomenclature to avoid confusion.

[13]The principle of charity should not be confused with intentional concepts like Grices's cooperative principle. The cooperative principle represents an element of an intentional mental state; a speaker intends to cooperate. The principle of charity, on the other hand, is the necessary precondition for all social communicative interaction. It is not an intentional feature of language or a manifestation of a mental state.

[14]Davidson's conception of the passing theory corresponds closely to Derrida's idea of iterability. Both stress the impossibility of reducing language to what Davidson calls a "framework theory" ("Derangement" 444).

[15]For a discussion of what Heidegger means by "equipment," see *Being and Time* 97.

Works Cited

Berlin, James A. "Contemporary Composition: The Major Pedagogical Theories." *College English* 44 (1982): 765-77.

Brodkey, Linda. "Writing Ethnographic Narratives." *Written Communication* 9 (1987): 25-50.

Bruffee, Kenneth A. "Social Construction, Language, and the Authority of Knowledge: A Bibliographical Essay." *College English* 48 (1986): 773-90.

Clark, H.H., and Susan H. Haviland. "Comprehension and the Given-New Contract." *Discourse Production and Comprehension*. Ed. Roy O. Freedle. Norwood, NJ: Ablex, 1977. 1-40.

Cooper, Marilyn M., and Michael Holzman. *Writing as Social Action*. Portsmouth, NH: Boynton, 1989.

Dasenbrock, Reed Way. "Do We Write the Text We Read?" *College English* 53 (1991): 7-18.

Davidson, Donald. *Inquiries into Truth and Interpretation*. Oxford: Clarendon, 1984.

——. "A Coherence Theory of Truth and Knowledge." *Truth and Interpretation: Perspectives on the Philosophy of Donald Davidson*. Ed. Ernest LePore. New York: Blackwell, 1986. 307-19.

——. "A Nice Derangement of Epitaphs." *Truth and Interpretation: Perspectives on the Philosophy of Donald Davidson*. Ed. Ernest LePore. New York: Blackwell, 1986. 433-46.

——. "The Myth of the Subjective." *Relativism: Interpretation and Confrontation*. Ed. Michael Krausz. Notre Dame, IN: Notre Dame UP, 1989. 159-72.

——. "Meaning, Truth, and Evidence." *Perspectives on Quine*. Ed. Robert B. Barrett and Roger F. Gibson. Oxford: Blackwell, 1990. 68-79.

——. "The Second Person." Unpublished essay, 1989.

——. "The Measure of the Mental." Unpublished essay, 1990.

——. "Afterthoughts, 1987." *Reading Rorty: Critical Responses to Philosophy and the Mirror of Nature (and Beyond)*. Ed. Alan R. Malachowski. Cambridge, MA: Blackwell, 1990. 134-37.

Derrida, Jacques. "Signature Event Context." *Glyph 1*. Ed. Samuel Weber and Henry Sussman. Baltimore: Johns Hopkins UP, 1977. 172-97.

Dewey, John. *Reconstruction in Philosophy*. Boston: Beacon, 1948.

Elbow, Peter. "Closing My Eyes As I Speak: An Argument for Ignoring Audience." *College English* 49 (1987): 50-69.

——. "Forward: About Academic Personal Expressive Writing." *Pre/Text* 11 (1990): 7-20.

——. *Writing Without Teachers*. New York: Oxford UP, 1973.

Faigley, Lester. "Competing Theories of Process: A Critique and a Proposal." *College English* 48 (1986): 527-42.

Fish, Stanley. *Is There A Text In This Class?: The Authority of Interpretive Communities.* Cambridge: Harvard UP, 1980.

Flower, Linda, and John R. Hayes. "A Cognitive Process Theory of Writing." *College Composition and Communication* 32 (1981): 365-87.

Flower, Linda, John R. Hayes, and Heidi Swarts. "Revising Functional Documents: The Scenario Principle." *New Essays in Technical and Scientific Communication: Research, Theory, Practice.* Ed. Paul V. Anderson, R. John Brockmann, and Carolyn R. Miller. Farmingdale NY: Baywood, 1983. 41-58.

Foucault, Michel. *The Archaeology of Knowledge.* Trans. A.M. Sheridan Smith. New York: Harper, 1972.

Grice, H.P. "Logic and Conversation." *Studies in Syntax, Vol III.* Ed. P. Cole and J.L. Morgan. New York: Seminar P, 1975. 253-65.

Halliday, M.A.K. *Language as Social Semiotic: The Social Interpretation of Language and Meaning.* Baltimore: University Park P, 1978.

Heidegger, Martin. *Being and Time.* Trans. John Macquarrie and Edward Robinson. New York: Harper, 1962.

Huckin, Thomas N. "A Cognitive Approach to Readability." *New Essays in Technical and Scientific Communication: Research, Theory, Practice.* Ed. Paul V. Anderson, R. John Brockmann, and Carolyn R. Miller. Farmingdale NY: Baywood, 1983. 90-108.

Kenny, Anthony. "Cartesian Privacy." *Wittgenstein: The Philosophical Investigations.* Ed. George Pitcher. New York: Anchor Books, 1966. 352-70.

Kent, Thomas. "Paralogic Hermeneutics and the Possibilities of Rhetoric." *Rhetoric Review* 8 (1989): 24-42.

Kinneavy, James, John Cope, and J.W. Campbell. *Writing—Basic Modes of Discourse.* Dubuque, IA: Kendall Hunt, 1976.

Kuhn, Thomas S. *The Structure of Scientific Revolutions.* Chicago: U of Chicago P, 1962.

Lewis, Clarence Irving. *Mind and the World Order.* New York: Dover, 1929.

Lyotard, Jean François. *The Postmodern Condition: A Report on Knowledge.* Trans. Geoff Bennington and Brian Massumi. Minneapolis: U of Minnesota P, 1984.

Nietzsche, Friedrich. *On the Genealogy of Morals.* Trans. Walter Kaufmann and R.J. Hollingdale. New York: Vintage, 1969.

Putnam, Hilary. "The Meaning of 'Meaning.'" *Mind, Language, and Reality: Philosophical Papers.* New York: Cambridge UP, 1975.

Quine. W.V. *From a Logical Point of View: Nine Logico-Philosophical Essays.* Cambridge: Harvard UP, 1961.

Ritchie, Joy S. "Confronting the 'Essential' Problem: Reconnecting Feminist Theory and Pedagogy." *Journal of Advanced Composition* 10 (1990): 249-73.

Root, Michael. "Davidson and Social Science." *Truth and Interpretation: Perspectives on the Philosophy of Donald Davidson.* Ed. Ernest LePore. New York: Blackwell, 1986. 272-304.

Rorty, Richard. *Contingency, Irony, and Solidarity.* New York: Cambridge UP, 1989.

Trimbur, John. "Collaborative Learning and Teaching Writing." *Perspectives on Research and Scholarship in Composition.* Ed. Ben W. McClelland and Timothy R. Donovan. New York: MLA, 1985. 87-109.

Walker, Jeffrey. "Of Brains and Rhetorics." *College English* 52 (1990): 301-22.

Wittgenstein, Ludwig. *Philosophical Investigations*. Trans. G.E.M. Anscombe. New York: Macmillan, 1953.

Young, Richard E., Alton L. Becker, and Kenneth L. Pike. *Rhetoric: Discovery and Change*. New York: Harcourt, 1970.

Interrupting the Conversation: The Constructionist Dialogue in Composition

JOSEPH PETRAGLIA

In "Current-Traditional Rhetoric: Paradigm and Practice," James Berlin and Robert Inkster make the important point that epistemological assumptions underlie every conception of rhetoric and composition. They suggest that we cannot demonstrate what it means "to persuade" or "to explain" without a tacit belief in what it means "to know." I believe they are also correct in acknowledging a general neglect of these assumptions on the part of those of us who teach writing: it is fairly easy for instructors of composition (indeed, most teachers) to buy into a dominant theory of knowledge unquestioningly.

Nevertheless, though awareness of the ways in which written and oral discourse contribute to what people believe they know (that is, how rhetoric may be epistemic) may seem marginalized in the contemporary writing classroom, it has been a central issue for philosophers and rhetoricians since Plato and Aristotle. From that classical period to the contemporary writings of Burke, Perelman, and Young, Becker, and Pike, the tradition of investigating rhetoric's role in producing rather than merely transmitting knowledge has remained intact. Though it is not surprising that composition studies should follow in the wake of rhetoric and begin investigating the knowledge-generating capacity of language, the writing field seems to have carved out for itself the distinction, and perhaps the burden, of being the first discipline to bring to the fore questions of how this theory of knowledge relates to classroom practice.

A problem has arisen in the field, however, in that most of the rhetoric-as-epistemic arguments have settled on a rather eclectic and politicized conception of the issue and its relevance to the teaching of writing. Composition theorists, working within what appears to me to be a closed dialogue, downplay or completely ignore a wealth of critical thought available in related disciplines—speech communications and social psychology in particular. My use of the term "dialogue" is intended both as a convenient shorthand for "a-community-of-writers-in-composition-who-have-introduced-and-continue-to-popularize-*rhetoric-as-epistemic*," and as a way to convey my sense of that community's insularity from the criticisms and controversies surrounding "social construction," the somewhat generic term for social knowledge-production that composition has adopted in arguing for rhetoric's epistemic powers. In this essay, I'd like to suggest some of the basic premises that seem to underlie composition's conception of social construction, and to critique those premises from the perspectives of theorists in related disciplines that are investigating the relationship of discourse to knowledge.

Rhetoric-as-Epistemic(s)

Briefly (and broadly), a social constructionist argues that knowledge is created, maintained, and altered through an individual's interaction with and within his or her "discourse community." Knowledge resides in consensus rather than in any transcendent or objective relationship between a knower and that which is to be known. The choice of social constructionism as the contemporary composition field's most high-profile conception of rhetoric-as-epistemic is not for lack of alternatives; Michael Leff's "In Search of Ariadne's Thread: A Review of the Recent Literature on Rhetorical Theory" offers a number of candidates. Leff classifies perspectives on the knowledge-generating potential of rhetoric into four major groupings.[1] The first acknowledges rhetoric's weakest claim to knowledge generation: its ability to create a place in an already accepted paradigm for a new particular (cf. Perelman and Olbrechts-Tyteca's notion basing arguments on the structure of reality). The second argues a stronger case for rhetoric's knowledge-making capability in noting its role in establishing consensus in order to create a social knowledge which complements personal knowledge (cf. Bitzer's conception of "public knowledge"). The third perspective views rhetoric as establishing the knowledge necessary to mediate the limitations of formal logic. The last notion of rhetoric-as-epistemic suggests that knowledge *is* rhetorical. It is this last view, argued forcefully in Robert L. Scott's seminal "On Viewing Rhetoric as Epistemic," that basically forms what the discipline of composition has come to term "social constructionism."

The term "social construction," however, is the rubric under which a number of theories of social knowledge are subsumed; almost as many variations of social construction exist as there are rhetoricians, philosophers, sociologists, and anthropologists to promote them. Different writers serve as the principal gurus behind particular versions of a social theory. Although Thomas Kuhn and Richard Rorty appear to be most often cited in composition scholarship, social-construction's modern form has been variously attributed to sociologists Karl Mannheim, G.H. Mead and Emile Durkheim, anthropologists Franz Boas and Clifford Geertz, linguists Benjamin Lee Whorf and Edward Sapir, literary critic Michel Foucault, and Karl Marx, to name but a few.

The Constructionist Dialogue in Composition

Though cohesive (if problematic) theories of social construction can be found in disciplines such as the sociologies of science and knowledge, philosophy of science, hermeneutics, and history, no one theory of social construction from any one discipline has been adopted by the field of composition *in toto*. For this reason, the variety of social constructions presented in this paper is actually the result of many social constructionisms«a phenomenon that merits its own lengthy investigation, but not one with which this paper is concerned.[2]

This paper's stipulative definition of the dialogue's conception of social construction is limited to the manner in which its best-known advocates in the field have presented it, especially as explicated in Kenneth Bruffee's 1986 article in *College English* entitled "Social Construction, Language and Knowledge: A Bibliographical Essay" and James Berlin's article in that same journal entitled "Rhetoric and Ideology in the Writing Class." Though I am arguing that the dialogue's "core" is reflected in these two works, both Bruffee and Berlin have applied a constructionist stance to a broad range of topics of interest to English studies. These two significant articles are inclusive of, but are by no means limited to, the following premises which I suggest form the basis of social construction in composition:

- Real entities ("reality") include knowledge, beliefs, truths, and selves.
- All reality is arrived at by consensus.
- Consensus, and thus knowledge, is "discovered" solely through public discourse (rhetoric).
- Reality changes as consensus/knowledge changes.

According to Bruffee, "A social constructionist position in any discipline assumes that entities we normally call reality, knowledge, thought, facts, texts, selves, and so on are constructs generated by communities of like-minded peers" (774). Without denying the existence of a physical reality, social constructionism is concerned solely with human perception of, and interaction with, that reality. To quote Bruffee again, "We generate knowledge by 'dealing with' our *beliefs* about the physical reality that shoves us around. Specifically, we generate knowledge by justifying those beliefs socially" (777). Thus, it is the social arena that produces what passes for knowledge, not "scientific inquiry" in any exclusively experimental sense. As linguistic interaction is necessary to establish and convey knowledge, rhetoric plays a central role in the discovery and solution of whatever problems a society believes it faces. Berlin's sketch of what he terms "social-epistemic" rhetoric summarizes the constructionist position as one which views reality as "located in a relationship that involves the dialectical interaction of the observer, the discourse community (social group) in which the observer is functioning, and the material conditions of existence" (488). The "observer," according to Berlin, "is always a creation of a particular and cultural moment" (489). Without explicitly *denying* the possibility of an individual's intellect existing apart from the communal public knowledge, social constructionists in English studies do not find a place for an individual who is not him or herself constructed by the environment.

For the teacher of composition, a social constructionist perspective has resulted in a focus on *discourse communities*—communities that share "values, objects of inquiry, research methodologies, evidential contexts, persuasion strategies and conventions, forms and formats, and conversational forms" in addition to conventions rooted in language (Reither 18). Much of the constructionist literature concentrates on the dynamics of such communities and the ways in which we as teachers can facilitate our students' entry into them (Bartholomae).[3] Consonant with Foucaultian and Freirean theories of knowledge as power, social constructionists in composition of all political persuasions have sought to promote access to knowledge-creating communities as a critical first step toward student empowerment. Compared to current-traditional and cognitive rhetorics which focus on the individual writer and how he or she can and/or should shape discourse to gain the audience's assent, one might say that constructionists focus on the ways in which the audience (that is, the community) shapes the discourse of its members.

An important theme in composition studies' dialogue is that a constructionist theory of knowledge heralds an overdue acknowledgment of a rheto-centric universe—a stance reminiscent of Kant's coronation of philosophy as "the queen of sciences" for its self-proclaimed ability to sit in judgment of the legitimacy of whatever knowledge sciences might produce. Bruffee has suggested that "it is possible to take the position that since knowledge is identical with language and other symbol systems, the problems presented by social constructionist thought are of a sort that humanists in general and English teachers in particular are especially well-equipped to cope with, if not solve" (778). The appreciation of rhetoric as a foundational discipline, critical for understanding any other academic enterprise, is thus a recurring theme in much constructionist literature, especially in English studies and rhetoric.

To speak of a constructionist dialogue is not to promote a conspiracy theory or to suggest that the political or pedagogical objectives of the dialogue's participants are identical or even similar. The theories of social construction held by Bruffee and Berlin do not overlap in many respects, particularly in terms of their sources.[4] Bruffee traces his ideas to Rorty and Vygotsky in order to provide a rationale for classroom collaboration; Berlin draws heavily on leftist literary theorists and Paulo Freire to advance the cause of "radical" pedagogy.[5] Instead, the term "dialogue" is meant to draw attention to the fundamental epistemic assumptions this conversation's participants appear to share as well as those they have commonly chosen to ignore. It is important to note as well that not all social constructionists in *rhetoric* are participants in *composition's* dialogue. Though writers such as Robert L. Scott and Barry Brummett are widely read in composition studies generally, they are not widely quoted by dialogists, nor do they in turn draw from the work of composition theorists to any great extent. The dialogue has no "card-carrying" members, of course, but one often associates social construction in composition with writers such as Berlin and Bruffee as well as Patricia Bizzell and David Bartholomae, as they are a few of the more frequent contributors.

In this paper, I make no pretense of critiquing any single dialogist, definitively characterizing any individual's full-blown conception of a theory of knowledge, trivializing any individual's contribution to our understanding of social construction, or taking a community of writers "to task." Rather, it is my belief that the constructionist dialogue (like *any* discourse among a fairly static group of participants), has a life of its own, especially from the perspective of people outside of the conversation. What I refer to as the "dialogue" is not the sum but a *subset*, a reduction, of its parts. It is this subset, these generalities, that have shaped the discussion of social construction in composition studies and which will be examined more closely. The remaining sections of this paper look at how each of the four constructionist premises listed above can serve as a focal point for critics seeking to resolve what they perceive as weak links in a social theory of knowledge.

An Issue of Ontology
Premise 1: *Real entities ("reality") include knowledge, beliefs, truths, and selves.*
In *The Strife of Systems*, Nicholas Rescher suggests that theories on any subject are comprised of premises which are independently plausible but inevitably inconsistent when taken together as a whole; theorists thus refine their disciplines by exploiting these inconsistencies. Premise 1 of social construction's definition presented here, however, demonstrates an instance in which a basic tenet of the theory has been criticized for being inconsistent within itself. Such a criticism comes from a viewpoint Richard Cherwitz and James Hikins call "perspectivist."

Cherwitz and Hikins note that the social constructionist claim that entities are created intersubjectively (through social interaction) requires an acceptance of the existence of objects (that is, the persons doing the "inter-subjectifying"). But this leads constructionists to the "inherently solipsistic" conclusion that "other persons must be regarded as the product of meaning too" and that "in the absence of any account establishing the objective existence of other subjects, intersubjectivity collapses altogether" (254). Similarly, Jeffery Bineham states, "An intersubjective position traditionally is assumed to result from the collision and consequent refinement of two subjective positions. The subjective mind thus becomes primary in importance" (54). Thus, the status of the knower to the known is indeterminate if one takes literally the premise "reality includes knowledge, beliefs, truths, and selves."

Another variation on the chicken-or-egg riddle this first premise poses is the related ontological issue of whether, temporally, one can posit theories of existence and knowledge simultaneously. Earl Croasmun and Cherwitz argue that "any human system of ontological beliefs presupposes a valid epistemology.... A general theory of what should be granted the status of knowledge precedes the consideration of any specific ontological statement. ... It makes no sense to suggest that we know something about the world unless we first determine what it means to 'know'" (8). Bineham too has suggested that the conflation of epistemic and ontological issues is one that will be central to future discussions of rhetoric-as-epistemic. Lack of a clear distinction between "reality" and "knowledge" is what many writers have discerned as social construction's most fundamental error.

The Need for Objective Reality
Premise 2: *All reality is arrived at by consensus.*
Criticism of premise 2 generally settles on the necessity of an objective reality or notion of transcendent "truth." At least three responses to this issue have surfaced in communications journals. Cherwitz and Hikins propose a perspectivist account of reality based on *relationality*. Cherwitz along with Croasmun offer a variation on the theme by resurrecting a notion of *objectivity* (as opposed to "objectivism"), and C. Jack Orr's suggestion that *critical rationalism* replace intersubjectivism offers a third articulation of the need for objective truth. A fourth argument relating to premise 2 does not make a case for objective truth, but instead goes further than the dialogists in the opposite direction: what can be called the hermeneutic perspective claims that not only reality, but *consensus itself*, is illusory.

The problem the first three positions find with a crude constructionist denial of objective reality is that it results in a relativist theory that ultimately must collapse under its own weight. As Orr makes clear, "Even if one insists ... that the world we know is a rhetorically constructed, interpreted world, we wish to recognize, exchange, criticize, and improve upon our interpretations. This enterprise is made intelligible through the presupposition of an independent reality, a common target, toward which our interpretations are intended" (268). H. Gene Blocker argues, "It is the concept of an objective reality that enables us to acknowledge the limitation of the human standpoint to completely reproduce the world in thought and deed. We recognize our constructions of reality as constructs by making reference to an objective reality which our constructs fail to capture!" (qtd. in Orr 267). In this way, the argument follows, the articulation of any position, including that of a constructionist, assumes an appeal to some objective reality or notion of truth. Of course, thoughtful constructionists do not deny that material reality "exists," but neither have they really engaged the issue of representation versus materialism as philosophers of science routinely must. The problems encountered by endorsing subjectivism, even if the "subjects" are entire communities, are as recurring as they are counter-intuitive, yet it is seemingly unavoidable given a premise as all-encompassing as this second one. Though constructionists (with the notable exception of Scott in rhetoric) assiduously avoid using the "r" word, basing reality solely on consensus does not rule out relativism; it merely pushes it to a higher plane.

Cherwitz and Hikins critique a less strident form of social construction which they label "mitigated subjectivity" that attempts to moderate somewhat both premises 1 and 2 to escape the intersubjective dilemma. Its proponents, notably many philosophers of science, set up a dichotomy in which some realities/entities (such as objects of the material world) are independent of a subject's perception of them, while others (such as values and beliefs) are constructed intersubjectively. Mitigated subjectivists do not escape the brand of solipsism any better than their unmitigating counterparts for, according to Cherwitz and Hikins, they "embrace the dualist [Cartesian] position in their separation of mental and physical entities, without commenting on the philosophical problems which such dualism engenders ... How does one account for the influence of one realm on the other? How is it that two so qualitatively distinct worlds coexist and interact?" (254).

Cherwitz and Hikins suggest that perspectivism offers a way out of this bind. Central to perspectivism is the concept of *relationality*, originally formulated by sociologist Karl Mannheim (see Berger and Luckmann), or the notion that "entities in the universe are what they are solely because of the relationships in which they stand to other entities" (Cherwitz and Hikins 252). This position allows that individuals' accounts of the world are going to vary as their relationships to other entities are unique. In terms of classical rhetoric, one might say it comes down to a question of *stasis*. Disagreement does not result from the existence of different realities, for there is only one reality. Rather, people appear to disagree only because they stand in different relationships to reality. Once *stasis* is agreed upon and the other's relationship is understood, conflict is resolved: "On this account, the apparently contradictory judgments are really not contradictory at all, *since they are judgments about different aspects of the same object*" (264).[6]

Croasmun and Cherwitz develop further the distinction Cherwitz and Hikins make between *objectivity* and *objectivism* in the formers' "Beyond Rhetorical Relativism." Here, "objectivity" is defined as a concept that "frames an ontological assumption about the objects of reality, including discourse," whereas "objectivism" "characterizes a specific epistemological methodology for gaining knowledge of that reality. To embrace 'objectivity' is not necessarily to accept the tenets of objectivism" (3). This seemingly self-evident distinction enables them to preclude the relativism constructionists themselves would prefer to avoid. One can maintain that reality is objective and at the same time hold that knowledge of reality is subjective.

A third critique of premise 2, closely related to perspectivism in its retention of objective reality, is that of the *critical rationalists*, represented by Karl Popper and C. Jack Orr. Because crude constructionism refuses to entertain the possibility of objective truth, "truth" for them is dismissed as another construct, another social myth humans have invented to assuage our fear of relativism. Nevertheless, the utility of a notion of objectivity is seen by critical rationalists as too important to be discarded. By holding the objective existence of reality as a constant, they say, we are able to *criticize*, a faculty that intersubjectivity denies us. Orr states that critical rationalism is unlike the intersubjectivity of social construction theory in that, "critical rationalism retains the concepts of objective reality and truth. Therefore, it becomes possible to relate knowledge and truth dialectically, that is, to question each consensually validated claim to truth in the name of truth which is beyond consensual validation" (273). Of course, frameworks for knowledge will differ from knower to knower, but if we can engage each other in critical debate by appealing to an objective reality about which some propositions must ultimately be true, then, critical rationalists maintain, we can "take a constructionistic social theory at least several steps beyond the perils of intersubjectivism." Popper's influence is clearly felt here, as critical rationalism privileges the rendering of theories *falsifiable*, or subject to disproof.

Finally, perhaps the most troublesome critique of this second premise has its roots within the dialogue itself, in what might be seen as the hermeneutic "stance." Part of the baggage the dialogue takes on when it aligns itself with intersubjectivist philosophers such as Rorty (and, to a lesser degree, literary theorists such as Foucault and Jacques Derrida) is a belief in the significance of the interpretive act and the assumption that knowledge is not only constructed, but inevitably *mis*constructed insofar as language is rooted in idiosyncratic and unsystematic interpretation even as it is communalized. A strong hermeneutic stance, one might think, would prove especially problematic for constructionist theorists of composition, as they have a tacit investment in the systematic nature of consensual knowledge (that is, they want knowledge to be predictable enough to be of use in achieving some pedagogical end) and yet are intellectually indebted to theorists such as Rorty and Derrida whose conceptions of social construction are anything but "user-friendly."[7]

Rorty is less insistent than many of his followers in composition on tying reality to consensus by admitting, and even privileging, the existence of knowledge that operates outside of consensus, which in *Philosophy and the Mirror of Nature* he has termed "abnormal," though he is unclear as to the where and how of its origins. For Rorty, the goal of philosophy is to "keep the conversation going rather than to find objective truth" (*Philosophy* 377). In Rorty's ideal system, the paradigm would be dialectically challenged and undermined, never allowed to wallow in stultifying, "normal" discourse.

It is at this point that the strain of juggling the concerns of social construction with those of education are most apparent. Perhaps in an effort to make Rorty's perspective more operational, social constructionists in composition talk about "the conversation" (by which Rorty invites abnormal discourses to engage normal discourse in perpetual "edification"), while at the same time suggesting a more normative, systematic approach to knowledge—that based on the consensus of the discourse community. This seems logical; if social constructivists are to direct the teaching of rhetoric and composition toward any end, they cannot have students running about discoursing abnormally. As a correlate, educators have to assume they have some more or less stable knowledge worth imparting to students, knowledge that can be assimilated and used until it is tested and perhaps abandoned.

Thomas Kent underscores the tension the hermeneutic stance causes for constructionist teachers of composition when he notes that Davidson's and Derrida's "analyses of discourse suggest that (a) both writing and reading require hermeneutic skills that refute codification, and, therefore (b) neither writing nor reading can be taught as a systematic process" (25). For this reason, social constructionists in composition seem to make strange bedfellows with less-constrained, edifying philosophers who do not face similar occupational hazards. Put another way (and not too glibly, I hope), the educable unit that educators deal with is the individual student: we do not teach bodies of consensus-builders; we can only teach their members. The dialogue's pervasive preoccupation with consensus, it might be argued, is at odds with the teacherly focus on individual interpretation and agency to which it also subscribes.

Distinguishing among Knowledges
Premise 3: *Consensus/knowledge is "discovered" solely through public discourse (rhetoric).*
A key, perhaps *the* key, argument in the dialogue's constructivist theory of knowledge rests upon the presumption that all reality is mediated through language. As I noted earlier, such a premise is central to discussions of rhetoric-as-epistemic and makes it easy to understand social construction's appeal to those of us whose job it is to teach language skills. Critiques of premise 3 can be leveled from at least two slightly different perspectives. Many writers in speech communications as well as the cognitive sciences maintain that emphasis on the discourse within the social environment as *the* generator of knowledge ignores the ways in which the human brain "produces" ideas and perceptions. Other critics fault premise 3 for ignoring the non-social aspects of the "self." Both groups, basically, are making the case for widening the term "knowledge" to include forms other than the social.

Cognitivists would be critical of constructionists such as Berlin for not taking into account the varying abilities and idiosyncrasies of individuals in constructing meaning. Berlin seems to suggest that drawing attention to differences in cognitive abilities is politically expedient and has as its result, if not aim, the perpetuation of corporate capitalism (483). However, cognitivists would say that such differences can and do exist independent of their political desirability. George Steiner has noted that there are "such subconscious, deliberately concealed, or declared associations so extensive and intricate that they probably equal the sum and uniqueness of our status as an individual person" (qtd. in Gregg 137). To cognitivists it may seem paradoxical that a constructionist holds the opinion, on the one hand, that any given event cannot have a single, objective meaning, while maintaining on the other, that individuals' processes of perception are identical or at least inconsequential. It is pointless, from a cognitivist perspective, to argue that qualitative (in terms of superiority) differences in cognitive abilities account for the variety of interpretations; equally capable people are still going to perceive things differently. These critics suggest, however, that it is likewise unreasonable to deny that individuals construct meaning based on private associations that may be withheld from public validation. Much of what I have already presented as the hermeneutic stance clearly ties into the positions of Steiner, Gregg, and others who argue for the primacy of individual cognition.

No contemporary cognitivist perspective that I am aware of supports an epistemology that could be labeled "positivist." Cognitivists generally concur that meaning is constructed both subjectively and socially and that there is a constant interaction between the environment of the mind and that of the outside world. There are psychological and physiological differences between individuals which suggest that neither associations nor knowledge can be constructed identically from subject to subject. Such features are crucial not only to personal knowledge but to social knowledge as well.

It is worthwhile, I think, to quote extensively from Richard Gregg's "Rhetoric and Knowing: The Search for Perspective." Drawing heavily on research in psycholinguistics, Gregg, a strong advocate of acknowledging the distinction between individual and social knowledge, claims that "on the one hand, individual neurological structures are prerequisites for the development of social meanings, and on the other, the development of systems of social meanings will have concurrent consequences both for the further development of the neurological structure and other systems of social meaning. There is constant interaction between individual systems of meanings and a system of socially shared meanings, with neither system effacing the other" (136). To cut away the individual dimension of meaning making and to try to create a purely "'social knowledge,' or 'public knowledge' or 'explicit knowledge' is to artificially render static the active processes of meaning" (142). Gregg says Steiner has noted that "meaning is full of associative matter constructed from personal experience and the subconscious, and that such associative contexts will vary from person to person" (137). It is our ability to form idiosyncratic associations and our attendant capacity to generate personal knowledge which define our individuality. On a slightly different note, Gregg alludes to research that is discovering the impact *affective states* and *motivation* have on cognition and meaning making (I'll discuss such research shortly). He concludes that "if personal meaning is an inherent part of human meaning, we ought to avoid distinctions which preclude rhetoric scholars from being able to consider it" (138). Thus, Gregg finds the constructionists' rigid separation of personal and social knowledge (and their neglect of the former) both artificial and unproductive.

Whereas Gregg has argued against the premise that knowledge can only be generated through public discourse by suggesting that knowledge is not always *public*, research presented by Linda Flower and John Hayes challenges the notion that knowledge is always in the form of *discourse*. Their "multiple representation thesis" suggests that ideas and their articulation fall somewhere on a continuum ranging from sensory perception to formal prose. In studying how writers represent knowledge to themselves, Flower and Hayes discovered that "different modes of representation can range from imagery, to metaphors and schemas, to abstract conceptual propositions, to prose" (129). Thus, "As writers compose, they create multiple internal and external representations of meaning. Some of these representations, such as an imagistic one, will be better at expressing certain kinds of meaning than prose would be, and some will be more difficult to translate into prose than others" (122). In other words, meaning, and therefore knowledge, may be represented and brought to bear on problem-solving in the writer's mind without the aid of linguistic articulation. Research in cognition has suggested that non-verbal representations may be stored as a *visual image or pattern* that mimics its material referent, a *perceptual experience*, such as might be useful in determining whether the red lifesavers are cherry- or strawberry-flavored, or as a *procedure* "in which perceptual cues play a large share in 'knowing' something (e.g. how to dance your way across a crowded floor)" (130). If constructivists concede that these abilities count as knowledge, it cannot follow that all knowledge is socially constructed.

A dispute between two constructionists, Thomas Farrell and Walter Carleton, proves instructive. Farrell, a "mitigated subjectivist" in Cherwitz and Hikins' parlance, distinguishes between social and "technical" (perceptual) knowledge. Carleton argues that Farrell is resurrecting a dualism that social construction has sought to eradicate, and presents an extended syllogism which he believes logically precludes Farrell's notion of personal knowledge. The first five premises of the syllogism argue convincingly that "selves" have a social "dimension," but the subsequent three premises suggest:

(6) The impossibility of being a wholly private self entails the impossibility of discovering or expressing wholly private knowledge.

(7) Yet there is knowledge.

(8) Therefore, the knowledge we have must be social knowledge. (325)

While the case that Farrell, Gregg, Flower and Hayes, and others make for the individual's potential to create knowledge is not undermined by the acceptance of social knowledge's existence, these scholars would suggest that Carleton's assertion—that as individuals are not wholly private beings, their knowledge is entirely social—fails to resolve the issues relating to the recognition of the role of individual cognition they have advanced.

Finally, research in social psychology is beginning to explore the relationship of affect to cognition and thus has created a whole new literature that undermines a conception of knowledge as entirely social. Although this scholarship is too extensive and varied to summarize adequately here, research on the ways in which emotion shapes knowing can be roughly categorized into three areas: emotion and perception, emotion and avoidance (both cognitive and behavioral), and emotion and memory. I will briefly touch on some key concepts in these areas that seem to have implications for a constructionist theory of knowledge.

The literature on emotion and perception is the least extensive but in some ways the most intriguing in that it focuses not on how individuals deal with or interpret information, but rather on the physical ability to acquire information itself. This research suggests that emotional arousal systems act to physiologically alter an individual's ability to use other sensory systems such as hearing and sight. Douglas Derryberry and Mary Klevjord Rothbart have called this phenomenon *perceptual defense*: "a tendency for stimuli of negative emotional tone to have relatively high recognition thresholds" (139). Psychologists have conducted a large number of experiments using very different designs to demonstrate that emotionally negative words, both written and spoken, more easily escape detection when placed subliminally in text than positive or neutrally toned words, suggesting that emotional (emogen) encoding prior to cognitive (logogen or imagen) encoding may circumvent the mind's cognitive perception processes. Thus, a sender's message is not only subject to personal interpretation, but to personal perception as well.

"Sensation-seeking and avoidance" is the term Marvin Zuckerman uses to describe the way affect motivates people to expose themselves, or avoid exposure, to information that enters cognition. Seeking or avoiding information is based on the "optimal level of arousal" theory proposed by Eysenck in 1967. Essentially, Eysenck, Zuckerman, and others have found that every individual has a level of emotional arousal at which he or she feels comfortable. When this "optimal" level is violated (that is, when the person feels over- or under-stimulated) cognition reacts accordingly by either seeking sensations to increase arousal to the optimal level, or avoiding sensation in order to reduce arousal to the optimal level. This affective-cognitive phenomenon has numerous implications, of course (see Pieters and Van Raaij), but for our purposes it suffices to note that every individual has his or her own level of arousal and thus seeks and avoids acquiring knowledge idiosyncratically, thus subverting the constructionist's tacit faith in discourse as the sole mediator of cognition.

The last area of research, emotion and memory, is the broadest and most complex literature in terms of the variety of claims and implications made by its researchers and theorists. Major contributors that composition and rhetoric theorists might find of most immediate interest include Gordon Bower, Margaret Clark, and Alice Isen and her coauthors. This area has witnessed tremendous growth over the last decade and continues to attract the attention of scholars throughout the field of psychology. A central theme in this literature is that of emotionally "toned" memory. As one might guess, the basic idea is that knowledge of words, situations, images, and so on may be encoded in long-term memory not only semantically, conceptually, and visually, but also emotionally. In other words, "cats" may be encoded in memory not only through the oral cue /kæts/ and other cognitive associations, but also in terms of one's emotional disposition toward cats. The memory of cats may then be retrieved through similarly emotionally-toned concepts; for instance, if one suffers from many phobias, being in a small, windowless room may invoke the thought of cats as the sensation of fear relates one's claustrophobia to one's aelurophobia. Though the *terms* that are being affectively linked (in this case "cats" and "enclosure") may ultimately be socially defined constructs, the link itself is not created through linguistic association. Clark's recent article "Moods and Social Judgments" demonstrates how such an emotional network may play a role in making simple judgments, but clearly such research has implications for more complex decision-making and knowledge-building.

The current research into affect is raising some exciting questions. Most fundamentally, it asks "what counts as knowledge?" If affect is not a discrete counterpart of cognition (as is commonly assumed) but actually *shapes* cognition by directing our attention to information and stimulating memory, what implications does this have for a conception of knowledge rooted in social discourse? It would seem to suggest that extra-linguistic phenomena play an enormous role in our mental lives. Though the realm of affect is by no means exempt from social construction in many respects, it certainly becomes more difficult to maintain an exclusively language-based theory of constructionism when affect is understood as critical to cognition.[8]

Questioning the Dynamics of Change
Premise 4: *Reality changes as consensus/knowledge changes.*
Central to social construction is the premise that reality changes as knowledge changes. Kuhn's phrase "paradigm shift" attempts to account for this change in the realm of science to an extent. As new observations and inexplicable phenomena challenge the existing paradigm, the paradigm must evolve so as to maintain the coherency and cohesiveness of the community. When the strain of the challenges becomes too great, however, the old

paradigm crumbles, giving way to a new paradigm capable of commanding the community's allegiance. Though constructionism thus grants that consensus is subject to change, critics of this fourth premise suggest that a fairly loose intersubjective theory of knowledge, such as the one constructionists in composition promote, does not explain how *inter-communal* knowledges negotiate new consensuses. It makes sense that an outsider's opinion, either that of an individual or of some other extra-consensual entity, must serve as a catalyst for change; yet social constructionists do not explain how a minority's knowledge can exist in the face of consensus, much less alter that knowledge. From where do individuals derive unconventional ideas, and how can the expression of this "abnormal" discourse be tolerated?

Greg Myers raises a similar question when he points out that Bruffee fails to explain how knowledges evolve, differentiate, and come together again as consensus. He notes that "bodies of knowledge cannot be resolved into a consensus without one side losing something" (167). Though this conclusion may seem self-evident, the dynamics of consensus are neither specified nor alluded to in the dialogue which has generally played up the positive aspects of consensus-building. Like Kuhn, composition's constructionists are often content to confirm that inter-communal consensus is subject to change but do little either to show *how* competing communities arrive at all-important consensus or to acknowledge that consensus-building may not always be a progressive, "liberatory" process, that it could involve coercion instead.

Donald Cushman and Lawrence Prelli's "action theory perspective" takes the Wittgensteinian premise that "for an idea to count as knowledge, rules must be provided which allow agents embracing different ideological systems to share the same thoughts" and concludes that "knowledge, therefore, consists of those observations and ideas which remain stable under transformation" (275). At first glance, this definition of knowledge seems to preclude social construction altogether, but Cushman and Prelli suggest that it is by virtue of rhetorical action that understanding and rational consensus between ideologies is possible, again making consensus the focal point of knowledge, but providing at least a theory of how communities interact. Although the action theory perspective presumes a much less structured, theoretically "clean" conception of knowledge and of community than social constructionists do, their article (which is not a criticism of social construction *per se*) goes some way toward raising questions that a coherent theory of constructionism must address.

Conclusion: Resuming the Conversation

The purpose of this paper has been to look at social constructionism from the perspective of those that have found it lacking rather than from the perspective of its champions; naturally the resultant picture of constructionism is unfairly skewed to some extent. Also, I've purposely streamlined the constructionist argument so that it may be used as a springboard for exploring the scholarship of other fields. Even so, many of the questions these other perspectives raise seem important to composition but remain inadequately or inaccurately represented by those composition theorists who have taken the lead in importing the constructionist conversation to our own discipline. This is especially disturbing as the issues raised in this paper "against" social construction are hardly new; most if not all of the points made by communications theorists and psychologists have been fairly common currency in rhetoric for quite some time.

The question is not whether the field of composition can gain anything from a constructionist perspective; clearly it can and has. In a sense, the constructionist dialogue in composition is a welcome reaction, a counterbalance, to a field that has for too long accentuated the role of the individual writer and ignored the social forces that shape the writer's perception of reality. Current-traditional rhetoric enforced a long period of neglect of traditional social considerations such as audience and *kairos*, and subsequent rhetorics (including those emphasizing cognition) which tacitly acknowledge that the writer is only part of a broader social matrix, have been slow in examining the implications of this. A by-product of this reaction, however, seems to be that social construction has often been construed in such a way as to give further impetus to a political agenda, common in contemporary English departments, that centers on issues of social justice and empowerment even though there is little in constructionist theory itself that suggests a moral or political stance. Still, though the relationship of their social aims to a theory of knowledge might give one pause, constructionists in English have nonetheless succeeded in pushing concern for the social constraints imposed on the writer to the forefront of many theoretical debates—not a bad thing.

Social construction and its advocates in the field of composition have provided valuable insights into rhetoric's relation to knowledge. They undoubtedly will continue to raise critical questions about what we are doing in the composition classroom and in our research, and they have suggested many new areas of inquiry in interpretation theory, especially those having to do with discourse communities. What should be of concern to everyone, both inside and outside the dialogue, however, is that if the conversation sidesteps the difficulties it engenders in the belief that political or educational agendas are thereby furthered, it will become less responsive to other voices, ultimately to the detriment of those of us in rhetoric and composition who look to our journals for fresh ideas and critiques. In other words, the problem I find with the constructionist dialogue is not that its perspective is incomplete; *that* criticism can be easily and accurately leveled at any position. Rather, it is the threat of insularity of which we must be mindful. Insularity is bred, perhaps, whenever a theory becomes so closely identified as a vehicle for social, political, or pedagogical values that a call for a review or for a reframing of the theory becomes associated (unnecessarily) with a repudiation of those values. Primarily for this reason, I would argue, critical thinking about social construction in composition is in danger of falling victim to the aura of political-correctness often associated with it.

In an article on hermeneutics, Rorty speaks of a "preoccupation with 'radicalizing' the terms in which . . . problems are described." He goes on to say of hermeneutics what I believe can be applied with equal acuity to the constructionist conversation hermeneutics has helped to generate in English departments: "To the extent that 'hermeneutics' becomes the name of a movement which tells students 'These concepts are now old-fashioned; use these new ones—the recently discovered *right* ones—instead,' that movement betrays its own origins . . . it will eventually become as sterile as the tradition of positivistic scientism has become" ("Hermeneutics" 14). Conversing with its critics can spare the constructionist dialogue that fate.[9]

Notes

[1]Jeffery Bineham similarly divides discussions of rhetoric-as-epistemic into four basic positions, each centered on either the "Objectivist Thesis," the "Critical Rationalist" position, the "Social Knowledge Thesis," or the "Consensus Theory." He argues that the four positions overlap in many ways, notably in their stance towards the "Cartesian" dichotomy pitting a Platonic conception of truth against unbridled relativism. Using Bineham's system of classification, I would place composition's dialogists in the Consensus Theorist camp along with Robert Scott, Barry Brummett, and Walter Carleton. Thus, Bineham's critique of the Consensus Theory from the perspective of the first three positions raises many of the same issues I am exploring here.

[2]Kenneth Gergen's widely cited article "The Social Constructionist Movement in Modern Psychology" offers an interesting account of the interdisciplinary roots of social constructionism. Although, as the title suggests, Gergen is primarily concerned with how social psychology can be situated in a constructionist framework, the article provides ample references to philosophy and rhetoric. Of particular interest to readers of the present paper might be Gergen's brief critique of social construction's assumptions on pages 271-73.

[3]The notion of "community" in composition studies has been reviewed by Joseph Harris. One of Harris' central arguments is that "one does not need consensus to have community" (20). The idea that communities are (to use his word) "organic" and rooted in the consensus of their members is commonplace in the constructionist dialogue, though Harris notes that "social theorists" in composition have begun to moderate their position on this issue. Nevertheless, I would argue that the characterization of communities as monolithic is so endemic to the dialogue (given its social and pedagogical commitments), that it is one that will continue to plague constructionists in composition whose emphasis remains on *inter*-communal conflict.

[4]Kenneth Bruffee has complained that his notion of social construction has been mistakenly termed "a theory," preferring, instead, that it be understood as "a way of talking, a language, a vernacular" ("Response" 145). Presumably, then, he might argue that to critique constructionism is to miss the point. However, for most purposes (including that of this paper), I think that it is reasonable to present social construction as a theory, especially since it has been used to critique the theories of others and is sufficiently systematic and complete (especially in its compositionist incarnation) to bear critique of its own.

[5]For a more detailed account of the sources of social constructionism and the various strains of antifoundationalism in composition studies, see Stanley Fish's chapter on composition in *Doing What Comes Naturally*. See also Patricia Bizzell's lengthier discussion and critique of both foundationalism and antifoundationism in rhetoric.

[6]Rescher has termed the perspectivist position "syncreticism" (belief that every theory is true to some extent) in opposition to "skepticism," the position that doubts that anything can be true. The syncretic/skeptic dichotomy is one on which he elaborates extensively in his book and is, I think, an interesting alternative to the Cartesian dichotomy (Bineham) or the exogenic/ endogenic dichotomy (Gergen) as a way of understanding the underlying tensions that spawn variations of social constructionism.

[7]In interviews with the *Journal of Advanced Composition* conducted by Gary Olson, both Rorty and Derrida make clear that writing teachers adopt the strong hermeneutic program at their own peril. As Rorty puts it, "Higher education should aim at fixing it so the students can see that the normal discourse in which they have been trained up to adolescence . . . is itself a historical contingency surrounded by other historical contingencies. But having done that, whether they remain happily embedded in the normal discourse of their society or not is something teachers can't predict or control" (Rorty, "Social Construction" 8). Addressing this issue further, Thomas Kent's notion of "paralogical" rhetoric is an interesting attempt at reconciling interpretation with the exigencies of the classroom.

[8]Rom Harré's *The Social Construction of Emotion* and Carol Stearns and Peter Stearns' *Emotion and Social Change* are two good sources for the constructionist perspective on affect. Chapters in both works demonstrate how language and social norms play a major role in how individuals understand their feelings. Although a continuing debate surrounds the issue of whether affect is post-cognitive (that is, exists only after it is assessed) or pre-cognitive (exists as an arousal that leads to low-level preferences of some sort *prior* to appraisal), both sides in the argument maintain that a feeling's eventual appraisal is subject to social forces and then re-enters the cognitive process as a socially constructed "artifact" of experience.

[9]I wish to thank Richard E. Young and Stuart Greene for their generous help and encouragement throughout the writing of this paper, as well as Gary Olson and Jasper Neel for their thoughtful and useful criticism of an earlier draft.

Works Cited

Bartholomae, David. "Inventing the University." *When a Writer Can't Write*. Ed. Mike Rose. New York: Guilford, 1985. 134-65.

Berger, Peter L., and Thomas Luckmann. *The Social Construction of Reality*. New York: Doubleday, 1966.

Berlin, James A. "Rhetoric and Ideology in the Writing Class." *College English* 50 (1988): 477-94.

Berlin, James A., and Robert P. Inkster. "Current-Traditional Rhetoric: Paradigm and Practice." *Freshman English News* 8 (1980): 1-14.

Bineham, Jeffery L. "The Cartesian Anxiety in Epistemic Rhetoric: An Assessment of the Literature." *Philosophy and Rhetoric* 22 (1990): 43-62.

Bitzer, Lloyd. "Rhetoric and Public Knowledge in Rhetoric." *Philosophy and Literature*. Ed. D. Burks. West Lafayette IN: Purdue UP, 1978.

Bizzell, Patricia. "Foundationalism and Anti-Foundationalism in Composition Studies." *Pre/ Text* 7 (1986): 37-56.

Bower, Gordon H. "Mood and Memory." *American Psychologist* 36 (1981): 129-48.

Bruffee, Kenneth A. "Social Construction, Language, and the Authority of Knowledge: A Bibliographical Essay." *College English* 48 (1986): 773-87.

——. "Response to the *JAC* Interview with Richard Rorty." *Journal of Advanced Composition* 10 (1990): 145-46.

Carleton, Walter L. "What Is Rhetorical Knowledge? A Response to Farrell—and More." *Quarterly Journal of Speech* 64 (1978): 313-28.

Cherwitz, Richard A., and James W. Hikins, "Rhetorical Perspectivism." *Quarterly Journal of Speech* 69 (1983): 249-66.

Clark, Margaret Sydnor. "A Role for Arousal in the Link between Feeling States, Judgments, and Behavior." *Affect and Cognition* Ed. Margaret Sydnor Clark and Susan T. Fiske. Hillsdale, NJ: Erlbaum, 1982. 263-89.

—. "Mood and Social Judgments." *The Handbook of Psychophysiology.* Ed. Wagner and Manstead. Chichester, UK: Wiley, 1989.

Croasmun, Earl, and Richard A. Cherwitz. "Beyond Rhetorical Relativism." *Quarterly Journal of Speech* 68 (1982): 1-16.

Cushman, Donald P., and Lawrence J. Prelli. "Rhetoric and Epistemology from an Action Theory Perspective." *Central States Speech Journal* 32 (1981): 273-78.

Derrida, Jacques. "Jacques Derrida on Rhetoric and Composition: A Conversation." By Gary A. Olson. *Journal of Advanced Composition* 10 (1990): 1-21.

Derryberry, Douglas, and Mary Klevjord Rothbart. "Emotion, Attention, and Temperament." *Emotions, Cognition, and Behavior.* Ed. Carroll E. Izard, et al. Cambridge: Cambridge UP, 1984.

Eysenck, H.J. *The Biological Basis of Personality.* Springfield, IL: Thomas, 1967.

Farrell, Thomas B. "Knowledge, Consensus, and Rhetorical Theory." *Quarterly Journal of Speech* 62 (1976): 1-14.

—. "Social Knowledge II." *Quarterly Journal of Speech* 64 (1978): 329-34.

Fish, Stanley E. *Doing What Comes Naturally: Change, Rhetoric, and the Practice of Theory in Literary and Legal Studies.* Durham: Duke UP, 1989.

Flower, Linda, and John R. Hayes. "Images, Plans, and Prose." *Written Communication* 1 (1981): 120-60.

Gergen, Kenneth J. "The Social Constructionist Movement in Modern Psychology." *American Psychologist* 40 (1985): 266-75.

Gregg, Richard B. "Rhetoric and Knowing: The Search for Perspective." *Central States Speech Journal* 32 (1981): 133-44.

Harré, Rom, ed. *The Social Construction of Emotions.* Oxford: Blackwell, 1986.

Harris, Joseph. "The Idea of Community in the Study of Writing." *College Composition and Communication* 40 (1989): 11-22.

Isen, Alice M., et al. "Affect, Accessibility of Material in Memory, and Behavior: A Cognitive Loop." *Journal of Personality and Social Psychology* 36 (1978): 1-12.

Kent, Thomas. "Paralogic Hermeneutics and the Possibilities of Rhetoric." *Rhetoric Review* 8 (1989): 24-42.

—. "Beyond System: The Rhetoric of Paralogy." *College English* 51 (1989): 492-507.

Kuhn, Thomas S. *The Structure of Scientific Revolutions.* Chicago: U of Chicago P, 1962.

Leff, Michael. "In Search of Ariadne's Thread: A Review of the Recent Literature on Rhetorical Theory." *Central States Speech Journal* 29 (1978): 73-91.

Myers, Greg. "Reality, Consensus, and Reform in the Rhetoric of Composition Teaching." *College English* 48 (1986): 154-71.

Orr, C.J. "How shall we say: 'Reality is Socially Constructed Through Communication'?" *Central States Speech Journal* 29 (1978): 263-74.

Perelman, Chaim, and Lucia Olbrechts-Tyteca. *The New Rhetoric: A Treatise on Argumentation.* Notre Dame: U of Notre Dame P, 1969.

Pieters, G.M., and W.F. Van Raaij. "Functions and Management of Affect: Applications to Economic Behavior." *Journal of Economic Psychology* 9 (1988): 251-82.

Reither, James A. "Academic Discourse Communities, Invention, and Learning to Write." ERIC, 1986. ED 270 815.

Rescher, Nicholas. *The Strife of Systems.* Pittsburgh: U of Pittsburgh P, 1985.

Rorty, Richard M. "Hermeneutics, General Studies, and Teaching." *Synergos* 2 (1982): 1-15.

——. *Philosophy and the Mirror of Nature.* Princeton: Princeton UP, 1979.

——. "Social Construction and Composition Theory: A Conversation with Richard Rorty." By Gary A. Olson. *Journal of Advanced Composition* 9 (1989): 1-9.

Scott, Robert L. "On Viewing Rhetoric as Epistemic." *Central States Speech Journal* 18 (1967): 9-16.

Sterns, Carol Z., and Peter N. Sterns. *Emotion and Social Change: Toward a New Psychohistory.* New York: Holmes, 1988.

Zuckerman, Marvin. *Sensation-seeking: Beyond the Optimal Level of Arousal.* Hillsdale, NJ: Erlbaum, 1979.

Defining Rhetoric–and Us:
A Meditation on Burke's Definitions

Richard M. Coe

As others have before, Paul Hunter chided us at the 1989 convention of the Conference on College Composition and Communication for honoring North America's greatest rhetorician, Kenneth Burke, more than we use him. Though many composition textbooks make an honorific bow in Burke's direction by including a simplified version of his Pentad in their treatment of heuristics, few composition texts or courses are informed by Burke's insights into language and rhetoric. Especially in advanced composition, a Burkean approach has much to offer.

Though Burke gets upset every time I suggest this, many composition instructors have difficulty reading his work. If we understood Burke better, we could better devise approaches to composition that embodied his insights. In hope of engendering such understanding, I will here meditate on a text Burke presented at the 1989 CCCC, about a half an hour after hearing Hunter's complaint.

Burke begins (and ends) with a definition of *humanity*. Not of *rhetoric*, *language*, *literature*, *culture*, or *discourse*, but of *humanness*. The first of the "five summarizing essays" in *Language as Symbolic Action* is "Definition of Man"—and it was a revised, expanded version of this definition that Burke presented at CCCC. Any comments on matters cultural, Burke asserts, must embody assumptions about the nature of the human beings who compose culture—and who compose themselves socially, rhetorically, in terms cultural (*Language* 2). One key to understanding Burke is understanding his conception of what makes us human.

If our purpose were merely to distinguish human beings from other beings, we might define people as animals that laugh, or as animals that use tools to make tools, or as erect, bipedal mammals with opposable thumbs, or in a variety of other ways. Though all these definitions can be derived from Burke's, he chooses none of them. Instead, he defines us like this:

Being bodies that learn language
thereby becoming wordlings
humans are

> *the symbol-making, symbol-using, symbol-misusing animal*
> *inventor of the negative*
> *separated from our natural condition*
> *by instruments of our own making*
> *goaded by the spirit of hierarchy*
> *acquiring foreknowledge of death*
> *and rotten with perfection*

From the fullness of this definition, we could, in principle, derive the totality of Burke's insights into the species that uses language (though probably no one but Burke would in actuality).

Though Burke does cite the standard rule that a definition should have "just enough clauses [to define] and no more," his is not a standard definition. The rule usually means to use only as many distinctions (*differentia*) as necessary to distinguish what is being defined from the rest of the universe. But any one of Burke's clauses, even the last, which he calls a "wry codicil" (*Language* 16), suffices to distinguish us.

A definition, Burke asserts, "sums things up." Definition may well be what comes last in a writer's discovery process, "the last thing a writer hits upon," for it is hard to "sum up" what has not yet been observed or invented. In retrospect, however, it should logically be possible to derive the properties of whatever is being defined from the definition. And, indeed, Burke's definition is finally summed up in the word *wordling*. From the implications of this pun—human worldlings are wordlings, bodies that, of their nature, learn words (thus becoming more than mere bodies)—the rest follows.

The clauses of Burke's definition are not "just enough" to define; they are, rather, "just enough" to serve as chapter headings, titles for categories under which his observations of human beings can "be assembled, as though derived from." Burke's aim is "to get as essential a set of clauses as possible, and to meditate on each of them" (*Language* 3).

Symbolic

For Burke, everything essentially human derives from our being symbol-making animals. This derivation is logical, not biological or historical; it is a statement about the present, about the structure (*logos*) of human reality, not about first causes or origins. Our very perceptions—as well as our interpretations, attitudes, judgments, choices and the actions that follow—are all mediated by the symbols we make, use, abuse and are, in this sense, used by. We are, to be sure, not alone in our use of symbols. Burke himself notes that any animal, insofar as it learns from experience—one of his more famous examples is a trout that learns to distinguish bait from food (*Permanence* 5)—must generalize, and hence must come to perceive individual events as signifiers for categories of events. But our use of symbols is qualitatively beyond that of any other animal. We not only use language and other semiotic systems, we make them and are made by them. As Noam Chomsky emphasizes, human individuals are born with special abilities to learn language; and we are made human, interinanimated as social individuals, through our interaction with cultural semiotic systems that are essentially linguistic, semiotic, rhetorical.

As historical and social groups, we make language (and other semiotic systems). As individuals, we are to a significant degree, made by language—a fact that has important implications for composition as both a social and an individual process. The limited literature on feral children makes suggestively clear that human beings raised outside of human language and culture do not develop the ability to think abstractly (for example, if integrated in human society as adolescents, they can learn arithmetic, but not mathematics) and *perhaps consequently* never develop the human ability to love or act morally (at least not beyond the sense in which dogs can love and act morally). An erect, bipedal, mammal with opposable thumbs that cannot think abstractly or love or act morally may be biologically human; but it is precisely such abilities that really define our humanness. For Burke, these abilities all follow logically from our ability to abstract, which follows from our use of language. Taken together, these abilities make our behavior symbolic action, motives mediated by symbols, not mere motion (see, for example, Burke's "(Nonsymbolic) Motion/(Symbolic) Action").

Our errors, too, are mediated by our terms and other symbols. Indeed, our errors are often motivated by erroneous terms and tropes. We misuse our symbols not only immorally to gain advantage over others (as in machiavellian rhetoric), but also in self-abuse, blinding ourselves to our deepest fears, hopes and insights. Our naming (and misnaming) not only helps individuals evade personally (as per Freud), misnaming also keeps ordinary scientists from the sort of breakthrough insights that mark the great scientists (see Gould, for example).

Everything we do is mediated by our symbols. And it is we (historically, socially, ecologically) who created these systems of symbols. They guide us to relevant insights but blind us to more radical insights. They conserve our traditions and lock us into those traditions. They help us evade what we wish not to see or understand. They function epistemically—and ideologically—to make us social as well as individual human beings.

Negativity

Language is the crux of our symbolicity. Human language is distinguished from various animal semiotics by the arbitrary relationship between signifier and signified. That is to say, among the various clauses used in defining language, the crucial one distinguishes semiotic systems where there is an analogy between signifier and signified from language where that relationship is arbitrary.

To use a currently popular metaphor, human semantics is primarily a left-brain function because of properties that follow logically from the use of arbitrary signifiers (but cf. Gardner 267 ff.). Another way to articulate the same distinction is to say that all animal communications are analog, but human semantics is digital. Analog systems can say "no" to what is present (can refuse what is offered), but only digital systems have the logical capacity to say "not" (as in "I am not writing now").

Thus, Burke's second clause is not a new defining feature; it is implicit in his first clause: it can be derived logically from the nature of the human symbolic, from our nature as "wordlings"; thus, it is technically redundant. Still, Burke is right to add this clause, for many crucial features of language, culture and humanness fall under the heading of "the power of negative thinking," which Burke calls "my positive negative."

Our culture—Burke's too—is in so many ways positive. We are for the most part logical positivists—even those of us (the vast majority) who don't know what the term means. We built our country by "thinking positively" to overcome obstacles to greatness. As inheritors of British empiricism (rather than French rationalism or German dialectics), we believe in the positive facts of practical realism and can grasp the virtues of negativity only with difficulty (often only with the aid of Asian spiritualism or Hegelian philosophy).

Burke thinks of the "positive negative" in terms of Greek drama, especially *Oedipus* and the *Oresteia*, juxtaposing Aristotle's *Poetics* with his *Rhetoric*. *Antigone* is Hegelian, he says. Pain is a "positive negative," as in catharsis—"a message, not an error," as when it tells us to remove our fingers from a hot stove (personal communication, 31 August 1989).

Part of what Burke has to offer is insight into the powers of negative thinking, which we lost (one time) when we accepted Plato's reactionary slanders against sophists and rhetoricians; which we lost another time when we reduced Aristotle's logic to his analytic logic (which includes the law against contradiction), thus deleting dialectic (which is founded on contradiction); and which we continue to lose because of our (anti-intellectual) mistrust of theory that cannot *immediately* demonstrate practical applications.

Having defined us in terms of our symbolic uses of language, Burke is absolutely right to define us next as "inventor of the negative." Linguistically, he is correct because what defines language, what separates human language from all other natural semiotic systems is its negative capacity. Other natural semiotic systems include a primitive, behavioristic *no*. A lion cub swatted across the head learns not to chew its mother's ears. After sufficient repetition of stern *no*'s, a puppy learns not to shit on the carpet (though it is the sternness, not the word, that embodies the primitive negative for the puppy). Even rats learn from psychologists' shocking negatives.

But the true propositional *negative* is uniquely linguistic. Only digital semiotic systems have true negatives, and the only natural digital semiotic systems on this planet are human languages. The logical negative allows human beings to conceive and communicate about what is not present. This means we can abstract and theorize—whatever else an abstract idea may be, it is not the concrete, positive reality it conceptually encompasses. This negative relationship—between positive reality and abstraction—is crucial to Burke's movement of mind.

Negativity also gives language its tenses, hence our ability to conceive and talk about what is *not* present because it is past or future. In a sense this is a form of abstraction, especially when, utopian, we speak of what does not, never has, and perhaps never will exist. Even to talk of the past is to negate the present (as various mystics have pointed out). Other animals are "just animals" in part because they lack this ability to communicate past and future. A dog, for example, can threaten—but only in the present perfect: a dog's raised hackles and snarl say, "I *am going* to bite you" (because they are the beginning of the process that actualizes as biting); but a dog cannot communicate, "I *will* bite you next week."

In addition to abstraction and tense, the negative allows basic logical functions that animals are incapable of communicating: *if . . . , then . . . .* and *either/or*. A dog can communicate desire ("I want to be fed") but not conditional action, not "If you don't feed me, I will bite you." Our ability to hypothesize about the future conceptually (instead of relying on trial and error) and our highly developed ability to conceive and make choices turn on these logical functions.

Without our ability to abstract, theorize, consider the distant past (historicize) and not-yet existent future (plan), to hypothesize and to weigh alternatives, we are not human. And all these cognitive abilities are part and parcel of our linguistic abilities.

Though he discusses this aspect of the negative, which he calls the "propositional negative," Burke emphasizes the "hortatory negative," the "Thou shalt *not*."[1] In the 1966 version of his definition, he added parenthetically that we are "moralized by the negative," for our morality turns on our ability to conceive abstract commandments. So again there is no real distinction: our nature as moral beings depends on our intellectual ability to abstract, which depends on the propositional negative we acquire with language. When people behave with extreme immorality—such as in Nazi extermination camps—we say they are inhumane, their actions inhuman. Upon moral imperatives, formally negative, we found our positive humanness.

Nature/Culture
Our experience is mediated by language, our actions moralized by the negative; thus we are removed from nature into culture. Indeed, "Thou shalt

not commit incest" is the minimal definition of culture. As Anthony Wilden asserts, "In every human society there is a rule about kinship that has no parallel in nature, a rule so universally accepted that it is not even mentioned in the Ten Commandments: the prohibition of incest" (102). Though exact definitions of incest (that is, precisely which relatives are forbidden) vary considerably from one society to another, no society, no human culture exists without an incest taboo. "Like language," Wilden emphasizes, "kinship is a revolution rather than an invention" (102)—a revolution that separated us from nature, a revolution that created culture.

Incest is not literally an "unnatural act"; the prohibition of incest is a social, not natural law. The prohibition of incest is "a *spoken* rule hemmed about by social sanctions" (Wilden 102; emphasis added). Contrary to popular belief and royal hemophilia, moreover, a moderate amount of incest would more likely help than harm the gene pool; indeed, such mating is common among farm animals. Incest is socially, not biologically harmful.

Though it appears to be a rule about who not to marry, the incest taboo is more importantly a rule about who to marry. Naturally, one is likely to mate with those who are nearest, hence most available. If the incest rule redefines those nearest as unavailable, people "marry out." By marrying out of the nuclear family, out of the extended family, even out of the band or clan, people create links of kinship over geographical and ecological space. These links encourage trade and mutual aid among neighbors. They ease movement of people from one group to another. They also diminish the probability, hence decrease the quantity, of wars. As a positive mandate for exogamy, the incest prohibition engenders cooperation, encourages social and cultural development (Wilden 107).

The *genus* of Burke's definition, "animal," is both true and false. We are, biologically, animals; but we are defined, distinguished from other animals, by our use of symbols (instruments of our own making), especially language (the tool that is more than a tool), which allows us to develop culture, to think abstractly and morally about our experience past, present and future. Our culture separates us from nature, creates the nature/culture boundary. It frees us—but in the process alienates us (from our natural condition). Our condition becomes more social than natural, shaped by culture within only very broad biological and ecological parameters.

Culture in this sense *negates* nature, though *negates* must be understood dialectically, for nature is not destroyed by our transcendence, and we remain in nature as we go beyond it. *Beyond* is a key word for Burke, who talks about "beyonding" (in part to evade the technical philosophical term, *sublate*.) Thus, separation does not mean we are not connected, just that a boundary has been drawn (hence the need for connection). The social is, in at least one crucial sense, natural, derived from nature, from the evolutionary process. We are "*bodies* that learn language/thereby becoming wordlings."

Since our connection-separation from nature is made by our symbolicity, Burke's third clause, too, is technically redundant—not a new defining feature but an additional heading for organizing our discussion of language, culture, and humanness. Indeed, the connection (between symbolicity, negative thinking, and the nature/culture boundary) is the insight. Not that we are social animals, separated from nature by our culture; but that this separation is a logical consequence of our languaging.

Order, Hierarchy, Levels

"Goaded by the spirit of hierarchy" is a rich metaphor, but it too is a logical consequence of our languaging, specifically of our language-based ability to abstract and sublate. For every abstraction is a sublation, which both conserves and transcends the concrete reality from which it is abstracted. As an abstraction, the term *love* in one sense is beyond the concrete experience of mother's love; yet, in another sense it en-compasses that experience (note the well worn metaphor of drawing a circle around). So any abstraction "beyonds" (to use Burke's verb) experience, puts my experience in relation with yours (which can be titled with the same word), thus makes it not only mine. But that abstraction is also grounded in experience, in reality, in nature.

Among the most important hierarchies, for Burke, are ladders of abstraction, hierarchies of even more encompassing titles, of abstractions that point at what disparate events share. Thus, Samson's suicide in Milton's *Samson Agonistes* (see Burke's *Rhetoric* 3-19) is a unique and concrete event. But naming it "suicide" puts it in a circle with all other suicides (hence the need for the modifier, "Samson's"). And suicide is a form of death, so a larger circle is drawn, another level of abstraction established. And death is a form of transformation. And so on, up the ladder of abstraction, in principle *ad infinitum*.[2]

Samson's suicide does not, of course, cease to be Samson's suicide just because we have reconceived it. It is conserved as his unique suicide; we do not forget that when we rename it. But we do not understand Samson's suicide in its uniqueness until we understand it also as a transformation, as a transcendence which makes Samson's ur-sainthood. That is Milton's point; we do not understand Milton until we understand how Samson's suicide both is and is not a suicide—that is, how it both breaks and, more importantly, does not break the commandment against suicide, how it is both death (an ending) and transcendence (a beginning). Explicitly or implicitly, articulately or inarticulately, we must read Samson's act on at least these two levels before we understand it; if we read it only on the level of suicide, we do not understand Milton's play.

For Burke, such hierarchies are in the very nature of human understanding. This is why he added parenthetically in the 1966 version of the definition that being goaded by the spirit of hierarchy means being "moved by the sense of order." We are moved by the sense of order every time we expect a concrete event to conform to our abstract conception of that type of event, every time we expect a student to act like a student, a professional to act like a professional, a civil servant to serve civic purposes. When we use words, we title events; and when we title events we understand them not only in their concrete particularity but also in relation to the abstract concept that is signified by the title. This is a *both-and* upon which Burke insists. It is also an important fact that belongs at the center of our teaching of diction.

Burke's insistence on thinking *both-and* rather than *either/or*, on thinking at once on several levels, is part of what makes him hard to read—at least for readers who were raised with the linear, analytic, either/or logic Aristotle articulated in his Law of [Non]Contradiction. So it is important to note that Aristotle said there were two types of logic, analytic and dialectic; but philosophers opted to formalize only analytic logic, thereby debasing both rhetoricians and dialecticians (Perelman 1-4).

On any one level, the Law of [Non]Contradiction holds: either/or is the correct procedure; *A* cannot be *not-A*. But as Bertrand Russell noted, certain paradoxes (some of which go back to Greek pre-Socratics and the sophists) can be resolved only by realizing what their apparently contradictory assertions mean on distinct levels. If *A* is Samson's suicide, then *A* (suicide) can also be *not-A* (transformation). This *A* and this *not-A* are not exclusive; rather, the *not-A* encompasses the *A*. Similarly, a horse can be both a horse and a symbol (of sexuality, for example, in a D.H. Lawrence short story).

Though we have no difficulty reading Lawrence on several levels (literal and symbolic), we who have been raised in a culture that stresses analytic logic are not very skillful when it comes to advanced thinking in terms of levels, hierarchical orderings. But one thing we can learn from Burke is how better to think about order, hierarchy, levels. Burke's value here is precisely that he negates one of the shortcomings of the dominant culture, teaches us another, fuller way to read reality.[3]

Rotten with Fore-Knowledge and Perfection

Burke explains that the clause "acquiring foreknowledge of death" was added from the perspective of his 90th birthday. In a sense, it too is redundant, for the ability to imagine our own deaths follows from the same propositional negative that allows us to abstract and to articulate the future tense. But Burke asserts that this clause

> reveals notable synergistic powers. Recall how zestfully Marx and Engels took to Henry Morgan's work on the development of the Greek clans. And recall Alban Winspear's *The Genesis of Plato's Thought*, which advises us that Plato was a member of the landed gentry, whose ancestors bequeathed them this particular acreage, and were honored by their descendants as tutelary deities. Death, immortality, and private ownership were thus all of the same parcel. (personal communication, 31 August 1989)

To say we are rotten with perfection not only evokes eternity and immortality, it is a particularly suggestive and powerful way to repeat that we are moved (motivated, goaded/go-ed/god-ed) by the sense of order, the spirit of hierarchy. For our abstractions become our ideals. At least in the abstract, we can conceive perfection, despite its being literally no-place (*u-topia*). Having conceived it, we strive for it, are moved toward it. Almost teleologically, the conception becomes the goad toward what is conceived. We conceive a potential and strive to actualize it.[4]

But this separates us from nature, from the here-and-now, makes us part of the fallen world, where things die and rot, leads us into all kinds of confusions and misapprehensions, this rotting within us, this dissatisfaction with what is, this humanness, our downfall and our wonder, our specialness, our potential to be more than what we are.

Rhetoric

For Burke defining humanness and defining rhetoric are hardly distinct tasks. What makes us human is our culture, which is founded in our unique form of symbolizing, our languaging, which is in its very nature rhetorical as it goads/gods us, moves/motivates us, makes us social, cultural (non-)animals, allows us to compose ourselves humanly. The study of language, culture, discourse, rhetoric, and humanity is one.

Burke's *Grammar of Motives*, *Rhetoric of Motives* and his unfinished *Symbolic of Motives* (studies toward which were collected in *Language as Symbolic Action*) were written because Burke had planned a book on human ethics, then decided he could not approach that subject except through a discussion of human motives, which for Burke necessarily meant a study of how our motives are mediated by our discourses. For Burke *Homo sapiens* is synonymous with *Homo rhetorica*; human wisdom is a discursive process.

Burke offers at least two types of definition for rhetoric. They are, of course, really two perspectives of one definition. One seems familiar: rhetoric as *addressed* (the traditional category of *audience*). Rhetoric is language used to have an effect on an audience, persuasive language. Thus, Burke begins by distinguishing *communication* from *expression* (etymologically, mere breathing out). But Burke, the dialectician, is never happy with the stasis of a dichotomous pair; his method is always to seek a third term. Consequently, the movement from *expression* to *communication* leads to *communion*, the state of identification with the community that is the logical outcome of persuasive communication. When an audience is convinced, they atone for their differences, stand at-one with the rhetor and with each other—in their agreement on how Athens should respond to the Persian fleet or in their agreement on how writing abilities should be developed.

To stand together with others is to be *consubstantial* with them: *stance* = stand; hence *substance* = that upon which one's stance is based, grounded; *con* = with; hence *consubstantial* = to stand on the same ground with. Thus,

Burke's definition of rhetoric as *identification*—the result of communally shared assumptions that allow us to work together, to cooperate, to identify even though we are not identical—is an implication of his definition of rhetoric as *addressed*.

Burke's most famous definition of rhetoric intertwines definitions of *language, symbolic, rhetoric,* and *humanness* to the point where all these terms define each other:

> For rhetoric as such ... is rooted in an essential function of language itself, a function that is wholly realistic, and is continually born anew; it is the use of language as a symbolic means of inducing cooperation in beings that by nature respond to symbols. (*Rhetoric* 43)

In its final phrase, this definition of rhetoric is grounded in Burke's definition of humanity: our essence is not that we have a particular essence but that we respond to symbols, define our own variable essences through discourse, language, rhetoric, culture. We are not, as capitalist ideology would have it, naturally selfish and aggrandizing; nor are we, as anarchist ideology would have it, naturally cooperative and sharing; we are, rather, beings who continually define and redefine ourselves through the symbolic processes of language, discourse, rhetoric, culture.

Burke's is an operational definition; rhetoric is defined by what it does. The key phrase in this definition declares rhetoric "a symbolic means of inducing cooperation." In his important but difficult essay on the origins of language, Burke founds language in the need of our ancestors to cooperate in order to survive (*Language* 419-79). Language allowed our relatively slow, weak, vulnerable ancestors to coordinate hunting and gathering, childcare, and protection from predators. Theories about the origins of language are inevitably speculative, but Burke is less interested in his theory's historical truth than in its mythic validity as a representative anecdote which captures the functional essence of our languaging.

Burke emphasizes that the phrase "inducing cooperation" presumes that cooperation must be induced, that we are not genetically, instinctively cooperative, that at best we may be said to have an inborn capacity to cooperate (including a capacity to learn language, which facilitates cooperation). Thus, for Burke, cooperation arises from division. We must persuade, must induce cooperation, must socialize our children into our communities because we are individuals—"in-divide-you-alls," as one schizophrenic pronounced the word for R.D. Laing, a "joycing" Burke would appreciate.

We are, in various ways, divided, alienated—from nature, from each other, from other cultures, even from ourselves. As there are levels of division, so there are levels of rhetoric. In Burke's reading of Freud, we are divided within ourselves, contain a parliament of voices which must be harmonized into an identity, an individual who acts in the world with some consistency (which we call the individual's personality or character). Socially, on various overlapping levels, we are divided from other people. And by our nature separated from nature, we must talk ourselves into patterns of action that embody ecologically valid strategies for survival—for if a culture talks itself into ecologically invalid strategies, its people fail to survive and that is the end of the culture; its discourse, its symbols disappear with the people who spoke them. (In the same sense that, biologically, all organisms, including people, can be interpreted as DNA's way of evolving and reproducing itself, so, rhetorically, people can be interpreted as cultures' ways of evolving and reproducing themselves.)

This dialectic of division and cooperation, individual and social, underlies Burke's definition of rhetoric—and us. When we convince an audience (or a subculture or a whole society) to share a perspective, we create at-oneness, togetherness, the basis of cooperation in action. Shared attitudes lead to cooperative actions, for attitudes are leanings, "incipient actions." In the nature of the rhetorical situation, however, we inevitably divide those we persuade from those who remain unpersuaded. When we socialize our children to share the broad values of our culture, we divide them from other children socialized in other cultures. When we teach our students to adopt the discourse of a professional community, we divide them from other communities. And then rhetoric is needed to bridge those divisions, to enable cooperation between people of distinct cultures.

If rhetoric is language used persuasively, then argumentation is just the tip of the iceberg. How language brings a community to share assumptions and perspectives is a much larger and more important rhetorical question. And one of Burke's major contributions to rhetoric, a contribution that virtually creates the New Rhetoric, is his broadening the subject of rhetoric by emphasizing the submerged seven-eighths of the iceberg.

Rhetoric becomes primarily the process whereby a community comes to share a symbolic discourse—or whereby a communally shared discourse creates consubstantiality, subliminally persuades individuals to identify with the community, even to sacrifice their lives for their country and flag (and what it stands for). Or to refuse to listen to, understand or publish nonstandard discourse. How do human individuals, with their "unique" perceptions, come to agree so often and so profoundly? Consider how much two people must agree upon in order to argue about whether a base runner was out at second base. Consider what leads millions of individuals to choose to wear their skirts at mid-thigh in 1927, at mid-shin in 1933, to wear their hair long and natural in 1969, clipped and greased into purple parody in 1989. These are all unique individuals with free will; surely the remarkable levels of agreement and conformity need more explanation than occasional differences.

In revising his definition of human beings, Burke has added to it. The second part (or verse) now reads,

> From within or
> from out of
> the vast expanses of the
> infinite wordless universe
> we wordy human bodies have carved
> many overlapping universes of discourse
> which add up to a
> pluriverse of discourses
> local dialects of dialectic

Thus, rhetoric, as a study of how wordlings word, becomes also a study of discourse communities and how they commune.

For Burke, the discourse of any community, in addition to whatever else it may do, represents strategies for encompassing situations: "These strategies size up the situations, name their structure and outstanding ingredients, and name them in a way that contains an attitude toward them" (*Philosophy* 3). The situations are real; a discourse is "an adjustment to a particular cluster of conditions" (*Counter-Statement* 107). Like Nietzsche or Derrida, Burke often uses a nihilistic perspective to work ideas, but Burke is no nihilist. A discourse must represent strategies that work, at least to such an extent that the community survives. The discourse must also work socially, must be persuasive and rhetorical, must produce consubstantial identification, must bring people into community—or it will be like a manuscript that no one but its author wants to read (or publish).

The third part of Burke's expanded definition, not yet fully formed (or versed) is about how wordlings are constituted. Burke has long been fascinated by constitution, the process of how we constitute ourselves. At the far end of his life (and his definition) he is looking at how we constitute ourselves both by masterpieces of verbal process—he cites both the U.S. Constitution and the "Communist Manifesto"—and by what he calls technological constitution, nowadays "fittingly defining itself by a mode of Artificial Intelligence."

I could continue—and I intend to elsewhere. But the point here is not to sum Burke up (or down—summaries really are down, reductive), just to provide a basis for reading Burke and for grounding our teaching of composition in some understanding of his critical insights into beings constituted as rhetorical animals.

Notes

[1]See "A Dramatic View of the Origins of Language" (*Language* 419-79). Commenting on a draft of this article, Burke said, "I feel uneasy [about the discussion of analog/digital] without reference to Gestalt psychology, computers, etc." See, therefore, my "Dracula" (236-40) and Burke's comment thereon. Burke also referred me to *The Harper Dictionary of Modern Thought*,

specifically to "synergy": "This concept reflects the classical opinion that 'the whole is greater that the sum of its parts.'... Synergy is formally studied as a property of systems by cybernetics. ... More generally still, the term is applied to the generation of unplanned social benefits among people who consciously cooperate in the pursuit of their own interests and goals."

[2]For an important distinction between abstraction and generalization, see my *Grammar* 22-25, 79-82, and works cited therein.

[3]Though this may seem difficult, it is pragmatically powerful; I have tried to suggest some implications for composition in the section on "negative invention" in the second chapter of my textbook. Also see Elbow, Part IV, "Contraries and Inquiry."

[4]See the Utopian U heuristic in Shor 155-80.

Works Cited

Burke, Kenneth. "A Comment on 'It Takes Capital to Defeat Dracula.'" *College English* 49 (1987): 221-22.

——. *Counter-Statement*. 1931. Berkeley: U of California P, 1968

——. *A Grammar of Motives*. 1945. Berkeley: U of California P, 1969.

——. *Language as Symbolic Action: Essays on Life, Literature, and Method*. Berkeley: U of California P, 1966.

——. "(Nonsymbolic) Motion/(Symbolic) Action." *Critical Inquiry* 4 (1978): 809-38.

——. *Permanence and Change: An Anatomy of Purpose*. 2nd ed. Indianapolis: Bobbs-Merrill, 1965.

——. *The Philosophy of Literary Form: Studies in Symbolic Action*. 1941. New York: Vintage, 1957.

——. *A Rhetoric of Motives*. 1950. Berkeley: U of California P, 1969.

Coe, Richard M. "It Takes Capital to Defeat Dracula." *College English* 48 (1986): 231-42.

——. *Process, Form, and Substance: A Rhetoric for Advanced Writers*, 2nd. ed. Englewood Cliffs, NJ: Prentice, 1990.

——. *Toward a Grammar of Passages*. Carbondale: Southern Illinois UP, 1988.

Elbow, Peter. *Embracing Contraries*. New York: Oxford, 1986.

Gardner, Howard. *The Mind's New Science: A History of Cognitive Revolution*. Rev. ed. New York: Basic, 1987.

Gould, Stephen Jay. "For Want of a Metaphor." *The Flamingo's Smile: Reflections in Natural History*. New York: Norton, 1987. 139-51.

Hunter, Paul. "Freire and Burke: A Pedagogy for the Non-Traditional Student." Conference on College Composition and Communication. Seattle. 17 Mar. 1989.

Perelman, Chaim. *The Realm of Rhetoric*. Tr. William Kluback. Notre Dame, IN: U of Notre Dame P, 1982.

Russell, Bertrand. "Mathematical Logic as Based on the Theory of Types." *American Journal of Mathematics* 30 (1908): 222-62.

Shor, Ira. *Critical Teaching and Everyday Life*. Boston: South End, 1980.

Wilden, Anthony. *The Rules Are No Game*. London, Routledge, 1987.

Winspear, Alban D. *The Genesis of Plato's Thought*. New York: Russell, 1940.

Afterword

LINDA BRODKEY

So much of composition is about what students do that we sometimes forget that what they write on Monday morning depends on what we think about on Friday afternoon, when teachers find some time to reflect on curriculum and pedagogy. Since I think of the essays in *Composition Theory for the Postmodern Classroom* as the labor of many such Friday afternoons, I read each as an attempt to make some kind of theoretical sense of writing and teaching practices. As I read the collection of essays, I was frequently reminded that despite seemingly indefinite variation in the circumstances of teaching, composition teachers do not treat theory as a refuge from practice, but value instead what it can tell them about writing and writing pedagogy.

Judging by the variety of theories invoked in the essays, postmodernity does not so much suggest a particular theory of writing, or writing pedagogy, as create enough intellectual uncertainty that old explanations either no longer suffice or require further justification. While some might consider a plethora of theories evidence that composition has lost its way, or is on the verge of losing itself in a miasma of theory, I'm inclined to see the theoretical excursions taken in the essays as intellectual sorties, and the sorties as harbingers of an emerging sense among us that our right to govern our intellectual lives depends on our willingness to theorize writing in the light of practice. That many of us presume practice to be the site of theory, and pedagogy to be foremost among the practices that concern us, seems to mean, among other things, a refusal to lease our classrooms as test sites for theories in which writing is an afterthought.

I detect in these essays a decided preference for theories in which writing already is, or easily could be, a critical component, and a reluctance to assume that the best theories necessarily keep a safe distance from practice. Some theories travel better than others. The ones that travel best in composition share not only our regard for writing and writers, but also for teaching and teachers. What I find particularly inviting about the theories introduced in these essays is that with each new definition of practice, I found myself considering a different set of issues and problems. In some instances, a theory or theoretical notion complicated already familiar concerns of composition—process pedagogy or collaborative learning. At other times, a particular theory or notion raised and elaborated seemingly new and specific concerns about the politics of pedagogy or the philosophical underpinnings of discourse. Taken singly or collectively, the essays therefore make a case for reading theory by conceptualizing a writing or teaching practice and articulating its theoretical possibilities.

The postmodern classroom is the one where the verities no longer hold. Just as theory is not a refuge from practice, a college classroom is not a sanctuary from life for students and teachers. What goes on in our classes, what students do and teachers do, depends in large measure on our ability to theorize writing in ways that invite students to see themselves as entitled to identify, analyze, evaluate, and ultimately propose alternatives to the social and political conditions that beset us all. In her address on receiving the Nobel Prize in Literature, Toni Morrison is reported to have argued for the importance of those who do "word work," and to have said, "We die.... That may be the meaning of life. But we do language. That may be the measure of our lives" (qtd. in Darnton B1). I would like to think that the comparatively recent and increasingly widespread interest in theory in composition will teach us that working with words *is* work and that not only individuals but societies are measured by their work with words. By this measure, we are enjoined to reconceptualize language, to invent, learn, and teach a version of "word work" that refuses to treat language apart from thought and reality.

While some theories come closer than others to articulating the intersection of language, thought, and reality, the difficulty lies in teaching ourselves and students to resist retreating to common sense because it is theoretically or practically more convenient to treat language as a thing in itself. Common sense is not necessarily good sense, not if it teaches students that grammar, spelling, punctuation, diction, and organization are the literal measures of good writing. That the eloquence of writing reflects an eloquence of mind and the clarity of writing a clear purchase on reality are but examples of appeals to common sense that have vexed writing and pedagogy from the outset. Spin doctors are nothing if not eloquent, and a sound bite is a model of clarity. But neither are measures of writing. They are measures instead of a bloated cynicism that has made a fetish of common sense. It is common sense to "conclude" that if Lani Guinier, a female African American who teaches law in an Ivy League university, writes law reviews articles about majority rule that she is the "quota queen" (see Branan; Guinier). And it is apparently also common sense for the president who nominated her for the office of assistant attorney general for civil rights to retract his nomination in the face of negative spins, but to attribute his withdrawal not to media spins but to his own reading of Guinier's work.

The turn to theory in composition expresses a desire above all for a little uncommon sense in the face of what sometimes seems an intentional but always a feckless rending of words from deeds. For I hear in these essays echoes of an inclination to reject precepts that ignore writing and teaching in the name of common sense, and I see traces on the paths taken of the uncommon intention to practice and teach writing—for a change. Yet, a refusal to return to business as usual also means suffering the awkward moments when the struggle to acquire the language of theory creates a kind of intellectual confusion that must be akin to that of students who take college writing classes and learn there is more to writing than five-hundred-word essays. One never just learns to speak a language, or learns to write, because both entail a set a cultural practices. In composition, the reading and writing of theory is a search for a language in which writing and teaching are valued cultural practices. The most powerful and craven among us could not spin with impunity if "word work" were an entitlement. Since the failure to provide "word work" has taken a higher toll than any of us can countenance, a world in which words count is not only preferable to one in which they do not, it might even be fit for human habitation.

Works Cited

Branan, Karen. "Lani Guinier: The Anatomy of a Betrayal." *Ms.* 4 Sept./Oct. 1993: 51-57.

Darnton, John. "Accepting Nobel, Morrison Proves Power of Words." *New York Times.* National Edition. 8 Dec., 1993: B1.

Guinier, Lani. "A Challenge to Journalists on Racial Dialogue." *Extra* 6 Nov./Dec. 1993: 7-9.

Contributors

Lynn Z. Bloom is professor of English and Aetna Chair of Writing at the University of Connecticut. Among her publications that practice what she teaches are *Doctor Spock: Biography of a Conservative Radical* (1972), *Fact and Artifact: Writing Nonfiction* (1994), *The Essay Connection* (1991, 1995), "Teaching College English as a Woman" (1992), "Growing Up With Doctor Spock: An Autobiography" (1993), and the forthcoming *Songs of Ourselves: Reading, Writing, Researching Autobiography*. "Why Don't We Write What We Teach? And Publish It?" appeared in *JAC* 10, 1990.

David Bleich is professor of English at the University of Rochester and one of the founders of reader response criticism. He is author of *Readings and Feelings: An Introduction to Subjective Criticism* (1975), *Subjective Criticism* (1978), *The Double Perspective: Language, Literacy, and Social Relations* (1988), and numerous articles on writing, teaching, and literacy. In 1994 he guest edited a special issue of *JAC* on Collaboration and Change in the Academy. "Sexism in Academic Styles of Learning" appeared in *JAC* 10, 1990.

Linda Brodkey is associate professor of literature at the University of California at San Diego and director of the Warren College Writing Program. She is author of *Academic Writing as Social Practice* and of journal articles on writing and literacy.

Mary Kupiec Cayton is associate professor of history and American studies at Miami University in Ohio. She is the author of *Emerson's Emergence: Self and Society in the Transformation of New England, 1800-1845* (1989), and co-editor (with Elliott Gorn and Peter Williams) of *The Encyclopedia of American Social History* (1993). She has also written on the problems of temporary and part-time faculty in the academy. "What Happens When Things Go Wrong: Women and Writing Blocks" appeared in *JAC* 10, 1990.

Richard M. Coe is professor of English at Simon Fraser University and has taught in China and the United States as well as Canada. His *Toward a Grammar of Passages* (1988) introduced an instrument for studying generic discourse structures and contrastive rhetoric. In 1990, Prentice-Hall published a thoroughly revised edition of his innovative textbook under the new title, *Process, Form, and Substance: A Rhetoric for Advanced Writers*. He is presently writing *How to Read Kenneth Burke* and planning *The Rhetoric and Ecology of Genre*. "Defining Rhetoric—and Us: A Meditation on Burke's Definitions" appeared in *JAC* 10, 1990.

Reed Way Dasenbrock is professor of English at New Mexico State University and author of *The Literary Vorticism of Ezra Pound and Wyndham Lewis* (1985) and *Imitating the Italians* (1991). His work in theory includes editing two anthologies: *Redrawing the Lines: Analytic Philosophy, Deconstruction and Literary Theory* (1989) and *Literary Theory after Davidson* (1993). He has published essays in *College English*, *JAC*, and *College Composition and Communication*. "Becoming Aware of the Myth of Presence" appeared in *JAC* 8, 1988.

Sidney I. Dobrin teaches composition, technical writing, and professional writing for graduate students at the University of South Florida, where he serves as associate editor of *JAC*. He has published articles on composition theory, writing across the curriculum, and popular culture, and he is currently working on a book on tensions between composition theory and pedagogy.

Thomas Fox is associate professor of English at California State University at Chico. He is author of *The Social Uses of Writing* (1990) and is currently writing a book about race and writing instruction. "Repositioning the Profession: Teaching Writing to African American Students" appeared in *JAC* 12, 1992.

Henry A. Giroux holds the Waterbury Chair Professorship at Penn State University, where he also directs the Waterbury Forum on Education and Cultural Studies. His recent books include: *Border Crossings* (1992); *Living Dangerously* (1993); *Education Still Under Siege* (1993); and *Disturbing Pleasures: Redneck Popular Culture* (1994). "Paulo Freire and the Politics of Postcolonialism" appeared in *JAC* 12, 1992.

Joseph Harris is associate professor of English at the University of Pittsburgh, where he directs the composition program. He has written several articles on English teaching and is the editor of *College Composition and Communication*. "The Other Reader" appeared in *JAC* 12, 1992.

Douglas Hesse is associate professor of English and Director of Writing Programs at Illinois State University. He has published essays on narrative, rhetoric, and nonfiction in *Writing Theory and Critical Theory*, *The Rebirth of Rhetoric*, *Literary Nonfiction*, *Narrative and Argument*, *College Composition and Communication*, and other books and journals. "The Recent Rise of Literary Nonfiction: A Cautionary Assay" appeared in *JAC* 11, 1991.

Thomas Kent is professor of English at Iowa State University, where he serves as editor of the *Journal of Advanced Composition*. He is the author of *Paralogic Rhetoric: A Theory of Communicative Interaction* (1993) and *Interpretation and Genre: The Role of Generic Perception in the Study of Narrative Texts* (1986). "Externalism and the Production of Discourse" appeared in *JAC* 12, 1992.

James L. Kinneavy is the Jane and Roland Blumberg Centennial Professor of English at the University of Texas at Austin. He is the author of *A Study of Three Contemporary Theories of the Lyric* (1956), *A Theory of Discourse* (1971, 1980), *Greek Rhetorical Origins of Christian Faith: An Inquiry* (1987), *Writing in the Liberal Arts Tradition*, with two coauthors (1985, 1990), and *Elements of Writing*, a high school textbook series for English from the sixth through the twelfth grades (1993). He has also written numerous articles on rhetorical theory, history, and practice. "The Process of Writing: A Philosophical Base in Hermeneutics" appeared in *JAC* 7, 1987.

Michael Kleine is associate professor of rhetoric and writing at the University of Arkansas at Little Rock. He has published articles on corporate, academic, and scientific writing, and also on ethnographic practice, rhetorical theory, orality and literacy, and collaborative approaches to teaching writing. "Toward an Ethics of Teaching Writing in a Hazardous Context—The University" appeared in *JAC* 12, 1992.

Carrie Shively Leverenz is assistant professor of English and director of the Reading/Writing Center at Florida State University. Her publications include *The Presence of Others: A Guide for Teachers* (1994) and collaboratively authored articles in *Rhetoric Society Quarterly* and *Pre/Text*. "Peer Response in the Multicultural Composition Classroom: Dissensus—A Dream (Deferred)" appeared in *JAC* 14, 1994.

J. Hillis Miller is Distinguished Professor of English and Comparative Literature at the University of California at Irvine. His most recent books are *Versions of Pygmalion*, *Ariadne's Thread*, and *Illustration*. A new book, *Topographies,* is forthcoming in 1994 in the Meridian Series of the Stanford University Press. "Nietzsche in Basel: Writing Reading" appeared in *JAC* 13, 1993.

Sandy Moore is a student in the graduate program in technical and expository writing at the University of Arkansas at Little Rock. She has taught introductory writing courses and has written extensively about free speech in the workplace. "Toward an Ethics of Teaching Writing in a Hazardous Context—The University" appeared in *JAC* 12, 1992.

Michael Murphy is a graduate student at Syracuse University, where he is working in both composition and cultural theory. He is completing a dissertation called *Camp Happens: Modernism, Post-Modernism, and Mass Culture* and is planning a book on composition and cultural studies. "After Progressivism: Modern Composition, Institutional Service, and Cultural Studies" appeared in *JAC* 13, 1993.

Jasper Neel chairs the English department at Vanderbilt University and is author of *Plato, Derrida, and Writing* (1988), *Aristotle's Voice: A Study of Rhetoric and Writing in America* (1994), and numerous articles on rhetoric, critical theory, and pedagogy. He is currently at work on a book entitled *Process Theory and the Revolution in Literary Studies in America.* "Dichotomy, Consubstantiality, Technical Writing, Literary Theory: The Double Orthodox Curse" appeared in *JAC* 12, 1992.

Gary A. Olson is professor of English and teaches in the graduate program in rhetoric and composition at the University of South Florida. His most recent book is *Philosophy, Rhetoric, Literary Criticism: (Inter)views*, published by Southern Illinois University Press (1994).

Joseph Petraglia teaches rhetorical theory and research methods at Bowling Green State University. He is currently editing a collection of essays on the disjuncture between contemporary writing research and theory and general skills writing instruction, and he is working on a book entitled *Rhetoric Real and Imagined: Rhetorical Sensitivity as a Goal of Formal Instruction.* "Interrupting the Conversation: The Constructionist Dialogue in Composition" appeared in *JAC* 11, 1991.

Jacqueline Jones Royster is associate professor of English at Ohio State University. Since 1983 she has been a member of the editorial collective of *Sage: A Scholarly Journal on Black Women.* In addition to their semi-annual journal, the collective has published an anthology, *Double Stitch: Black Women Write About Mothers and Daughters.* Her other publications include *Writer's Choice*, a textbook series in language arts for middle school students, and various articles in books and scholarly journals in literacy studies and women's studies. Currently, she is completing a book, *Traces of a Stream: Literacy and Social Change Among African American Women.* Royster is associate chair of the Conference on College Composition and Communication and a member of the executive committee of the Division on Teaching Writing of the Modern Language Association.

David W. Smit is associate professor of English at Kansas State University, where he teaches courses in composition theory, modern drama, and Henry James. He is the author of *The Language of a Master: Theories of Style and the*

Late Writing of Henry James (1988), and he has published articles in the *Journal of Advanced Composition*, *Style*, the *Henry James Review*, *WPA*, and *Rhetoric Review*. "Some Difficulties with Collaborative Learning" appeared in *JAC* 9, 1989.

Patricia A. Sullivan is assistant professor of English and director of the Freshman English Program at the University of New Hampshire. She is coeditor of *Methods and Methodology in Composition Research* (1992) and *Writing and Reading (in) the Academy: Pedagogy in the Age of Politics* (forthcoming). "Writing in the Graduate Curriculum: Literary Criticism as Composition" appeared in *JAC* 11, 1991.

John Trimbur is associate professor of English and co-director of the program in technical, scientific, and professional writing at Worcester Polytechnic Institute. He is coauthor of *Reading Culture* (1992) and co-editor of *The Politics of Writing Instruction: Postsecondary* (1991), which won the CCCC Outstanding Book Award. "Articulation Theory and the Problem of Determination: A Reading of *Lives on the Boundary*" appeared in *JAC* 13, 1993.

W. Ross Winterowd, who is on the verge of retirement from his position as Bruce R. McElderry Professor of English (Rhetoric, Linguistics, and Literature) at the University of Southern California, admits defeat: his literary colleagues have assiduously dismantled the graduate program that he founded, rhetoric and composition in their view having no place in a department of English. "Rediscovering the Essay" appeared in *JAC* 8, 1988.

Robert G. Wood is a graduate student at Michigan Technological University, where he is currently completing his dissertation, *Contending with Multi-Subjectivity in the College Composition Classroom*. His earlier publications include: "Review of Children of Promise," Writing Center Journal (1992), and "Response to Maxine Hairston," *College Composition and Communication* (1993). "The Dialectic Suppression of Feminist Thought in Radical Pedagogy" appeared in *JAC* 13, 1993.

Index